צָדְקָה מִמֶּנִּי

THE *Jewish Ethic* OF *Personal Responsibility*

VOLUME I

Steven Pruzansky

Copyright © Steven Pruzansky
Jerusalem 2014/5775

All rights reserved. No part of this publication may be translated, reproduced, stored in a retrieval system or transmitted, in any form or by any means, electronic, mechanical, photocopying, recording or otherwise, without express written permission from the publishers.

Author photo ©2013 David Beyda Studio, NYC

Cover Design: Leah Ben Avraham/Noonim Graphics
Typesetting: Benjie Herskowitz, Studio Etc.

ISBN: 978-965-229-649-8

1 3 5 7 9 8 6 4 2

Gefen Publishing House Ltd.	Gefen Books
6 Hatzvi Street	11 Edison Place
Jerusalem 94386, Israel	Springfield, NJ 07081
972-2-538-0247	516-593-1234
orders@gefenpublishing.com	orders@gefenpublishing.com

www.gefenpublishing.com

Printed in Israel   *Send for our free catalog*

Library of Congress Cataloging-in-Publication Data

Pruzansky, Steven, author.
   Tzadka mimeni : the Jewish ethic of personal responsibility / Rabbi Steven Pruzansky.
      volumes ; cm
   Includes index.
   Contents: Volume 1: Breisheet-Shemot.
   ISBN 978-965-229-649-8
   1. Responsibility in the Bible. 2. Bible. Pentateuch--Criticism, interpretation, etc. 3. Ethics in the Bible. 4. Responsibility--Religious aspects--Judaism. 5. Choice (Psychology)--Religious aspects--Judaism. I. Title. II. Title: Tsadkah mimeni.
   BS1225.6.R39P78 2014
   296.3'6--dc23
                               2014022887

Rabbi Dr. Sholom Gold

Av 5774

Rabbi Pruzansky's *sefer* (I can't call it a book) is of vital importance. People have always tried to divest themselves of blame and cast it on others. In recent years we have been witnessing an unprecedented flight from responsibility and an abandonment of accountability. For some people, transferring decision making to others is seen as a virtue to be pursued. It is not perceived as weakness but rather as strength. It does, in fact, mean relinquishing the essence of one's humanity, which calls upon us to exercise the divine gift of free will in an intelligent and responsible way.

Once, while driving through Har Nof with some fine gentleman, I innocently asked him (since it was election time) for whom he was planning to vote. He responded that he didn't know yet because he hadn't asked his *rav*. With all the emotional strength I could muster I continued driving responsibly and calmly, and said to him, "When the Sanhedrin had completed their deliberations in a case where a human life hung in the balance, voting would begin from the youngest member, not from the head of the court. Torah wants the honest opinion of each member, devoid of the inevitable powerful influence of the senior members. Voting in Israeli elections is always an act that involves questions of life and death. We need your own opinion, not someone else's." I doubt that my words were understood or appreciated.

The classic work of Jewish ethical literature, the *Mesillat Yesharim*, opens with that famous first line:

> The foundation of saintliness and the root of perfection in the service of God lies in a man's coming to see clearly and to recognize as a truth the nature of his duty in the world and the end toward which he should direct his vision and his aspiration in all of his labors all the days of his life.

The pivotal word is *duty*, which means "responsibility." Rabbi Pruzansky's *sefer* is dedicated to clarifying the profound significance of that term. This, as he demonstrates so effectively, finds its expression throughout Torah. The reader who studies his *sefer* will be richly rewarded. His insights are creative, incisive and wise. Rabbi Pruzansky opens up a vast Torah panorama that is so desperately needed.

I commend him for having made that hasty, off-the-cuff remark years ago about writing a book on the topic, and indeed bringing it to life in this *sefer*. Y'yasher kochacha.

Rabbi Dr. Sholom Gold
Founding Rabbi, Kehillat Zichron Yoseph, Har Nof
Dean, Avrom Silver Jerusalem College for Adults, OU Israel Center

Yeshiva University in Israel
RIETS Kollel – Gruss Institute
Bayit Vegan, Jerusalem Israel

Rabbi Dr. Aaron Rakeffet

לכל מאן דבעי מידע

My dear student Rabbi Steven Pruzansky has once again authored a volume which synthesizes his deep knowledge and the contemporary challenges. Rabbi Pruzansky is an articulate speaker and writer who provides profound guidance for the manifold challenges which confront עם ישראל today. "Responsibility" is a key word in his discourses on the first two volumes of the Pentateuch.

May I add that I yet knew his grandparents. Rabbi Pruzansky is a true credit to their memory. May he continue להגדיל תורה ולהאדירה in health and happiness, together with his wonderful wife Karen and their extended family.

החותם למען כבוד התורה ולומדיה
עש"ק פ' ראה תשע"ד
August 22, 2014

Aaron Rakeffet – אהרן רקפת

☙❧

*In loving memory of
Dr. Oscar (Riley) Hausdorff, z"l,
my father-in-law,
who infused his life
and the lives of those who knew him
with love, meaning, joy and goodness*

and

*Abigail Ginsberg, a"h,
my granddaughter,
whose short life
reminded all of the preciousness of life.*

*May their memories
continue to inspire those
who loved them.*

☙❧

This book is lovingly dedicated by my parents,
Sylvia and Wallace Pruzansky,
may Hashem bless them with long life,

સ

in memory of their parents, my grandparents,
of blessed memory.

સ

My grandfather Rav Efraim (HaRav Efraim Michel ben Zev Nechemia Halevi) Pruzansky was born in Brisk on June 15, 1904, into a family of *shochtim* (ritual slaughterers). As a child, he befriended a young Yosef Dov Soloveitchik when the latter would visit his grandparents in Pruzhana. In his teen years, he studied at the prestigious Reb Mailes Yeshiva in

Vilna, returning in his older teenage years (after his father's death at a young age) to learn in the Slonimer yeshiva. There he received *smicha*, and within a few years, received his *kabbala* for *shechita* from the revered Rav Eliyahu (Feinstein) Pruzhaner, in the town of Pruzhana where the family home was located. He became a *shochet, mohel, baal tokeia* and *baal korei*.

His wife, my grandmother Pesha Wolinetz, was born on November 8, 1911, in Antipolia, Poland (today, Belarus), a town not far from Brisk and Pruzhana. She was the daughter of Tamar and the esteemed Rav Ahron Osher Wolinetz, a young prodigy and the author during his lifetime of more than fifteen *sefarim*. The couple married on November 14, 1929, and for the next decade resided in Pruzhana, where my grandfather was one of the town's *shochtim*.

After my grandfather was arrested several times for violating Poland's ban on *shechita*, my grandparents escaped Poland on one of the last ships to leave before the outbreak of World War II. Their voyage was made possible only through the intervention of Rav Ahron Osher, who, in a providential tale famous in our family, helped a local politician (a stranger who appeared in shul unannounced) say Kaddish on a *yahrtzeit*. He, in turn, interceded with the local congressman, James Fitzpatrick, who wrote two letters to the American embassy in Warsaw requesting visas for the Pruzansky family. My grandparents and their three oldest children (including my father) arrived on American shores on Lincoln's birthday in 1939.

After taking a job as a *shochet* for several years in Freehold, New Jersey – employment arranged by Rav Moshe Soloveitchik – my grandparents moved to the Bronx, with my grandfather taking a job as a *shochet* at half pay, in order to allow their children to attend yeshiva in the Bronx. My grandfather often said, by way of explanation, that he "did not run away from Hitler so that his children should grow up as *goyim* in America." There they raised their children – my father, his two sisters Vela and Evelyn, and his late brother Rabbi Jerry Pruzansky, a"h. In his later years, my grandfather was a regular *maggid shiur* at the Young Israel of Pelham Parkway.

My paternal grandparents were people with great *mesirut nefesh* for Torah, people of enormous intelligence and sophistication, whose lives were rooted in acts of kindness and the rhythms of Jewish life. My grandmother returned her soul at a young age on 19 Tishrei 5735 (October 5, 1974) and my grandfather passed away on 5 Tevet 5743 (December 21, 1982).

My maternal grandfather Hyman Schneider (Chaim Dov ben Uziel) was born on January 21, 1905 (Tu b'Shvat), in Wysokie Mazowieckie, Poland, not far from Bialystok. He learned in the famed Lomza Yeshiva until he was sent to America by his parents in 1922. (His father Uziel Schneider, *Hy"d*, died in the Bialystok ghetto in 1941, and his mother Rivka, *Hy"d*, was murdered in Treblinka in 1942, together with several of my grandfather's siblings.) In the late 1920s, my grandfather opened a butcher store in the Bronx, where for the next four decades, he was one of several kosher butchers but the only one that was *shomer Shabbat*, hard to imagine by modern standards. Many of the rabbis in the Bronx were his regular customers, and most were never charged for their purchases.

For years, my grandfather was assisted in his store by my grandmother Lillian (Leah bat Ephraim HaKohen), who was born in Brooklyn on July 26, 1909 (Tisha b'Av), and raised in the Bronx by her grandmother after her mother's untimely death when my grandmother was just two years old. They married on December 16, 1928, and raised their two daughters, my mother and her older sister Ann, in the Bronx.

My grandfather was a daily shul-goer, morning and evening, and his life revolved around shul, *minyan* and *shiurim*. For forty years, he was president of his shul, the Chevra Mishnayos Anshe Emes in the Bronx, apparently the only president that shul ever had. He was a noted *baal tzedaka*, who regularly provided free meat to the indigent and who was once audited by the IRS for five years in a row because his charitable contributions were disproportionately high relative to his income. He was a person of unparalleled integrity.

My grandparents' kindness was legendary. They were tremendous *machnisei orchim*, with an open home that would welcome guests who would sometimes stay for months at a time. Perhaps remembering his own youth in Lomza, my grandfather was especially generous with young yeshiva students who needed meals or lodging. For more than a decade, they too lived in Pelham Parkway, and my two grandfathers sat next to each other in shul. In 1972, my grandparents made *aliya*, and lived in Netanya for the balance of their lives. There my grandfather, always an early riser who would recite *tehillim* and *maamadot* long before Shacharit, spearheaded the early morning *shiur* in his shul, which began at 6:30 AM and then was moved to 5:30 AM when 6:30 AM was deemed "too late." He went to his eternal reward on 7 Kislev 5753 (December 2, 1992), and my grandmother died on 18 Tevet 5758 (January 16, 1998).

☙

All my grandparents were extremely loving and devoted to their families. May their memories be a blessing and source of inspiration for all their children, grandchildren, great-grandchildren and now great-great-grandchildren, and may the Torah thoughts recorded here bring everlasting merit to their souls.

– Steven Puzansky

Contents

Acknowledgments xix
Introduction xxi

BREISHEET 1
The Book of Genesis 1

Breisheet 3
    Creation 3
    The Creation of Man 4
    Conquering the World 5
    Good Enough 6
    Marriage 7
    Adam in the Garden of Eden 10
    Work 12
    My Brother's Keeper 15
    Lemech 17
    God's Limits 18

Noach 19
    The Collapse of Mankind 19
    The Choice 19
    Perfect in His Generation 20
    Objectively Flawed 22
    The Ark's Passengers 24
    The Raven 24
    The Evil Inclination 26
    The Covenant 27
    Noach's Children 28
    The First Dictator 30
    The Follower 31

Lech Lecha 33

- Independence 33
- Cult of Personality 34
- Self-help 36
- Ten Trials 38
- Wealth 40
- Concern for Others 42

Vayera 45
- The Way of Kindness 45
- Lot 47
- Lot's Redemption 50
- The Evil of Sodom 51

Chayei Sarah 55
- All Good 55
- Seize the Day 56
- Integrity 57
- Excessive Speech 59
- Finding a Spouse 61
- Idle Chatter 63
- Modesty 65

Toldot 67
- Yitzchak's Path 67
- Prayer: Together but Apart 69
- Yitzchak and Esav 70
- No Excuses 71
- Initiative 73
- Consequences 76
- Humility 78
- The Rebirth of Marriage 79

Vayetzei 80
- Impressions 80
- Two Lives 81
- Warring Stones 83
- The Vow 85
- Marriage 86
- Rationalization 88

    Work and Marriage 89
Vayishlach 93
    Self-defense 93
    Small Jars 94
    Left Alone 95
    Wrestling for Eternity 97
    Complete 98
    Blaming the Victim 99
    Royalty 101
Vayeshev 103
    Serenity Now 103
    Appearances 106
    Sibling Rivalry 107
    The Long Wait 110
    Good Intentions 111
    First Signs of Greatness 113
    Flight from Responsibility 114
    "Tzadka Mimeni!" She Is More Righteous Than Me 114
    "Everybody Does It!" 118
    Yosef in Prison 120
Mikeitz 123
    God's Role 123
    Yosef and Pharaoh 124
    No Man Is an Island 126
    Flaunting 127
    "We Are Guilty" 129
    Fools Can't Be Trusted 131
Vayigash 133
    Fateful Approach 133
    The Day of Judgment 135
    Communal Responsibility 136
    Surviving Egypt 139
    Private Property 140
Vayechi 143
    Influence 143

The Oath	145
Rachel's Death	146
Yosef's Sons	146
Sibling Rivalry Revisited	148
The Evil Eye	149
The Blessings	151
The Midlife Crisis	154
Reconciliation	156

SHEMOT 161
The Book of Exodus 161

   Shemot 163

Redemption	163
Gratitude	164
Chosen People	166
The Courage to Say No	167
Finding a Spouse	168
The Enemy of the Good	169
Moshe	171
Prince of Egypt	172
Rod of Action	174
Control of Emotions	177
The Walking Dead	178
God's Many Agents	180

   Va'era 182

The Price of Exile	182
Marriage Check	183
Loss of Free Will	185
Plagues	187
The Limits of Gratitude	189
Business Opportunity	191
Sanctifying God's Name	193
The Circle of Fault	194

   Bo 196

The Process	196

- Children 197
- Light in the Darkness 199
- Time 201
- Spoiled by Wealth 202
- Parenting Skills 204

Beshalach 206
- Armed but Not Ready 206
- Don't Wail, Do Something! 207
- Religious Cop-out 210
- The Gift of Certainty 211
- Small Things 213
- Manna from Heaven 215
- Shabbat 217
- Filling the Void 219

Yitro 222
- Loneliness 222
- Abundant Kindness 223
- The Community's Torah 225
- Limits 227
- Beneath the Mountain 228
- Individual Acceptance of the Torah 230
- The Right Ideas 231
- The Father Figure 232
- Homicide 234
- Torah from Heaven 236
- Fairness 237

Mishpatim 239
- The Mentsch 239
- Slave Mentality 241
- Flying Solo 244
- Man and His Torts 245
- An Eye for an Eye 246
- De-fueling the Fire 247
- The Optional Requirement 248
- The Cult of the Victim 249

The Burden of Enmity..250
Living in the Moment 251
Terumah 253
The Inner World of Prayer..253
The Precious Stones of Individual Initiative 255
Our Torah 256
The Permanent Joys of Youth...258
Tetzaveh 261
Self-Effacement 261
Clothes Make the Man 262
On Our Hearts..264
The Ideal, Part I..265
The Ideal, Part II 266
Ki Tisa 269
My Share 269
The Holy Shekel 270
Stage One Thinking...272
Stunted Growth..273
Quick Slide 275
One Man 277
The Minority 278
The Book and the Sword...280
Vayakhel 283
The National Project...283
Centrality of Shabbat...284
The Wise-Hearted..287
Hesitation..288
Happiness..289
Mirror Image..291
Pekudei 292
The Lingering Sin..292
Trust but Verify..293
Repetition 295
Between Heaven and Earth 297
About the Author 301

☙Acknowledgments

As I complete twenty years as the spiritual leader of Congregation Bnai Yeshurun in Teaneck, New Jersey, I am deeply grateful for the profound Torah commitment and sheer goodness of the membership, as well as the stimulating intellectual environment the shul consistently provides. Not least, my gratitude extends for the mini-sabbatical that was granted me in 2013, during which most of this book was written. The time was spent in the burgeoning city of Modiin, amid neighbors whose interest in Torah and commitment to Religious Zionism helped refine these thoughts.

My thanks as well to Gefen Publishing House, Lynn Douek and Kezia Raffel Pride for their dedication and professionalism, and to Ilan Greenfield and Michael Fischberger for their success in making Gefen one of the most prominent publishers in the world today of Jewish and Zionist works.

I continue to be inspired by my teachers and rabbinical mentors, Rav Berel Wein, now of Yerushalayim but who enormously influenced me as a teenager and beyond, and to Rav Yisrael Chait of Yeshiva Bnei Torah, Far Rockaway, New York, my *rebbe muvhak*, whose Torah ideas I still ponder daily. May Hashem grant both strength, good health and peace of mind to continue their propagation of Torah.

Of course, I am blessed every day to be part of a loving, warm and supportive family. My wife Karen continues to amaze with her infinite empathy for others, a selflessness that benefits all who know her. My beloved parents, Sylvia and Wallace Pruzansky, are worthy children of their parents, Lillian and Hyman Schneider, and Pesha and Rav Froim Pruzansky, *a"h*, to whom this book is dedicated, and who set an admirable standard for building Torah homes in less than hospitable climes. Their reward in Gan Eden is continuous. May Hashem bless my parents with continued good health and *nachat* from their children, grandchildren and great-grandchildren, and so too my mother-in-law, Sue Hausdorff, who displays an inner strength that matches her outer decency and who enjoys the love and respect of all who know her.

Most of what I learned in life about personal responsibility I learned from my parents, and often heard their voices as I was writing. Many of the issues raised were frequent topics of discussion in my formative years, such that the conclusions drawn herein seem natural, at least to me.

Since my last book was published, we have been shaken by the death of my father-in-law, Dr. Oscar (Riley) Hausdorff, *a"h*, whose physical presence is sorely missed but whose emotional presence lives undiminished, and of our granddaughter, Abigail Ginsberg, *a"h*, taken from us at a young age but who remains a vivid part of our lives. May their souls be bound in the bond of eternal life.

And Karen and I have been blessed with an expanded family that has branched out across the world. Our children Ayelet and Shmuly Katz live in Ramat Shilo, Israel, with our grandchildren Yona Leah Katz, Ari Katz, Ahava Katz and Yehuda Katz. Tamar and Rav Ari Ginsberg keep us company on this side of the pond, with their sons Asher Ginsberg and Shaya Ginsberg. New to Israel (Ramot) are Dina and Hillel Weingarten, and their children Amalya Chana Weingarten, Kayla Leah Weingarten, and Noam Weingarten. And rounding out the American contingent are (soon to be Rav) Ari and Lauren Pruzansky and their daughters Meital Avigayil Pruzansky and Gavriela Brahna Pruzansky. They have brought us only joy, itself a gift from God. May Hashem continue to bestow His kindness, favor, grace and blessings on all of them, and may their tribe continue to increase.

Certainly my brothers and sisters and their children and grandchildren (now numbering more than three dozen, divided between the United States and Israel) complete a family that has appreciated Hashem's blessings and seeks every opportunity to better His world and His people.

The ideas expressed herein are solely my own, notwithstanding that much has been inspired by the greatest and holiest thinkers in Jewish life, past and present. To be sure, there are many lessons about personal responsibility in the first books of the Torah that were not included here, and the reader is invited to supplement this book with his or her own findings. But this was written with love for every Jew, and with the hope that every single Jew can find his or her way to worship God, study Torah, perform mitzvot, love each other and the people of Israel, protect and preserve the land of Israel, and take responsibility for our lives, our destiny and our divinely entrusted mission.

– Steven Pruzansky
Teaneck, New Jersey
Sivan 5774 – June 2014

Introduction

They were the two words that changed history.

In the episode of Yehuda and Tamar (Breisheet 38), a pregnant and unmarried Tamar was accused of conceiving illicitly and was sentenced to death by the local court. Rather than publicly shame the father of her child – her ex-father-in-law Yehuda, who acted innocently and unknowingly – she simply brought out the pledges entrusted to her in lieu of payment and said, "I conceived through the man to whom these belong," adding, "identify these, please, whose are this signet, cloak and staff?" (Breisheet 38:25).

Yehuda could have remained silent – he was reluctant to have Tamar marry into his family again, having had two sons die while married to her – and could have thereby avoided humiliation. Instead, he stepped forward and claimed responsibility with these two words: "*Tzadka mimeni*" (She is right; it is from me; 38:26). In so doing, Yehuda saved Tamar from execution – but he also was thereby awarded the future monarchy of Israel. It is through these events that the royal house of Israel was formed, through the birth of Yehuda and Tamar's son Peretz. That royal house began with King David and will eventuate in the coronation of his descendant, the Moshiach.

As I expounded this chapter several years ago, I realized how refreshing was Yehuda's embrace of personal responsibility, and how exceedingly rare it was by modern standards. It is much more common for leaders (and laymen) to deflect responsibility, to shift blame to others, and to never admit mistakes (except in the passive sense, as in "mistakes were made").

At that time, I articulated a litany of other areas in which modern man – Western and Jewish – has been trained to avoid personal responsibility: by parents who blame teachers for their child's misdeeds or educational weaknesses, and never the child; by parents who would rather not allow their children to make mistakes and learn from them, and often not even to make their own decisions in life; by "children" who become adults and have little interest in marrying, raising children or earning a living, coddled by a society that labels them children until well into their twenties;[1] by adults who delegate to others the responsibility for finding themselves spouses to avoid having to deal with the pain of rejection, notwithstanding its importance in the maturation process of any human being; by adults who delegate fundamental and personal decisions about their lives (e.g., whom to marry, when to marry, what career to choose, where to live, what to name their children, etc.) to mystics and others, rather than just seeking their advice or guidance; by American CEOs who looted the assets of their companies in financial peril by paying themselves (with board approval) inflated salaries, pensions and perks – and then declaring bankruptcy and leaving the companies' creditors and shareholders without recourse; by other CEOs who ran their companies into bankruptcy with flawed business models and/or poor decisions and then turned to the government (i.e., the taxpayer) for bailouts;[2] by those who castigated the so-called "predatory lenders" who were, essentially, forced or induced to lend money to people who could not afford the homes they were purchasing – but *never* criticizing those who applied for those loans in the first instance, knowing both that they could not afford repayment and that the government (i.e., the taxpayer) would foot the bill for their profligacy; by therapists who discover new pathologies in order to enable people to avoid taking responsibility for their plights in life;[3] by the cultural imperative of "never blame the victim," even when the victim is negligent and contributes to his own fate; by the Israeli architects of the failed Oslo peace process that strengthened the enemy, weakened their own country and unleashed an unprecedented wave of terror – and who never paid a political price for their blunders and flawed conceptions; by the "entitlement" mentality that finds people demanding that others support them almost without limit; etc.

The list goes on and on. While addressing this topic that Shabbat morning several years ago, I blurted out, in an unguarded moment, that I should write a book that goes through the entire Torah and highlights the Torah's perspective on personal responsibility. This is the first volume of that book, and it extracts the lessons to be gleaned from a study of the books of Breisheet and Shemot, the first two books of the Torah. Yehuda's two momentous words – "*Tzadka mimeni*" – gave this book its title.

---

[1] American parents with family health insurance policies can now keep their "children" on these policies until age twenty-six (!), a symptom of the problem.

[2] "Bailout" is a euphemism for a rejection of personal responsibility in the business context.

[3] The great American economist and thinker Thomas Sowell wrote: "Many of the people in the 'helping professions' are helping people to be irresponsible and dependent on others." See Thomas Sowell, "Random Thoughts," *Jewish World Review* (December 21, 2010), http://tinyurl.com/23jc3o8.

To some of an older generation, "personal responsibility" sounds like a platitude, so obvious that it needs no elaboration. It is a character trait that is associated with maturity, reasoned decision making, acceptance of consequences for one's actions, admissions of guilt and wrongdoing when appropriate, thrift and decency, concern for others and for society at large. An older generation might think it is too obvious even to mention, much less to discourse about at length.

But it has gone missing from Western and American society and to a great degree from Jewish society as well. The abandonment of the ethic of personal responsibility has transformed the way we live and look at the world. And it needs to be revived for the good of the Jewish world and the world at large.

Personal responsibility is at the very heart of the Torah. One of the fundamental doctrines of Jewish thought is the concept of "free choice." Rambam characterizes that as a "great principle" and a "pillar of Torah," to know that we have the unfettered freedom to choose good or evil: "The Creator neither forces man nor decrees upon him to do good or evil; rather it is all given over to him."[4] Without free will, the laws of the Torah are incomprehensible and the doctrine of reward and punishment is illogical.

In this first volume, we will encounter the Jewish ethic of personal responsibility in areas as diverse as marriage, parenting, family life, employment, divine service, military service, acts of kindness, repentance, private property ownership, wealth, *mitzvot*, modesty, justice, gratitude and the like. Many of these themes will recur, as befits such an essential principle. To be sure, it is clear that many more examples of personal responsibility can be derived from the Torah than have been recorded here, and the reader is invited to duly note his or her own. But these examples suffice to illustrate how elementary this value is to Torah, and how its centrality in our lives must be restored.

---

[4] Rambam, *Hilchot Teshuva* 5:3.

BREISHEET

The Book of Genesis

Breisheet

CREATION

In the beginning, God created the heavens and the earth. (Breisheet 1:1)

The Torah begins with an account of Creation not to teach us science but to teach us theology – and especially the relationship of God to His creation. Without acknowledgment that God is the Creator of the universe and the Source of all life, man is inevitably overcome with haughtiness and finds moral subservience to God's will unnecessary.

That is why secular society is obsessed with disconnecting God from His creation, and preaches to its young through the public school system that the universe emerged from an unguided evolution in which the dominant force was "randomness," a notion that is as speculative as it is inherently unscientific. It is interesting that the Hebrew word for science is *mada*, whose root is "knowledge." Knowledge encompasses far more than what is verifiable in a laboratory. While it is certainly reasonable to concede that the public school is not the ideal forum to discuss what are ultimately theological questions, overtly erasing the divine role is itself a theological choice, one that advances secularism over religion. In essence, as conservative commentator William Murchison once wrote, the educational choice is not between "intelligent design" or "evolution" but rather between "intelligent design" and "accidentalism" – the notion that the universe, and our lives, are nothing more than cosmic accidents.

Only the person who acknowledges a divine creation can relate directly to the Creator and see his life as ultimately consequential. It is only such an individual who can make moral choices, have an objective sense of good and evil, and influence others for the good. The perception of man as a morally responsible being is rooted in the recognition that "in the beginning, God created the heavens and the earth."

The Creation of Man

And God created man in His image, in the image of God He created him; male and female He created them. (Breisheet 1:27)

The Torah underscores that man was created to be a thinking, free-willed and rational creature, who could control his instincts and thereby attain saintliness. "And God said, 'Let us make man in our image, after our likeness…' And God made man in His image, in the image of God He created him; male and female he created them."[5] Rashi comments that *demut* – form – refers to man's power of understanding, i.e., man's intellectual gifts,[6] what Rambam characterizes as "man's distinction…his intellectual perception…the Divine intellect with which man has been endowed…[that enables him to] distinguish between the true and the false," and after Adam's sin, between "right and wrong."[7]

In that capacity, man "imitates" a dimension of God, who is the ultimate free-willed Being.[8] And the entire Torah rests on one foundation: man's capacity to make free-willed choices, and then to assume responsibility for those choices. As Rambam teaches:

> Every man has permission to incline to the way of goodness and become righteous, and if he desires to incline to the way of evil and become wicked. The choice is his…. Do not contemplate even for a moment what fools and the vacuous say that "God decrees from the moment a person is created whether he will be righteous or wicked." It is not so! Every person can be righteous like Moshe or evil like Yerovam, or wise or foolish, or compassionate or cruel, or generous or miserly, and the same with all other traits…[9]

Indeed, "this is a fundamental principle and the pillar on which the Torah and all the commandments rest…. If God decreed that a man be righteous or wicked, or that he would be compelled in either direction…then how could He have commanded us through His prophets 'do this' or 'do not do that' or 'improve your ways,' if from birth it had been dictated or he had been coerced by something to do something that he could not possibly resist?"[10]

---

[5] Breisheet 1:26–27.
[6] Rashi, Breisheet 1:26.
[7] Rambam, *Moreh Nevuchim* 1:1–2.
[8] Rav Ovadia Sforno, Breisheet 1:26.
[9] Rambam, *Hilchot Teshuva* 5:1–2.
[10] Ibid. 5:3, 4.

The Torah not only promotes the notion that individuals are responsible for their own actions, but this is also the very foundation of the principle of "reward and punishment" that is the eleventh of Rambam's Thirteen Principles of Faith.[11] Without personal responsibility, there can be no commandments, no expectation of virtuous conduct of man, and no retribution for failure to adhere to the divine moral code.

This idea did not just arise at the creation of man, but in fact was the very essence of the creation of man: a being created "in the image of God" who is therefore accountable for his deeds.

Conquering the World

Be fruitful and multiply, fill the earth and conquer it…
(Breisheet 1:28)

Man is charged with subduing the earth, using his God-given intelligence to explore it, master it and develop it – but also to preserve it.

The Midrash states that "when God created the first man, He took him around to all the trees in the Garden of Eden and said to him, 'See My handiwork, how beautiful and praiseworthy they are…. Be careful not to ruin and destroy My world, for if you do ruin it, there is no one to repair it after you.'"[12]

In truth, nature is quite resilient and has frequently rebounded from man's exploitation of the world's resources. All past predictions of the imminent depletion of nature's bounty have not come to pass, and even the extent to which man can permanently impair the environment is debatable.

But man is not simply an animal with a better brain whose entire focus in life is the fulfillment of his animalistic desires. Man is a thinking being whose mandate is to use society's resources to serve God and enjoy pleasure in moderation. The environmentalist movement, which often uses apocalyptic language and exaggerated claims to sound its alarms, is at its core a moral movement. Its unreasonable assertions and outlandish policy prescriptions should not obscure that basic point: man has a responsibility to ensure the planet's survival, for ourselves and for future generations.

"For He rested on [the seventh day] from all the work that God created *to do*" (2:3). The Midrash comments that "to do" means that God subsequently

---

[11] Rambam, Commentary on the Mishna, Masechet Sanhedrin, Perek Chelek.
[12] Kohelet Rabba 7:13.

partnered with man, the righteous and even the wicked, in order to bring the world closer to perfection.[13] There is still much left to accomplish.

Good Enough

> *And God saw that it was good… (Breisheet 1:10, 12, 18, 21, 25)*
> *And God saw everything that He had made, and behold, it was very good… (Breisheet 1:31)*

The world as created was "good" and "very good," but not perfect.

The creation story itself admits to certain changes – compromises, in a sense – that God made in concession to man's moral weakness. Thus, the primeval light of creation was actually hidden,[14] the trees themselves did not have the same taste as their fruit – as originally intended,[15] and the "two great luminaries" (1:16), the sun and the moon, were reduced to just one luminary – the sun – with the moon merely a reflection of the sun. What went wrong?

Rav Moshe Chaim Luzzato writes that there is an ideal physical world in which man can grow and thrive spiritually, but man cannot appreciate that world until he is perfected, until he becomes adept at choosing properly.[16] The original plan called for perfection, but at the instant of creation, flaws were implanted in the system, and man's task is to rectify them, one flaw at a time, one generation at a time, one person at a time.

The hidden, primeval light contained dimensions of knowledge that will only be accessible to man well in the future. If the wicked had been given access to this knowledge, the world could not have survived. Knowledge was hidden to be released slowly over time, as history itself demonstrates. Man, while dominated by his evil inclination, cannot be entrusted with this knowledge.

Nor could imperfect man appreciate a tree whose bark and fruit had the same taste. In such a scenario, impetuous man with his craving for immediate physical gratification would never allow fruit to grow. Why wait for the fruit when you can eat the tree? Nothing would have grown, so God concluded that "a tree yielding fruit" (1:12) – a tree that produces fruit but is not itself fruit – would have to suffice.

---

[13] Breisheet Rabba 11:10.
[14] Rashi, Breisheet 1:4.
[15] Rashi, Breisheet 1:11.
[16] *Daat Tevunot: The Knowing Heart*, trans. Shraga Silverstein (New York: Feldheim, 1982), pp. 20–22.

Nor could man, with his arrogant tendencies, serve God in a world with two luminaries. The universe has many suns, but our galaxy has only one, as a lesson for man. Two kings cannot share one crown. Subservience and humility are virtues to be cultivated – or man will become not a creator but a destroyer.

That is our world. We have to possess an image of perfection for which we can strive. We have to know what we can be and what the world can look like – and then, through the Torah, endeavor to refine it and restore it to its original luster. That is the responsibility of mankind and of every individual, and that is why man's role as God's "partner" in completing His work continues throughout history until today.

Rav Yitzchak Hutner[17] added a penetrating insight. The Midrash comments simply that the Hebrew word *me'od* (very) consists of the exact same letters as *adam* (man), as if to say, "and behold, man is good."[18] What is the import of this cryptic comment?

Rav Hutner[19] explains that man's creation was unique because only man – of all creation – has free choice and therefore unlimited potential for good or evil. The rest of creation is essentially fixed within the boundaries of natural law. Only man is capable of *me'od* – accomplishing something that transcends his physical nature – and simultaneously capable of endangering his spiritual existence and severing his connection with his Creator.

Thus, of all the creatures in God's universe, it is only about man that we can argue "whether or not it was better for him to be created."[20] Only man can stumble so grievously that he renounces his uniqueness and lives an animalistic existence, and only man can exceed his natural limitations, access divine secrets and live an angelic life. That is the fundamental choice in life.

Marriage

Therefore shall a man leave his father and mother, and cleave to his wife, and become as one flesh. (Breisheet 2:24)

A child is, by definition, a dependent. He is born incapable of caring for himself, and slowly, over the course of many years, he begins to assert his independence. As an infant, the child is nourished, sustained, bathed and coddled by his

---

[17] Twentieth-century American *rosh yeshiva* at Yeshivat Chaim Berlin in Brooklyn, New York.
[18] Midrash Breisheet Rabba 8:5.
[19] *Pachad Yitzchak*, Rosh Hashana 7:9–11.
[20] Masechet Eruvin 13b.

adoring parents, who can do no wrong in his eyes (and vice versa). As a toddler, the child begins expressing – sometimes quite vehemently – his likes and dislikes about food, bedtime and the like. By the time the child reaches adolescence, his rebellion is full-blown. His tastes become more pronounced and he begins to challenge his parents' value system, testing the limits of their patience, endurance and ethical guidelines – all to prepare him for the moment when he will marry and, together with his wife, establish their own home.

Marriage is the ultimate act of independence and requires the young couple to carve out a new joint identity that is no longer merely an extension of their respective families. It requires maturity, autonomy and discipline.

Yet the modern marriage challenges the Torah's conception in a number of ways. Often, adult children have given little thought to self-sufficiency, and prefer to live as financial wards of their parents. The younger the couple – and religious Jews tend to get married younger than the norm in the secular world – the less they are prepared for the mundane aspects of marriage: creating a budget, living within one's means and finding jobs that can underwrite their financial requirements. Conversely, there are many parents who are enablers of that very dependency and prefer to control the purse strings so as to unduly influence the young couple's life choices – especially where to live, when to have children and even what to name those children.

Neither dynamic is particularly healthy, but the problem is to some extent unavoidable. Those young people who are still learning Torah on an advanced level lack the wherewithal to support themselves but still feel a need to marry, and the Torah certainly encourages both men and women to marry while relatively young.[21] Torah study is so valued that, in some communities, a young man with a job is considered an undesirable catch, strange as that sounds. In other cases, the young person – man or woman – is still in professional school and is several years away from gainful employment, and the parents' financial support is not only a necessity but a negotiable element in the marriage proposal.

Our Sages debated what should be the proper order in life for a man – whether it is better to first learn Torah and then marry, or marry first and then learn Torah.[22] The working assumption was that in the former case, the demands of earning a living and of married life would greatly limit a young man's capacity to learn Torah effectively, whereas in the latter case, the physical pleasures of marriage would at least ensure that he was not distracted by

---

[21] Masechet Kiddushin 29b.
[22] Ibid.

unquenched desire. The clear answer in this context was…it depends: "A man should always learn Torah and then marry, for if he marries first, his mind will not be free to learn Torah – there will be a millstone around his neck; but if he will be overpowered by his instinctual drive so that he will also be incapable of learning Torah, then he should marry first."[23]

The unanswered question is that of self-sufficiency during that period of time, and undoubtedly this financial burden falls on the wife or the parents (or in-laws) – sometimes quite willingly and other times less so. That is a problem in itself, for two reasons: Judaism has always seen the man as the primary breadwinner, even as women – even in ancient times, and certainly today – worked outside the home; additionally, one of the primary obligations of a father is to teach his son a profession so that he will be able to support himself and his family.[24]

An arrangement that is understandable and agreeable to all is, of course, acceptable – but with one caveat: it does not necessarily meet the Torah's test of leaving one's father and mother, and cleaving to one's wife. The longer the newlyweds live in a dependent state – essentially playing house while their parents are footing the bill – the less they will feel and act fully married, and the less capable they are of asserting the personal autonomy that is the true sign of adulthood and the inner capacity to build one's home and pursue one's destiny.

On the other hand, parents also have to learn to let go, to allow married children to make their own decisions – and even to make their own mistakes, as frustrating as that can sometimes be. Parents are always available for advice and guidance, and children are usually wise to heed that advice, but the decisions have to be made by the child. Perhaps the clearest indication of the Torah's attitude in this area is the law that the demands of honoring parents are overridden in several matters, especially including the choice of a spouse.[25] The child has the absolute right to choose a spouse; it is the child and not the parents who will be living with this person. Parents can advise but should never insist, threaten, intimidate or insinuate dire consequences if their will in this matter is not obeyed, and parents should always avoid trying to relive their lives through their children.

---

[23] Rambam, *Hilchot Talmud Torah* 1:5, *Shulchan Aruch*, Yoreh Deah 246:2.

[24] Kiddushin 29a.

[25] Rema, *Shulchan Aruch*, Yoreh Deah 240:25; cf. Netziv (Responsa Meshiv Davar 2:50) who gives the parent veto power if the child's mate will cause the parent "embarrassment and pain," a standard that is largely undefined.

Whether or not we fully embrace the Torah's directive here on the implications of marriage, its message is at least clear: childhood is all about dependence, while marriage is defined by independence. "Leaving parents," to be sure, does not mean abandoning them, but it does mean clearly delineating the parameters by which each new married couple is able to seek its inimitable path in life basking in parental love but free of undue parental interference.

Adam in the Garden of Eden

And Adam said, "The woman You gave me, she gave to me from the tree, and I ate." (Breisheet 3:12)

The Torah's narrative is a pendulum that swings back and forth between accounts of individuals who fled from the practice of personal responsibility and those majestic souls who became role models of contrition and accountability. Human beings are naturally defensive and self-protective, and the story of the first man and woman in the Garden of Eden established a pattern for future conduct that remarkably endures.

Adam was created as a singular creature and provided with a wife who would be his *ezer k'negdo* (his helpmate; 2:18), someone to bring out his strengths and to curb the pursuit of his vices. The newlyweds were placed in the Garden of Eden and Adam was given but one commandment: "You may surely eat of every tree in the garden; but of the Tree of Knowledge of good and evil, you shall not eat therefrom…" (2:16–17).

As the Sages relate, Adam sinned within one hour of receiving this command.[26] The serpent seduced the woman into eating from the tree, "and she also gave to her husband with her," and he ate" (3:6). When confronted, Adam immediately shifted blame away from himself. "And the man said [to God], 'The woman whom You gave to me, *she* gave to me from the tree, and I ate'" (3:12). Certainly, Adam's ingratitude stands out.[27] His wife was a gift; as the only creature with a psychological nature similar to his, to whom he could relate on an intellectual and emotional level, she relieved his sense of loneliness. But Adam's headlong plunge into denial mode stands out.

And Chava reacted the same way. "And the woman said, 'The serpent deceived me, and I ate'" (3:13). Thus, mankind's denial of personal responsibility for our own misdeeds tarnished our very first day on earth – predating even

---

[26] Masechet Sanhedrin 38b.

[27] Rashi, Breisheet 3:12, from Masechet Avoda Zara 5b.

the first Sabbath – and has continued to color our conduct in all the millennia since.

The very foundation of personal responsibility is the confession of misdeeds, and a clear sign of a lack of personal responsibility is the attribution of fault to others in an attempt to rationalize or diminish one's crimes or sins. History is so replete with such examples that the Torah taught us a fundamental lesson in the very first account of human life: just as man's instinctual nature inclines him to seek gratification of his physical desires, so too his psychological makeup is hard-wired to obfuscate and conceal his errors and assign his failures to others. And just as we are mandated to control our instinctual yearnings – "its desire is toward you, yet you can dominate it" (4:7) – so too we are obligated to overcome our natural desire to blame others for our misfortune or sins.

Chava clearly partook of the same malady and blamed her downfall on the serpent. But she took it a step further, and in her eagerness to avoid being the only guilty party ensnared her husband in the same net. She provided Adam with the same fruit of the tree, "so that she should not die [alone], leaving him to live and marry another woman."[28] Sinners routinely believe that there is a safety in numbers, that if "everyone is doing it" then either it cannot be wrong or it cannot be penalized. People can easily escape a sense of personal responsibility by linking their fortunes with a group of like-minded malefactors. That is why our Sages admonished us that "a confederacy of wicked people does not count [as a group]";[29] it is only the opinions of honorable people that are considered in making decisions or moral choices.

That, indeed, was the great failing of the *ir hanidachat*, the wayward city whose inhabitants all worship idols, and which is therefore to be destroyed in its entirety.[30] People – especially neighbors – are drawn to live in proximity to each other in order to benefit one another, to elevate each other's lives and reinforce their virtues instead of degrading each other and eroding our pursuit of ethical goodness. An entire city that is devoted to corruption, human degradation and rejection of God cannot be allowed to endure. In a sense, man and woman transformed Gan Eden from what it was – the first Mikdash (Temple), in which every element in that society could be used to serve God – into the first *ir hanidachat*, a society that was defined by its sinful character. The only difference was that rather than destroy the place,

---

[28] Rashi, Breisheet 3:6.
[29] Masechet Sanhedrin 26a.
[30] Devarim 13:13–19.

mankind was barred from that place – and tasked with discovering the road back through self-perfection.

On the sixth day of creation, and the first day of Adam and Chava's existence, the Torah introduced us to man's powerful tendency to castigate others for his own failings and to seek out the company of fellow sinners – even inducing others to sin – in order to mitigate his own misconduct. Both tendencies are alive and well, and we must be alert to their subtle influences, and – when confronted with our own guilt in any matter – pause, reflect, think, recognize these inclinations and respond in a way that reflects our more admirable qualities.

Work

> *By the sweat of your brow you shall eat bread… (Breisheet 3:19)*

The Torah never uses the word *punishment* to describe the changes wrought to Creation after the sin of Adam and Chava, although it is certainly perceived as such – especially the requirement that man would have to work, gruelingly, in order to provide for his sustenance. The first man lived in an idyllic environment in which all his physical needs were easily obtainable. The world was his for the taking – except for the one item over which, naturally, he obsessed and fantasized, and then sinned. In context, Adam's capacity to seek constant gratification from the physical world had to then be limited by his need to support himself, otherwise his pursuit of pleasure would have been unending. In practice, Adam's world post-Eden was still enviable: "They would sow for one year, and be sustained for forty years."[31]

Is there a "Jewish work ethic"? The "Protestant work ethic," a term coined by the German sociologist Max Weber in 1904, saw a religious value in humble origins and hard work that lifted an individual to a higher socioeconomic level. "The so-called Protestant Ethic," wrote the libertarian intellectual Frank Chodorov, "…held that man was a sturdy and responsible individual, responsible to himself, his society, and his God. Anybody who could not measure up to that standard could not qualify for public office or even popular respect."[32] That tradition informed American life for well over a century but is in recession today.

---

[31] Midrash Tanchuma, Breisheet 40.

[32] Frank Chodorov, "The Radical Rich," in *Out of Step: The Autobiography of an Individualist* (New

For Jews, work is not an inherent value, like, for example, Torah study, but the absence of work and the spurning of gainful employment is a sign of moral weakness. And even work itself is extolled for its redemptive qualities. "The one who enjoys [the fruit of] his own exertions is greater than one who is God-fearing," states the Talmudic Sage known as Ulla. "'When you eat the labor of your hands, you are praiseworthy and it is well with you' (Tehillim 128:2), 'praiseworthy' in this world and 'well with you' in the world-to-come."[33]

There are two approaches to understanding this extraordinary claim. One is reflected in other Talmudic statements: that "idleness leads to boredom,"[34] which invariably leads to thoughts of sin, and that "Torah study goes well with work [*derech eretz*], for involvement in both causes sin to be forgotten. And any Torah that is not accompanied by work will be nullified and generate iniquity."[35] The combination of work and Torah study fills a person's day to the extent that the time for mischief is limited, and the exertions in both satisfy our yearnings for physical and intellectual gratification. The day devoted to prayer, study, work and good deeds leaves little opportunity for rebellious behavior.

Additionally, work is humbling, and the attainment of humility is a prime Torah objective in the pursuit of moral perfection. The worker endures occasional failures and enjoys temporary successes. He identifies more closely with others who are engaged in the same process, so work itself builds character. The alternative, sad to say, nurtures a sense of entitlement that afflicts even (especially?) religious people – that work is beneath them, something for the masses but not the spiritual elites. That arrogance is as personally off-putting as it is morally corrosive. Rav Yechezkel Landau[36] questions the Gemara cited above, asking how a worker can be greater than one who is God-fearing.[37] If he is also God-fearing, then that should be the best status of all, and if the worker does not fear God, then how can the work itself be virtuous?

He answers that as a youth he would joke that it must mean that the one who enjoys the fruit of his own physical labor is greater than the one who seeks to enjoy the product of his spiritual accomplishments, i.e., the person

---

York: Devin-Adair, 1962).

[33] Masechet Berachot 8a.

[34] *Kalla Rabbati* 9:20, *Psikta Zutreta*, Shemot 5.

[35] Masechet Avot 2:2, and see Rambam and Bertinoro thereon. Both interpret *derech eretz* as *parnasa*, livelihood.

[36] Rav Landau was the chief rabbi of Prague during much of the eighteenth century.

[37] In his commentary, *Tzlach*, on Berachot 8a.

who says to his contemporaries "[you must] support me because I am a God-fearing person."

One of the more lamentable aspects of modern Jewish life has become an open disdain for self-support among certain groups. There is a burgeoning mendicant class. Rare is the synagogue or community that is not visited regularly – even daily – by individuals, many of them relatively young, who are incapable and/or unwilling to provide for themselves and their children, who are not educated in any functional way to be able to find and hold gainful employment and who see nothing improper in becoming public charges. In essence, they have "chosen" poverty rather than having it thrust upon them due to some misfortune, or fall into penury because of a lack of education, skills or opportunity. They require community support for basic needs in life: rent, food, clothing, health care, tuition assistance, weddings, child support, etc.[38]

That lifestyle is as distressing as it is abnormal, and reflects a failure to inculcate basic Torah values – not necessarily of work but of self-support, which for most people (excluding wealthy heirs) means the same thing. It is the gloomy Jewish equivalent to the multigenerational welfare families that dot the bleak American urban landscape.

Jews do not maintain that one's occupation defines the individual and should be the source of one's self-esteem. Our self-esteem comes from being part of an eternal and chosen people and is measured by our fidelity to God's law, our commitment to His service, and our success in pursuing moral greatness. Thus, many Talmudic giants engaged in manual labor – as blacksmiths, shoemakers, wood hewers, and the like. Several leading *rishonim* (medieval authorities) were physicians. It did not detract from their greatness; on the contrary, it added to it, as they did not exploit their lofty spiritual positions for financial benefit.

"Work," therefore, is embraced as part of the reality of the world that God created and in which we live. It also provides opportunities for spiritual growth, and that itself is ennobling.

---

[38] Certainly the Jewish community has always been exceptional in providing financial assistance to the downtrodden who have suffered involuntary blows – illness, unemployment, death of a breadwinner, dislocation, etc. Helping those people is a natural and expected element of membership in the Jewish community.

My Brother's Keeper

And [Cain] said: "I don't know. Am I my brother's keeper?" (Breisheet 4:9)

The first two children born to man had different personalities, different motivations for divine service, and very quickly their relationship descended into conflict and violence. Cain brought his offering to God "from the fruit of the ground" (4:3), and his brother Hevel provided "from the firstlings of his flock and from the most desirable" (4:4). When God spurned Cain's offering and accepted Hevel's, a vengeful Cain lured his brother into an argument in an open field and stabbed him to death – the world's first homicide.

The brief dialogue that follows between God and Cain is among the most ominous and far-reaching in the Torah: "And God said to Cain, 'Where is Hevel your brother?' And he said, 'I don't know. Am I my brother's keeper?' And He said, 'What have you done? The sound of your brother's blood cries out to me from the ground'" (4:9–10).

Rashi notes that God asked Cain a simple rhetorical question in order to gently engage him in dialogue, and perhaps prompt him to confess his crime.[39] If Cain had done that, it would have been a discernible improvement over his father's castigation of others for his own sin and would have marked mankind's progress in the realm of personal responsibility. Instead, Cain's denial upped the ante and reflected a peculiar – but not uncommon – application of personal responsibility: I am responsible, but only for myself. "Am I my brother's keeper?"

The Torah's obvious answer is that, indeed, we *are* our brother's keeper – and our sister's, our neighbor's, our fellow Jew's, and even the world's keeper. Man has an obligation to pursue righteous conduct on his own, and to strive to positively influence those in his immediate circle and the world beyond. That is a substantial part of personal responsibility – feeling an obligation to assist others, to inquire after their welfare, to take responsibility for their personal well-being, and to act upon it. Cain failed this basic test, and his punishment was, essentially, banishment from civil society: "You shall be a drifter and a wanderer on the earth" (4:12).

Cain's crime has deeper implications as well. The Midrash suggests three possible themes for the brothers' fatal argument.[40] One opinion states that

---
[39] Rashi, Breisheet 4:9.
[40] Breisheet Rabba 22:7.

they divided the world's resources between them, with Cain seizing the real property and Hevel possessing the movable property. They then fought over the disposition of the land on which Hevel stood, and the clothing that Cain wore! A second opinion finds that they each shared the world's resources, but argued over the location of the Holy Temple in Yerushalayim, with each claiming sovereignty over that place (a very modern argument, to be sure). The third opinion teaches that the brothers were each born with a twin sister (whom each married), but Hevel was born with two sisters. Cain – as the firstborn – claimed that sister was his rightful possession, and Hevel maintained that she was rightfully his, having been born together with him.

On one level, the Midrash is imparting – in its typically enigmatic way – the three causes of enmity in the world: wars over money, religion and power. Our Sages, with their keen insight into human nature, perceived this dynamic in the very first interaction between human beings. But, on second glance, we are being reminded of the extension of personal responsibility into three realms of existence. We are obligated to concern ourselves with the financial welfare of others, with their spiritual well-being, and with their personal and familial satisfaction.

Cain's rhetorical question – "Am I my brother's keeper?" – reverberates throughout history, and is the hallmark of the self-centered, egotistical individual who cannot and will not see beyond himself. In the end, one who does not feel responsible for others will not be concerned at all how he treats others – even to the extent of homicide. Such a person is unfit to live in civilized society, and Cain was abruptly banished to wander the earth.

Rav Chaim Shmulevitz, the venerable *rosh yeshiva* of Mir, added another compelling point.[41] The Midrash states that Cain responded to God by saying, essentially, why are You asking me where my brother is? "You are the guardian of all creatures, and You are asking me?"[42] How could Cain be so obtuse as to think he could deceive God?

The answer is that Cain was not looking to deceive God but to fool himself. Man's need to justify his own misdeeds and avoid responsibility is so powerful that Cain persuaded himself that he was not at fault – it was God's fault for not protecting His creatures. *You, God, permitted me to kill him because You didn't protect him… You, God, are responsible, because You did not accept my offering as You accepted Hevel's offering.*

---

[41] *Sichot Musar*, maamar 20.
[42] Tanchuma Breisheet 9.

Rav Shmulevitz elaborated that the primary punishment of man is not necessarily for the crime he commits but for his refusal to accept responsibility for his actions. Thus, God later castigated the people of Israel: "Behold, I will judge you [harshly] because you have said, 'I have not sinned.'"[43] Its modern equivalent, and the downfall of politicians from Watergate until today, is not the crime itself but the cover-up that destroys careers and reputations.

LEMECH

Have I slain a man by my wound and a child by my injury? (Breisheet 4:23)

After punishment was pronounced, Cain expressed grief and remorse – itself significant progress for humanity. "And Cain said to God, 'My sin is too great to bear'" (4:13).[44] He feared that his life would now be meaningless, and, as the one who introduced murder to the world, he would be a target for any avenger. So God assured him that he would be protected: "'Therefore, whoever slays Cain before seven generations have passed will be punished.' And God placed a mark on Cain so that none who met him would kill him" (4:15).[45]

But Cain's repentance and acceptance of personal responsibility were not completely sincere. He had learned from his father the form of repentance, but lacked the substance. "And Cain left the presence of God" (4:16), the text informs us, and Rashi notes that he walked away "in feigned humility, as if he could deceive God." That is why Cain was protected for only seven generations, and soon afterwards death would come upon him abruptly, albeit inadvertently, at the hands of his great-great-great grandson Lemech.

It is another cryptic tale in the story of creation, related in just two verses: "And Lemech said to his wives, 'Adah and Tzilah, hear my voice, wives of Lemech, give ear to my words, for have I slain a man by my wound, and a child by my injury? If Cain suffered vengeance at seven generations, then Lemech at seventy-seven!'" (4:23–24).

Rashi explains that Lemech was blind, and led by his son, Tuval-Cain, shot an arrow at what Tuval-Cain identified as an animal. In reality, it was Cain

---

[43] Yirmiyahu 2:35.

[44] Some commentators (Rashi, Targum Onkelos and others) construe Cain's statement here as a question: "Is my sin too great to bear?"

[45] This verse is also ambiguous and subject to varying interpretations. Ramban (4:23) and Radak (4:15) both explain that Cain's murderer would be punished "sevenfold."

himself whom Lemech had accidentally killed. When he realized his error – and his future fate – Lemech slapped his hands together and accidentally killed his son, Tuval-Cain.

It was certainly a tragedy, but Lemech's greatness emerges from his prompt admission of guilt, abetted by his realization that his action – unlike Cain's crime – was unintentional.[46] He accepted responsibility for his offense, and only compared it contextually to Cain's crime. By comparison, Lemech pleaded with his wives, he is no Cain: "If Cain suffered vengeance at seven generations, then Lemech at seventy-seven!"

Cain's story begins with the fratricide he committed and ends with his death at the hands of his own offspring. Lemech's confession was a partial rectification of Cain's deed – Lemech *was* his brother's keeper – but Cain's descendants would all perish in the flood, and the world would begin anew with Noach, the descendant of Cain's brother Shet.

God's Limits

And God said, "My spirit shall not strive forever with man, for he is but flesh…" (Breisheet 6:3)

Rav Ovadia Sforno comments that "it is not appropriate that God should have limitless patience with man. That would give license to conclude that man gets a free ride because he was created in the 'form and image' of God, but because he is also 'flesh,' he should be given the opportunity to repent."[47]

Man is the only creature whose existence depends on his moral development and ethical strivings. All other creatures are compelled to follow their instincts. The duality of man's existence as soul and body forces him to strive upward for greatness while simultaneously feeling the earthly pull of his instinctual drives. He is constantly being tested and can often stumble, and repentance is always a possibility as well. But man always remains accountable for his actions, and this generation's commitment to evil foreshadowed its doom.

---

[46] Rashi, Breisheet 4:24.
[47] Sforno, Breisheet 6:3.

Noach

The Collapse of Mankind

These are the generations of Noach… (Breisheet 6:9)

Man's spiritual descent was swift and relentless. Only ten generations separated Adam, God's handiwork, from the righteous Noach, and those generations were conspicuously rebellious and defiant against God.[48] Enosh and his contemporaries embraced idol worship, based on a false conception of God.[49] The strongmen of that era forcibly seized women, robbed and stole private property; victims had no recourse to any societal institution. The social order had collapsed, and man's dichotomous nature – body and soul – seemed incompatible with the capacity to consistently choose good over evil. "And God said, 'My spirit shall not strive forever with man, who is but flesh, and his days shall be one hundred twenty years.' …And God saw that man's evil was great on earth, and every inclination of his thoughts was perpetually evil"(6:3, 5).

Man would have a grace period of a little more than a century in order to rectify his deeds, after which – if he persisted in his evil ways – he would be destroyed. In this decadent milieu, one man stood out for his righteousness: Noach.

The Choice

This one will bring us rest from our work and from the toil of our hands… (Breisheet 5:29)[50]

---

[48] Mishna, Masechet Avot 5:2.

[49] Rashi, Breisheet 4:26; Rambam, *Hilchot Avodat Kochavim* 1:1.

[50] Technically, this verse appears in Parshat Breisheet but is included in this chapter for its thematic

His very name reflected his parents' hope for mankind and their generation – and a challenge to all generations. "And he [Lemech[51]] called his name Noach, saying, 'This one will comfort us from our work and the toil of our hands from the ground that God has cursed'" (5:29). Every child evokes optimism in his parents and the general community, in that he represents new life, new opportunities and the chance for a new direction.

The Talmud notes metaphorically that the angel responsible for conception brings the drop that will form the embryo before God and asks: "'This drop, what will come of it? Will it be strong or weak, smart or simple, wealthy or poor?' But whether the drop will be righteous or wicked is not mentioned…because everything is in the hands of Heaven except awe of Heaven."[52] Man's tendencies – left unchecked – will always incline him toward seeking instinctual gratification of every urge that he possesses. Yet man is equipped with a counterforce that he can access in order to pursue the higher elements of his nature – the life of the intellectually stimulating and the morally uplifting. Much in life is given to us as our genetic makeup, and much else is a matter of opportunity, such as the intellectual or financial gifts we are granted and the manner in which we utilize them. But moral choices are never prearranged, and every human being struggles with instinctual drives in order to harness those predispositions that tend to drive us away from the holy. This is a personal preference, and therein lies the primary and enduring test in life and the realm in which one's sense of personal responsibility will either be exalted or denigrated.

Perfect in His Generation

Noach was a righteous man, perfect in his generations; Noach walked with God… (Breisheet 6:9)

The Torah describes Noach as singular in his age, "a righteous man, perfect in his generations, [who] walked with God." Rashi famously comments that our Sages were equivocal about Noach's righteousness. He was "perfect in his generations" but "some maintain this was praise of Noach; he was righteous, and had he lived in a generation of righteous people he would have been

---

connection.

[51] Noach's father, of course, was not the Lemech mentioned above who was a descendant of Cain, but the progeny of Shet.

[52] Masechet Nidda 16b.

even more righteous. But others were critical of Noach; he was righteous in his generation but had he lived in the era of Avraham he would have been considered a nonentity."[53]

It is certainly strange for our Sages to criticize anyone this harshly, and especially so when the Torah extols that very person. Who are we to castigate an individual whom the Torah characterizes as one "who found favor in God's eyes" (6:8) and who is defined as virtuous? And if Noach was only "relatively" virtuous, owing to the awful deficiencies of his generation, then how does the Torah without elaboration assert that he was a "righteous man"?

The answer says less about Noach than about us, and the ethical obligations of every human being. Noach was a flawed hero, as we shall shortly discover. He was subjectively righteous; when compared to the rest of his peers, he was outstanding. But morality is neither subjective nor relative; man is obligated to heed the moral norms decreed by our mutual Creator – 613 commandments for Jews[54] and seven for non-Jews.[55] So Noach in the generation of Avraham would have been insignificant.[56]

What, then, made Noach a "righteous man, perfect in his generations"? Noach lived in his time and had the fortitude and internal strength to challenge his entire generation – and that was his righteousness. It is emotionally difficult for a person to stand alone, to be the only honest businessman in an industry of thieves, to be the only faithful spouse in a world where infidelity is accepted, to be the student who does not cheat in a class of cheaters, to be the person who eschews conversation in a synagogue of rampant chatter. The common refrain that "everyone does it" is the death knell of any aspiration to moral greatness and the obliteration of any concept of personal responsibility. We are obligated to be moral even in an immoral society and to pursue justice even in a world fraught with injustice. Noach had weaknesses, but his greatest strength – and the reason why the Torah described him as unequivocally upright – was his courage in defying his generation, obeying the call of God, and confronting his peers over their wicked ways.

---

[53] Rashi, Breisheet 6:9, citing Masechet Sanhedrin 108a.
[54] Masechet Makkot 23b–24a.
[55] Masechet Sanhedrin 56a.
[56] This is literally true. Noach died when Avraham was fifty-eight years old, and yet, after the immediate post-flood era, and certainly after the birth of Avraham, Noach is never mentioned again.

Objectively Flawed

Noach was a righteous man, perfect in his generations…
(Breisheet 6:9)

Where did Noach go wrong? What flaw did he possess that would engender such an equivocal characterization? The clue is hidden in a reference to Noach by the Prophet Yeshayahu: "For this is to Me like the waters of Noach; as I have sworn to never again pass the waters of Noach over the earth, so too I have sworn not to be wrathful with you or rebuke you."[57] But why was the flood referred to as the "waters of Noach"?

The *Zohar* states that when God commanded Noach to "enter the ark, you and your household" (7:1), Noach reasoned that since "he and his family would be saved, he did not pray for the rest of the world, which was destroyed. For this reason, the waters of the flood were termed 'the waters of Noach.'"[58] The flood, in essence, was partly blamed on Noach, as he was indifferent to the fate of his contemporaries.

Clearly, God's intention was that Noach attempt to influence his generation to abandon their evil ways. Rashi comments that the construction of the ark took 120 years and was done in plain sight, so "his peers might ask him, 'What are you building?' Noach could then respond, 'God will in the future bring a flood to the world [as retribution for evil],' and maybe they would repent."[59] That very expression – "maybe they would repent" – indicates Noach's casual feelings toward the survival of his fellow human beings.

Noach's insouciance was a grievous error and revealed a character flaw that even a "righteous person" might possess. It is not uncommon for pious individuals or Torah scholars to feel spiritually or psychologically detached from their friends and neighbors who do not fully share their knowledge, commitments or values. In the worst scenario, this attitude engenders an unbecoming haughtiness on the part of that individual who prefers to bask in his personal relationship with God and pursuit of moral perfection, and fears that such can only be compromised by too much involvement with the world at large.

---

[57] Yeshayahu 54:9. This chapter is read as the *haftara* for Parshat Noach.
[58] *Zohar*, Parshat Noach 54b.
[59] Rashi, Breisheet 6:14.

This is not the way of the righteous Jew, as epitomized by the woman of Shunem who told the prophet Elisha, "I dwell among my people."[60] The righteous Jew does not live in an ivory tower or alone in the wilderness, but in the midst of the people – feeling their pain, assuaging their grievances and tending to their needs. Indeed, Noach had been told to build an ark with a "window" (6:16)[61] – even in the ark he was not to be detached from his surroundings. Similarly, we are instructed to build synagogues with windows.[62] Noach's attitude, which diminished his standing as a righteous individual, stands in marked contrast to that of Avraham, who dedicated his life to spreading God's word across the world, often at great personal sacrifice.

It is hard for us to blame Noach. When corruption, promiscuity, violence and denial of God swirl around us, there is a natural temptation to want to circle our wagons and protect ourselves, our families and our own little society. But even that is no guarantee of ultimate success. So when the world is crying out for an Avraham, it is not sufficient to be a Noach. That is why our Sages stated so sharply that "had he lived in the generation of Avraham, Noach would not have been considered anything."[63] Noach was righteous "in *his* generation," a generation of flawed sinners who could not be saved.

Personal responsibility does not mean that a person is fixated only on his own needs and deeds – but rather requires acknowledging our obligations to our fellow creatures. This point is underscored in the aftermath of the flood, when God admonishes Noach that He will "demand the blood of every human being" (9:5) from the one who sheds it. "Whoever spills the blood of man, his blood shall be spilled by man, for man was made in the image of God" (9:6). We have inherent worth because we were created in the image of God – but so was our fellow man. In the Talmud's expression, "I am a creature and my friend is a creature."[64] We each have our tasks in the world, tasks that only we can perform. The ethic of personal responsibility demands that I not only fulfill my task in life but try to facilitate my colleague's fulfillment of his task as well.

---

[60] II Melachim 4:13.
[61] Per Rashi's first explanation.
[62] *Shulchan Aruch*, Orach Chaim 90:4.
[63] Rashi, Breisheet 6:9.
[64] Masechet Berachot 17a.

The Ark's Passengers

And from every living thing, of all flesh, bring two of each kind into the ark to keep alive with you, male and female they shall be. (Breisheet 6:19)

Shortly thereafter, God revised His command and told Noach to take "seven pairs, a male with its mate" (7:2) of all pure animals. These species would be kept alive in the enormous ark that took Noach 120 years to build.

Yet Ramban comments that the ark contained all these animals and birds only "miraculously; what was small held the many."[65] But if the ark functioned only through a miracle anyway, then why was such a large one built? Wouldn't a smaller one have sufficed?

The answer is that it was critical for Noach to become involved in building the ark and caring for the world's creatures. Man is God's partner in creation only when he assumes responsibility for others and appreciates what God has provided. God did not need an ark to save the remnant of His world; man did, and does, in order to enrich our existence and energize our spirit. Every person is asked to play the role of God's partner.

The Raven

And [Noach] dispatched the raven, and it kept going out and returning until the waters dried from the earth. (Breisheet 8:7)

Why was the raven "going out and returning"? What was its mission? Later, the dove was given a specific mission: "to see if the water had receded" (8:8). But why was the raven sent by Noach out into that watery world?

Our Sages explain that the raven was distressed. Every time it returned to the ark, Noach slammed the window shut, and so it flew out again. Its "grievance" was legitimate: "Not only did God make me an impure bird, but you – Noach – were told to take into the ark seven of every pure species but only two of an impure species. Thus, if I fail to return, will not the world be missing me? Will not ravens become extinct?" And Noach answered, "So what? What are you good for anyway – neither for food nor for an offering!"[66] *What does it matter if you survive? Who will care, besides Edgar Allen Poe?*

---

[65] Ramban, Breisheet 6:19.
[66] Masechet Sanhedrin 108b; Yalkut Shimoni, Noach 58.

God then told Noach to save the raven, as in the distant future there would be a righteous prophet named Eliyahu (Elijah) who would flee for his life and be kept alive by food brought to him by ravens.[67]

What is the deeper meaning of these conversations?

The "dialogue" between Noach and the raven was actually an internal dialogue Noach was having with himself over an issue that undoubtedly troubled him throughout the ordeal of the flood. The greatest danger to Noach after the flood was nihilism, the belief that nothing has value or importance. The danger was that Noach would emerge from the ark after having been spared the fate of his contemporaries and become desensitized, inured to death, suffering and human misery. Noach was saved – but all around him was devastation. Everything he had seen and every person he had lived with outside his family was now gone forever. No wonder he was depressed (and turned to wine); it would not have been shocking if Noach also became hardhearted and callous.

The same Midrash continues that Rabbi Akiva once expounded in Persia over the fate of the generation of the flood, "and no one cried." Then he began teaching about the sufferings of Iyov (Job) – and "they all cried." Sometimes, it is easier to cry for one person than to cry for six million people. The evil dictator Josef Stalin is said to have remarked in a related context that a single death is a tragedy, while a million deaths is a statistic.[68] Such pitiless indifference to life is the death of true humanity.

And, as we know, Noach had already been guilty of a lack of genuine concern over the fate of his generation, and had refrained from reaching out to his contemporaries and encouraging their repentance.

To avert the potential for apathy, God placed Noach in charge of caring for creation – to force him into daily exercises of empathy for all the animals in his care. When he learned his lesson, then the Torah teaches that "God remembered Noach and every living thing and all the cattle that were with him in the ark" (8:1). And when he was dismissive of the raven – "*ma tzorech la'olam b'cha?*" (for what does the world need you?)[69] – God reminded him that "every person has his time and every creature has its place,"[70] even the raven. The world needs every person and every part of creation. Thus, Jewish law

---

[67] Yalkut Shimoni, Noach 58.

[68] While it is debatable whether Stalin actually uttered this line widely attributed to him, he certainly behaved violently enough to have heartily endorsed it.

[69] Midrash Breisheet Rabba 33:5.

[70] Masechet Avot 4:3.

states that every person present when someone dies must rend his garments because we are all diminished by the death of every person.[71] The death of a human being is compared to the burning of a Torah scroll; in both cases, a holy expression of God's divinity – His image and His word – is lost.

In today's world in which, again, "he who slaughters an ox is as if he slays a man,"[72] in which homicide is rampant, Islamic terror still rages and life itself is trivialized, we always need to look afresh at God's world and our role in it – in protecting human dignity and preserving life.

The Evil Inclination

...for the inclination of man's heart is evil from his very youth... (Breisheet 8:21)

Rashi cites the Midrashic statement that man is inclined toward instinctual gratification – "evil" only relative to the sublime pursuits that gratify the soul – from "the time he begins to emerge from his mother's womb."[73] The infant's body needs oxygen and sustenance immediately, and the infant's early life is defined by little more than satisfying those needs as soon as they arise. That is the *yetzer hara* – the part of man that seeks physical and psychological enjoyments. The *yetzer hatov* – the part of man that inclines him to spiritual satisfactions – does not take up residence in the person until maturity, defined as the age of acceptance of *mitzvot* (bat or bar mitzvah).

The *yetzer hara* has an enormous head start – twelve or thirteen years – and the natural response of some parents is often to indulge it, to gratify every childish need and fulfill every childish whim. Such pampering only strengthens the *yetzer hara* and makes it much more difficult for the *yetzer hatov* to take root. The "evil inclination" can easily become one's master, especially in people who are never taught boundaries and in children who never hear the word *no* (when "no" is appropriate). Reining in the *yetzer hara* and activating the *yetzer hatov* is a primary responsibility of parenting, and exercising that self-control is the major test of adulthood.

It is no excuse to argue that the "evil inclination" is stronger than the good one and its gratification more immediate. That is man's challenge – to strive for godliness even as he is being pulled to earthiness.

---

[71] Masechet Moed Katan 25a; *Shulchan Aruch*, Yoreh Deah 340:5.
[72] Yeshayahu 66:3.
[73] Breisheet Rabba 34:10.

The Covenant

And I will establish My covenant with you; never again shall all flesh be cut off by waters of a flood, and never again shall there be a flood to destroy the earth. (Breisheet 9:11)

The question presents itself: If the original flood was an ethical necessity because the world had reached a state of utter turpitude, then how can God commit Himself not to bring another flood? Indeed, the moral condition of Noach's generation is not that dissimilar from many others historically, including our own. The sins of that generation – especially promiscuity, violence and theft – are certainly not unknown to us. So how could God make this promise?

The essence of the covenant was that God guaranteed that there would always be good in the world – good people who would do good things. And no matter how much evil would exist and does exist, and no matter how many people tolerate it, accept it, ignore it, extol it or are indifferent to it, there will always be righteous people to sound the alarm, to fight it and to mobilize society against it.

Thus, God implanted in creation a historical provision that pure evil might still exist in the world, but rather than be a cause for the earth's destruction it would instead be perceived as an opportunity. Man will have the capacity to challenge it and the strength of character to oppose it. He need only mobilize that strength of character and avoid becoming either enamored of evil or simply complacent. The covenant is only breached if mankind in its entirety accommodates or surrenders to depravity.

Noach started a new world of individuals who would try to redeem mankind, preach about God and goodness, and remind mankind that God's moral norms are as substantive as are the laws of nature – and that the two are intertwined. And he would be succeeded – in his lifetime – by Avraham, and by a nation that would come into existence for that purpose alone.

The Midrash avers that the world cannot endure unless every generation has thirty righteous people like Avraham – or perhaps just twenty, ten, five, or two such righteous people.[74] Rabbi Shimon bar Yochai adds that perhaps, even if there is only one virtuous soul, that will also suffice to validate God's decision and justify His world – and even if the people are Rabbi Shimon himself and his son. In other words, if the world has only one righteous person, then you

---

[74] Breisheet Rabba 35:2. Masechet Succa 45b records that there are thirty-six righteous people who receive the Divine Presence every day.

be that one. If it has two or ten or twenty or thirty – if there is a support system for *tzaddikim* – then you be in that group too. It is much more difficult to be the only *tzaddik* – but even then one cannot flinch from that obligation.

To be a *tzaddik* is a choice – a choice that is made every moment of every day. We are fortunate to be part of a people that was groomed for righteousness, but every individual must choose wisely and cannot simply rely on the choices of others.

Noach's Children

And Shem and Yefet took a garment, laid it upon both their shoulders, walked backwards and covered their father's nakedness; their faces were turned away and they did not gaze upon their father's nakedness. (Breisheet 9:23)

The bestial treatment of Noach by his son Cham earned Cham everlasting scorn but elicited from his brothers Shem and Yefet dignified and appropriate treatment of their father. They protected his modesty as best they could, and were rewarded for their sensitivity for all eternity, even as shameless Cham was sentenced to a life of servitude. But why was Shem, the younger brother, mentioned before Yefet?

Rashi states that Shem was more assiduous in fulfilling the commandment of honoring parents; it was his idea to preserve Noach's dignity, and so his descendants were rewarded with the *mitzva* of *tallit* – the *tzitzit* that Jewish males wear every day. The descendants of Yefet, who followed his brother's lead, will merit the dignity of burial after the climactic war of Gog and Magog. Their bodies will be treated with respect. The Midrash suggests further that Yefet's descendants were also rewarded with a distinguished garment – the Roman toga.[75] How is this connected to the story?

It is difficult to lead, to be a pioneer, to be the first person to do the right thing. It is much easier to be a follower. This was the greatness of Shem: he saw the degradation of his father at the hands of his brother Cham and rather than turn away and remain uninvolved, he acted, in effect rebuking his brother for his reprehensible conduct. Shem took the initiative. He had an inner sense of right and wrong, and therefore merited the *tallit* – the garment that connects us to God and is a constant reminder of our obligations to Him. The *tzitzit*

---

[75] Breisheet Rabba 36:6.

enable us to remember to do what is right because God has said it is right, and for no other reason. It shapes our inner world, which greatly influences our behavior.

Yefet was a follower. He did respond initially but only acted when he saw Shem act. He had a correct notion of right and wrong, but it was only activated by an external trigger. Yefet joined Shem because it appeared to be the right thing to do, and he did not want to be perceived by others as less caring or devoted to their father. So Yefet, who was concerned with appearances, and his descendants merited things that deal with the external reality but are meaningless in substance. Accordingly, they merited either burial (the physical disposal of the body, the shell of the human being) or the toga (which was an outward sign of one's status in Roman society). Yefet's world – the world of Greek, Roman and Western civilization – is one that, for all its contributions to mankind, has often presented a veneer of refinement, and enlightenment that scarcely concealed the barbarism that raged within and that too often targeted the descendants of Shem for special, brutal treatment.

There are people who are prime movers in the world of ethics, and there are others who are their followers. In truth, both groups are necessary, but the prime movers are more valued and make a greater difference. They are the leaders who influence others for the good.

The worlds of Shem and Yefet collide in another sphere as well – in divine service. How many people serve God and observe the *mitzvot* not necessarily in order to obey God's will but because of fear of what others – parents, teachers, rabbis or the community – will say if they don't observe? That service is the world of Yefet, and invariably, children begin their Torah observance with that mindset. However, we all must graduate from that at some point – and the age of bar mitzvah is the ideal time for the implicit recognition of the obligation to serve God like Shem – not for the sake of others but rather to inform our spiritual growth and refine our attachment to God.

Ultimately, we are defined by our thoughts and our actions, which make an everlasting imprint on our souls.

The First Dictator

And Cush begat Nimrod. He began to be a mighty one on earth. He was a mighty hunter before God; therefore, it is said, Nimrod was a mighty hunter before God. (Breisheet 10:8–9)

How was Nimrod a "mighty hunter before God"? Everything in the universe occurs "before God."

Rashi and Ramban both explain that Nimrod was the first religious rebel. He ruled with demagoguery and an iron fist and fomented a rebellion against God. In essence, he ordained himself as the most powerful force on earth in place of God.

Interestingly, Avraham ibn Ezra comments that Nimrod was "mighty before God" in that he hunted animals, caught them, and offered them before God on altars that he built. Ramban rejects this interpretation, because it paints Nimrod in a positive light, whereas our Sages deemed him an inveterate evildoer. So why would ibn Ezra "praise" Nimrod?

Rabbi Yisrael Chait[76] explained that all three interpretations complement each other. Rashi states that Nimrod waged war against the idea of God, and Ramban adds Nimrod was successful by dint of his forceful personality. He was both physically powerful as well as charismatic – a deadly combination in a wicked person. But how did he succeed in rallying others to his cause?

That is the focus of the ibn Ezra's commentary – that Nimrod would construct altars and offer sacrifices on them. Nimrod was the first human being to harness the power of religion to inflame and then subdue the masses. He exploited the attraction of religion – its connection to the Almighty and its definition of the purposeful life – and created around himself a cult of personality.

Nimrod was the first but not the last individual to realize the powerful hold religion has on people's lives; he has many heirs, from Pharaoh and Nevuchadnetzar in biblical times to medieval kings who claimed a divine right to rule and Adolf Hitler, who saw himself as a creature of Providence. Today's Muslim radicals who promise paradise to individuals who explode themselves trying to kill Jews and others continue the same ghastly tradition. Nimrod invented the ploy of using God's name to justify murder, theft, marauding, conquest and abuse.

---

[76] *Rosh Yeshiva* of Yeshiva Bnei Torah, Far Rockaway, New York, my Rebbe Muvhak.

It is hard to combat this weapon which has led many individuals to reject religion altogether; it was nearly impossible in ancient times as well. No wonder Nimrod perceived Avraham as such a dire threat to his empire. Avraham represented the true idea of God, and could prove it as well.

Nimrod's descendants are alive and killing still. The task of the God-fearing is not to shirk from this conflict but to confront it, to speak in God's name and to represent God's interests in the world. Every moral individual has the responsibility to propagate the true ideas of a God of justice, mercy and righteousness – a God that bequeathed to man an objective morality that that both guides and inspires his life. Despair is not an option, nor is shirking that responsibility. As the eighteenth-century Irish-British statesman Edmund Burke purportedly said, "The only thing necessary for the triumph of evil is for good men to do nothing."

If Nimrod falsified God in order to reduce man to an animalistic level, Avraham (and his heirs) proclaimed God's name to all in order to elevate man. That remains our historic role and the realization of our destiny.

The Follower

And Haran died during the lifetime of Terach his father, in the land of his birth, in Ur Kasdim. (Breisheet 11:28)

Rashi recounts the distressing family drama that unfolded in these few verses. Terach snitched to Nimrod about the heresies of his own son, Avraham, which prompted Nimrod to confront Avraham publicly and menacingly. When Avraham did not renounce his faith, Nimrod tossed him in the fiery furnace of the Chaldees – from which Avraham miraculously emerged unscathed.

Haran, Avraham's brother, sat and watched this spectacle, and calculated: "If Avraham is victorious, then I will be with him; but if Nimrod triumphs, then I will be with him."[77] When Avraham escaped, Haran proclaimed his allegiance to Avraham. Nimrod then threw Haran into the furnace – and Haran was burned to death. Why wasn't he saved as well?

Avraham's faith was complete and sincere. He had the courage of his convictions, even before God reached out to him in prophecy! Avraham had the logic of faith.

---

[77] Rashi, Breisheet 11:28.

Haran had the logic of the businessman – no convictions, no substance, no depth and no faith at all. His belief system was purely utilitarian – support for whoever or whatever seems ascendant at any particular time. Haran was a classic frontrunner.

If Haran had also been saved from the furnace, just like Avraham, and then joined his brother in Canaan, the result would have been disastrous and might even have undermined Avraham's mission. At the first setback – and for Avraham, there were many – Haran would have deserted, and desecrated God's name through his lack of faith.[78]

Jewish life – personal responsibility – demands that we not follow the herd and their trends, but use our judgment independently and fearlessly to do what is right and just.

---

[78] Heard from Rav Yisrael Chait.

Lech Lecha

Independence

Go for yourself from your land, from your birthplace and from your father's house to the land that I will show you. (Breisheet 12:1)

Our forefather Avraham was an extraordinary human being, but his greatness is distorted if we don't appreciate the events in his life as he lived them. He was the paragon of faith, following God's command to uproot himself and travel to an unknown land, to separate himself from the only society that he had known in order to reestablish himself elsewhere. And Rashi explains the word *lecha* (for yourself) as "for your pleasure and benefit."

How was this voyage to the unknown for his "pleasure and benefit"?

There is an excitement in seeking one's own destiny and carving out for oneself a path on which no one else has trodden. Often, people – especially religious people – see conformity as a virtue, and undoubtedly it is when matters of practice are concerned. We do not have the luxury of choosing which *mitzvot* to fulfill and how to fulfill them. The 613 commandments all come with rigid guidelines as to their form and substance; that is the essence of what makes them commands and not suggestions.

Yet every person possesses a unique soul that shapes a unique personality. "The Holy One, Blessed be He, imprinted every human being with the stamp of Adam, and yet no person is like any other."[79] So, too, our Sages ordained a special blessing to be recited when one sees six hundred thousand Jews gathered in one place: "'Blessed is the Knower of Secrets' – because no two personalities are identical and no two faces are identical."[80] Individuality is not

---

[79] Masechet Sanhedrin 37a.
[80] Masechet Berachot 58a.

only a blessing but a fulfillment of God's will in creation. We are allowed – even encouraged – to pursue our individual talents and destinies, all within a Torah framework. We may become Jewish doctors, lawyers, artists, musicians, inventors, scientists, businessmen, entrepreneurs and thinkers. To live in a box stifles creativity, and the attempt to produce cookie-cutter children eventually grows stale. The enormous variety of personal expression in Israeli life is a joy to behold, with committed Jews reviving facets of life, art and culture that were dormant throughout the long exile. God's message to us, as well, is "go for yourself," for your pleasure and benefit. Seek to do what is fulfilling to you, and also what benefits the society at large.

We do not have the luxury of hearing a direct command from God to "go," but God's communications with Avraham were also limited. God appeared to Avraham in Elon Moreh and promised the land of Israel to his descendants, as yet unborn.[81] His mission was set; "he built there an altar to God, and called out in the name of God" (12:8). And then? "And Avram journeyed on, traveling steadily to the south" (12:9). No further guidance was offered, nor were detailed instructions needed.

Our personal tendencies and proclivities are innate – God-given. It is our choice whether to explore and actualize them or allow them to remain undeveloped, whether to suppress them when they might be harmful or rechannel that energy and use it productively to further God's will.

Cult of Personality

> *…and all the families of the earth shall be blessed through you. (Breisheet 12:3)*
>
> *A man will say to his son, "Be like Avraham." (Rashi, Breisheet 12:3)*
>
> *And Avram took…the souls he had made in Charan… (Breisheet 12:5)*

In his homeland, Avraham had defied Nimrod and preached about the existence of one incorporeal God Who created the universe and decreed how man should live. Rashi comments that these individuals were drawn to Avraham and accompanied him to Canaan, "for he brought them under

---

[81] Breisheet 12:7.

the wings of the Divine Presence; Avraham converted the men and Sarah converted the women." These were the souls that Avraham "made" in Charan. To teach people Torah, values and morality not only gives them purpose in life, but also molds their souls and literally creates them, their essences.

So what happened to these souls that Avraham shaped – these courageous individuals who also left their homes, families and birthplaces to join Avraham on his journey? Indeed, these people did not even have the benefit of a divine communication, and still they escorted him to his unidentified destination!

Unfortunately, they disappeared after Avraham's death as Yitzchak was unable to retain their allegiance. These precious souls – Avraham's converts – were too tied to Avraham's personality and were lost in the mist of history.

Rav Avraham Yitzchak Kook wrote that people should take care never to identify too closely with the personality of (even) their rabbi lest they take on his good *and* less than good characteristics.[82] A total identification with another's personality is never healthy, both because even great people are bound to disappoint here and there and the slightest misstep can lead to complete disillusionment, and because it is never prudent to abandon one's individual judgment. Even a teacher's word and thoughts must be scrutinized and weighed carefully, if only to be understood properly and to know when to ask questions – and when to (respectfully) disagree.

The Talmud notes that when Rabbi Shimon ben Lakish (Resh Lakish) died, his teacher and companion, the outstanding sage Rav Yochanan, fell into a deep depression. His friends sent an especially sharp disciple to learn Torah with Rav Yochanan in order to lift his spirits, and that disciple validated every point that Rav Yochanan made with an additional proof. That made Rav Yochanan even *more* despondent: "Previously, when I studied with Resh Lakish, on everything I said he would ask twenty-four questions and raise twenty-four objections, and *that* is how we explicated the matter. All you do is agree with me and support what I am saying. Do I not think that what I am saying is correct?"[83]

The truth of Torah emerges through dialectic, but more to the point, Resh Lakish was not so intimidated by Rav Yochanan's sublime stature that he forfeited his independence of thought. For some reason, that autonomy has been mislaid in our generation, and many Jews identify with their spiritual leaders to the point of self-effacement, incapable of (or unwilling to) make the smallest decision in life without consultation or guidance. And these decisions

---

[82] *Orot*, Orot Yisrael 3:3.
[83] Bava Metzia 84a.

are frequently not about matters of Jewish law – which obviously is the natural and proper sphere for rabbinical guidance – but usually about personal issues for which guidance is best sought but ultimate decision making left to the individual.

The danger inherent in such an approach is self-evident, as no human being is infallible. Avraham's disciples were lost because they identified more with him than with the ideas he was preaching. The Kotzker Rebbe, on the Mishnaic recommendation "Raise up many students,"[84] observed that the primary function of a teacher is to "raise up" students, to create the environment in which students can stand on their own two feet.

That is the Torah way. It is not that rabbis do not have great wisdom to offer; many, if not most, do. It is rather that each person can only live his own life and not the life of another. Individual decision making, after receiving ideas and recommendations from a number of sources, is part of maturity. This approach does protect against possible disenchantment, but more importantly, it enables the development of healthy, well-adjusted people who can think for themselves and act appropriately as free-willed beings.[85]

We cannot "be like Avraham" in the sense that we can replicate his life's experiences. Those were exceptional events. Unlike most people, Avraham was not the product of his times. He was reared by an idolatrous father in an idolatrous country – and yet was able to follow his mind and pursue truth until he concluded that his father's faith was false, and he discovered God. We can "be like Avraham" in maintaining our independence of thought, following our minds and developing the uniqueness of our characters all for the purpose of better serving God and spreading His word.

Self-help

> *Please say that you are my sister, so that it will go well with me for your sake and that I will live because of you. (Breisheet 12:13)*

Avraham twice, and his son Yitzchak once, employed the ruse of pretending that their wives were their sisters in order to prevent a potentate from simply murdering them and seizing their wives. The theory was that an "unmarried"

---

[84] Mishna Avot 1:1.

[85] Questions that relate to specialized areas – e,g., should one have surgery? should one invest in a particular stock or business? – are best left to experts in those areas.

sister would be wooed rather than have her "brother" killed. That the scheme never worked does not inherently invalidate its logic. But why continue to use a ploy that consistently fails?

The answer is that sometimes in life there are no perfect answers, only a variety of options that range from poor to best and from which one must choose the best. That was Avraham's predicament. He was brought by God to the land of Israel, and almost immediately after receiving God's promise that the land would be his in perpetuity, he was forced to leave it in order to avoid the effects of a devastating famine. It was one of the ten trials that he had to endure.[86]

What were Avraham's options? He could not stay in the land of Canaan without any means of sustenance. He could not return to his homeland; that would be a betrayal of God's command and an admission of failure. The only realistic choice was to go to Egypt, which presented its own problem: the decadent nature of that society in which men leered at women, who were perceived only as objects for male gratification. He could try to smuggle Sarah in, and if that did not succeed, try to save them both by pretending to be brother and sister. That would theoretically induce a potential suitor to want to charm Avraham rather than incarcerate or execute him; even reprobate societies have some redeeming qualities and try to present a façade of decency. That would allow Avraham to buy time, wait out the famine in Egypt and then return to Canaan at the earliest opportunity. All his plans failed.[87]

Avraham's actions here were rooted in one of the great standards of Jewish life: do not rely on miracles.[88] We do not rely on miracles not because we believe that God cannot perform them; on the contrary, we have long been the beneficiaries of God's compassion and Providence. Much of the Torah relates God's interventions on behalf of our forefathers.

But no individual has the right to expect a miracle, or even to remain passive when confronted with a desperate situation and allow a miracle to be the only means of escape. One has to be worthy of a miracle, and even the most righteous people – Avraham, Yaakov – feared that sin had detracted from their merits.[89] If they deemed themselves unworthy, what can we say about ourselves?

---

[86] Radak, on Breisheet 12:10, citing *Pirkei D'Rabbi Eliezer* 26.
[87] Rashi, Breisheet 12:11, 14. See also Ramban, Breisheet 12:11.
[88] Masechet Pesachim 64b; Radak, Breisheet 12:12.
[89] Radak, Breisheet 12:12.

Nevertheless, the broader reason for not relying on miracles is that God created a system in which we live, a system that encompasses both the natural and the political order. We have been given all the tools – the wisdom of Torah and minds to comprehend it – necessary to resolve most situations in life, albeit not all. Those who sit and wait for salvation under the guise of piety are actually denying a fundamental Torah principle. Taking responsibility for our own destiny is critical to the Torah personality.

Ten Trials

Our father Avraham was tested ten times by God and withstood every test, to teach us the extent of his love [for God]. (Masechet Avot 5:4)

Although there are several different calculations of the ten trials, most of Avraham's life easily fits into that category: his attempted execution by Nimrod in the furnace of the Chaldees,[90] his departure to Canaan, the famines, the turmoil with his ne'er-do-well nephew Lot, the wars, the infertility, the covenant of circumcision, the Akeidat Yitzchak (binding of Isaac), the death of Sarah, and so on. His life as the Torah records it seems to move from one trial to the next, seemingly without a moment's peace – chased from his birthplace, hounded in the land of Israel, embraced and then distanced by his contemporaries – all of which would seem to belie the Torah's benign characterization of Avraham as "blessed with everything" (24:1), and dying "old and content" (25:8), i.e., satisfied. He was old – but satisfied? How could he be satisfied – childless for almost a century, troubles from one son (Yishmael), a wife who is kidnapped twice and then dies suddenly? How can one be "satisfied" after such a life?

A *nisayon* is more than a test or a trial. We all face challenges – but ours are usually not the *nisyonot* of Avraham.

Avraham's trials were all tests for which there is no ready answer, no clear-cut solution, no one correct approach. A plausible argument can be made for either side: does he obey God's command of "go forth" even if that means abandoning his elderly father? Is that moral?[91] Should he journey to Egypt

---

[90] This is not enumerated by most of the commentators as it is not explicitly mentioned in the Torah.

[91] Rashi (11:32) suggests that was the reason why the Torah "concealed" the death of Terach, placing it "before" the command of *Lech Lecha* even if it actually occurred much later, so that people will not readily deduce that Avraham did not appropriately honor his father.

or stay in Canaan – stay and starve or journey and risk capture of death? Not much of a choice.

Should he go to war against four powerful despots to save Lot, or not endanger himself for what looks like a hopeless quest? Should he plead for the sinners of Sodom, or let them receive their just desserts? Should Avraham expel Hagar to preserve Yitzchak's spiritual integrity – and, if so, what is his responsibility to his son Yishmael? Should Avraham obey God's call to offer his son Yitzchak at the Akeida, argue that this violates God's promise that Yitzchak will be his heir (and that this therefore cannot be God's will) or simply protest that child sacrifice is objectively abhorrent?

Not only was there no simple answer to these quandaries, but we lack even a barometer to know which moral choice was right or wrong. How then can the Mishna conclude that Avraham "withstood all of them," that he chose correctly each time?

Each of Avraham's trials tested his faith. They were nothing more than opportunities to complain to God. At any point, Avraham could have protested: "Why are You doing this to me? What do You want from me? You dispatch me to the land of Canaan, only to be greeted by a famine and a war; You promise me a noble lineage, and make me childless; You offer me no guidance on how to protect my own wife from the marauders of my generation; You demand I sacrifice my son as an offering before You; and then my wife dies from the trauma. What do You want from me?"

To us, it seems natural. Modern man is filled with grievances – against God, against parents and grandparents, against spouses, against children, against the boss, against the rabbi and the shul, against nature, against the government, against the doctor and lawyer and accountant, against the service in a restaurant and against the other drivers on the highway. We are filled with complaints, and will air them to anyone who will listen, and to many who will not. It is a sign of a weakness in our souls.

The response to a trial is not measured by right or wrong, but by the decision-making process, the motivation, and the ultimate goal. Every choice Avraham made was motivated by one goal: which option would contribute more to the proliferation of God's name? Which would reflect better on God's ultimate objectives for mankind?

With that goal, decisions in life become clearer. We are told quite directly that if we wish to complain about anything in life, we should complain about our failings. "About what should a living man complain? Each man for his sins!"[92]

Our forefathers never whined, complained, doubted or had any grievances. They were spiritual giants. From that perspective, it is clear why Avraham's life was filled with contentment despite its superficial hardships. He only had to decide which approach furthered God's will the most. He always had one purpose in life: "And he proclaimed there in the name of God, God of the universe" (21:33). If we really looked at our lives with any objectivity, we would realize we have so little to complain about. Our real trials are miniscule and exceedingly rare. We can acquire the same contentment in life if we remove the sources of discontent – ego, greed, jealousy, and frustration – and realize their insignificance when compared to the reality of our lives and our sacred mission.

Wealth

> *And Avram was heavily laden, with cattle, with silver and with gold. (Breisheet 13:2)*

Few tests are as challenging as the test of wealth. To people bereft of values or purpose in life, riches can be destructive. The disproportionately higher rate of suicide among lottery winners (who suddenly have great wealth thrust upon them) is so striking that one would think it would decrease the number of people who buy lottery tickets.[93]

"The crown of the wise is their riches but the foolishness of fools is just foolishness."[94] When the acquisition of money is internalized so that the bearers of that wealth attribute to themselves great powers of success, intelligence and divine favor, then wealth can devastate the soul, not to mention ruin marriages, families and friendships. But when wealth is perceived as a tool – as a gift from God in line with "it is the blessing of God that enriches"[95] – then the righteous and wise, and the world generally, benefit from that wealth.

This is not only a function of the righteous being able to distribute their bounty to the disadvantaged. Rabbeinu Yona writes that when a wise person attains wealth, he has even greater power to inspire and promote reverence for

---

[92] Eicha 3:39.
[93] It doesn't, because most people think that *they* will not be affected negatively, only *others* will.
[94] Mishlei 14:24.
[95] Mishlei 10:22.

Heaven.[96] The average person respects the wealthy, if only because he aspires to wealth himself. The wealthy who are righteous – and our forefathers were all affluent people – are able to gain an audience and influence others to listen to their message.

Of course, the dangers are apparent as well. Rabbeinu Bachye comments, as the verse indicates, that wealth is a crown to "the wise" but to the fool it will just add to his foolishness. Wealth that distorts the soul and is used only for the acquisition of luxuries, placing undue pressure on the person to maintain that inflated standard of living, is corrosive to life and to one's pursuit of moral perfection.

Wealth is thus just an instrument that one can use for good or ill; it is morally neutral. How it is used, and what effect it will have on the holder, is a personal choice. The examples are before us. "And also Lot, who went with Avram, had flocks, cattle and tents" (13:5). Lot was exceedingly wealthy, and all because of his proximity to Avraham.[97] But Lot was corrupted by his prosperity, chafed under the moral restrictions of Avraham's household, and was easily seduced by the allures of Sodom.[98] He defined himself by his worldly goods: "And [the kings] captured Lot and his possessions the son of Avram's brother..." (14:12). He wasn't "Lot the son of Avram's brother" but rather "Lot *and his possessions* the son of Avram's brother"! His entire sense of self-worth emerged from his resources.[99]

Conversely, Avraham's wealth was a vehicle for him to better fulfill his mission in life. He hated dependence and abhorred the notion that his wealth would be perceived as acquired from others, telling the king of Sodom whom he had liberated: "[I will not take from you] as much as a thread or a shoe strap...or anything of yours, so you shall not say, 'I enriched Avram'" (14:23). To be perceived as a taker would have diminished Avraham's ability to preach God's message. His wealth was part of him and enabled him to fulfill his divinely ordained role, but did not define him.

Would that we were able to embrace the same approach to life!

---

[96] Rabbeinu Yona, Mishlei 14:24.

[97] Rashi, Breisheet 13:5.

[98] Rashi, Breisheet 13:7. Despite Lot's great wealth, his shepherds still stole from others.

[99] Similarly, "And Haman recounted to them the glory of his wealth and of his many sons..." (Esther 5:11), putting his wealth before his children in the hierarchy of importance. Examples of this phenomenon are legion, both ancient and modern.

Concern for Others

And Avram heard that his kinsman was taken captive, and he armed his disciples who had been born in his house – three hundred eighteen – and he pursued [the kings] as far as Dan. (Breisheet 14:14)

Personal responsibility should never be conflated with selfishness, an awful character trait that materialistic societies often breed. Avraham had fame and fortune, a good life, a divinely inspired life, and risked it all to rescue his nephew who had betrayed him and taken up residence in an environment that was the antithesis of everything revered by Avraham. The natural instinct would have been to tell Lot: "Sorry, but I told you so, not to mention that you deserve it." A sharp political instinct would have concluded that, even if Lot's fate is unfortunate, any attempt to save him from the clutches of the four powerful kings who had just been victorious in the first world war was a quixotic and hopeless quest – even with the 318 disciples who constituted Avraham's army. Had Avraham desisted, and we merely read of Lot's untimely demise, we would not have thought any less of Avraham.

Nor did Avraham leap into battle because of his love of combat and adventure. On the contrary, Avraham fretted about the necessity of going to war and feared that the loss of life caused by war – and the gift of his own survival – had consumed any divine reward to which he was entitled. "After these events, the word of God came to Avram in a vision, saying, 'Do not be afraid, Avram, I am your shield; your reward is exceedingly great'" (15:1).[100] Avraham was a reluctant warrior.

Avraham went to war at tremendous personal sacrifice because of two values that burned within him: love of justice and loving-kindness. Both of these qualities engendered a fierce commitment to look beyond himself and to concern himself at all times with the needs of other people. That other people could possibly accomplish the same goal is irrelevant to an Avraham; the obligation to help others is personal, not just societal. His engagement in this battle reflected on Avraham, and his personal responsibilities to others, especially family, and especially when the aggressors were evildoers who threatened the vision Avraham had for society.

---

[100] See Rashi, Breisheet 15:1.

Indeed, the *Zohar* states that the kings kidnapped Lot in order to lure Avraham into a battle in which he would be easily killed, or so they thought.[101] Avraham was a threat to the existing world order, in which these despots ruled based on might and cruelty.[102] They were being undermined by Avraham's popularity wherever he traveled, preaching of the one God, His universal morality and the dignity of all mankind. Avraham had to be eliminated, and in a way that would be manifestly fair – as, presumably, just another casualty of war. Indeed, Avraham surely realized that his participation in this war might even undercut his image as a man of peace and kindness, and impair his broader message.

All those calculations paled before the injustice that drew Avraham into battle. He showed that there is no contradiction between being a warrior and a man of God, between being a Torah scholar and a soldier.[103] One must be zealous in fighting God's battles, even if the struggle is lonely and unappreciated by others. That there are religious groups in Israel today who cannot bridge the gap between those two roles – the scholar/warrior – is a sign of weakness, not strength. It is the emasculation of Torah, not its fulfillment, even discounting the societal discord and hatred for Torah it generates.[104]

Certainly, Avraham, Moshe, Yehoshua, David and many other spiritual giants were no less dedicated to Torah study and service of God than today's young men who eschew military or national service for the sake of their Torah learning. They were able to adjust their priorities when the needs of the nation so demanded. An abundant love of Torah must always be combined with love and concern for others. It is surely not impossible to fulfill both mandates – Torah and national service; many, in fact, do so with distinction. In general, modern Western society with its extensive welfare and social services apparatus has fostered a system of givers and takers. There are those who give – work, earn, contribute, fight, build, teach – and those who take. Inevitably, that system produces strife, discord and unrest, until it finally collapses.

---

[101] *Zohar*, Breisheet 86b.

[102] Rashi (14:1) notes that the first king mentioned – Amrafel – was Avraham's old nemesis Nimrod.

[103] Although Avraham willingly went into battle to rescue his nephew, one Talmudic sage states that Avraham was punished for "impressing scholars [his disciples] into military service" (Masechet Nedarim 32a). Other disagree with that conclusion, and one later authority (the *Shitah Mekubetzet* of Rav Betzalel Ashkenazi, sixteenth-century rabbi in Egypt and Israel) asserts that Avraham was criticized not for conscripting his disciples but for not paying them an appropriate wage for their service.

[104] See Parshat Matot for an additional discussion of this phenomenon. The controversy surrounding the military or national service of Haredim in Israel rages as this is being written.

It would be extremely misleading to suggest that those involved in serious and sustained *talmud Torah* do not also contribute in a meaningful way to the spiritual state of nation. The ideal, though, remains contributions in both spheres – spiritual and physical. Avraham prided himself on being a giver, and abhorred "taking" to the extent that he shunned even the spoils of war to which he was entitled.[105] We should know better than to construct a society on the same inequitable foundation, if only because we are the "people of the God of Abraham."[106] The ideal must be to give rather than take, and to contribute to society in as many different ways as is necessary to sustain a healthy polity. We know, as well, that those who are Avraham's descendants inherited not only the land promised to our illustrious ancestor but also his passionate and tireless commitment to justice, loving-kindness and the sanctification of God's name in all that we do.

---

[105] Breisheet 14:21–24.
[106] Tehillim 47:10.

Vayera

The Way of Kindness

> *And behold there were three men standing before him, and [Avraham] saw and ran toward them from the entrance of the tent, and he bowed to the ground. And he said: "My lord, if I find favor in your eyes, please do not go away from your servant." (Breisheet 18:2–3)*

> *Avraham came forward and said, "Will You also eliminate the righteous along with the wicked?" (Breisheet 18:23)*

> *And Avraham prayed to God, and God healed Avimelech, his wife, his maidservants, and they [again] gave birth. (Breisheet 20:17)*

Avraham's concern for others reaches its apex in this Torah portion. In a variety of situations, Avraham is confronted with the choice to act or to remain passive, and in each situation he acts, notwithstanding that there are cogent and even moral reasons to remain disengaged.

In the midst of a prophetic vision from God, Avraham is visited by three strangers, dressed like Arab nomads and in the guise of idolaters – and Avraham begs leave from God (!) to tend to the needs of his visitors. "Rav Yehuda said in the name of Rav: welcoming guests is greater even than greeting the Divine Presence,"[107] as this story indicates. Avraham took time out from his prophetic vision – that would shortly inform him of the birth of his son one year hence – in order to fetch water, bread, butter, cakes and meat for his guests. But why should the rather humdrum *mitzva* of welcoming guests take precedence over an exalted and extraordinary divine revelation?

---
[107] Masechet Shabbat 127a.

The Netziv comments that only one who is filled with love of God will even merit the Divine Presence, but one of the foremost (and substantive) expressions of love of God is to show love for His creatures.[108] Avraham, in essence, did not forsake God mid-prophecy but rather exchanged one form of divine service for another. In the Netziv's formulation, he momentarily passed up an expression of love of God that is timeless for an expression of love of God that is time-bound, i.e., the presence of wayfarers who needed his kindness.

So, too, Avraham's pleas for Sodom had a dual purpose: to understand God's attribute of justice and ascertain the point at which man's existence becomes utterly counterproductive to God's plan and therefore must end; and to demonstrate his own love of humanity, even for people whose lives reflected the very opposite of the benevolence that characterized Avraham. In the end, Avraham realized that, of course, the "Judge of all the earth [shall] do justice" (18:25). The ineluctably wicked, the irredeemably guilty, will be punished – but those whose wickedness is incomplete and who have redeemable qualities, like Lot and his family, will be saved. But Avraham had to see beyond himself and even beyond his values to perceive the potential good in his contemporaries in Sodom and environs.

If Avraham could gaze down on Sodom from a safe distance, he was forced to confront the immorality of Avimelech and his people up close and personal. Again confronting a local famine, and again resorting to the old standby of "my wife is really my sister," Avraham went to Gerar (in today's Gaza Strip) and again Sarah was seized by the local potentate. There was "no fear of God in this place" (20:11); rather, Avraham noted the peculiar moral culture of Gerar in which a traveler was greeted not with questions about his need for food and lodging but with questions about his wife.[109] Indeed, Avimelech's kingdom had its own ethical code: it abhorred adultery but tolerated homicide.[110]

Yet despite the decadence, egocentricity and hypocrisy that defined Gerarian society and its king, Avraham made peace with Avimelech and prayed for his recovery from the malady with which Avimelech and household had been afflicted as punishment for his debauchery. *Ichpatiyut* (concern for others) is the very foundation of Jewish society, even if those "others" do

---

[108] *Ha'amek Davar*, Breisheet 18:2.

[109] Rashi, Breisheet 20:11.

[110] Lest that strike one as bizarre in the extreme, do note that Western society today abhors homicide but is quite tolerant of adultery. The Torah deems both to be cardinal sins and capital crimes.

not measure up to our standards of decency. And that concern is a personal responsibility, and not simply the obligation of the community.

Ichpatiyut also defines the Jewish people as a whole, and descendants of Avraham as individuals. "Whoever has compassion for other creatures, it is obvious that he is a descendant of Avraham, and whoever does not have compassion for other creatures, it is obvious that he is not a descendant of Avraham."[111] It is the same compassion that he showed even to his wife Hagar and son Yishmael, under trying circumstances, when he was forced by Sarah's command (confirmed by God) to send them away to ensure the survival of Yitzchak. Avraham's kindness – the constant theme of this *sedra* – is a by-product of his love of God, and therefore admits no exceptions or deviations.

LOT

> *And the two angels came to Sodom in the evening, and Lot was sitting at the gate of Sodom. And Lot saw and rose to greet them, and bowed down, face to the ground. (Breisheet 19:1)*

Avraham's nephew[112] is one of the more tragic figures in the Bible. Although he lived in Avraham's shadow (an exalted residence, to be sure), Lot struggled for his own identity but made one misstep after another. He was successful, but his wealth was strictly inherited, a matter that no doubt grated on him. It was his proximity to Avraham that merited him all his financial bounty,[113] and his separation from Avraham that led to one trauma after another. But Lot chose not to remain faithful to Avraham's way, and paid a steep price.

Lot left Avraham's company and chose to reside in Sodom, infamous for its wickedness and depravity. "And the people of Sodom were exceedingly wicked and sinful to God" (13:13), and still Lot did not hesitate to move there.[114] Even his captivity during the War of the Kings did not cause Lot to reevaluate his life's choices. The Sodomites were the polar opposites of Avraham, and even though Lot did not fully embrace their ideology (he retained a superficial

---

[111] Masechet Beitza 32b.

[112] Lot was also Avraham's brother-in-law (Sarah's brother) based on Breisheet 11:27, 29, and Rashi's commentary to 11:29. Both Lot and Sarah were children of Haran, Avraham's brother who died in Nimrod's furnace.

[113] Breisheet 13:5, with Rashi's commentary.

[114] Rashi, Breisheet 13:13.

form of *hachnasat orchim* that he had learned in Avraham's house[115]), he was nonetheless accepted by Sodomite society, to the extent that he was appointed a municipal judge.[116]

Yet unlike his wife, whose identification with Sodom was so complete that she could not break away and literally became an eternal part of the city,[117] Lot retained enough self-awareness to recognize the moral morass in which he was living. He freely admitted to the angels who came to save him that the "majority [of Sodomites] are evil."[118] He desperately wanted acceptance, even respect, but received neither. When he resisted handing over his guests for typical Sodomite treatment, his townsmen scorned him. When he told his sons-in-law of the looming catastrophe, they mocked him. His wife rejected him. Only his daughters accompanied him out of the city. Avraham, his patron, remained a distant presence; even now, Lot refused to return home.

Lot's typology is not an unfamiliar one. That he decided to create his own destiny, away from Avraham's house, is fairly conventional. Few adults want to live their lives as adjuncts of someone else. In the best of circumstances, Lot could have been a quasi-Avrahamic outpost in the five evil cities of the region, mitigating some of their iniquitous excesses and bringing some semblance of civilization to that barbarous district. Yet we find no instance of Lot rebuking his townsmen, or at all trying to influence them for the good. His moral code, to the extent that he practiced it, was private.

"Whoever can protest [the sins of] his household, or fellow citizens, or the entire world and refrains from doing so is ensnared [in the fate of] his household, fellow citizens or the entire world."[119] Like the company officer who looks away from illegality and says nothing, or the quiet person who sits in the company of scoffers and talkers and does not seek to rebuke them, Lot preferred popularity to reproach, knowingly selling his soul in order to acquire status among some of the most repulsive people who ever lived. But why?

There are people whose self-esteem is based on the world of the relative. They feel better about themselves living among moral and ethical inferiors. They turned our Sages' statement on its head: "Rav Matia ben Charash said: Better to be a tail to lions than the head of foxes."[120] It is better to serve those

---

[115] Rashi, Breisheet 19:1.

[116] Ibid.

[117] Breisheet 19:26. Lot's wife was turned into a pillar of salt, obviously a hardened criminal.

[118] Rashi, Breisheet 19:4.

[119] Masechet Shabbat 54b.

[120] Masechet Avot 4:20.

who are greater than you – where you will gain in knowledge and personal perfection – than to lead those who are worse than you. There, you will not gain at all but will be brought down to their level.

Lot chose the exact opposite of our Sages' advice. He chose to be the head of foxes, and was nearly destroyed in the process. When the angel told him to flee to the mountain – i.e., return to Avraham[121] – Lot demurred: "Behold your servant has found favor in your eyes, and your kindness done to me was great to save my life, [but] I cannot escape to the mountain lest the evil that clings to me kills me" (19:19). "In Sodom, God saw my deeds and those of my fellow inhabitants, and I looked like a righteous person and worthy of salvation. But when I go to the *tzaddik* [Avraham], I am like a wicked person."[122] For Lot, the jig was up. It was an admission of clarity about his life and his life's choices.

We are always influenced by our surroundings, but no one has the right to rationalize his moral failings by blaming them on those around him. Absent exigent circumstances, we choose where we live and with whom we interact. A prospective homeowner typically searches schools, synagogues, infrastructure and the like before purchasing a particular home; he even does a title search to verify that his ownership will be unassailable. But one should do – to the extent feasible – a "search" on the ethical level of his neighbors as well – what are their values, commitments and aspirations in life? How materialistic are they? These are all valid questions; it is a shame that too often people are content to gauge the righteousness of others based on superficial trivialities (a particular style of dress seems to be a prominent guidepost, or the presence or absence of a television) rather than discover, to the extent possible, their true values. [123]

"Better a nearby neighbor than a distant brother."[124] The neighbor who adjoins your house will have a far greater influence on your life – and your children – than relatives who live far away. That is why we prefer to attach ourselves to lions – people on a higher level – than to choose the opposite, as Lot did. That choice defined and ruined his life, and we can learn from his example. We are responsible for our environment – and no one else.

Lot could never really break away from Avraham, as much as he tried. Even his hasty escape from the cauldron of Sodom was due to Avraham's merit.[125]

---

[121] Rashi, Breisheet 19:17.

[122] Rashi, Breisheet 19:19.

[123] Granted that one can never truly know another person's deepest allegiances, and certainly not upon a superficial acquaintance. Perhaps that is why the trivilialities noted are employed as shorthand guidance to another person's character, even if they can easily be misleading.

[124] Mishlei 27:10.

[125] Rashi, Breisheet 19:19.

But rather than acknowledge his special relationship with Avraham and all the potential good it could afford him, Lot was a master of poor choices. His main problem was that he was active when he should have been passive, and passive when he should have been active. He left Avraham's household when he should have stayed, and he did little or nothing to inspire his contemporaries. Even with his daughters, in the odd story that ends his active life, Lot is nothing but a vessel that they used, the first time without his knowledge and the second time with his knowledge.[126] He was the "simpleton [who loved] his folly."[127] He enjoyed his passivity and became exactly what he strove not to be – just an accessory to others.

Lot's Redemption

> *And when God destroyed the cities of the plain, and God remembered Avraham, He sent out Lot from the midst of the upheaval when He overturned the cities in which Lot had lived. (Breisheet 19:29)*

Why was Lot saved? Granted that it was in Avraham's merit, and that Lot was the best of a bad lot of human beings, but what was his redeeming quality? What did he bring to the world, such that his rescue was mandated on High?

Rashi is troubled that the verse states that "God remembered Avraham" when in fact, in context, God "remembered" Lot and therefore saved Lot.[128] Rashi explains that Lot's merit was that "Lot knew that Sarah was Avraham's wife, and when he heard Avraham say in Egypt that 'Sarah is my sister,' Lot did not reveal the secret. Because he had pity on Avraham, so God had pity on him" and saved him from the destruction of Sodom.

Rav Nosson Tzvi Finkel, the legendary Alter of Slabodka, commented that Lot's hospitality was a habit that was ingrained in him from being raised in Avraham's household. He did it by rote and couldn't even stop himself in Sodom despite the strictures there against kindness. But Lot's silence in Egypt was a matter of conviction; it was a moral choice he made. Even though Lot stood to inherit a large fortune if Avraham were killed – he was the only

---

[126] Rashi, Breisheet 19:33.
[127] Mishlei 1:22.
[128] Rashi, Breisheet 19:29.

kinsman eligible – Lot held his tongue and overcame his natural greedy, materialistic tendencies.

Thus, the Alter concluded, even a small good quality acquired on one's own, as a result of forethought and commitment, outweighs a greater deed done out of force of habit. The former is a greater attainment and more reflective of the real person. The only act of moral greatness on Lot's part that resulted from his own personal achievement was his silence in Egypt.[129]

Certainly this represents a challenge to every Jew and every Jewish family. The virtues we inculcate in our children can often lead to rote observance; probably, with small children, that is the inevitable starting point. It is when the child matures and leaves home and even starts his own family that parental education on particulars may be insufficient, and the child must be capable of making moral choices in areas that are not identical to the ones he learned at home. This acquisition of moral intuition is essential to education and indispensable to adulthood.

It was Lot's redeeming quality, and the one that earned him salvation from the disaster of Sodom.

The Evil of Sodom

> *One who says, "What is mine is mine and what is yours is yours," that is the average person, and some say that is the attribute of Sodom; [one who says,] "What is mine is yours and what is yours is mine" is an ignoramus; [one who says,] "What is mine is yours and what is yours is yours" is pious; [one who says,] "What is mine is mine and what is yours is mine" is wicked. (Masechet Avot 5:13)*

There appears to be a chasm between the two opinions that define the assertion "What is mine is mine and what is yours is yours." At first glance, it appears quite reasonable – even normal. If "what is mine is mine, and what is yours is yours," then society can function fairly smoothly. There will be no envy, no crimes against persons or property, no resentment, and no sense of entitlement that what someone else has should really be mine, in whole or in part. Granted it is not the epitome of kindness that is exemplified by the

---

[129] Even his protection of the angels in his home – at risk of his life – was rooted in the education he had received from Avraham.

quality of the pious one: "What is mine is yours, and what is yours is yours." *That* is selflessness: I have no claims against you and no material ambitions at all for your property, and I do not seek to retain any permanent interest or have any lingering attachment to my own wealth. "What is mine is yours."

The first statement is realistic and neutral, even if a bit self-centered. But how do we traverse the gulf from that understanding to labeling it as the "attribute of Sodom"?

Rav Avraham Yitzchak Kook[130] wrote that the dilemma in the Mishna in Avot is the titanic struggle between individual property rights and selfishness. Without individual property rights, man is stripped of the possibility of doing good for others with his possessions. He becomes simply a tool of the state, and looks then to the state to provide welfare and public assistance to the needy. In the commentator Dennis Prager's classic formulation, "the bigger the state, the smaller the citizen." The smallness of the citizen is not just a function of the power and reach of the behemoth state that encroaches on every aspect of its citizens' lives, but also a reflection of the citizen himself and his diminished capacity to both internalize and externalize the good.

Notice how the Mishna derisively dismisses the socialist ideal: "[One who says,] 'What is mine is yours and what is yours is mine' is an ignoramus." What seems quite attractive on the surface – a life of sharing and mutual concern, free of the rat race, competition and material strivings – simply does not accord with human nature. The socialist experiment has failed in every place it has been tried, notwithstanding its enduring appeal, and has even failed to create a classless society. Invariably, the socialist elites have prospered, afforded themselves luxuries unavailable to commoners, and seen their economies collapse. And the average person has usually suffered inordinate hardships under socialist regimes. Winston Churchill articulated the capitalist/socialist dichotomy best: "The inherent vice of capitalism is the unequal sharing of blessings; the inherent virtue of socialism is the equal sharing of miseries."[131]

There are people who pride themselves on the equal sharing of miseries and aspire to nothing more. They, indeed, had a difficult time emerging successfully from the cradle-to-grave (albeit substandard) care of the Communist regimes in Europe into the world of freedom, free enterprise and unlimited opportunities. But most people embrace freedom, even with the hardships it can engender, i.e., the personal responsibility it demands of its proponents. Just as there is an illusory safety in numbers, there is an illusory

---

[130] *Igrot Hare'iya* 1:99.

[131] Speech in the House of Commons, October 22, 1945.

comfort in seeing all others equally miserable; often, they won't even know what they are lacking or that there is a better way.

But capitalism – the private ownership of the means of production and the opportunities thereby afforded for widespread prosperity outside the framework of government control – engenders its own problem, Rav Kook wrote: the possibility of excessive greed, selfishness and self-interest – the "'what is mine is mine' and I don't care at all about you" syndrome. That egocentricity is deadly to one's pursuit of moral perfection, as one who is consumed by his material ambitions can both run roughshod over others in his race to fortune as well as ignore the cries of still others who need his assistance. That is the attribute of Sodom. In its worst expression, "what is mine is mine and what is yours is mine" – the credo of the "wicked person" – is actually that of the rapacious capitalist, who wants everything for himself and perceives the wealth of others as merely awaiting his conquest. He defines himself by his assets, and wants not only to take over his competitors but also to have their lunch.

Nevertheless, the "what is mine is mine" approach can also lead, in the moral person, to philanthropy and expansive concern for others. One who has nothing can give nothing, or at least nothing material; he can certainly offer prayer and psychological support. But someone who needs a meal or a job will not be substantially benefited by another who merely offers prayers and kind words. Neither activity, meritorious in their own right, will feed or provide. The highest form of charity, as perceived by Judaism, is "bolstering the Jew who has fallen, by giving him a gift, a loan, becoming his partner or finding him a job."[132]

The handout is a lesser form of assistance, as it both degrades the recipient and does not at all enable him to provide in the future. Finding the unemployed a job is the epitome of charity,[133] as it maintains his dignity in the short-term and the long-term. But only a person who *has* something – who has his own possessions or owns his own business – can provide support to the needy or a job to the unemployed. One bereft of possessions because the state owns everything cannot do *tzedaka*.

How realistic is the way of piety, "what is mine is yours and what is yours is yours"? Understood properly, it is very realistic. Such an approach

---

[132] Rambam, Laws of Gifts to the Poor 10:7.

[133] I note parenthetically the well-known observation that *tzedaka*, "charity" as it is loosely defined, actually means "righteousness." It is considered obligatory and bears none of the discretionary characteristics implicit in the English word *charity*.

actually exemplified King David's chief of staff, Yoav ben Tzruyah, who was so unconcerned with wealth that "his home was like the wilderness; just like the wilderness is ownerless, so too his home was ownerless."[134] Yoav freely allowed the poor to sustain themselves from his assets. Lest one think that Yoav's wealth could have been depleted in a short time, it is important to understand the Talmud's statement. It does not mean that Yoav possessed nothing, but rather that he did not attach any personal significance to his possessions. He was not "possessive," in the sense of selfish and domineering. He did not feel he was losing anything by supporting the poor, nor did he even have the benefactor's occasional feelings of satisfaction at…well, being a benefactor. Whatever Yoav owned was for his use, and for others who needed it. He had more important matters that concerned him, like fighting the wars of King David and ensuring the survival of the Jewish people.

That is the approach of the pious one. The ethical level of "what is mine is mine and what is yours is yours" ultimately depends on perspective and implementation. In the worst scenario, it is the attitude of Sodom: Leave me alone and I will leave you alone – and you are on your own like I am on my own. But in its most edifying sense, that statement articulates a capitalist ideal – that individual property rights are the foundation of liberty, because ownership enables to me to do what I want with my possessions, to both enjoy life and help others as needed. It is "neutral" only in the sense that it is fraught with danger –the danger of selfishness and material overindulgence.

How one navigates that narrow bridge is one of the great tests of life in the modern world and one of the timeless challenges in embracing personal responsibility.

---

[134] Masechet Sanhedrin 49a.

Chayei Sarah

All Good

And Sarah's lifetime was one hundred years, twenty years and seven years; the years of Sarah's lifetime. (Breisheet 23:1)

Rashi's commentary herein reads at first glance like revisionism: the repetition at the end of the verse of "the years of Sarah's lifetime" teaches us "that all were equally good."

But by what standard were Sarah's years "equally good"? On the contrary, one can make a cogent argument that Sarah lived a difficult, even sometimes tragic life. She was kidnapped twice by foreign despots, suffered from infertility for ninety years, endured almost all of Avraham's trials at his side, underwent domestic strife several times, and finally died suddenly upon hearing the news that her beloved son Yitzchak had a near-death experience at the Akeida. So how were her years "all equally good"? Her life's struggles might have found vindication – but "good"?

Rav Dovid Hofstadter explains that "good" means "successful," and applies in a spiritual context.[135] One who lives through hardships in life and overcomes them is bettered by the experiences, even if he or she would not initially choose to undergo them. There is no greater good than to be spiritually elevated by surmounting obstacles, because that culminates in the greatest good of perfection of the soul.

He cites a well-known story of the late *rosh yeshiva* Rav Nosson Tzvi Finkel of Mir,[136] who asked a visiting group of successful American businessmen their opinion on what was the most important lesson to be derived from the Holocaust.[137] Each answered as can be expected: the importance of Israel and a

---

[135] *Darash David*, vol. 1, p. 141.

[136] He was the great-grandson (and namesake) of the Alter of Slabodka mentioned above.

[137] I have seen elsewhere that one of the principals in the story was Howard Schultz, the founder of

strong military, combating evil, "Never Again," etc. He told them that what they had said was all true, but to him the most important lesson of the Holocaust was that "suffering has a purpose," and that those victims of the Holocaust who saw a divine hand in their suffering retained the "image of God" within them – their dignity, their humanity and their concern for others.[138]

The "good" that Rashi referred to is ultimately an attitude that shapes much of our lives and that all people should embrace: *we often cannot control what happens to us, but we can control how we respond to it.* Paradoxically, what shatters one person often strengthens another person. It depends on background, temperament, psychological state, moral code and, above all, religious values. If the Jewish people had ever used hardship as an excuse to compromise our values and succumb to the moral level of our tormentors, we would never have survived spiritually intact. Our foremother Sarah epitomized the woman of valor and inner strength whose steely will enabled her to triumph over every misfortune she encountered in life, "all equally good."

SEIZE THE DAY

> *...one hundred years, twenty years and seven years; the years of Sarah's lifetime. (Breisheet 23:1)*

Rav Shlomo Aviner offers a related but distinct thought.[139] Sarah lived a majestic, inspired and good life because she did not get bogged down in the travails of the moment, lamenting what was and speculating what will be. Such an approach to life – a choice that people make – is debilitating. We can be as guilty of mourning the past as we can be of fearing the future, and in both cases the present – the timeframe in which we actually live – is neglected.

To live in the present does not mean that we ignore either the past or the future; rather, it is the realization that "on each and every day, we offer God the appropriate blessings."[140] Today is a new and special day of divine service, unlike yesterday and tomorrow. We are well aware that "it is not our responsibility to finish the work, but nor are we allowed to remain idle from

---

Starbucks. (See Howard Schultz, "A Blanket of Trust," http://www.aish.com/ci/be/48880957.html.)

[138] He noted that in the concentration camps, often, only one person out of six was given a blanket at night. That person faced a choice – to keep the blanket for himself or to share it with others.

[139] *V'halachta Bi'drachav*, pp. 482–83.

[140] Masechet Berachot 46a.

it [because we can't finish]."¹⁴¹ And we internalize that "Blessed is God, day by day He loads us."¹⁴² Each day brings new opportunities and challenges; only death puts an end to this quest. No wonder then that the Torah portion that underscores this idea is called Chayei Sarah, the "life of Sarah," even though it relates to us only the death of Sarah and its aftermath. The "life of Sarah" is summarized succinctly in the opening verse and its interpretation: *carpe diem*, seize the day, each and every day.

And Sarah saw her life in stages: "one hundred years, twenty years and seven years." She did not act like a seven-year-old when she was twenty, nor look at the world when she was twenty as she did later when she was one hundred years. In her wisdom, she appreciated childhood, adulthood and old age. She had no desire to be the same person in each stage, but grew through her experiences and life's work. That was a full, fulfilling and satisfying life, worthy of our illustrious ancestress.

INTEGRITY

Listen to us, my lord, you are a prince of God among us…
(Breisheet 23:5)

Avraham, grieving over the sudden death of his wife Sarah, approached the children of Chet to procure a burial spot. They sensed his greatness, calling him a "prince of God." But how did these pagan idolaters discern this princely godliness in Avraham?

The Netziv wrote that the book of Breisheet is called by the prophets *Sefer Hayashar*, the Book of the Upright, for it describes in detail the lives and personalities of people who were defined by their integrity.¹⁴³ The Netziv noted that the Jews of the Second Temple era were "righteous, pious and toiled in Torah, but they were not upstanding in the ways of the world.… Especially their baseless hatred caused them to suspect anyone who was not identical to them in fear of God as being a Sadducee and a heretic."¹⁴⁴

There are two related qualities integral to *yashrut*. One is tolerance – the idea that not only do all people not think alike, but that all people need not think alike. Truth can only emerge through a multiplicity of views, and sometimes

---

¹⁴¹ Masechet Avot 2:21.
¹⁴² Tehillim 68:20.
¹⁴³ Netziv, *Ha'amek Davar*, Introduction to Breisheet.
¹⁴⁴ Ibid.

truth too can be multifaceted. Rav Kook commented on the well-known (and occasionally challenging) aphorism that "Torah scholars increase peace in the world"[145] that, indeed, Torah scholars increase peace through their study of Torah because such includes, by definition, disagreement, argumentation, and divergence of opinions.[146] But since every opinion is heard, and since every opinion should be respected, the truth of Torah emerges from that dialectic. "Peace" cannot be achieved through the suppression of views, comments, opinions or questions, but rather through reasoned dialogue that produces a decision, or at least an approach.

The Avot were extremely tolerant of their society, even if they categorically rejected its idolatry and immorality. That tolerance engendered the second quality inherent to *yashrut* – the honesty and decency with which they related to their fellow man. "This is also praise of the forefathers, that aside from the fact that they were righteous, devout, lovers of God to the extent that is humanly possible, they were also *yesharim* who conducted themselves with others – even with distasteful idolaters – with love, and sought their good and welfare as that ensures the continuity of civilization."[147]

"God," the Netziv continued, "has little tolerance for 'righteous' people who are crooked," corrupt and mean-spirited, even if they claim their motivations are pure.

That is why Avraham was so respected by his contemporaries, even if they did not necessarily share his ideals or worldview. They saw – throughout his life and in all his dealings – truthfulness, reliability, sensitivity, compassion and kindness. Those were traits that were not prevalent then and hence could only come from one source. "You are a prince of God among us," they declared. They saw how Avraham dealt with Lot, Sodom and Avimelech; how he endured trials and tragedies with grace and faith; how his peers admired him and how people flocked to him because of his legendary goodness.

Punctiliousness in the laws of Shabbat or *kashrut* or *tzniut* was never the definition of a good Jew, until perhaps recently, and only in some limited precincts of our people. As important as these *mitzvot* are and as all the *mitzvot* of the Torah are, these are, frankly, relatively easy to fulfill and do not always define the person's essence. *Yashrut* does; integrity is demanding and requires more effort in overcoming challenges that complicated questions about Shabbat and *kashrut* rarely will present.

---

[145] Masechet Berachot 64a.

[146] Rav Kook, *Ein Ayah*, Masechet Berachot 64a.

[147] Netziv, *Ha'amek Davar*, Introduction to Breisheet.

The surest indicator of a person's spiritual standing is his general reputation for goodness. "Rabbi Chanina ben Dosa said: Those with whom people are pleased, God is pleased; and those with whom people are not pleased, God is not pleased."[148] It is a fairly straightforward equation. "He who is beloved below is obviously beloved on High."[149]

This does not necessarily mean universal acclamation; no human being is beloved by everyone. But it does mean that one's general reputation is usually an accurate barometer of his real character. You can't fool all the people all the time. There is nothing in life that is more controlled by every person than his deeds, behavior and interactions with people that will create his public reputation. It is never helpful to protest that "they are all wrong about me. No one understands me." If that is so, then the fault lies not with "them," but with "you," to determine why they are so mistaken and what can be done to correct it.

That was Avraham's essence – and why his generation knew him best, appreciated him for who he was, and to a great extent were drawn to acknowledge the God of Avraham. He was, indeed, *av hamon goyim* (17:5), the father of many nations.

Excessive Speech

> *And Efron replied to Avraham, within earshot of the children of Chet, saying, "No, my lord, listen to me, I have given you the field and the cave in it I have given to you; in front of my townspeople I have given it to you, bury your dead." …And Efron replied to Avraham, saying, "My lord, listen to me, the land worth four hundred shekels, between me and you, what is it? Bury your dead." …And Avraham weighed out to Efron… four hundred shekels in negotiable currency. (Breisheet 23:10–11, 14–16)*

The Talmud teaches that "the wicked say a lot and do not do even a little,"[150] as we see from Efron, who expansively and publicly gifted to Avraham his field of Machpela – and then accepted four hundred shekels in the foremost currency

---

[148] Masechet Avot 3:13.
[149] Commentary of Rav Ovadia Bertonoro, ibid.
[150] Bava Metzia 87a.

of the time. He contrasts poorly with Avraham himself – "the righteous say little and do much"[151] – who offered his visitors just water and bread, but actually brought them an elaborate meal with a variety of delicacies.[152] But why does the Talmud maintain that the wicked "do not do even a little"? After all, Efron did deliver the field in Hevron to Avraham in exchange for the money he received – and Avraham insisted on paying. And why can't the righteous just say what they will do, and then do it – why must they minimize their offers and maximize their offerings?

Rav Yisrael Chait explained that the righteous and the wicked (here simply meaning a person with corrupt ideas about life) both operate according to a value system. But therein lies the difference between the two. The wicked will not engage in kindness for the sake of kindness but out of expedience, and in order to gain some personal benefit.

All Efron wanted was popularity and public acclaim for his actions. He was extremely gracious and extravagant in public. Everything he did was for public consumption. Efron's statements were made "within earshot of the children of Chet"; his initial offer was "before the eyes of the children of Chet" (23:11). The satisfaction that Efron sought was not the performance of a kindness but the approval of his friends and peers. Thus the emphasis is on what he *says* – "a lot" – but once the applause dies down and the microphones are switched off, once the wicked receives what he wants, he will not do "even a little." The motivation to act is gone.

The righteous, like Avraham, are drawn to kindness for its own sake. Avraham pleaded with the visitors to stay.[153] No one else was present. He did not need to put on a verbal show for an audience of admirers, but his performance was unparalleled in its scope. Avraham always did what was right because it was right, not because it was or might be popular. An Avraham does not require the gratuitous praise of sycophants, nor does he require the human observer to provoke him to action.

"Say little and do a lot," said Shammai the Elder.[154] It is the way of the righteous. Personal responsibility often requires self-motivation, or at least the motivation to do God's will. Other human beings are unreliable sources of motivation; they can just as easily induce the bad or half-hearted as they can the virtuous and the passionate. The way of the righteous requires strength

---

[151] Ibid.
[152] Breisheet 18:4–5.
[153] Breisheet 18:3.
[154] Masechet Avot 1:15.

of mind and character, all qualities that we can possess if only we desire to possess them.

Finding a Spouse

Rather, to my land and to my birthplace shall you go, and take a wife for my son, for Yitzchak. (Breisheet 24:4)

Our forefather Yitzchak was completely passive in the search for his spouse, relying not only on his father's judgment but especially on his father's servant's judgment. Is this a paradigm for Jewish dating practice, or is this an exception?

The question is of more than theoretical interest. The Jewish world, which knows only crises and never mere problems, frequently agonizes over the "*shidduch* crisis," the rising number of single men and women who cannot seem to meet their mates, commit, marry and settle down to build Jewish families. What is to explain this phenomenon?

One technical answer might be demographics – that females slightly outnumber males in the Jewish world, as in the world at large. But that can account for only a small part of the problem. It strikes me that a broader answer lies in the emasculation of today's male as confirmed by the *shidduch* system as it currently operates.[155]

The Talmud states that "it is the way of man to seek after a woman, and it is not the way of woman to seek after a man."[156] That is why in the Jewish marriage ceremony the man gives the ring to the woman. Men are supposed to be conquerors – active, vigorous, even aggressive in pursuing their goals.

Yet today's man is more likely to have subcontracted the challenge of finding his future wife to a variety of agents who do the work for him. These agents – matchmakers, parents, relatives, lawyers, accountants and others – screen the potential candidates, adhere to a very rigorous list of marital criteria that disqualifies almost all women, serve as intermediaries between the couple if perchance they should ever go out, and need to hold their hands throughout the process, up to and including the *chuppa*.[157]

---

[155] Although the problem exists, it should be emphasized that these issues arise in a minority of cases. The majority of young Jews meet on their own, are introduced by friends, or are set up by well-meaning people, and they marry with a minimum of aggravation. Nevertheless, the problem does exist.

[156] Masechet Kiddushin 2b.

[157] I exaggerate, but only slightly, and in some cases not at all.

When added to that sad reality the fact that, in many communities, opportunities for men and women to meet socially even for purposes of potential marriage are greatly restricted and often frowned on, it is clear why the problem exists. Men are not being men – not only because today's marriageable man is upon marriage usually unable to support his wife,[158] but also because he has ceased to be the prime mover in building his own home. That is not normal. It is the *man* who is commanded to procreate, not the woman: "it is the way of man to conquer, not the way of the woman."[159] What has happened to the Jewish male?

Like in many other areas of life, personal responsibility has here too been diminished and even delegitimized. It is little wonder then that men who have delegated the process to others of finding appropriate marital candidates do not know how to be men, seal the deal, commit and get on with their lives. They live in a prolonged adolescence. Part of the process has been designed to shield young people from the sting of rejection, as if somehow rejection is not part of life. That has become a failing of parents and educators, so concerned with developing children's self-esteem that they have neglected to shine the light of reality on their true talents and abilities, their hopes and expectations in life, and their assumption of responsibility for their own futures.

Yitzchak *was* unique – an *olah temima*, a "perfect offering" whose life took a dramatic turn to passivity when he was bound on the altar of Moriah by his father. He was entirely dedicated to God's service and lived in the world of ideas, not people. His interactions with others were limited. He was completely holy, could not even leave the land of Israel, and so was not capable of choosing his own spouse.

There are no "Yitzchak's" today, and the rigid rules of meeting and dating have handicapped the entire process, and also made it deeply unpleasant to many. Living, breathing, interesting human beings are reduced to criteria on lists and blurbs on a resume, not to mention the inconsequential matters that too often preoccupy the handlers. Young men who would not allow others to choose for them a *lulav* and *etrog* do not hesitate to delegate others to find them a spouse. For some, it unduly delays their fulfillment of the commandment of procreation. And something is not normal, and frankly, unfair, when young women have to sit by the phone for weeks and months waiting to be

---

[158] At weddings when I read the *ketuba* in which the husband declares "I will support my wife..." it is hard to suppress a smile. Some are years away from supporting their spouses, others light years! May Hashem bless their homes.

[159] Masechet Yevamot 65b.

contacted by agents. As well-meaning as the system's intentions are, this must be demeaning and deflating – worse than even the rejection that happens after casual encounters.[160]

Avraham and Yaakov met their spouses through their own initiative, even granting that they married relatives. So did Moshe, and many others, then and now. The numerous well-meaning people involved in *shidduchim* cannot obscure the simple fact that infantilizing and emasculating the Jewish male has impaired the dating scene, not improved it. As is frequently the case, passivity breeds hesitation, then insecurity, and then paralysis.

We know better and we should do better for our young men and women by promoting a system of casual but wholesome interactions that allows them to meet informally and encourages them to take responsibility for their own lives.[161] God's salvation comes in an instant, but we have to prepare ourselves properly to recognize it when it comes.

Idle Chatter

Rav Acha stated: The idle conversation of the servants of our forefather is more precious to God than the Torah of their children, as the portion of Eliezer is repeated in the Torah, while there are Torah fundamentals that are only alluded to. (Rashi, Breisheet 24:42)

What was so cherished about Eliezer's mission that the Torah reviews every detail of the story at great length? Elsewhere, Rashi notes that Eliezer, Avraham's servant, "had a daughter, and was seeking a pretext whereby Avraham would [ask his daughter to marry Yitzchak]."[162] His plan was thwarted because Avraham did not want Yitzchak to marry a Canaanite – even Eliezer's daughter – because of the low moral caliber of that people. In other words, Eliezer deeply desired to perpetuate his share in the household of Avraham but was rejected outright.

And nevertheless, his loyalty to Avraham was undiminished. Avraham's devoted servant sublimated his own desires and carried out Avraham's

---

[160] Conversely, and paradoxically, the popularity of meeting on the Internet in another segment of our world has given young people far too many choices, and the prospect of playing an unlimited field has also engendered a reluctance to find one's soul mate and settle down.

[161] Such encounters can occur at a *kiddush*, after a public *shiur*, and the like.

[162] Rashi, Breisheet 24:39.

instructions fully and faithfully. His dedication was such that the Torah repeats every detail of the story, the plan and its execution, thereby highlighting Eliezer's self-sacrifice and commitment – two indispensable qualities to living the Torah life.

It is incompatible to a Torah life for a person to ask "what's in it for me?" or to set himself up as the arbiter for what is right or wrong. Fidelity to God demands that we conform our desires to the Torah, and not vice versa. That is one message of the "idle conversation" of our fathers' servants: before anything else, we must be able to subdue our desires before God's will. If not, then the "children's Torah" becomes vapid and hollow, an empty performance that lacks spiritual substance.

There is a second message implicit in the above citation. Rav Kook wrote that there are two ways of absorbing spiritual lessons.[163] One way is through a book, a method with which we have become quite familiar today. The how-to books that are in abundance tell us about the details of the *mitzvot* and the proper means of fulfilling them – what to do, and when to do it – the "Torah in Ten Easy Lessons." The book is important and available, but cannot quite convey the experience of Jewish life, or what to think and feel, and especially how to act when the answer is not forthcoming in a book.

The Midrash records that even the "feet-washing of the forefathers' servants is more precious than the Torah of the children,"[164] because the Torah sees fit to mention that as well! Very often, Rav Kook said, we learn more from good examples than we do even from good books.

We learn more from the Avot and even from their servants about the foundations of Torah and the building blocks of the perfected human being than we do from just knowing the raw *halacha*, the technicalities of what to do. From Eliezer we understand self-abnegation, loyalty, dedication, faith and what it means to have a constant awareness of God even while dwelling temporarily in the house of idol worshippers. From Eliezer we can learn how to speak to people and how to live a truly God-centered life.

The idle chatter and mundane actions of the ancients teach us in ways that books often cannot. This is not at all a disparagement of Torah; rather it *is* Torah, in the expression of the Talmudic sage Rav Kahana, who followed his master, Rav, into a number of private, intimate situations, and said, "This too is Torah, and I need to learn it."[165]

---

[163] *Maamarei Hare'iya* I, Derech Hatechiya, pp. 6–8, cited in Rav Shlomo Aviner, *Tal Chermon*, p. 55.
[164] Breisheet Rabba 60:8, cited by Radak in Breisheet 24:32.
[165] Masechet Berachot 62a.

A great thinker once said "you can observe a lot just by watching."[166] The greatest influences on our lives are not necessarily people who teach us this law or that custom but rather the people who convey to us the inner experience of Torah, inspire us to feel God's presence, radiate goodness, and teach by example. Parents, especially, teach mainly by example, as children absorb their values and priorities over the years – far more than from any lecture or teacher. We learn about priorities, values and the essence of God's message.

We have a responsibility to seek out those good influences, and to be those good influences for others.

Modesty

And [Rivka] said to the servant, "Who is that man who is walking in the field toward us?" And the servant said, "He is my master." And she took the veil and covered herself. (Breisheet 24:65)

The Jewish laws of modesty in dress are certainly controversial today, if only because they are countercultural. The Western world attributes to dress and deportment no moral significance at all. For some modern Jews, they are a non-starter, an encroachment by the Torah on an area of life in which men should have no say, an opinion that has been voiced quite often in the last few years. Indeed, male enforcement of female modesty standards does seem inherently immodest.[167]

For others, *tzniut* (modesty, but better translated as privacy) is determined by hems and sleeves, and meticulously regulated by inches and limbs. The longer the merrier, to the extent that not only do the guidelines seem to increase in length and specificity every few years, but there are Jewish women today sporting the Muslim *burka* – a head-to-toe covering that implicitly indicts prior generations that relied on more lenient standards.[168]

This entire area of Jewish life is best understood not as *tzniut* or modesty, and not exclusively in terms of sleeve or skirt lengths, and socks and stockings, but with another term entirely: *pnimiyut*, the inner life. There is a

---

[166] It was the immortal Yogi Berra.
[167] The institution of *tzniut* applies to both women and men, but as the context here is Rivka, the focus is on women. This matter will be revisited in a more general way later.
[168] I recognize that the rabbinate even in the Haredi world has decried this new look, but specifically why they oppose it – aside from the fact that it was not the custom of our foremothers – is unclear.

straightforward equation that guides our thinking: how a person looks on the outside is a reflection of one's inner world and values, and the public statement one wishes to make. The shallower someone's inner world actually is, the more that person needs attention or approval from outsiders. The deeper the inner life is, the less the appeal to others' recognition has to be made.

One who dresses for attention – whether objectively immodestly or, frankly, too modestly, like the *burka* women – is essentially exposing a superficial, one-dimensional inner world, in which only looks matter, and in which the wearer feels that he or she will be judged not based on values, ideas or substance, but rather on appearance.

Our foremother Rivka understood that very well, and wanted Yitzchak's first impression of her to be not what she was wearing but who she was – personality, character, values and the like. So "she took the veil and covered herself."

Each individual has a private inner world. It belongs to no one else, and cannot be understood by anyone else. It is unique and personal – and so it is to be developed, nourished and cherished. The impression that others have of us should always emerge from that profound inner world…and then the clothing will take care of itself. Girls (and women, and men!) with a healthy sense of self will naturally dress appropriately, in a way that brings them dignity and respect.

Toldot

Yitzchak's Path

And these are the offspring of Yitzchak son of Avraham – Avraham begat Yitzchak… (Breisheet 25:19)

The Netziv observed that Yitzchak was Avraham's authentic son, as Avraham's ways and values were perceivable in Yitzchak but not in Yishmael, Avraham's other son. Yet by no means was Yitzchak simply a clone of his illustrious father, as no child can ever be just a replica of his or her parents.

Rav Eliyahu Dessler defined the differences between the two men that transcended their personalities.[169] Avraham served God through *chesed* (kindness), and brought the ideas of God to a wide audience through his embrace of loving-kindness. On a personal level, Avraham successfully transformed his *yetzer hara* (evil inclination) into a *yetzer hatov* (good inclination). That is, all of Avraham's energies were focused on divine service, as noted: "And his heart was found to be faithful before You."[170] It seemed effortless, and he was whole and at peace.

Yitzchak's method of divine service came through the *midat hadin*, the attribute of justice. He subjugated all his desires through *gevura*, internal strength and greatness. There was not one movement or activity in Yitzchak's life that did not reflect surrender to the will of God. His self-sacrifice at the Akeida both defined him and shaped him. His relationship to the world around him was based on the need for justice,[171] and, unlike Avraham whose quest for perfection brought others into his sphere of influence, Yitzchak was more inner directed.

---

[169] *Michtav Me'Eliyahu*, vol. 2, pp. 204–5.
[170] Yerushalmi Masechet Berachot 9:5, citing Nechemia 9:8. See also *Meshech Chochma*, Devarim 34:8.
[171] See Breisheet 26, where Yitzchak battles the shepherds of Gerar to retain the wells dug by Avraham.

Ultimately, there is no one right way (Yaakov would blaze a different path as well), and that recognition informs both our divine service and our capacity to become independent personalities. Rav Dessler noted that Yitzchak did not simply imitate his father's path. Too often, that is a recipe not only for personal bitterness and frustration but also an obsession with external appearances and rote performances. To "look like" and to "act like" is not the same as to "be like." Yitzchak toiled to acquire his own inner world, and to make it uniquely his. Thus he is not merely a son but a father – a forefather.

Too often parents see their children as clones, and even try to relive their lives through them. It is a great mistake. Very often, as well, children try to carve out their own identities by renouncing their parents' values or otherwise engaging in self-destructive or antisocial behavior. That is usually an even greater mistake. There are children who, disenchanted with their parents for real or imagined sins, live their lives in anger, in opposition and in unhappiness. They think they are punishing their parents, which they are to an extent, but mostly they are punishing themselves, ruining their own lives and often transmitting their dysfunction to the next generation.

Poor parenting can explain but never justify poor decision making on the part of the children. As progressive as it is today to rationalize bad behavior because of troubled origins, it is one of the primary factors in the evasion of personal responsibility that afflicts modern life. "[Someone else] made me do it"; just fill in the blank. One may need years of therapy and patience to overcome an unfortunate childhood – but that then becomes the person's obligation in order to live a productive, fulfilling and responsible life.[172]

The Avot were great models of independence. Yitzchak had his own personality, identity and particular path to divine service, and yet did not hesitate to re-dig his father's well that had been clogged by the Philistines.[173] It was a healthy balance, worthy of one of the giants of Jewish life. It is a balance to which we should aspire in our own lives: eternal gratitude and appreciation to our parents for the life they gave us as well as for the opportunity to seek divine service and happiness in line with our unique personalities.

---

[172] It is a sign of maturity to seek therapy when necessary, but it is unsuccessful if the therapy never allows the person to progress; permanent wallowing is not productive.

[173] Breisheet 26:18.

Prayer: Together but Apart

And Yitzchak pleaded with God about his wife, for she was barren, and God was entreated by him, and his wife Rivka conceived. (Breisheet 25:21)

Rashi comments that "he stood in one corner and prayed, and she stood in the other corner and prayed." But why didn't they just pray together?

Yitzchak and Rivka came from different moral universes. Rashi continues that "God responded to Yitzchak's entreaties, because there is no comparison between the prayer of a righteous person descended from a righteous person [Yitzchak] and that of a righteous person descended from a wicked person [Rivka]."[174] They understood their current plight differently as well, and each sought to take responsibility for his or her share of the problem.

Public prayer is a fundamental of Jewish life. Without the proper *minyan* (quorum), there are certain prayers or readings that cannot occur. But even as we stand together, we stand individually as well. The essential prayer – the Shemoneh Esrei – is said individually before its communal recitation, and the quality of one's prayer is most individualized, depending entirely on the *kavana* (intent, focus) that one can muster and sustain.

Both dimensions of prayer – communal and personal – are indispensable. There are some for whom communal prayer is a distraction, while for others it is an inspiration. Much depends on the place and the people. One cannot simply rely on the prayers of the community, but so too one should not think that private prayer is loftier. Rambam codified: "The prayer of the community is always heard, and even if there are sinners in their midst, God never despises communal prayer. Therefore, one should always seek to join the prayer of the community and never pray individually as long as he can pray with the public."[175]

Yitzchak and Rivka prayed together in the same room, but apart, in different corners of the room, to reflect both their individuality and their relationship. Yitzchak's prayer was successful, but it was Rivka who received

---

[174] Perhaps this reflects a child's natural instinct to break away from his parent as he matures. If so, one with evil parents can "rebel" and become righteous through oppositional behavior. That is often easier than the dilemma of one with righteous parents whose "adolescent rebellion" can distance him from God. Thus, the child of righteous parents can struggle more, and that is reflected in the attitude of God toward their respective prayers.

[175] Rambam, *Hilchot Tefilla* 8:1, citing Masechet Berachot 7b–8a.

the fateful prophecy that clarified the special qualities of the twins she was carrying and the eternal conflict they would wage.

Yitzchak and Esav

> *And Yitzchak loved Esav, for game was in his mouth; and Rivka loved Yaakov. (Breisheet 25:28)*

How could Yitzchak have loved Esav, who in moral commitment and temperament was the antithesis of his father? And how could the Torah describe such eminent people as having distinguished so blatantly between their children?

There are numerous answers to these most pressing questions. Rav Shamshon Raphael Hirsch asserts that Yitzchak and Rivka erred in making their preferences known[176] and in not abiding by the benchmark of "Educate your child according to *his* way."[177] Each requires unique parenting, because each child is unique. Those who compel their children to wear the same clothing, attend the same schools, engage in the same hobbies and like the same things usually do their children (and themselves) a great disservice.

It is likelier that our ancestors did not err, but rather made a calculation as to what was most necessary for their children. Note, of course, that stating that one parent "loved" one child does not preclude that parent from loving the other child or children as well.

Yitzchak perceived that his son Yaakov was perfected within and without, and needed less of his attention. Rivka too, more sensitive to degenerate tendencies (having grown up in a disreputable family), saw Yaakov's innate goodness and was drawn to it but also saw Esav's character and was bewildered, if not disconcerted. What did Yitzchak see in Esav?

Rav Dessler argued that Yitzchak saw a kindred spirit, a person who was out in the fields and had the potential to do what Yitzchak could not: sanctify the material world.[178] "Each kind loved its own."[179] Yitzchak realized that Esav's external world was troubled, and so gave him more love and more attention.

---

[176] Rav Shamshon Raphael Hirsch, Breisheet 25:28.

[177] Mishlei 22:6. The Vilna Gaon comments there on the obligation of parents to guide their children in accordance with the *child*'s "temperament, inclinations and personality," rather than those of the parents.

[178] *Michtav Me'Eliyahu*, vol. 2, p. 208.

[179] Ibid, citing the *Zohar*.

"Love," Rav Dessler wrote, "is a product of giving." Yitzchak was drawn to Esav not because Esav was wicked, but because he invested much in his upbringing, and never – never – gave up on him. The more Yitzchak gave to Esav, the more he loved him.

A father once came to Rav Kook and sadly reported that his son had abandoned Jewish life. The father asked if he still had an obligation to love this wayward child.

"Did you love him when he was religious?" asked Rav Kook. "Of course," replied the father. "Well, then," Rav Kook replied, "now love him even more." Sometimes love can do what disapproval, rebuke and certainly rejection cannot.[180]

Parenting, for the most part, never ends. It takes on different forms and must be applied in different ways, but it never ends. It is a life's work, and the responsibility that transcends many others.

No Excuses

And the youths grew up and Esav became a hunter, a man of the field, and Yaakov was a wholesome man, a dweller of tents. (Breisheet 25:27)

The Torah does not provide much pejorative information about Esav, and none that would merit his given last name in Jewish tradition – *harasha* – "the evil one." He was a hunter, sold his birthright (which held little meaning to him) to his brother, married women of whom his parents disapproved – but also was a doting and respectful son. Where is the evil? Why doesn't the Torah mention explicitly what our Sages taught – that Esav was a murderer, an idolater and a lecher?[181]

Rav Shimshon Pincus[182] explained that people often find themselves in challenging situations, especially spiritual ones, and say "it's not fair."[183] *If only I had been given greater intellectual capabilities; if only I lived next door to the Vilna Gaon or the Chofetz Chaim; if only I had a more sedate and refined spirit, I would not be tempted and I would not sin. If only this stimulating*

---

[180] Well-known story drawn from different sources, related by Chief Rabbi Jonathan Sacks, "Toldot (5771) – Why Did Isaac Love Esau?" http://www.rabbisacks.org/covenant-conversation-5771-toldot-why-did-isaac-love-esau/.

[181] Masechet Bava Batra 16b.

[182] Twentieth-century American-Israeli *rosh yeshiva*.

[183] Rav Shimshon Pincus, in his Torah commentary.

conversationalist did not sit next to me in shul, I would never talk. If only God gave me more money than I need, then I would give copious amounts of charity. If only I had more time, or a better mind, then I would be able to learn more Torah. If only…

Rav Pincus writes that almost every circumstance in which we find ourselves is neither a blessing nor a curse; what matters is what we do with it. A person with intellectual limitations might exert himself more than others – and the mind he was given is a blessing. If he gives up entirely, then it was a curse. So, too, if the person with intellectual gifts uses them, it becomes a blessing; if he squanders them, then in retrospect it was a curse.

Someone may have neighbors who are not spiritual assets, but who can induce him to watch his children more carefully. Then, the degenerate society in which he lived will turn out to have been a blessing; but if he lets his children roam free, then it will have been a curse.

The Talmud states that much in life is given, especially our physical, intellectual and financial constraints, but the moral choices we make and our responses to our circumstances are entirely ours.[184] Man is the determinant of his own destiny.

Had the Torah told us explicitly the full story of Esav – the propensity for paganism, the belligerence, the dishonesty, the contemptuous rejection of all ethical norms – then we might have thought that Esav had no choice. He was a bad seed from the womb, devoid of any spiritual sensitivity and incapable of ever living a civilized life. But, like all of us, Esav did have a choice; he was born with tendencies that he could have harnessed and channeled more productively.

In that sense, he was just like Yaakov, who also had tendencies; Yaakov was a "wholesome man, a dweller of tents." But he could have squandered that as well, reasoning that the life of Torah would therefore come easy to him, and that he would naturally evolve into a moral person without any effort on his part. Instead, Yaakov exerted himself – fourteen years at the Academy of Shem and Ever – in order to build on his innate qualities and not dissipate them. Yaakov became Yaakov Avinu (our forefather Yaakov) neither because of how he was born nor because of his inherent gifts, but rather because of what he did with them. And Esav became Esav *harasha* not because of how he behaved in the womb, but because of what he did on this side of the womb.

---

[184] Masechet Nidda 16b.

There is no more pernicious doctrine in Western society today than defining people by their "group" or their "given circumstances" in life – advantaging or disadvantaging people by their skin color, race, sex, religion or background. That is a grievous distortion of human potential. Similarly, the willingness of some elements of our society to excuse certain conduct or lifestyle choices prohibited by the Torah on the grounds of their alleged innateness fundamentally misstates the Torah's position on human nature.

If the true goal is service of God, then we need to recalculate who is blessed and who is cursed, who is advantaged and who is disadvantaged; all our traditional formulas and equations must be reevaluated. Then we will all be able to access the greatness that lurks within all of us and engross ourselves in the Torah of truth that is our lifeblood.

INITIATIVE

> *And Yaakov said, "Sell me, as of today, your birthright." (Breisheet 25:31)*

> *And Rivka said to Yaakov… "Listen to my voice, to what I am commanding you…and bring [the delicacies] to your father and he shall eat, so that he may bless you before his death." (Breisheet 27:6, 8, 10)*

Yaakov, whom the Torah describes as "a wholesome man, a dweller of tents" (25:27), and who serves God through an uncompromising commitment to truth,[185] finds himself in two compromising situations. In the first, he exploits his brother's physical weakness and moral infirmity by purchasing from Esav his birthright in exchange for lentil soup. In the second, Yaakov is a diffident, reluctant participant in his mother's scheme to wrest away Yitzchak's blessings from Esav and steer them to Yaakov. How can Yaakov's image and the reality of his conduct be reconciled?

These events are so familiar to us that it is often extremely difficult to step back and view them afresh. Certainly, there can be no implications drawn from here for standard business practices. Yaakov's implicit threat to Lavan conveyed to Rachel – "if he tries to deceive me, I can be his 'brother' in duplicity, but if he deals with me honestly, then I am the son of Rivka, his upright sister"[186] – is

---
[185] Micha 7:20.
[186] Rashi, Breisheet 29:12.

no primer on how to deal with unscrupulous business partners. So, too, these events cannot be removed from their context – the internal family dynamics of a family whose destiny was guided by Providence.[187]

From that perspective, both events become more comprehensible. We are almost always obligated to take the initiative to try to better our spiritual state (and our material condition). Passivity is usually a formula for stagnation and decline, and only warranted when any action will damage prospects for improvement. Thus, on the day of Avraham's death,[188] when Yaakov was contemplating the implications of Avraham's passing on his own life and on the future of Avraham's mission, he was jarred by the contrast between his own grief and spiritual longings and Esav's reaction to his holy grandfather's death. The Midrash records that Esav spent that sad day in the field, raping, marauding, pillaging, plundering and murdering.[189] Yaakov, then, sought to impress upon Esav his unsuitability for leadership in the tradition of Avraham. It was not a hard sell. "And Esav said, 'Behold, I am going to die, so of what use to me is the birthright?' …And Esav scorned the birthright" (25:32, 34), notwithstanding that later Esav would, on some level, regret his decision, even claiming – quite conveniently – that Yaakov "took away" his birthright.[190]

Here, Yaakov seized the opportunity to impress upon Esav their different destinies; that Esav later lamented what he had lost is indicative not of any impropriety on Yaakov's part but of the anguish of Esav's realization of his unsuitability for the life's mission of Avraham and Yitzchak.

Similarly, Rivka's intervention to secure the "blessings" for Yaakov must be understood in the unique context of that event. Yitzchak was granted by God the one-time opportunity to convey to one of his sons the blessings of material prosperity and political power. These were not the "blessings of Avraham," which were bestowed upon Yaakov by God and were in any event not Yitzchak's to give away.[191] The blessing of Avraham was the heritage of Jewish life – the Torah, the land of Israel, the designation as the chosen people; this blessing was given only by God, first to Yitzchak after Avraham's death[192] and then to Yaakov.

---

[187] Rav Hirsch (his commentary to 25:34) goes so far as to understand the "sale of the birthright" as something akin to adolescent hijinks that had no practical import but merely exposed the spiritual inclinations of each brother.

[188] Rashi, Breisheet 25:30.

[189] Breisheet Rabba 63:12; see also Masechet Bava Batra 16b, which adds Esav's embrace of heresy to his busy day.

[190] Breisheet 27:36.

[191] Breisheet 28:4.

[192] Breisheet 25:11.

Yitzchak's desire to give the material blessings – "the dew of the heavens and the fatness of the earth, abundant grain and wine. Nations will serve you and regimes will prostrate themselves before you…" (27:28–29) – to Esav was quite logical on the surface. Yitzchak envisioned an eternal partnership between Esav and Yaakov, in which Esav would use the blessings of bounty and power to protect and support Yaakov, the heir to the spiritual blessings and legacy of Avraham. Together they would project the ideas of God to the rest of mankind – Yaakov the teacher and Esav the "muscle." And the plan had the additional bonus of keeping Esav within the family of Avraham. Besides, of what value really would be wealth and dominance to Yaakov, "the dweller of tents" (25:27)?

The plan had only one flaw, which Rivka perceived and to which Yitzchak was understandably blinded: Yitzchak underestimated the extent of Esav's irrational hatred for Yaakov. Rather than sustain Yaakov, Rivka saw that Esav would use his material superiority to crush and even destroy Yaakov. Hence, Rivka intervened, both to ensure that these blessings – granted through prophecy – would go to Yaakov and to awaken Yitzchak to the true danger of Esav.

Indeed, Yitzchak was shaken. "And Yitzchak trembled – greatly, exceedingly agitated…" (27:33) when he realized Esav's real nature, and how he – Yitzchak – had almost imperiled the mission of Avraham with which he had been entrusted. Rivka saved the moment – but Yitzchak also knew that henceforth the vocation of the heirs of Avraham would change. No longer would it suffice to remain in the tent and rely on the support and protection of others. And, in fact, Yaakov never again returned to the tent but had to struggle in the real world, and maintain Avraham's principles and values there. So, too, Yitzchak then gave one final blessing to Esav – "when you are aggrieved, then you may cast off his yoke from your neck" (27:40), i.e., when the Jewish people sin and are deemed unworthy of these blessings, then you will dominate them.[193] And that has been the synopsis of Jewish history – Esav is a counterforce to ensure the loyalty of the Jewish people to the Torah. When we stumble, Esav's might, nurtured with resentment, seeks to crush us.

These events were truly unique, and part of the formation of the House of Israel. In most mundane situations in life, passivity is not unwelcome. One need not react immediately to every problem, incident, slur or insult. As the thirtieth president of the United States, the taciturn Calvin Coolidge, was fond

---

[193] Rashi, Breisheet 27:40.

of saying, "If you see ten troubles coming down the road, you can be sure that nine will run into the ditch before they reach you."[194]

In spiritual matters, though, the opposite is true. To sit and do nothing is not always preferable.[195] The parent responsible for a child's education cannot simply delegate and hope for the best, but must act in his best interests. The person who wants to learn Torah or do *chesed* must actively seek opportunities and not wait for the perfect circumstances to come his way.[196] Shuls are built, *yeshivot* are founded – and even the State of Israel was established – by people who are active, not passive, people who take the initiative in the spirit of Rivka and Yaakov.

Consequences

> *And Yaakov said to his mother Rivka, "…Perhaps my father will feel me and I will be in his eyes like a deceiver, and I will bring on me a curse rather than a blessing." And his mother said to him, "Your curse will be on me, my son, now listen to me and go bring [two choice young goats] to me." (Breisheet 27:11–13)*

> *When Esav heard his father's words, he screamed a great and bitter scream, and he said to his father, "Bless me also, my father." (Breisheet 27:34)*

The flip side of the joys of activism is the ritual sniping that comes from those who would have done nothing, or would have done it better. A sign hangs in my office: "For every action, there is an equal and opposite criticism." Actions have consequences, and even good and necessary actions have consequences that are far-reaching and profound. In God's perfect system of justice, every aspect is weighed precisely – the deed itself, every minute detail, and the overall objective.

---

[194] Cited in Hugh Rawson and Margaret Miner, eds., *Oxford Dictionary of American Quotations* (New York: Oxford University Press, 2006), 676.

[195] A paraphrase of Masechet Eruvin 100a. Note that in the performance of certain *mitzvot,* we can frequently be told *not* to act – "*sheiv v'al taaseh adif*" – a phrase that occurs thousands of times in the responsa literature. But those refer to the technicalities of performance rather than the larger, global issues that confront Jewish life.

[196] Masechet Avot 2:5. "Do not say, 'When I have time, I will learn,' because maybe you will never have time."

Rivka forced her unwilling son to engage in a subterfuge, one that was necessary to ensure the survival of her posterity. But they did cause anguish to Yitzchak, who "trembled – greatly, exceedingly agitated" (27:33), and it was both Rivka and Yaakov who suffered unanticipated sorrow as a result of their scheme, required as it was.

Yaakov and Rivka parted company at the end of this *sedra*; it was Yaakov's first trip away from home. And he would never see his mother again, as Rivka would die before Yaakov's return from Charan.

Moreover, Yaakov's fear of a curse befalling him as a result of his duplicity – "and I will bring on me a curse rather than a blessing" – unfolded in a most unexpected and heartbreaking way. The Vilna Gaon commented that the word *alai* (on me), consisting of the Hebrew letters *ayin*, *lamed* and *yud*, is an acronym for the three great tribulations of Yaakov's life – his ordeals with his brother Esav, his father-in-law Lavan, and his son Yosef. Later, Yaakov will use the same word in reflecting on the misfortunes of his life – "*alai hayu kulana*" (all [of these troubles] have fallen *on me*; 42:36).

Similarly, Esav's cry upon realizing that Yaakov had preempted him and received the blessings from Yitzchak has reverberated through the ages. "Whoever says that God overlooks anything, may his intestines melt, for God is patient but ultimately collects. Yaakov caused Esav to scream bitterly, and that cry was recompensed in Shushan, as it says, 'And [Mordechai] cried a loud and bitter cry' (Esther 4:1)."[197]

On a simple level, Esav's moment of sincere anguish evoked divine sympathy. Repentance can occur in a variety of ways, and even incomplete repentance deserves recognition. On a deeper level, when Esav "screamed," we were forced eventually to "scream" as well. Esav's loss to the family of Avraham is really our loss, as is the disappearance of every Jewish child from today's world of Torah. Certainly, it was worse in Esav's case, as he became the progenitor of our tormentor Amalek who reared his head through his descendant Haman in the story of Purim. If Esav is not with us, he will be against us, and we will pay a price for not keeping him in the fold – whether or not that was feasible.

Such is the measure of divine justice that everything is accounted for – every action, every particular, every objective. It is the spiritual equivalent of the "butterfly effect," in which a small, seemingly insignificant act in one place has a profound impact on events in another place and at a later time. Because

---

[197] Esther Rabba 8:1.

all actions have consequences, we are obligated to mind our actions, large and small, and concentrate on both what we intend to do and how we do it.

Humility

And Yitzchak sent Yaakov and he went to Padan Aram to Lavan son of Betuel the Aramean, the brother of Rivka, mother of Yaakov and Esav. (Breisheet 28:5)

I do not know what this teaches us. (Rashi, Breisheet 28:5)

The Torah's reference to Rivka as the "mother of Yaakov and Esav" seems superfluous, prompting Rashi's comment that he does not know what this teaches. His words are astonishing, especially when we consider that Rashi could have remained silent; he doesn't comment on every word or phrase of the Torah.

Interestingly, there is no shortage of explanations for this cryptic phrase. We can note that it places Yaakov before Esav, confirming Yaakov as the "real" firstborn. Or, it can acknowledge Rivka's special relationship with Yaakov,[198] or that Yaakov was fleeing to Aram because of his mother's actions. She acted first as Yaakov's mother, so Yaakov is placed first, but she acted in both their interests, so she is "mother of Yaakov and Esav."

Why then does Rashi emphasize his ignorance of this verse's meaning? Indeed, a cursory study reveals that Rashi employs this disclaimer seventy-seven times in the Bible and forty-four times in the Talmud. So why mention this again and again?

Surely Rashi could have embraced one of the suggestions above, but it would not have sounded true. The question would have remained better than the answer, and there is a broader point to be taught here about methodology. The admission of "I don't know" is not only an expression of humility but also a prerequisite to learning anything, but especially Torah. One who knows it all cannot learn anything else or from anyone else. It is good to know what we know and reinforce it constantly with review. But it is also good to know what we don't know and to seek appropriate guidance and constant study.

In modern culture, to admit ignorance of anything is shattering. The world is filled with experts ("talking heads") who spout their opinions on every issue; right or wrong, they continue to sound off on every matter under

---

[198] Radak, Breisheet 28:5.

the sun, and several above it. Pseudo-knowledge can even be more powerful than knowledge. "Being wrong" is not a deterrent; what can never be said, though, is "I don't know."

But it is the "I don't know" that defines our quest for Torah and makes us true servants of God. The Talmud declares: "Teach your tongue to say 'I do not know,' lest you be caught in a falsehood."[199] We cannot know, nor are we supposed to know, everything. Our responsibility is to make ourselves receptacles for the infusion of Torah knowledge. That requires the humility taught to us by Rashi, in one of his greatest (albeit subtle) lessons.

THE REBIRTH OF MARRIAGE

And Esav went to Yishmael and took Machalat the daughter of Yishmael...for himself as a wife. (Breisheet 28:9)

The Talmud states that there are three individuals whose sins are immediately forgiven: the wise man, the bridegroom and the prince.[200] The proof text for the atonement of the bridegroom is derived from here: "Was Machalat her name? Really her name was Basmat! But she was called here Machalat[201] to teach us that all his sins were forgiven." But why is a bridegroom forgiven on the day of his wedding, a point reinforced by the general obligation that a bridegroom fast on his wedding day and recite the Viduy, the confessional prayer as recited on Yom Kippur?[202]

Rav Chaim Shmulevitz explained that the uniqueness of the bridegroom is that on his wedding day he assumes responsibility for his new wife, and there is nothing greater than a person taking responsibility for someone else.[203] The bridegroom is forgiven all his sins so that nothing in his past should impair or encumber his relationship with his new spouse. Thus, even Esav was forgiven! How much more so when we marry, take on a new role and embrace new obligations for another human being, and then for the children with which God blesses the couple.

And it all starts with the foundation of marriage: personal responsibility.

---

[199] Masechet Berachot 4a.

[200] Yerushalmi Masechet Bikkurim 3:3.

[201] The root of *machalat* means "forgiveness."

[202] Rema, Yoreh Deah 61:1, who teaches that both bridegroom and bride fast, unlike the opinion of some older authorities like Rokach, chapter 353.

[203] *Sichot Musar*, maamar 23. Note that according to the prevalent custom that both parties fast, the acceptance of responsibility is mutual, even if the obligations of each party to the other are not identical.

Vayetzei

IMPRESSIONS

And Yaakov departed from Beersheva and went toward Charan. (Breisheet 28:10)

Rashi comments that the first half of the verse is unnecessary; what is important is that Yaakov went to Charan, not that he left Beersheva. So why was it mentioned? "It was to teach us that the departure of a righteous person from a locale makes an impression. When a righteous person dwells in a place, he is its majesty, radiance and glory, but when he leaves, he takes with him the town's majesty, radiance and glory."[204]

One person can have a tremendous impact on other people and on his community. One person dedicated to the study of Torah or the performance of acts of kindness influences others. One person who conducts himself reverently in shul, or who is known for his integrity, very subtly sways the behavior of those who respect him. A righteous person can inspire others to follow him, or even just limit the enthusiasm of the wicked to pursue their folly. Even one person can accomplish that, an inducement to all to become that one person and not simply seek to blend in to the norms of that society.

The Kli Yakar asks an interesting question: this is not the first time that someone left a place. Avraham and Sarah left Charan, and Yitzchak left his town temporarily to move to Gerar. So why does the Torah emphasize Yaakov's departure?

He answers that when Avraham, Sarah and Yitzchak left on their journeys, there were no righteous people who remained behind. Obviously, then, their departure made an impression on others. But when Yaakov embarked on his journey, he left behind his righteous parents. Nonetheless, "the departure of

---

[204] Rashi, Breisheet 28:10.

a righteous person from a locale makes an impression." Every honorable individual makes a difference through his presence, and, if it happens, through his absence. The world itself becomes different and loses some of its luster and radiance.

We should never underestimate the power of an individual for good, and unfortunately, the opposite.

Two Lives

And Yaakov departed from Beersheva and went toward Charan. (Breisheet 28:10)

In a very real sense, Yaakov lived two separate and distinct lives of almost equivalent duration. For his first seventy-seven years, he was a "tent dweller," who lived at home and learned with his father and then with his teachers. Then he left fairly abruptly, and for the next seventy years until his death at 147 years of age, Yaakov almost never finds himself sitting in a tent. He is always on the move, and sometimes on the run, facing dangers, challenges and troubles. Yaakov has a Beer Sheva existence, and a Charan existence. Which is the real Yaakov? Which paradigm resonates with us or speaks to us more? Which Yaakov is our role model?

One of the most challenging issues of modern times has been the use and abuse of the Internet. Stories are legion – and usually true – of people whose lives, marriages and families were destroyed because they succumbed to the worse excesses and vices that the Internet offers. By the same token, we know that a new world has dawned – by now, it is late morning – and the clock is not going to turn back. The Internet offers manifold opportunities for spiritual growth as well, with Torah resources available in an unprecedented way. What should a thinking Jew do?

This conundrum was highlighted not long ago in the Jewish media by symposia held separately by two Orthodox Jewish organizations representing different wings of the Torah world. One group was uncompromising: the Internet is bad, immoral, degenerate, a waste of time, and devastating to families and spirituality. Filters are desirable but insufficient; best would be a complete ban on Internet use (one rabbinical leader advocated a ban on computers generally), or at least safeguards involving supervision by other people to ensure that the Internet is not corrosive.

The other organization, while not oblivious to the dangers, had a completely different focus. It perceived the Internet as an infinite world of opportunity and discussed the challenges of harnessing its vast potential in spreading Torah through this wondrous mechanism that can transmit information across the globe in an instant. Overall, their approach was more positive than the other organization.

Which is better? Those who want to ban, proscribe and condemn, or those who want to benefit from the flame but not be burned? Is it more desirable to fear and avoid sin – or exploit the tremendous opportunities offered at the very real risk of potential sin?

In the cocoon of Beer Sheva, life is great – there is Torah and the observance of *mitzvot*. There are few challenges, little corruption, and a chance for unfettered personal and spiritual growth. In Charan, the potential to impact others' lives is enormous and the potential to spread Torah is unlimited. But in Charan, you also have to live with Lavan and his family; in Charan, Yaakov has to work, cut corners, deal with knaves and thieves and unsavory characters who have no use for ethics, morality or Torah. Once we leave the tent, we have to meet Esav on his turf and deal with Shechem,[205] Pharaoh,[206] and all sorts of people that we would never encounter in the house of study.

Is it better to be in the tent with the righteous or be in the field with everybody? Is it better to say about the Internet – something that is morally neutral but inherently dangerous – that it is simply forbidden or that it is permissible with certain constraints?

How one decides this questions may reveal where we see ourselves on the spectrum of Orthodoxy, but it need not. We benefit from having two prototypes – the Yaakov of Beer Sheva and the Yaakov of Charan. Yaakov's role demanded a long period of preparation in the tent and then as a forefather of the Jewish people, a period of passionate development and activity. It is easy but harmful to trivialize fear of sin and belittle the damage it causes, which grievously impairs our pursuit of holiness. It is unbecoming for us to minimize it as if it is not real.

But there is a price to be paid by those who live in the "tent" and never emerge – a price in terms of their ability to be self-sufficient, to influence others and propagate Torah in the world. Likewise, there is also a price to be paid by those who toil in the "field" with Lavan, Esav and others right alongside – a price in terms of purity of thought and deed. It is easy to become

---

[205] Breisheet 34.
[206] Breisheet 47.

soiled working in close proximity with a Lavan; very subtly, we are susceptible to adopting his worldview, values, entertainment, patterns of speech and lifestyle. There are dangers and rewards no matter which way we turn.

Jews of different background, personalities and temperaments will be drawn to one or the other. Ultimately, the choice is individual, and it is therefore the responsibility of every individual to choose wisely, with forethought, being mindful of the dangers that lurk regardless which approach is selected. No safeguard or filter will protect the corrupt soul, nor is there any failsafe "guardian [against] immorality."[207] Some Jews aspire only to the holiness of heaven, while others want to implant that holiness on earth as well.

Perhaps the dilemma of finding the right balance is what perplexed Yaakov as he slept on his journey, and beheld "a ladder fixed on earth with its top reaching to the heavens, and the angels of God ascending and descending on it." (28:12) Indeed, Yaakov never again returned to Beer Sheva – except once: as he steeled himself for his exile in Egypt, he stopped there, brought an offering to the God of his fathers, basked in the warmth of the Divine Presence and girded himself for the adventures ahead.[208]

Warring Stones

And [Yaakov] took from the stones of the place and arranged them around his head. (Breisheet 28:11)

Rashi notes that Yaakov "made a sort of gutter around his head because he was afraid of wild animals [attacking him]. [Those stones] began to argue with each other, each saying, 'On me shall the *tzaddik* rest his head.' The Holy One, blessed be He, then made all those small stones into one large stone, as it says, 'and he took the stone [singular] that he placed under his head' (28:18)."

A number of interesting observations emerge from Rashi's commentary.

First, we should note that Yaakov placed the stones "around his head" to protect himself from animals of prey. But how would that protect him? The wild animal could still attack his body and legs! Rav Simcha Zissel Ziv, the Alter of Kelm, explained that Yaakov's life was entrusted to Providence. "If God will be with me, and will guard me on this path I am traveling..." (28:20). Yaakov's ultimate security was in God's hands. Yet he was obligated to make his own effort, by doing what was feasible – protecting his head – even though his method was not infallible.

---

[207] Masechet Ketubot 13b.
[208] Breisheet 46:1–5.

We are always obligated to do our own *hishtadlut* – our own effort – in order to be worthy of divine protection.

Second, the stones around Yaakov's head actually symbolize an approach to life that is salubrious and rewarding. Stones represent the material world; a stone is among the rawest of the raw elements of nature. In essence, Yaakov knew that once he had left the bubble of his parents' hallowed home and entered the world, the confrontation with nature, man, indecency, dishonesty and pleasure would be a constant challenge. He therefore took the stones – the material world – and used them to protect his "head," the source of wisdom and connection to God. That, indeed, is the very function of the material world – not to seduce us with its attractions and ubiquity, but to serve as support for our spiritual lives. That realization – our attitude toward *gashmiyut* (physicality) – is one of the fundamental challenges of the modern world.

Yaakov sensed the danger – the wild animals of the marketplace and the general world – and knew he had to fortify his mind by erecting barriers that the material world could not cross.

Third, Rashi continues that the stones feuded with each other; each wanted to merit being Yaakov's pillow for the night. How do stones fight with each other? We can suggest somewhat whimsically that when Yaakov saw the stones fighting, that is when he realized he was in a "Beit Elokim" (28:17) in God's home, like a shul! Often, shuls bring out the worst in people,[209] as people who are bored, angry or otherwise frustrated with their lives and are having problems at home, work or with life generally seek to release their energy in this public and holy setting. They can whine and complain, find fault with almost everything, stoke the flames of controversy, and offer a running commentary on what is right and wrong and remediable, if only their words would be heeded.

It is a divine undertaking to make those diverse and discordant stones into one stone that rests under the righteous one. Thus, each Jew has the responsibility – especially in a shul – to defuse tensions, to overlook personal insults, to reduce the demands of the ego, and to ensure that the Beit Elokim is a place of peace, harmony and true divine service.

---

[209] Usually, though, they bring out the best!

The Vow

> *Then Yaakov took a vow, saying, "If God will be with me, guard me on this path that I am traveling, give me bread to eat and clothing to wear, bring me back to my father's house, and will be for me a God, then the stone that I have set up as a pillar will become a house of God, and whatever You give me I shall surely give a tenth to You." (Breisheet 28:20–22)*

The condition was not that if God provides Yaakov with sustenance and security then he will accept God;[210] that would be heretical. But if God fulfills His commitment to Yaakov, including protecting Yaakov from the potential harm of the outside world, then Yaakov will return and build this altar and serve God again in the land of Israel.[211]

What, then, is added by Yaakov's vow?[212]

A vow is an addition to the system that God gave us. It is undertaken by one who needs reinforcement against stumbling, for whom the usual safeguards are insufficient. Abused, vows can become building blocks for haughtiness, and a religion unto themselves.[213] Used properly, they are bulwarks created by a person who knows himself and his weaknesses – fences against sin that provide protection by accessing a secondary aspect of a person's relationship with God.[214] For some, a prohibition itself is not forceful or compelling unless it is combined with a vow. The vow adds a personal dimension of seriousness to the prohibition's compulsory nature.

Within reason, the Torah affords us the opportunity to carve out additional areas of prohibition to guard us from sin, or, as here, incentives to serve God faithfully. The responsible individual is contemplative, studies his nature assiduously, and knows his strengths, weaknesses and – especially – his motivations. In a sense, a vow is a personal stringency that one adopts that is justifiable and even praiseworthy – as long as it doesn't displace the Torah's system and as long as one doesn't seek to impose his stringencies on others.

---

[210] Mizrachi, explaining Rashi to Breisheet 28:21.

[211] Ramban, Breisheet 28:21.

[212] The subject of vows will be discussed in greater detail in Parshat Matot.

[213] Masechet Nedarim 22a.

[214] Masechet Avot 3:13. It is "secondary" to the extent that it supplements the essential relationship between man and God that is founded on the 613 commandments.

Yaakov here needed the external vow in order to give him the inner strength and self-confidence to weather the storms ahead, especially life in Charan with its intrinsic risks to his spiritual state.

Marriage

And Yaakov said to Lavan, "Give me my wife for my term has been fulfilled, and I will live with her." (Breisheet 29:21)

Yaakov's manner, somewhat gruff,[215] is understandable in light of the fact that he is now eighty-four years old, and extremely desirous of starting the family that would be heirs to the legacy of Avraham. Nonetheless, the marriages of our forefathers do strike a modern reader as unconventional. Yitzchak's wife was chosen for him, and Yaakov sought the hand of the very first woman he saw when he came to Charan (not to mention that his intended, Rachel, was switched at the last moment for her sister, Leah).

What can we learn from our forefathers and foremothers about marriage? Certainly, marriage can always use strengthening, for individuals and for the institution itself. Fewer Americans marry today than ever before, and still Americans marry in far greater numbers than do Europeans. In many circles, it is assumed that a person will have multiple spouses in a lifetime; after all, no one is the same at twenty-five years old as he or she is at fifty-five years old – so why retain the same spouse? This attitude reflects a spiritual and psychological malady that plagues modern man.

If there is one word that unfortunately characterizes the modern marriage, it is not *love*, but rather *me*. What's in it for me? What service or benefit can my spouse provide for me? Such a marriage becomes a very utilitarian institution of two people each looking to obtain some benefit from the other.

How long can such a relationship last? Sometimes as long as the returns are there, and sometimes not even that long. There can always be others who provide – or might provide – greater benefits. That is why there are so many prominent thinkers today who suggest that it is unrealistic – even unwise – to remain married to the same person for your whole life. Similarly, people can become jaded in their marriages, and they fall prey to what our Sages described as *"libo gass ba"* (an arrogance born of over-familiarity).[216] The couple can stop being kind and sensitive to each other, and politeness becomes an afterthought – something reserved for others, but not for the home. That is

---

[215] Rashi, Breisheet 29:21.
[216] For example, Masechet Eruvin 47a.

what happens when marriage becomes all about *me*, *my* needs, *my* wants – and how *you* will fulfill them.

The Torah has a different view. Marriage is not about finding your own happiness, but about making the other person happy. It's about giving, not taking. Interestingly, many modern marriages classically include a double-ring ceremony, and that has even infiltrated fringe parts of the Orthodox world. But the Torah world generally rejects the double-ring ceremony, and not only because of the technicalities of Jewish marriage but for a deeper reason that pertains even if a ring is given by the bride to the husband at the end of the ceremony. A double-ring rite is classic utilitarianism: *I give you something, and I get something in return*. That is not the Jewish marriage, which is defined by "what can I give?" The Jewish marriage is effectuated by the husband giving – and the wife not taking but *accepting*. And that becomes the basis for the marriage – each gives to the other, and each concentrates on giving to the other.

The root of *ahava* (love) is *hav* (give). The foundation of marriage is giving, not taking. To love is to find someone to give to, not someone to take from (that's self-love) – and that is the primary affliction of the modern marriage.[217] Self-absorption is fatal to marriage, as it is generally to happiness. Yaakov's declaration to Lavan becomes more understandable – "*hava et ishti*" (*give* me my wife). In essence, "give me" the person to whom I will become a giver. Let me have the focus of my attachment, so that I will have someone in life to whom I can give.

Our illustrious ancestors may not have had what we think of today as conventional courtships but they taught us the essence of marriage and the very foundation of the Jewish home. In a world where secular homes take on many different forms, and where the very premise of marriage is different – a relationship of expedience instead of a spiritual union designed to foster mutual perfection – the Jewish home is still an oasis, the envy of others, if we do not succumb to the same narcissism, the same obsessive self-love that destroys people, families and societies. Rather, our homes should be noteworthy for their love, mutual respect, and the pursuit of happiness for the other.

That, of course, depends on the assumption of personal responsibility by each spouse for the success of the marriage – to give to the other, to maintain the love, respect and devotion that usually characterizes the early years and then can wane because of boredom, weariness, cynicism or selfishness. It need not wane, but can and should grow, mature and bring a lifetime of satisfaction to each other.

---

[217] See *Michtav Me'Eliyahu*, vol. 1, pp. 32–39, for a lengthy and inspirational discussion of this concept.

Rationalization

And [Yaakov] said to Lavan, "What have you done to me? Did I not work for Rachel for seven years? Why did you deceive me?" And Lavan said, "Such is not done in our place, to give the younger [in marriage] before the older…" (Breisheet 29:25–26)

And where is this vaunted place where agreements are routinely voided and one need not keep his word – yet then proceed to claim the moral high ground? It is the world of Lavan.

Lavan represents a new type of enemy in the Torah. He is the first evildoer who is also clever, devious and sophisticated. He uses his intelligence to achieve his underhanded goals. He can say anything, do anything and speak out of both sides of his mouth. He cannot be defeated in argument, because he is adept at changing the terms of the debate and putting his interlocutor on the defensive. Yaakov is given a different wife than the one for whom he had worked? It is Yaakov's fault for not fully understanding the local mores. Lavan tries repeatedly to cheat Yaakov out of his duly earned wages? No matter, it is still Yaakov's fault. *He* is the one who is cheating Lavan![218] Lavan sells his daughters like chattel? You, Yaakov, fled in haste, "and did not give me a chance to kiss [them goodbye]" (31:28). Lavan has an answer for everything.

All the evildoers to this point have been unrestrained brutes who made no pretense about their desire for power, pleasure and domination. Lavan is a new force, and most difficult to oppose. He does not perceive himself as wicked and is able to rationalize his ignoble actions. It is a dynamic very familiar to us through Israel's dealings with the Arabs for the last forty years. They admit no wrongdoing and lodge with great facility the most outrageous accusations. When Arabs are killed, it is the fault of the Jews, they argue. When Jews are killed, it is also the fault of the Jews. If the Arabs kill, they were only forced into it by the Jews, in their twisted reasoning. They lament an "occupation" that never existed at all,[219] but they are rarely challenged on the weakness of their arguments.

To their way of thinking, Arabs can fire rockets and missiles at Israeli towns with impunity, but Jewish self-defense is always a war crime. The Arabs feel

---

[218] Breisheet 31:1, 7, 41, 43.

[219] Jews cannot be illegal occupiers of their own God-given country. Additionally, the acquisition of territory in a defensive war is a common standard under international law and throughout history for justified possession.

they are allowed to engage in any type of duplicity and malevolence, because "such is...done in their place." Confronting such an enemy is wearisome emotionally and intellectually, and ultimately requires divine assistance. It was God Who "visited" Lavan and told him to back off: "Beware of speaking to Yaakov, either good or evil" (31:29). The exile presents us with two prototypes of evildoers – the brutish "Esav" who tries to overwhelm us physically, and the conniving "Lavan" who tries to destroy us psychologically and emotionally. Thus, even the "Aramean tried to destroy my father."[220]

An evildoer is one who rejects responsibility for any of his actions, and who seeks to shift the blame onto the innocent victim. One who cannot admit his own guilt when appropriate lacks the capacity to lead a moral life, and rushes headlong away from ethical perfection. Man's gift of rationalization is exquisitely honed, and its prevalence must be understood and countered in order to aspire to integrity and good character.

Work and Marriage

> *[Yaakov exclaimed:] This is my twenty years in your house: I worked for you fourteen years for your two daughters and six years for your flocks and you changed my wages one hundred times. (Breisheet 31:41)*

It is well known, although not mentioned explicitly in the Torah, that Yaakov went to study for fourteen years in the academy of Shem and Ever immediately after leaving home.[221]

My learned colleague Rabbi Allen Schwartz[222] has pointed out the curious notion that Yaakov's study in this academy is celebrated and considered worthy of emulation, even though it not written in the Torah. Yet the fact that Yaakov *worked* for twenty years before and after he married is cited openly in the Torah, but receives no acclaim or fanfare and is not considered instructive

---

[220] Devarim 26:5, as explained by Rashi, Targum Onkelos and others.

[221] Rashi, Breisheet 28:9. Shem was the son of Noach, and Ever was Shem's great-grandson. It is important to note that both were blessed with the longevity of the early generations. What sounds fanciful – that Yaakov studied with descendants of Noach – is validated chronologically. While Shem died in the year 2158 (he outlived Avraham, and died when Yaakov was fifty years old), Ever actually lived until the year 2187, when Yaakov was eighty years of age – three years after Yaakov left the academy. In that academy, students were taught metaphysics, the nature of the one incorporeal God and His universal morality for mankind.

[222] Distinguished Rabbi at Congregation Ohev Zedek in Manhattan.

to anyone. That *is* curious. Many in our world know only of the former and do not talk at all about the latter.

We are living through a remarkable transformation in Jewish history, in which a growing segment of the population (at least in Israel, but it is burgeoning in the United States as well) eschews work and self-support and prefers to be supported by the community. This concept was so unknown in Jewish life historically that it was considered impious: "Whoever reasons that he will engage in Torah study and support himself from charity has desecrated God's name, scorned the Torah, extinguished the light of the faith, brought harm to himself, and removed his soul from the world-to-come. For it is forbidden to benefit from the Torah in this world."[223]

The problem is not only that the continuing subsidies paid to the proliferating number of full-time Torah students are economically unsustainable by the people of Israel or the Jewish community abroad. The greater problem is the corrosive effect such support has on the students, who see themselves as entitled, and superior to others. It forces them to look for wives whose main qualification is her father's wealth or her ability to support him. Some of their leaders have made a virtue of poverty – something that again is unprecedented in Jewish history – and have insisted on an elementary education that effectively leaves their students incapable of ever earning a living.[224]

The other devastating result is the repugnance toward Torah that the ennobling of handouts has engendered in the general Jewish world. Rather than perceive the Torah as a "tree of life,"[225] as God's sacred word that permeates every aspect of life, this philosophy has unwittingly made Torah into an academic exercise that is irrelevant to the world, essentially saying that one who genuinely wants to live a Torah life has to be segregated from society and cannot work or support his family. Thus, the "light of the faith

---

[223] Rambam, *Hilchot Talmud Torah* 3:10. This assertion of Rambam, rooted as it is in numerous statements in the Talmud, has been stripped of its potency by a number of modern authorities. It is astonishing that such an explicit and obvious conclusion has been watered down, in a way that – if done in most other areas – would have subjected those same authorities to accusations of heresy. It is indeed a *"shverrer Rambam"* (a most difficult Rambam.)

[224] "Poverty in a home is worse than fifty plagues" (Masechet Bava Batra 116a). Nor does it help a person come closer to God: "Excessive poverty…deprives a person of his own senses and knowledge of his Creator" (Masechet Eruvin 41b). Yet, others point to this statement: "Be careful of the children of the poor, for from them the Torah emerges" (Masechet Eruvin 81a). But this adage, firstly, refers to the children of the poor, and, secondly, it extols the spiritual benefits not of poverty but of a non-materialistic lifestyle.

[225] Mishlei 3:18.

is extinguished," because it is not allowed to illuminate outside the house of study.

Certainly the Talmud has a concept of *"Toratam umanutam"* (their Torah *is* their profession), and Jewish society extols those who learn (and teach) Torah. But it is arguable whether that designation still applies today, and even if it does, it does not preclude self-support.[226] What exacerbates the controversy is the great esteem in which Torah study is held in Jewish life. Advocates of change to the current system are therefore routinely perceived as "anti-Torah" and lambasted as being among those who will "prosecute Torah scholars" at the end of days,[227] even if they are often Torah scholars and lovers of Torah themselves (and sometimes part of the Haredi community).

Unquestionably, the Holocaust and the obliteration of much of the Torah world (and the Jewish world generally) has been a compelling factor in the redefinition of the Torah ideal. The need to rebuild from the devastation provoked a dramatic change in the way the Torah leaders of the time perceived the balance between Torah study and gainful employment. But with almost four generations passed since the end of the Holocaust, another reevaluation is necessary, and again, for the honor and majesty of Torah.

"It is a great virtue to support oneself with one's own hands."[228] "The greatest of the Sages of Israel were wood hewers and water carriers, and some were blind, and still they were involved in Torah day and night…"[229]

Certainly, on an individual level, one can forge a relationship with another – a Yissachar-Zevulun partnership, an affable father-in-law – and dedicate oneself to unending Torah study. The problem rests in the institutionalization of that model. It was never meant to be normalized or to become a mass phenomenon. The general society cannot sustain it; indeed, the Torah itself becomes alienated from those same masses when something meant for special individuals is standardized – and then becomes both an ideal and an expectation. The attraction of Torah is such that, despite the injunctions in

---

[226] The Rambam (*Hilchot Tefilla* 6:8) states that such people do not stop their learning even to pray. I doubt there are such individuals extant today. Furthermore, the *Shulchan Aruch*, Yoreh Deah 243:2, his second opinion, does not preclude the possibility that even someone "whose Torah is their profession" can still engage in some trade or business in order "to sustain himself but not to become wealthy." Today's *talmid chacham* would then typically be someone who makes "his Torah study permanent and his work provisional" which is a statement of priorities, as Rambam notes in his commentary to Masechet Avot 1:15 – "'make your Torah study permanent,' and whatever is needed for your business is subsidiary to it."

[227] Masechet Ketubot 112b.

[228] Rambam, *Hilchot Talmud Torah* 3:11.

[229] Ibid. 1:9.

the Talmud and early authorities against such a lifestyle, many people – inside and outside that world – admire it and perceive it as an act of great piety, a fulfillment of a Torah ideal rather than a deviation from it.

Notice how one problem begets another. The expectation that a man learn full-time and indefinitely for much of his adult life compels that he evade conscription (in Israel), have no ordinary means of employment, rely on his wife, family or society to support him, and transmit the same message to his children. It is a cycle of poverty that is not sustainable. Any life that mandates that responsibility for one's basic needs is shifted from the individual to others is a distortion of Torah and thereby undesirable.

We will experience a true renaissance of Torah when it is learned, internalized and fully implemented in society, when everyone who is not involved in pressing personal or professional needs is naturally lured to Torah study. Then it will become a *Torat chaim* – a Torah of life – as it was always envisioned, and as Yaakov carried out in his own life in the tents and the fields, in the exile and in the land of Israel.

Vayishlach

Self-defense

And [Yaakov] said, "If Esav comes to one camp and strikes it down, then the remaining camp will survive." (Breisheet 32:9)

Yaakov, fearful of his brother and terrified of the potential outcome of their confrontation, devised a plan to divide his family into two separate camps. He would first be able to assess Esav's mien and then respond accordingly. But Yaakov did something else that was even more elaborate.

Rashi cites the Midrash: "Yaakov prepared himself in three ways, with gifts for Esav, with prayer and for battle." The division into camps was the battle plan. And the gifts and prayer?

Yaakov taught us a basic lesson in our obligation of *hishtadlut* – of doing our own preparations and engaging in our own efforts in order to meet any challenge. It is not that we cannot rely on God, but exactly the opposite. We *do* rely on God for our ultimate success, and He is the One who trained us that our success depends on our efforts as well.

The brilliance of Yaakov's approach – and by extension, any type of individual or group effort – is that it appealed to three different modes of salvation.[230] Prayer seeks salvation in the spiritual realm and is indispensable to success. Prayer has accompanied the Jewish soldier into battle from the time of the Torah[231] through the stories of the Maccabim and until this very day. The recognition that God controls our destiny is both humbling and liberating (our mere survival as a nation is ample evidence of that).

Yaakov had to deal with Esav directly, and he chose to be deferential to him, even submissive. The substantial tribute he offered – hundreds of cattle

---

[230] We cannot draw any conclusions as to priority, as the various Midrashim list the three in different orders.

[231] See Devarim 20:1–4.

to be delivered sequentially, as if gifts were coming that would never stop – was a psychological appeal to Esav's insecurities about Yaakov and an attempt to defuse lingering resentments from their troubled past. In essence, Yaakov was demonstrating that he too was wealthy but he perceived his assets as a resource that could benefit Esav. Yaakov punctuated those gifts with persistent references to himself as "your servant." Indeed, Esav's heart melted when he saw the offerings and the prostrations and sensed the obsequious tone in Yaakov's message.[232]

But the danger of a physical confrontation was also present, and Yaakov did what was most rational under the circumstances. He could not avoid Esav, but he could minimize the danger of annihilation if their meeting went poorly by dividing his camp into two. This became a pattern in Jewish history as well: "God acted righteously to the Jewish people by scattering us among the nations," so that no enemy could ever eradicate all Jews at one time.[233] Moreover, the preparation for war is not a sign of moral weakness, but of moral strength and a keen understanding of human nature. The ancient Romans proclaimed, "*Si vis pacem, para bellum*" (If you wish for peace, prepare for war). It is an adage that Western man – and especially the Jewish community – ignores at his peril.

Yaakov did not sit back passively waiting for redemption. He used his intelligence to plead with Esav – an intriguing combination of deference and strength, bribes and a willingness to fight. Esav saw him both as a person of distinction worthy of respect and a brother who posed no threat to his regional hegemony. It was what the situation demanded.

Small Jars

> *And Yaakov was left alone, and a man wrestled with him until dawn. (Breisheet 32:25)*

Rashi cites the gemara that Yaakov, despite being part of a large camp of family and servants, was temporarily left alone on the east bank of the Yabbok stream because "he forgot some small jars and went to retrieve them."[234] From here

---

[232] Yaakov was even criticized by some of the Sages for adopting such a humiliating posture. See Breisheet Rabba 75:2.

[233] Masechet Pesachim 87b, with Rashi's commentary.

[234] Masechet Chulin 91a.

we learn, continues the Talmud, that "the righteous consider their possessions more precious than their lives, as they do not steal from others."

Surely people can value money without construing it as more important than their lives. Of what value is money if the owner loses his life protecting it?

Obviously, had there been a real and foreseeable danger, Yaakov would have forfeited those small jars and purchased others. The Talmud is teaching us that money and wealth *do* have value and importance. A person's earnings and assets represent his investment of time and energy, his "sweat equity" that consumes man's most precious and irreplaceable resource: his time. A person who never works, earns, purchases or owns can afford to be nonchalant about material wealth; after all, it is the wealth of others in which he has no interest.[235]

The mature individual values his assets because of what he did to acquire them, and because of the good that he can perform with them. Even "small jars" have a meaning and purpose that are not to be trivialized. They, too, represent part of the bountiful gifts that God has bestowed on the righteous.

LEFT ALONE

...and a man wrestled with him until dawn. (Breisheet 32:25)

The struggle with the angel (the "man" in the Torah text) is one of the seminal events in Yaakov's life and in Jewish history. It is interesting that while most commentators understood the event as literal – after all, Yaakov walked away limping – the Rambam explained it as a prophetic vision that Yaakov experienced, and from which he walked away limping because of the psychosomatic trauma that he endured.[236]

How then can we understand the struggle from Rambam's perspective? Why indeed was Yaakov left alone, to confront an unknown assailant that was an angel of God – Esav's guardian angel?

Yaakov on that fateful night was alone, tormented and terrified by the morrow's encounter with his brother. Undoubtedly, on some level, his voyage across the Yabbok was a subtle attempt to flee from his destiny – to avert the meeting with the pugnacious brother from whom he had fled decades earlier.[237]

---

[235] When a glass or plate breaks at a wedding banquet, and people yell "*Mazal tov*," I have often thought that their shouts of joy take into account that it is not *their* property that was broken, but the caterer's. It is easy to be philosophical about someone else's loss. So, too, those who find something and then lose it are less perturbed than those who have worked for something and then lost it.

[236] *Moreh Nevuchim* 2:42; Ramban vehemently disagrees in his commentary to Breisheet 18:1.

[237] See Rashbam 32:25, where he intimates that Yaakov was looking for an escape after having secured

Yaakov had a deep-rooted fear of his brother, some of it quite rational. Esav hated him and was not constrained in his behavior by any moral code. Yaakov had spent decades on the run, and on this night, God forced him to confront his fears – fears that, if continued unabated – would jeopardize the future of the nation that Yaakov would lead.

That was the nature of the prophetic vision he had. The tussle with "Esav's angel" was the struggle with his own insecurities. On this night, the "running" stopped and Yaakov assumed his role as leader of a nation and not just patriarch of a family.

The scuffle with the "angel" was intense, as our inner torments are the most difficult adversaries we ever face. The dust of this struggle reached the "divine throne of glory,"[238] i.e., it touched upon Yaakov's very faith and his commitment to his mission. He fought through the darkness of the night, until "the dawn," when the world becomes clearer. It was then that Yaakov was told that he had triumphed, and merited a new name: "And he said, 'Your name will no longer be Yaakov, but Yisrael, for you have striven with God and with man and prevailed'" (32:29). No longer would he be known as Yaakov, a name that implies a heel, downtrodden and timid, but Yisrael, a prince of God, who battles the mighty and triumphs, who will generate a mighty and eternal nation.

The dangers that loomed left an imprint – "and [Yaakov] was limping on his hip" (32:32) – but Yaakov had overcome his worst trepidations. A nation paralyzed by fears and anxieties cannot survive for long. Jews especially often dread the future – the power of our enemies, the persistence of their hatred, the internal struggles that weaken the people of Israel. Those fears are the "limp" that slows us down and hampers our capacity to embrace the glories ahead.

What Yaakov did in his own life on a national level is certainly true on an individual level. People are often beset by irrational fears that leave them unable to break away from self-destructive patterns or to seize new opportunities. It takes the utmost courage to confront our inner demons, but that courage is demanded of anyone who wants to maximize his talents and take responsibility for the fulfillment of his life's aspirations.

Since this nocturnal skirmish between Yaakov and the angel, that courage is the hallmark of the people of Israel.

---

his family's future, confident that Esav wished to harm him, not them.

[238] Masechet Chulin 91a.

Wrestling for Eternity

And Yaakov was left alone, and a man wrestled with him until dawn. When he saw that he could not overcome him, he struck his hip socket, and Yaakov's hip socket was dislocated as he wrestled with him. (Breisheet 32:25–26)

Of our three forefathers, only Yaakov had to wrestle an angel as part of his personal development. His name was even changed as a result of this confrontation to Yisrael (Israel), for "you have striven with God and with man and prevailed" (32:29). Why is it that only Yaakov had this experience, and not Avraham or Yitzchak?

The Chofetz Chaim, in his Torah commentary, quotes the *Zohar* that defined Yaakov's "hip socket" as *tmachin d'oraita*, the supporters of Torah – those who uphold it and enable it to withstand all the blandishments and threats of Esav and his cohorts.[239] The other Avot were never challenged like this because Avraham was the man of kindness and Yitzchak the epitome of self-effacing divine service. Yaakov, though, was the paragon of Torah who spent much of his life involved in ideas – the study of God and His morality – with his father and with his teacher Ever in the academy. Yaakov was the first selfless student of Torah.

The angel of Esav does not mind when Jews do acts of *chesed*, or even when we engage in divine service – for example when we pray and fast and wear *tztitzit* and the like. The angel of Esav is only disturbed when Jews study Torah, which has a transformative effect on the soul. It is the "hip socket of Yaakov," the point on which everything else in Jewish life hinges.

It is impossible to imagine a day without Torah study; it is the oxygen for the Jewish soul. And that is why Torah study is the tip of the spear of our enemies, both external and internal. The Greeks, Romans, medieval Christians, Communists and Nazis all targeted Torah study, and often made it a capital crime for Jews to learn Torah. So, too, our instinctual drives often kick into gear when we want to learn Torah. It is then that the phone or doorbell will ring, the food will boil over on the stove, the baby will cry, the children will need a bath and the office will call (and sometimes all of the above). The distractions that intrude on our Talmud Torah are diverse and uncanny – all of which points to the preciousness of Talmud Torah and the struggle to overcome the magnetic pull of the world of physical pleasures.

---

[239] *Zohar* 3, 243a. This is cited also by *Bnai Yissaschar*, Maamarei Kislev-Tevet 2 and 3.

We all have the ability and multiple opportunities for Talmud Torah – the only question is do we have the desire and the will? We can eschew mindless entertainment, make one fewer phone call, have one fewer inane conversation, and especially wrestle with Esav's angel when he comes dressed in fatigue – and instead strive to enter a different realm, challenge our minds, cultivate our souls, go to a *shiur* (Torah class), open a *sefer* (Torah book), and connect with generations of Jews past and present.

That is why the angel attacked Yaakov's hip socket – the supporters and lovers of Torah. We are admonished by the great Hillel, "Do not say, 'When I have time, I will learn,' because maybe you will never have time."[240] The opportunities today are literally limitless: through the Internet, one can learn Torah from teachers across the globe and around the clock (not to mention attend a local class taking place live).

The Jewish world has two camps – those who regularly learn Torah and those who do not. That is a fundamental choice we make that, more than anything else, determines our spiritual destiny. It is the responsibility of every Jew to choose wisely.

COMPLETE

And Yaakov arrived at the city of Shechem in the land of Canaan complete… (Breisheet 33:18)

Yaakov survived the encounter with his brother, and even his hip injury, made his way to Canaan, and arrived there "*shalem*" (whole, intact, complete). Rashi quotes the gemara that Yaakov came "whole physically, whole materially and whole spiritually."[241]

He was healed from his wound, his assets were replenished after the tribute given to Esav, and he had not lost his Torah commitment after his two decades with Lavan.

But didn't Yaakov have this same sense of completeness at the beginning of the *sedra*? Before he met Esav, he was not injured at all, he had all his wealth, and he had successfully survived the spiritual hazards of Lavan's house. So what had Yaakov gained now that he did not have before?

To be "complete" does not mean that life has no challenges, setbacks or tragedies. On the contrary, *shleimut* is an internal state that exists when one

---

[240] Masechet Avot 2:5.
[241] Masechet Shabbat 33b.

confronts obstacles and overcomes them. Yaakov survived his sojourn with Lavan, but he was not "complete" until he had resolved all his outstanding difficulties – until after he had faced physical danger, financial ruin and spiritual collapse – and withstood them all.

Rav Avraham Yitzchak Kook wrote that the three perfections – body, property and soul – ideally work in harmony with each other but if the emphasis is misapplied, then each one branches off from the other and takes on a life of its own.[242] Thus, people can focus on staying healthy but require money to maintain that vigor. Then, the pursuit of money becomes self-justifying, until looking after that money and increasing it detracts from one's health. So too one who has health and wealth has a great foundation from which to pursue spiritual greatness. But how often do health and money become enemies of spirituality, as people expend excessive energy maintaining their physiques or use their money to pursue luxuries that dull their spiritual sensibilities?

Yaakov showed us that these three types of perfection are symbiotic. Each one ideally strengthens the other and the three need not necessarily be antagonistic to each other. "One type of perfection need not alienate the others," Rav Kook wrote.[243]

One who wants to live a full life will seek completeness in every realm – but never succumb to the temptation to allow the pursuit of health or wealth to encroach on spiritual matters. That balance is another compelling choice in life.

Blaming the Victim

And Dina daughter of Leah, whom she had borne to Yaakov, went out to look at the daughters of the land. (Breisheet 34:1)

Rashi notes that Dina was referred to here as the "daughter of Leah," not as daughter of Yaakov, because she was a gadabout like her mother and got herself into trouble. Dina wandered out from Yaakov's house, too curious for her own good, and met with a terrible, brutal fate – kidnap and rape. Rashi's innocent observation is jarring from a modern perspective, in which it is considered mean-spirited and repugnant to blame the victim at all, even slightly, and even when the victim has somehow contributed to his or her own victimization.

---

[242] *Ein Ayah*, Shabbat 33b.
[243] Ibid.

What changed? Certainly, sympathy for any victim is natural, and especially for a crime victim. No one has the right to assault, assail, molest or harass another person; there is no such concept as the "victim had it coming." Yet something else has changed as well. Rashi's old-fashioned principles recall a time when personal responsibility was the norm and not the exception. And even an innocent victim has to ponder whether acting differently in some way might have helped avoid an unfortunate fate. That such an approach does not resonate with the modern reader is an indication of how much the Torah ethic of personal responsibility has evaded us, or has been eradicated from public discourse.[244]

Since the Torah promotes the ethic of personal responsibility, our Sages never shied away from "blaming the victim," even for slight missteps that barely contributed to the victim's fate. They fervently advocated introspection when anyone encountered any personal difficulty. Thus, "if a person is beset by troubles, he should examine his deeds; if he finds nothing unbecoming in his conduct, he should attribute his suffering to his lack of Torah study."[245]

The Rambam takes this concept to a higher level, positing that of the three types of evil that can befall a human being, the most prevalent are those we bring on ourselves.[246] We victimize ourselves through the vices we indulge; the foods we eat; the alcohol, tobacco or drugs we ingest; and the reckless conduct (known as "thrill seeking") in which many people engage. In effect, we are victimized mainly by the poor choices we make in life.

Too often in the modern world, people make knowing, conscious decisions, destroy their lives and then expect society (or the government) to pick up the pieces and the expense of rebuilding their shattered lives. Society seeks to avoid "blaming the victim" not because it necessarily loves or sympathizes with the victim but because it abhors individual responsibility and accountability. We are quick to deny the consequences of moral lapses, even as many also deny any notion of absolute morality. That is a deadly combination.

---

[244] There was a time when people avoided walking in "bad neighborhoods" after dark (perhaps that time still exists). Certainly, a person who defied that convention has not waived his right to walk unharmed. He is guilty of nothing, except bad judgment – but bad judgment is also a reflection of character. So, too, a victim of lung cancer naturally and properly evokes great sympathy, but if that tragic victim was a chain smoker for several decades, it is hard to conclude that he did not contribute to his demise in a significant and substantive way. Thus, secular law recognizes a doctrine of contributory negligence.

[245] Masechet Berachot 5a. Those "sufferings" can be anything – physical, financial, personal – the entire gamut of human experience, and include the trivial and the momentous. See Masechet Arachin 16b–17a.

[246] Rambam, *Moreh Nevuchim* 3:12. The other less prevalent "evils" are acts of God (unfortunate natural occurrences) and evil committed by people against each other.

Nothing justifies the dastardly assault on Dina, period, but our Sages perceived it as morally convenient but hypocritical to absolve the victim who contributes to his own misfortune. They fought the philosophy of the "cult of the victim" with all the intellectual strength they could muster – and found slivers of guilt in the most unlikely places.

For example, not only is Dina criticized for "going out," but Yaakov is also criticized. The Torah says that when Yaakov prepared to meet Esav, "he arose that night and took his two wives, two maidservants, and eleven children, and crossed the ford of Yabbok" (32:23). But, of course, Yaakov then had twelve children: eleven sons (Binyamin was yet to be born) and one daughter, Dina. Rashi asks: "And where was Dina? [Yaakov] placed her in a box and locked her in it, so that Esav should not set his eyes on her. For that Yaakov was punished, because he kept her from his brother, for perhaps she could have inspired his repentance. And [Dina] fell into the clutches of Shechem."

Inevitably, this repression of Dina backfired. Living in a house with all brothers, and sheltered from all potentially harmful influences, Dina undoubtedly felt stifled and did what came naturally to her: she went out, and innocently enough. Our Sages saw a smidgeon of fault in what Dina did and in what Yaakov did. The choices of both should not be overlooked simply because of the great evil perpetrated by Shechem.

In fact, Shechem's evil is a given; that is why he wound up on the wrong side of a massacre. But to blame Shechem (or other evildoers) and end the discussion is misleading. We have to always examine our actions, responses or conduct that provided the opening that allowed their evil to affect us.[247]

ROYALTY

And Dina...went out... (Breisheet 34:1)

How can we avoid our children succumbing to the most harmful influences (or substances) in the general society? There is no foolproof answer but one approach, inculcated from their earliest youth, poses a greater chance of success.

---

[247] Certainly we recognize that Yaakov's intentions were good, as were Dina's, and the Torah – again, in this instance – does not provide us with a ready, facile solution to their dilemmas. The question of how much we can properly shield our children from harmful influences, and at the same time prepare them to deal with a world that can be unsavory, does not lend itself to an easy, homogeneous answer. Ultimately, all parents draw a line, even knowing that the outcome of their decision will not be evident for decades.

The Netziv comments that Dina "went out" from her sense of dignity and self-worth.[248] She lowered herself. It was degrading that a daughter of Yaakov needed the approbation of the "daughters of the land." Certainly, curiosity is healthy, but not curiosity that demeans the person, debases the soul and devalues the innate worth of a member of a royal family.

Dina therefore went outside the bounds of propriety, which are not judged by the standards of society (and sometimes not by the standards of parents who should know better but are perhaps fighting demons of their own or trying to relive their own adolescence) but by the standards of the Torah, the requirements of Jewish life and our expectations of a member of a holy people.

Rav Yitchak Hutner famously said that the most important idea parents can convey to children is that they are princes of God, royalty, especially chosen to serve the King of kings. That idea, reinforced constantly, gives children a sense of self-worth, an awareness of their destiny and their potential for greatness. A child who grows up with that consciousness will never lose it, and that alone can embolden a person to withstand all types of pressure in every sphere of life.

Every Jewish parent is therefore mandated to transmit to their children not only the dos and don'ts of the Torah but also the knowledge that their offspring are heirs to a princely people and a proud tradition and must always live in a way that reflects that exalted status.

---

[248] *Ha'amek Davar*, Breisheet 34:1.

Vayeshev

Serenity Now

And Yaakov settled in the land of his father's sojourning, in the land of Canaan. (Breisheet 37:1)

After more than four decades on the run, Yaakov finally attempts to settle down into a graceful old age. It is not to be. Rashi comments: "Yaakov wished to dwell in serenity, but the vexation of the story of Yosef engulfed him. [When] the righteous wish to dwell in serenity, the Holy One, blessed be He, says: 'Is it not enough what is prepared for them in the world to come that they also wish to dwell in tranquility in this world?'"[249]

The travail of Yosef – his sale by his brothers, his absence from Yaakov's life for almost twenty-three years – was undoubtedly the greatest trauma of Yaakov's life, which certainly knew its share of hardships. Was it so wrong that Yaakov, having fled from his brother and his father-in-law and finally returning to his father's home bereft of his mother, now sought some peace of mind? Why is it that the righteous do not, or are not supposed to, desire contentment and equanimity? Doesn't the Talmud state that "quietude for the righteous is a pleasure for them and for the world"?[250]

There are two points worth noting that give us an insight into Yaakov's mindset. From what exactly was he seeking this psychological and physical repose? Rav Shimon Schwab commented that Yaakov wanted a break from parenting. He thought that he was finished teaching and guiding his children, most of whom were grown. They were old enough to make their own decisions and find their own paths in life. He assumed that, upon maturity, the sibling rivalries between them would cease and they would make common cause.

---

[249] Rashi, Breisheet 37:2.
[250] Masechet Sanhedrin 71b.

Yaakov was brutally awakened by the anguish of Yosef. Suddenly he realized that parenting never ends; that perhaps for him, it might not have even started yet; and that his children were still lacking the basic tools to carry forward Jewish destiny. It was too early for Yaakov to retire to his backyard and play with his grandchildren.

Parenting indeed is a lifelong process, and never really ends, even though it assumes different forms as children age. The old adage "you're only as happy as your unhappiest child" is true throughout life. And although children who are adults must be allowed to make their own decisions, the wisdom of their elders should always accompany them on their life's journeys (and perhaps also the realization that the worrying of their parents never ceases). The responsibilities of parenting are eternal.

From the context, another point of discontent emerges as well. Yaakov settled "in the land of his father's sojourning." He was content to dwell in security and peace in the land in which his father was only a *ger*, an alien and sojourner. In other words, Yaakov was tired of fighting for the land of Israel. He had struggled with Esav and warred with Shechem and triumphed. He was now ready to stake his claim to the land through accommodation – enough fighting, enough suffering.

"The torment of Yosef overwhelmed him." It is natural and understandable to be tired after years of struggle, both in life generally and especially in the land of Israel. The drumbeat of bad news – terror, explosions, casualties, death and suffering – surely wore down many Israelis in the first decade of the twenty-first century, a sentiment best articulated by its former prime minister (then vice prime minister) Ehud Olmert, who said in 2005: "We are tired of fighting, we are tired of being courageous, we are tired of winning, we are tired of defeating our enemies. We want to be able to live in an entirely different environment of relations with our enemies."[251]

It is surely an understandable attitude, albeit detached from the reality of the Middle East, and precipitated the expulsion of Jews from Gaza and years of incessant missile attacks and instability in southern Israel. Yaakov also wanted some peace and quiet, to which "the Holy One, blessed be He, says: 'Is it not enough what is prepared for them in the world to come that they also wish to dwell in tranquility in this world?'"[252]

---

[251] Ehud Olmert, speech to the Israel Policy Forum in New York, June 9, 2005.

[252] Rashi, Breisheet 37:2. Note that our text of the Midrash (Breisheet Rabba 84:3) attributes this statement to a different, internal force: "Satan comes and charges, 'Is it not enough what is prepared for the righteous in the world-to-come that they wish to dwell in serenity in this world?'" If so, then the yearning for serenity is an instinctual drive that stifles the *tzaddik's* capacity to serve God,

To be "tired" of life and its challenges is harmful, counterproductive, and self-destructive. We are tested in life not to debilitate or weaken us, but in order to challenge and strengthen us. Through our trials, we uncover our latent potential and achieve new heights of faith and service. If Yaakov was tired, that was not good for him or the Jewish people. One who is tired of being tested is tired of life itself, and to surrender to difficult trials (personal, financial, emotional) is a sign of a debilitating despair. Ultimately, it is self-defeating.

Conversely, the measure of greatness is even to take a single step toward overcoming the difficulty and escaping the danger. Yaakov had to be awakened by his personal ordeal (and go down to exile in Egypt), but later in our history, most Jews who lived during the Syrian-Greek exile were also tired. Greek culture had already permeated the land of Israel when Antiochus captured Yerushalayim and defiled the Beit Hamikdash. Most Jews had already accommodated themselves to Syrian occupation, if not culture and values. The national fatigue was pervasive.

The Jewish people were revitalized by one act: the rebellion of Matityahu and his sons in Modiin. The greatness of Chanuka is its eternal message to the Jewish people against despair, despondency, dejection, wallowing in self-pity, and indulging tired clichés and failed solutions. Chanuka was defined by its flames. From one jar of pure oil, a *menora* can burn; from one candle, thousands of others can be lit and spark a renaissance of Jewish life and identity, of fealty to Torah and Jewish destiny.

In our national lives, we are sometimes taught that lesson the hard way. In our personal lives, it is critical to realize that people possess enormous reservoirs of internal strength that can be tapped when crises arise. Those are the ultimate tests of righteousness.

The rewards are born our in real life. In his best seller *Outliers*, Malcolm Gladwell traces the source of the disproportionate financial success of Jewish immigrants in the twentieth century to their origins, but in the opposite way from what one might imagine.[253] They achieved prosperity not *despite* their humble, impoverished backgrounds but *because* of them. As refugees, they learned the value of initiative, practical intelligence and social savvy – and applied it. They saw, as did their children, a close connection between effort and reward.

---

perfect his soul and better the world – as tempting as it is on the surface.

[253] *Outliers: The Story of Success* (New York: Little, Brown and Company, 2008).

The Midrash states: "'Do not rejoice over me, my enemy; for though I fell, I shall rise!' If I had not fallen, I could not have risen. 'Though I sit in darkness, God is a light to me.' If I had not sat in darkness, I would have had no light."[254]

It is because we sometimes sit in darkness, and experience setbacks and hardships and are forced to make choices and decisions that God becomes our light and our salvation.

Appearances

These are the chronicles of Yaakov: Yosef was seventeen years old, and he was a shepherd with his brothers by the flock, and he was a youth with the sons of Bilha and Zilpa his father's wives... (Breisheet 37:2)

Yosef was a "youth," Rashi wrote, in the sense that "he would act like an adolescent, grooming his hair and primping his eyes so he should look beautiful."[255] That also did not endear him to his older brothers but it was a trait that Yosef found hard to uproot. Later, after he had been sold into slavery and climbed the ladder of success in Potifar's house, he resumed his excessive concern with his appearance: "And Yosef was beautiful in form and in appearance" (39:6), and Rashi notes that once again, "finding himself a ruler, he started eating and drinking and grooming his hair...."[256]

Certainly, none of this speaks well of Yosef, and in both cases his self-absorption created enormous problems for him – first with his brothers and then with Potifar's wife, who began to pursue him immediately following this renewed concern with his appearance.[257] But in that particular weakness of Yosef, a valuable lesson is learned.

Rav Moshe Ganz of Yeshivat Sha'alvim wrote that the young Yosef, on the surface, was a flawed individual from whom little could be expected.[258] He looked like a teenager who cared about nothing else other than superficialities – clothing, hair, appearance, recreation. But at the same time, he had tremendous spiritual depth: even as a teenager far from home and suffering from acute rejection by his family, he was able to retain his inner sense of right and wrong and resist the entreaties of Potifar's wife.

---

[254] Yalkut Tehillim 628, commenting on Micha 7:8.
[255] Rashi, Breisheet 37:2.
[256] Rashi, Breisheet 39:6.
[257] Ibid.
[258] *Pnei Shabbat*, pp. 91–92.

Too often we judge based on external appearances and completely miss the other person's essence. It is not that surprising: as God told the prophet Shmuel when he could not fathom how a young David was suitable as God's anointed king, "for it is not as a man sees, for man sees according to his eyes, but God sees into the heart."[259] What we see on the surface is as superficial as our evaluation of a person's real character – a hint, but often misleading. What people wear on the outside is less important than who they are on the inside. But modern Jewish society has unfortunately made a fetish of external appearances, presuming that people's true character, observance, religiosity and ethical commitment can be judged by the size and color (and shape) of one's hat or *kippa*, by the presence or absence of a beard, or by the style or color of one's clothing. The Talmud decries those who wrap themselves in *tallitot* to feign piety but are actually corrupt and dishonest.[260]

Moreover, a person's outward tendencies can even fool him into thinking that he *is* what he desires, and that a particular weakness or limitation defines him forever. That is also demonstrably false, as Yosef teaches us. Whatever our tendencies – and we all have illicit tendencies; that is how we were created – our souls remain pure and in search of the proper sustenance and development. We must recognize, therefore, that our inner world is always under our control, and therein lies the path to perfection, no matter how many obstacles are encountered along the way: free choice, personal responsibility, and relentless efforts to enhance our character.

Sibling Rivalry

> *And his brothers saw that their father Yisrael loved [Yosef] more than all his brothers, and they hated him, and could not speak to him peaceably. (Breisheet 37:4)*

There is perhaps no story in the Torah that is as troubling as the sale of Yosef by his brothers. How could a band of brothers sell another brother into slavery – and how could Yaakov's righteous sons, children of Avraham and Yitzchak and the progenitors of the Jewish people, commit an act that is unimaginably despicable?

Certainly, the hand of Divine Providence was at work, bringing the family of Yaakov into exile from which it would emerge as a Godly nation with the

---

[259] I Shmuel 16:7.
[260] Masechet Sota 22b, with Rashi, s.v. "*d'mitamra mitamra.*"

Torah as its constitution. Yosef, who inexplicably was dispatched by his father to the distant fields to inquire after the welfare of the brothers who hated him, lost his way and was only guided toward his brothers by a mysterious "man" (37:15), identified as the angel Gavriel.[261] Clearly, it was not a random event, but one that accorded with the will of God. Yet why was God's will effected in such a disconcerting way that so disturbed Yaakov and reflected such poor character on the part of his sons?

The formation of the Jewish people required more than the procreation of twelve tribes. It demanded superior moral and ethical greatness, and character above reproach. The sale of Yosef took place in Canaan and was a necessary prequel to the rise of the Jewish nation. In Canaan, in our nascent state, each principal of the future Jewish people (Yaakov, Yosef and his brothers) had a shortcoming that, if not rectified, would have had deleterious and long-term consequences for Jewish life.[262]

Yaakov's weakness was his attachment to Yosef above and beyond his relationship with his other sons. Yosef was the son of Yaakov's preferred wife Rachel, who had died young after an ill-fated and relatively brief marriage. Yaakov's affection for and commitment to Yosef was boundless, and their special relationship grated on his other sons. The favored treatment was blatant: Yaakov saw Yosef as the wisest of his sons and transmitted to him the teachings of the Academy of Ever;[263] Yosef's visage reminded Yaakov of himself;[264] and Yaakov therefore made for Yosef only a special multicolored coat that reflected his elevated status over his brothers.[265] The Talmud states: "A person should never show favoritism among his children, for because of the little extra silk that Yaakov put in Yosef's garment, his brothers were envious of him and the matter unfolded until we were exiled to Egypt."[266]

That is good advice in itself, but the Talmud is not referring merely to the chronology of events; rather it is addressing cause and effect. Yaakov's favoritism forced the exile to come about as it did because such an obvious differentiation between children would have generated untold and permanent

---

[261] Rashi, Breisheet 37:15. Yaakov himself is said to have sent Yosef based on "the profound counsel of the righteous one buried in Hevron" (Rashi, Breisheet 37:14, from Masechet Sota 11a), i.e., in order to fulfill the destiny set forth by God for Avraham's descendants.

[262] Heard from Rav Yisrael Chait.

[263] Rashi, Breisheet 37:3.

[264] Ibid.

[265] Breisheet 37:3.

[266] Masechet Shabbat 10b.

strife between his children long after his demise.[267] Yaakov's preferential treatment had to end in order for the tribes to remain one unit and become one nation. That fateful moment – and the rectification of Yaakov's flaw – came about unexpectedly: When the brothers returned from Egypt without Shimon and with the news that the peculiar vizier of Egypt insisted on seeing the youngest child Binyamin, Yaakov at first refused to send Binyamin, the last vestige of his beloved wife Rachel, with this other sons. When Yaakov relented,[268] he essentially equated Binyamin with his other sons and overcame the emotional complex that had undermined the unity of his family.

Similarly, the young Yosef was also flawed, beset by arrogance that repelled his brothers and resulted naturally from his exalted status in the family. He did everything wrong: "he was a youth with the children of Bilha and Zilpa, his father's wives, and Yosef brought bad reports about his brothers to his father" (37:2). Yosef was obsessed with his appearance,[269] and routinely slandered his brothers in order to curry even more favor with his father. Yosef's narcissism was uncontrollable and insufferable; worse, as Yosef was being groomed for leadership, his miscalculations in relating his dreams demonstrated that he was tone-deaf in his dealings with other people – disastrous in a leader. Yosef had to be humbled in order that he should learn the fundamental truth of the good leader: identification with his people, and not artificial separation from them.

Indeed, Yosef was humbled and then some, made a slave, and then imprisoned for a long period of time with the dregs of society. By the time he emerged from incarceration and was elevated suddenly to royalty, Yosef was a different person, chastened, humbled and selfless, tasked with providing nourishment to the entire civilized world. In time Yosef's failing – the haughtiness of youth that would have disqualified him from leadership – was also rectified.

And Yosef's brothers had their emotional burdens that needed to be lifted. The intense jealousy and hatred they felt for Yosef did not bode well for the budding nation; unresolved, that nation would have split apart at the earliest opportunity (it later did, anyway, during the reign of King Shlomo's son,

---

[267] As it is, the rivalry between the sons of Rachel and the sons of Leah has characterized Jewish life from the very beginning of our existence, through the monarchies of the First Temple period, and will endure until the Messianic Age when complete unity will be brought about with the rise first of Moshiach son of Yosef and then Moshiach son of David (Yehuda). See Yeshayahu 11:13 and Rashi, ibid., and the haftarah for Parshat Vayigash, especially Yechezkel 37:19.

[268] Breisheet 43:14.

[269] Rashi, Breisheet 37:2.

Rechavam). Nonetheless, their jealousy, grounded in real events, bordered on the irrational. They should have perceived, and acceded to, Yosef's superior wisdom and talents and submitted themselves to his dominion. But their hatred blinded themselves to that conclusion; indeed, they were so blind to their brother's true nature that they did not recognize him even when he stood right in front of their eyes.[270] At the end of the story, they were overcome with remorse, humbly accepted Yosef's leadership and were the beneficiaries of his compassion – and the Jewish people were ready for the crucible of Egypt.

Those are the ways of Divine Providence, which works through people's choices and characteristics in order to bring about its desired objectives. And so it works in our lives as well: we are shaped by our character, which in turn is tested by events and circumstances in our lives. Ultimately, we are defined in life by our character, which is completely under our control. Providence operates in the world through people – with their flaws, talents, weaknesses, and strengths – in order to achieve its aims.

The sale of Yosef is perhaps the greatest primer in the Torah about taking responsibility for one's actions. Each party recognized what trait needed to be corrected for the benefit of the individual and the nation. Each party was given the opportunity – forced into it, as it were – and drew the appropriate conclusions. As in our lives, this acceptance of personal responsibility did not happen immediately, nor did it happen without great personal distress to all concerned. But it did happen.

The Long Wait

> *And his brothers were jealous of him, but his father kept the matter in mind. (Breisheet 37:11)*

The phrase describing Yaakov's reaction to Yosef's dream – *shamar et hadavar* – bears understanding. He "kept the matter in mind," or "preserved it," or "watched over it." All are true. The Midrash states that Yaakov, indeed, preserved the moment: "Yaakov took a quill and recorded the day, time and place where he heard Yosef interpret his dreams.… The Holy Spirit advised him to mark down these [dreams] that would eventually be realized."[271] Notwithstanding Yaakov's sharp criticism of Yosef's interpretation, he knew something unusual was afoot. And then he waited.

---

[270] Breisheet 42:8.
[271] Breisheet Rabba 84:12.

What Yaakov did not do was tell his other sons about his sense of Yosef's impending greatness, or otherwise try to resolve their outstanding issues. He did not divulge to them what he had learned through divine inspiration; rather he let the matter rest. Yaakov was reactive – waiting to see what would happen – rather than proactive; perhaps his intervention might have somewhat tempered his other sons' hostility to Yosef.

There is a time for passivity and a time for action. Usually, family disputes fester through inactivity or apathy and are exacerbated over time. Perhaps Yaakov was waiting for the "right time" to engage his angry sons, or perhaps his unfortunate dispatch of Yosef to inquire about his brothers was Yaakov's desultory attempt at reconciliation.

Family feuds are mostly healed not through the passage of time, but through the involvement of one person who takes responsibility for ending them.

Good Intentions

> *And Reuven heard, and he rescued [Yosef] from their hand, and said, "We will not kill him!" And Reuven said to [his brothers], "Do not shed blood. Throw him into this pit in the wilderness, but no hand should touch him" – he intended to save Yosef from their hands and return him to his father. (Breisheet 37:21–22)*

Reuven, Yaakov's firstborn, was characterized throughout the Torah by events that reveal his good intentions but poor execution. He always has the right idea but is also always missing something that makes his actions seem heavy-handed, awkward or misguided.

Twice Reuven involved himself in his father's intimate relations with his wives, by retrieving the mandrakes for his mother Leah and moving Yaakov's bed into her tent.[272]

Later Reuven will guarantee Binyamin's safe return to Yaakov by offering to kill his own two sons if he fails, an offer that Yaakov silently rejected as the blathering of a fool.[273] Here, too, Reuven means well: "he intended to save Yosef from their hands and return him to his father." But what did he

---

[272] Breisheet 30:14 and 35:22.
[273] Breisheet 42:37–38, with Rashi's commentary on 42:38.

actually do? He announced they would not kill him, wrung his hands, left to tend to his father – and returned to find Yosef sold into slavery.[274] The goal he had announced – returning Yosef to his father – had not succeeded. Good intentions only go so far.

The Midrash quotes Rav Yitzchak bar Maryon who said that "one who does a *mitzva* [here meaning any good deed] should do it with a full heart, for had Reuven known that God would record in His Torah 'Reuven heard, and he rescued him from their hand,' then Reuven would have carried Yosef on his shoulders back to his father."[275] That sentiment conforms to the old adage that has largely fallen into desuetude: "Anything worth doing is worth doing well."

The antediluvian hero Chanoch was praised as a righteous person because as a shoemaker, with "each stitch he unified God's name."[276] Chanoch's every stitch was a praise of God, for each stitch was an honest stitch, performed to the best of his abilities. Yet how often do we throw ourselves wholeheartedly into what we do?

We can try to just "get by" with anything. In service of God, we can just do the *mitzva* to "fulfill one's obligation."[277] In our relations with other people, we can be cordial and perfunctory – the minimum that assures that we won't be perceived as cold and churlish but without evincing true love and respect for other people. As employees, we can perform our tasks to pick up a paycheck, rather than taking pride in our work and attempting to produce the best product, student, outcome or profit. As spouses and parents, we can remember the birthdays and anniversaries, and not much else. Politicians can focus on the next election, rather than solving society's current problems. We can always do the minimum, just enough.

Similarly, we can be filled with the noblest motives, but if we do not act – or act ineffectually – we will accomplish little. And ultimately, good intentions that do not come to fruition usually reflect poorly on the real "goodness" of the intentions. The intentions might not have been "good" in the first place, but rather designed to attract attention and acclaim.

Reuven, as was his wont, meant well, but did little to avert the catastrophe that befell his brother Yosef. Indeed, his abandonment of the crime scene

---

[274] Breisheet 37:29, with Rashi's commentary.

[275] Midrash Ruth Rabba 5:6. So, too, if Boaz had known that the paltry menu he offered Ruth ("parched grain," as in Ruth 2:14) was being recorded for posterity, he would have offered her a meal of the choicest fattened calves.

[276] Midrash Yalkut Reuveni, cited by Rav Tzadok Hakohen, *Likutei Maamarim*, p. 169, with the comment of Rav Yisrael Salanter found in *Tenuat Hamusar* of Rav Dov Katz, vol. 1, p. 359.

[277] To be "*yotzei*," in the Jewish vernacular.

at the most crucial moment imaginable – when the brothers were debating Yosef's fate – was typical of his desultory approach to life, notwithstanding that he had returned to care for his father. He meant well in that also, as he did in assuming the responsibility of the firstborn to make decisions – "do not kill him" – afraid that blame for Yosef's demise would be placed on him.[278] He was, in American parlance, always "a day late and a dollar short." And he always realized his shortcomings; after his failure to prevent the sale of Yosef, "Reuven was preoccupied with his sackcloth and fasts,"[279] mourning his failures and the family trauma to which he had contributed.

He always meant well. But usually in life, more than "meaning well" is required. Indeed, anything worth doing is worth doing well, and worth doing right, and worth doing well and right the first time.

First Signs of Greatness

And Yehuda said to his brothers: "What profit is there in killing our brother and covering up his blood?" (Breisheet 37:26)

Yehuda's statement seems cold and calculated, especially in contrast to Reuven's good intentions. Yet our Sages taught that Yehuda's argument was the first that would qualify him for royalty.[280] What exactly did he say that was so noble?

Rav Chaim Shmulevitz cited Rashi's explanation that Yehuda's reference to "covering up his blood" meant that they would have to "conceal his death."[281] To hide Yosef's death obligated them to deny responsibility for what was their "judicial decision" to execute him. If they could not take responsibility for their verdict, then it was not a just verdict.[282]

These were Yehuda's first stirrings of accountability that would fully mature in the episode with Tamar that set the stage for Yehuda's later assumption of kingship, whose first qualification is personal responsibility.

---

[278] Rashi, Breisheet 37:22.
[279] Breisheet Rabba 85:1.
[280] Tosefta Berachot 4:16.
[281] Rashi, Breisheet 37:26.
[282] *Sichot Musar*, maamar 20.

Flight from Responsibility

> *They sent the [bloody] colored tunic and brought it to their father, and said, "We found this. Please identify: Is this the tunic of your son or not?" (Breisheet 37:32)*

Ramban (and Radak) both state that the brothers sent a messenger with Yosef's tunic and commanded the messenger to ask their father that ominous question. In other words, their plan, devised in order to save their family from Yosef's excesses and made with deliberation, called for deception. And something else: they did not even have the decency or courage to look their father in the eye, and certainly not to explain to him their reasoning.

In truth, there was no justification they could offer their father, and among their miscalculations was their assumption that in time Yaakov would come to terms with Yosef's death. That never happened: "And all [Yaakov's] sons and daughters came to console him and he refused to be comforted, saying, 'I will go to my grave mourning for my son'" (37:35). They were so convinced of their righteousness that they took the twenty silver pieces for which Yosef was sold and bought shoes with them, shoes that they wore every day even knowing that Yosef their brother was enslaved somewhere.[283] Yosef's brothers never sought to rectify their sin – never even thought it was a sin until long after their reconciliation – but nothing more typifies their rejection of responsibility for their actions than their unwillingness to confront their father with the information about Yosef's "demise."

"Tzadka Mimeni!"
She Is More Righteous Than Me

> *And Yehuda recognized [the pledges] and said, "She is more righteous than I am, as I did not give her to Shelah my son." (Breisheet 38:26)*

This decisive event in Jewish history gave this work its name, as it is one of the most illustrious and obvious examples of personal responsibility in the Torah;

---

[283] *Pirkei D'Rabbi Eliezer*, chapter 38. Our Sages taught (Masechet Shabbat 129a) that a person should better sell the beams of his house and buy shoes than walk barefoot. Shoes afford us stability, confidence, and the security to walk without fear of getting injured. Wearing shoes is the sign of a person who is secure and treads the earth boldly, without misgivings or fears. The brothers felt no guilt, and yet could not speak openly to their father. Clearly, they had some lingering doubts about their actions, at least on a subconscious level.

no other had such far-reaching consequences. After the sale of Yosef, the brothers resorted to recriminations and bitterness. "Yosef, Reuven and Yaakov all grieved and fasted, and Yehuda went to find a wife – and God set about creating the light of the Moshiach."[284] From this sordid episode (mitigated only in that it took place before the giving of the Torah at Sinai), the royal house of Israel that endures for all eternity came into existence – and all because of one choice that Yehuda made.

Tamar, twice Yehuda's daughter-in-law but now alienated from him, schemed to remain part of his household by dressing as a harlot and enticing him at a highway junction. The plan worked, and she conceived. Brought to trial and sentenced to death for her apparently scandalous conduct (she was still nominally waiting to be assigned in marriage to Yehuda's third son, but was now pregnant with another man's child), she delicately brought out the pledges that she had taken from the paramour in lieu of payment. "As she was taken out, she sent word to her father-in-law, saying, 'I am pregnant with the child of the man to whom these [items] belong'; and she said, 'Please identify: To whom belongs this signet, seal and staff?'" (38:25).

Notice how coy and discreet was Tamar, never identifying Yehuda by name, and thereby leaving her fate to his moral judgment and sense of responsibility. "It is better for a person to be thrown into a fiery furnace than to embarrass another individual in public," the Talmud derived from Tamar's conduct here.[285] And Yehuda could have remained silent, avoided the public humiliation, and permitted Tamar to be executed. No one would have been the wiser, and Tamar, widow of two of his sons, would have been gone forever.

At this perilous moment, Yehuda stepped up and assumed responsibility for his actions. "*Tzadka mimeni!*" Rashi explains the phrase to mean, "She is right; it is from me [that she is pregnant]." In other words, *the items in question belong to me; I, Yehuda, am the father of her child.* Ramban and Rashbam explicated the phrase differently: "She is more righteous than I am." *Her deeds are more honorable. She is virtuous, and I am a sinner, for I failed to give her in marriage to my son Shelah.*[286]

"Yehuda confessed without any hesitation, and in the end merited eternal life. And what was his reward in this world? He merited royalty, the monarchy

---

[284] Breisheet Rabba 85:1.
[285] Masechet Bava Metzia 59a; Rashi, Breisheet 38:25: "Tamar said to herself: 'If he confesses on his own, he confesses, but if not, they will burn me, and I will not have embarrassed him publicly.'"
[286] Ramban, Breisheet 38:26.

of the Jewish people."[287] And the Talmud elaborates further: "Yehuda, who sanctified God's name in public, merited having God's entire name included in his own."[288] It was at that moment of contrition – of acceptance of personal responsibility – that Yehuda became the tribe of royalty, the progenitor of David, Shlomo and the Moshiach himself, through Peretz, one of the twin sons born from the liaison between Yehuda and Tamar.

While the family of Yaakov grieved over their irresponsibility and mutual alienation, "God was preoccupied creating the light of Moshiach"[289] through the nobility of spirit demonstrated by Yehuda in one fateful act.

Yehuda's response at this pivotal moment in history – personal and national – stands in marked contrast to the norms of life in the modern world, in which abdication from personal responsibility is the rule, not the exception. Politicians and public figures, rather than admit personal wrongdoing, will take refuge in the passive voice: "Mistakes were made," they will say, rather than admitting, "I made a mistake," as Yehuda did here, and as King Shaul did (finally) to David,[290] and as King David himself did after the sin with Bat Sheva.[291]

That is the essence of leadership.

Yehuda's conduct is remarkable because accountability is no longer in vogue. Fault for every misstep or calamity must always lie elsewhere, and to confess wrongdoing when it is unprompted by the media or the legal authorities – simply because it is the right thing to do – is astonishing. Yet the Torah consistently mandates that we look at ourselves first and recognize our contributions to any offenses.

To take but one modern example, surely Bernard Madoff was a scoundrel and a thief – Charles Ponzi was a small fry compared to him – but how many of his investors turned a blind eye to the "returns" they were getting from him at triple or quadruple the investment yields in the rest of the marketplace? How many people are drawn to get-rich-quick schemes – and then to get-even-more-rich-quicker schemes? How many young men today look for a quick killing in something, the lure of "easy" and sometimes unethically earned money being irresistible, and preferable to working and building a business?

---

[287] Masechet Sota 7b.
[288] Masechet Sota 10b. The four letters of God's ineffable name are all included in Yehuda's name.
[289] Midrash Breisheet Rabba 85:1.
[290] Ramban, Breisheet 38:26.
[291] II Shmuel 12:13.

Madoff was a crook, but was he not enabled by others, for years, as long as the good news was rolling in?

In the first decade of the twenty-first century, the American business world was defined by flight from responsibility – euphemistically known as the "bailout industry." Few, if any, were held accountable for bad business decisions, looting assets; many executives took exorbitant bonuses as workers were being laid off or benefited from golden parachutes as they fled their failing companies. Unions, originally created to prevent the exploitation of workers, now exist to exploit employers and shield workers from accountability or from having their pay based on their performance. The raison d'être of today's unions is to milk as much as they can in as short a period of time as they can from those who own the business and have assumed the financial risk in maintaining it.

The people of modern Israel have a peculiar habit of recycling failed politicians, hoping that they have grown in the interim. Few have, however (they usually just become more adept at handling the media and projecting an image of leadership). On a personal level, the avoidance of personal responsibility affects our lives dramatically, as people and parents.

Parents, today, for example, are much more likely than even two decades ago to argue with teachers rather than reprimand their own children. We have moved from an age in which "the teacher is always right" to "the teacher should be fired, and the principal too, for disciplining or criticizing" my child. A student's poor performance is often blamed on the teacher's inability to properly motivate rather than some deficiency in the child that needs to be addressed.

Some parents will baby their children into adulthood (and beyond) and vet their proposed mates as if they are not mature enough to make those decisions on their own. Others will allow children to marry before they have the means of self-support, a state of affairs that Rambam characterized as the way of "fools."[292]

The whole Torah is about personal responsibility. To the Rambam, it was a "great fundamental" and a "pillar of Torah" to know that we have free will to make our decisions and to live with the consequences.[293] Rabbeinu Bachye admonished us that a person should always admit his wrongdoing, and "not

---

[292] Rambam, Mishneh Torah, *Hilchot De'ot* 5:11.
[293] Rambam, *Hilchot Teshuva* 5:3.

scurry after excuses to defend himself and justify himself, [but rather should admit his errors] as did Yehuda who said *'Tzadka mimeni.'*[294]

Yosef's brothers ran from responsibility and said to Yaakov when he was presented with Yosef's bloody tunic, "*haker na*" (please identify).[295] What a subtle and sublime challenge was placed before Yehuda, who was confronted by Tamar with the exact same words: "*haker na*" (please identify).[296] And Yehuda responded with the greatness of true royalty: she is right, I am wrong.

Yehuda's admission reverberates throughout our history. His acceptance of responsibility is something we should demand of ourselves and our children, of Jewish leaders and leaders everywhere. We are always accountable for our actions and decisions, and bad acts and decisions must be acknowledged and rectified. This is a challenge confronted daily, in many different ways, and like Yehuda, we are always at a crossroads.

"Everybody Does It!"

And so, every single day, [Potifar's wife] enticed Yosef, and he did not listen to her, to lie next to her, to be with her. (Breisheet 39:10)

The Talmud relates that that the hedonist will be asked in the next world why he did not dedicate himself to the study and practice of Torah, and he will answer: "Because I was so handsome and attractive, and my desires were insatiable."[297] He will be told, "Were you better looking than Yosef? Did you ever confront the same temptation that he did?" And the Talmud continues that "every day, Potifar's wife tried to seduce Yosef when her husband was gone for the day. She would change garments during the day to get his attention, threaten him with incarceration or loss of his position in their home, threaten him with bodily harm, and then offer him a substantial bribe – and even just to lie down next to her." Yosef refused every such entreaty – even when she invoked eternity and her desire to be with him in the world-to-come. Yosef refused to succumb, and at the moment of greatest challenge, when arguably he was ready to give in to temptation, "she grabbed his garment, saying, 'Lie with me,' but he left his garment in her hand, fled and went outside" (39:12).

---

[294] *Chovot Halevavot*, shaar 6, the Gate of Submission, chapter 7.
[295] Breisheet 37:32.
[296] Breisheet 38:25.
[297] Masechet Yoma 35b.

The Talmud concludes that "Yosef indicts all [pleasure seekers]."[298]

No person can ever rationalize his conduct by saying that "everyone does it," "I'm only a human being," "the law is too difficult to observe," "nobody's perfect," "it's not my fault, I couldn't resist," or "what I do in private is no one's business." Yosef quashes all those arguments. If he could resist, so can we.

There are few people who have the opportunity and motivation to sin as did Yosef. He was abandoned by his family, putatively heirs to the religious tradition of Avraham. No one had come to find him. He had worked his way up from the mailroom of Potifar's house to become the chief administrator of his household. He was handsome and successful. The boss's wife was imploring him, and threatening him with the imminent loss of everything he cherished, especially including his freedom. She even offered Yosef theological justifications for their relationship, and he then lived in Egypt, a den of iniquity and immorality where such conduct was fairly conventional.

Why wouldn't he sin?

The Talmud relates the turning point: "At that moment, the image of his father appeared to him in the window, saying, 'Yosef, in the future your brothers' names will be inscribed on the stones of the breastplate of the High Priest. Do you want your name to be erased, and instead be forever known as a patron of prostitutes?'"[299]

Yosef wrestled internally with all of the aforementioned rationalizations. Two points overwhelmed him: he had an inner sense of his own moral aspirations and knew that sinning with Potiphar's wife was beneath him; and he also knew that his actions had consequences far beyond the immediate moment, and that the instant gratification he would experience paled before the long-term harm he would cause to himself and his destiny. So he stopped.

And Yosef had something else as well. He recognized that values and ideals are the most important and definitive dimensions of the human personality. Without values, we are shells of people, just bodies of tissues and fluids not very distinguishable from animals. To betray his own high calling was to betray his sense of self, and that enabled Yosef to leave that unnamed woman and not look back with any regret about his decision, despite the long incarceration that was his fate.

"Everybody does it" or "I had to do it" are sad euphemisms for lack of self-control and a dearth of core values. No man is perfect, and the Torah affords the sinner ample opportunity to confess, repent and recover his moral

---

[298] "Evildoers," in the text, i.e., those who seek illicit pleasure.
[299] Masechet Sota 36b.

equilibrium. But the time is somewhat limited: "He who sins and repeats the sin convinces himself that it is permissible."[300] Our powers of rationalization and our inability to live with guilt eventually compel us to devise a system in which our conduct is deemed not sinful and even virtuous and proper. That becomes the death knell of any moral aspirations.

Yosef is forever known to us as "Yosef Hatzaddik," Yosef the Righteous, not because he wasn't tempted but rather because he was tempted and refused to yield, forever indicting those who feel that they "can't" when they really mean they won't.

Yosef in Prison

And the chief cupbearer did not remember Yosef, and he forgot him. (Breisheet 40:23)

Yosef was incarcerated for ten long years, during which time he again rose to prominence – in prison! – as the warden's assistant. He was respected by his fellow prisoners to the extent that when two top ministers to the Pharaoh were jailed for various offenses and were beset by perplexing dreams, they turned to Yosef for interpretation, guidance and comfort. And Yosef delivered, offering them interpretations of their dreams that seemed plausible and were in due course realized: the chief baker was hanged, and the chief cupbearer was restored to his post.[301]

Immediately before the sentences were executed, Yosef requested a favor of his new friend, the chief cupbearer, that he should appeal to Pharaoh for Yosef's freedom, "For I was indeed kidnapped from the land of the Hebrews, and even here I did nothing and yet was placed in the pit" (40:15). It was that favor that induced the chief cupbearer to forget Yosef, almost as soon as he was liberated, and not to think about him until Pharaoh needed dream-interpretation as well.[302]

Why did the chief cupbearer ignore Yosef's plea?

Moreover, Yosef seems to have done the right thing in taking the initiative and trying to win his freedom. Yet he is harshly criticized, even punished

---

[300] Masechet Yoma 86b.

[301] Although both positions sound like cartoon characters, Rav Yosef Soloveitchik explained them both to be emblematic of security personnel. Those tasting and delivering food and drink were part of the security services in which Pharaoh had to have complete trust. Hence, the severe treatment of their offenses.

[302] Breisheet 41:9–13.

for it. "Because Yosef relied on the chief cupbearer to remember him [and gain his release], he was forced to spend another two years in prison, as it is written: 'Praiseworthy is the man who trusts in God and does not turn to the arrogant...' (Tehillim 40:5)."[303]

What did Yosef do wrong? Human initiative is one of the foundations of personal responsibility, the polar opposite of the passivity that afflicts the apathetic and irresponsible. How can Yosef be castigated for trying to better his lot? And why did the chief cupbearer forget him so precipitously?[304]

On the simplest level, Yosef had assured his fellow prisoners that all he would do was relay God's interpretations of their dreams. He would reveal their fate but could not influence it at all: "Do not interpretations belong to God?" (40:8). Their fates were determined already; if so, all Yosef did was relieve their anxieties for a few days, but he was not their deliverer or redeemer.[305] Why then should the chief cupbearer repay Yosef with freedom, when Yosef had not provided him with freedom?

There is a deeper message here as well. Certainly, Pharaoh's imprisoned officers were duly impressed with Yosef and likely wondered how such a talented individual, imbued with the divine spirit, could be languishing in the Egyptian dungeon. Undoubtedly, they had heard of his rise to prominence in Potifar's house and then again in the prison hierarchy, and felt that Yosef was a special individual worthy of assistance. That perception of Yosef changed in an instant when he begged for the assistance of the chief cupbearer and whined like a victim about all the injustices done to him in his life.[306] In a moment, Yosef was transformed from a nobleman of intelligence and sophistication into just another jailed convict protesting his innocence and railing against the unfairness of life. The chief cupbearer lost any respect for Yosef, and so discounted Yosef's role in his freedom, and without even a pang of guilt.[307]

What did Yosef do wrong? Certainly, man is allowed to take the initiative and use all his resources to try to better his position in life. Rashi indicates

---

[303] Rashi, Breisheet 40:23.

[304] Heard from Rav Yisrael Chait.

[305] Rav Avraham ibn Ezra, Breisheet 40:8.

[306] Breisheet 40:15. Note that Yosef tells them that he was placed "in a pit," echoing the original injustice done to him by his brothers. Rav Moshe Ganz (*Pnei Shabbat*, p. 98) remarks that, analogously, Gechazi in an instant caused the Aramean general Naaman to lose the holy image he had of the prophet Elisha, when Gechazi sought to profit (in Elisha's name) from his miraculous healing (II Kings 5:20–27).

[307] The chief's later reference to "my sins" (Breisheet 41:9) in not earlier recommending Yosef to Pharaoh can be attributed to his desire to make himself look good before Pharaoh and not to any real remorse on his part.

that what happened here is that Yosef became enamored with his ingenuity and thought he was in control of his destiny. That Rashi quotes the verse "Praiseworthy is the man who trusts in God" means that Yosef had completely discounted the help of Heaven and assumed he was all alone with his resourcefulness. He forgot about God, and so the chief cupbearer forgot about him.

Yosef needed another two years of "schooling" to recognize that his destiny was in God's hands and that his freedom would come unexpectedly, unpredictably, and completely as the result of Providence. When, indeed, Yosef was liberated from prison, he was not an independent mover but a passive object of other people's actions: "and they rushed him from the pit" (41:14).

We are obligated to be creative and imaginative in improving our lot in life. God created a system wherein the enterprising person can succeed and thrive as long as he is assiduous on his own behalf. But one should never feel that ultimate success or failure is dependent on our own efforts; that is God's realm. It is true that passivity usually leads to failure, but it is equally true that individual effort that takes place within a framework in which God's role is dismissed or excluded will distance a person from God rather than intensify man's attachment, and that is a net loss for one's spiritual state.

That is why prayer accompanies our endeavors in every sphere of life in which we are active – in learning Torah,[308] in seeking medical assistance, business success, peace, etc.[309] Yosef's mistake was not invoking God's assistance –and that was the last vestige of the haughtiness that had afflicted Yosef as a youth and until this very moment.

---

[308] Masechet Berachot 28b, the prayer of Rabbi Nechunia ben Hakana.
[309] The text of the Shemoneh Esrei prayer.

Mikeitz

God's Role

It is about this matter that I have spoken to Pharaoh. What God is about to do He has shown to Pharaoh. (Breisheet 41:28)

When Yosef interpreted the dreams of Pharaoh's ministers, he began with a reference to God, and included himself in the process: "Do not interpretations belong to God? Please tell it to me" (40:8). In his subsequent plea for assistance, "God" was completely excluded from Yosef's plan. That self-centeredness, as noted, harmed Yosef and kept him in prison another two years in order for him to learn the balance between individual initiative and the will of God. Yosef learned well, and in interpreting Pharaoh's dreams, Yosef consistently detached himself from the process and just as consistently directed all of Pharaoh's attention to God.

Now, Yosef saw himself not as the interpreter but simply as a vehicle that God might use to effect His will: "And Yosef said to Pharaoh, 'It is not me; it is God Who will respond to Pharaoh's welfare'" (41:16). While Yosef explained the significance of Pharaoh's dreams and proposed a system to deal with the coming famine, he referred to God another four times, finally leading Pharaoh to exclaim: "Could we find such as this – a man in whom [rests] the spirit of God?" (41:38).

That was the dramatic change in Yosef that enabled him to achieve his destiny. The references to God were not perfunctory, as they occasionally are with people who frequently say "Thank God" or "With God's help" when the reality of God's presence is not otherwise a compelling factor in their lives. Yosef's expressions were sincere, internalized only through his long years of imprisonment and his meteoric and unexpected rise to power.

Nothing is more important in life than recognizing that God controls the ultimate success or failure of an endeavor, nor is there any inherent contradiction in simultaneously acting on one's own behalf. Rav Haim Druckman[310] expounded this idea in reference to the following familiar verse: "Some with chariots, and some with horses, but we call out in the name of God!"[311] Those who rely on the chariots and horses are enamored with their own power. And we? Do we not also require chariots and horses to prevail? Yes! "We call out in the name of God" that our chariots and horses are from Him, that our strength and our abilities come from Him – and therefore "God will save! The King will answer us on the day we call on Him."[312]

In the celebration of Chanuka, Jews are quick to acknowledge the miracle that God gave over "the strong into the hands of the weak."[313] The Maccabim were weak, outnumbered and overmatched by the army of a global empire; their triumph was only due to their self-perception as tools of God, instruments to carry out His will on earth.

That self-perception engenders both humility and a fierce desire to carry out the role each of us has in fostering God's rule in our world.

Yosef and Pharaoh

Now let Pharaoh seek out a discerning and wise man and place him [as ruler] over the land of Egypt. (Breisheet 41:33)

Yosef was rushed from prison to interpret Pharaoh's dreams and soothe his perturbed spirit, and he did so splendidly. But what possessed Yosef to then begin to offer Pharaoh unsolicited advice – to segue from being a newly freed prisoner to becoming the chief counselor to Pharaoh, advising him on the best preparations for the upcoming famine and its aftermath? It certainly seems presumptuous, notwithstanding that Pharaoh was overwhelmed by it and immediately appointed Yosef to fill the position that Yosef had himself just created!

Yosef here acted in the spirit of all wise people imbued with knowledge of God and a sense of responsibility for others – and seized the moment. It was a singular and fleeting opportunity. Had Yosef stopped with the meaning of

---

[310] Modern Israeli Torah teacher and political leader.
[311] Tehillim 20:8.
[312] Tehillim 20:10.
[313] From the Al Hanisim prayer.

the dream and left Pharaoh to devise a plan to deal with the famine, he might have been returned to prison, or in the best circumstances, given his freedom. He would have seemed like a bright person, maybe too clever by half (after all, he *was* in prison), but not someone with whom Pharaoh would have any association after that moment. He might have been appointed to be one of Pharaoh's astrologer-advisers, who had just failed him in this matter.[314]

The "spirit of God" that Pharaoh saw in Yosef was not only because of Yosef's interpretation of the dream, but primarily because Yosef – on the spot – laid out for Pharaoh an entire plan that would both ameliorate the effects of the famine in Egypt and boost Pharaoh's standing among the people. Surely a "divine monarch" like Pharaoh who could not even provide bread to his own people was not very divine after all. Yosef, in his wisdom, intuited Pharaoh's insecurities and instinctively knew how to counter them and to strengthen Pharaoh in Pharaoh's own eyes.

Indeed, that is why Pharaoh impulsively elevated Yosef to become his viceroy.[315] Pharaoh could not interpret his own dreams[316] because they dealt with his megalomania, as seen in the peculiar wording "he was *standing on the river*" (41:1).[317] In his dream, he was even more powerful than the Nile, the source of Egypt's prosperity, but that majesty was devastated by the sight of gaunt cows emerging from that same river. He could not face up to his own weaknesses, having become so comfortable projecting only mastery and greatness.

Pharaoh discerned in Yosef a different force from anything he had ever encountered before – a person who uses wisdom, not mysticism, to analyze events, solve problems and plan the future. Yosef showed Pharaoh that the famine could ravage Egypt and Pharaoh's self-image, or it could be turned to Pharaoh's advantage and lead to Egypt's prosperity and preeminence in the world despite the coming famine. If Pharaoh handled supply and demand properly, then he could become even more powerful.

In an instant, Yosef sized up the situation, now imbued with the realization that nothing was coming from him: "The wisdom is not mine but [only] God will answer..."[318] He saw this as his moment, a divine gift, and advised

---

[314] Rashi, Breisheet 41:8.

[315] Heard from Rav Yisrael Chait.

[316] Nor would his astrologers have the gumption to tell Pharaoh the true meaning of his dream, even if they truly understood it.

[317] Notice how when Pharaoh related the dream to Yosef, Pharaoh saw himself "standing on the *bank of the river*" (41:17), not on the river itself. He could not even bring himself to say what he had actually seen in the dream, so poorly did it reflect on his self-perception.

[318] Rashi, Breisheet 41:16.

Pharaoh on both the problem and the solution. And then, Yosef asked for nothing, the precise opposite of his pleas to the chief cupbearer. The victim card remained in the deck, for otherwise Pharaoh too would have lost respect for him. Instead, Pharaoh immediately saw him as an "equal" (or almost an equal – "only by the throne shall I outrank you"[319]), and a personality who was somehow, incredibly given his origin, schooled in the ways and mindset of royalty.[320]

Benjamin Disraeli wrote: "Man is not the creature of circumstances. Circumstances are the creatures of men. We are free agents, and man is more powerful than matter."[321] For Yosef, opportunity knocked, and he responded with self-assurance and assertiveness that was grounded in humility, and a deep understanding that his salvation came from God.

No Man Is an Island

> *Two sons were born to Yosef before the year of famine began, borne to him by Asnat daughter of Potifera the priest of On. (Breisheet 41:50)*

Immediately after his appointment to high office, Yosef began to manage the Egyptian economy, prepare for the oncoming famine by stockpiling grain, and settle into Egyptian life, marrying and fathering children. But the Torah underscores that Yosef's children were born "before the year of famine began." Why is this important?

The Talmud states that a person is forbidden to engage in marital relations during a famine in order to empathize with those suffering: "When the Jewish people are engrossed in distress, one should not say, 'I will go to my home and eat and drink and all will be well with me,'…rather a person should cause himself to suffer along with the community."[322] A responsible person cannot feel that life should be normal for him if it is abnormal for most others. Although Tosafot averred that there is no explicit prohibition[323] – after all, Levi's wife gave birth to a daughter, Yocheved, mother of Moshe, while en route

---

[319] Breisheet 41:40.

[320] Yosef was renamed Tzofnat Paaneach, he who explains what is hidden (Rashi, Breisheet 41:45).

[321] Benjamin Disraeli, *Vivian Grey* (London: G. Routledge and Sons, rev. ed. 1853), book 6, chapter 7.

[322] Masechet Taanit 11a, cited by Rashi here. The ban on procreation is waived for one who has not yet been blessed with children.

[323] Ibid.

to Egypt[324] – the Meiri lambasted the gravity of displaying indifference to the plight of others: "During years of famine, a person should never intentionally satiate himself, so he should not forget the suffering in his friend's home which will cause him to become callous to the pain of another and not to worry about him. He should not indulge himself with luxuries or pleasures."[325]

The notion that one can live emotionally aloof from his contemporaries and ignore their needs or fate is anathema to the Torah, nor is the sentiment unknown in the broader world; it was aptly memorialized by the seventeenth-century British poet and cleric John Donne: "No man is an island, entire of itself; every man is a piece of the continent, a part of the main..."[326] To ignore the pain of others reveals a great emptiness in the soul.

When part of the Lithuanian town of Brisk burned to the ground in the early 1900s (not an uncommon experience, unfortunately), dozens of families were left homeless and were forced to sleep in the Great Synagogue of Brisk. Rav Chaim Soloveitchik, the great Brisker Rav, left his home and slept with them – not only demonstrating his concern but recognizing that the contractors would hasten to rebuild those homes if they knew the *rav* of the town was being inconvenienced by their slow pace.

Every Jew has to realize the impact of his actions on himself and on others. He must always weigh the appropriateness of his actions, purchases, lifestyle and luxuries on his neighbors – and even of his words and conversations. One should not talk of his acquisitions in the company of someone who is unemployed, nor of pregnancy and children in the presence of those suffering from fertility problems. We must always be aware of our environment and recognize that we may have to delimit otherwise permissible conduct simply because of its effect on others.

FLAUNTING

And Yaakov saw that there was grain in Egypt, and Yaakov said to his sons, "Why should you make yourselves conspicuous?" (Breisheet 42:1)

When the famine began, Yosef's stockpile of provisions made Egypt the world's granary. People from across the famine-afflicted region flocked to Yosef to

---

[324] Rashi, Breisheet 46:26.
[325] *Beit Habechira* (Meiri), Masechet Taanit 11a.
[326] "Meditation XVII," *Devotions upon Emergent Occasions* (1624).

purchase food – but Yaakov and his family were in no rush to seek grain from Egypt. Apparently, they were well stocked to endure the famine, except for one moral failing that Yaakov sought to avert.

"Why should you make yourselves conspicuous?" Rashi cites the gemara that has Yaakov telling his sons, "Why should you stand out in the face of the children of Esav and Yishmael? [Since we have grain,] it will only arouse their jealousy."[327] As in the previous passage, it is obvious that our actions or inactions influence others, and to be disconnected from the misery of others is not only spiritually debilitating but also physically dangerous. A supply of unused grain will attract enmity, marauders and pillagers, and leave Yaakov's family depleted and endangered.[328]

Making ourselves conspicuous, standing out, or flaunting our wealth (where it exists) is a problem for many Jews today and has been for centuries. The Kli Yakar explains that a Jew who is fortunate enough to acquire wealth in the exile should conceal it from public view and not flaunt it through extravagant living.[329] That only elicits envy and hatred from those who will claim that the Jews are stealing their money. This is why Yaakov here insisted that his sons assume a low profile and go down to Egypt to buy food just like everyone else. The Kli Yakar adds that such reticence has not been the historical norm for Jews. "Rather, Jews with money purchase fancy clothing and build luxurious mansions, and thereby incite the hatred of our enemies." The Kli Yakar is not saying anything that we do not ourselves know very well today; he just wrote it in early seventeenth-century Prague.

Certainly, even a tawdry lifestyle does not justify a physical assault on the person or property of a flamboyant family. The attacker is always wrong in such an instance! But personal responsibility means examining our own deeds to see whether we might have done anything to awaken the beast. In many cases, and in many places where we have been subjected to the brutal assaults of our enemies, that has been the sad reality. We have sometimes lived beyond our means, and even more frequently beyond the standard of living to which the non-Jewish society was accustomed. For that we have paid a steep price, and we will continue to be tormented by the enemies we inflame through our

---

[327] Masechet Taanit 10b.

[328] Rashi here states that "at that time, they still had grain," implying that Yaakov's food supply was extant but limited and could not be shared with others. Nonetheless, Yaakov did not want them to stand out from their neighbors who were already anxious about the famine, so he decided to send his sons to Egypt to procure grain.

[329] *Kli Yakar* (Rav Shlomo Efraim Lunschitz, seventeenth-century Poland, Prague), Devarim 2:3.

deeds and lifestyle until we internalize the lesson that Yaakov taught his sons when they first saw the effects of the famine.

We must distinguish, of course, between success or prosperity and ostentation or pomposity. The State of Israel is reviled by much of the Arab world for many reasons, mostly rooted in religion and some in politics, but also because the relative affluence of its citizens galls the Arab world in which there are pockets of extreme wealth contrasted with widespread poverty and servitude. The sophisticated among them see the benefits of freedom, education and opportunity, and both admire and envy Israel's superior standard of living. Nonetheless, not all resentment is justified, and the advantages of the life Jews have created in the land of Israel can be obtained by the Arab world as well, if only they focus on building, not destroying, and educating their youth instead of filling them with abhorrence of anything Jewish.

Thus, this Arab revulsion born of umbrage at the economic success of the Jews is completely unjustified. Yaakov's lesson relates not to prosperity, which a person is entirely allowed to pursue, but to grandiosity, a gaudy lifestyle in which a person seeks to be defined by others not because of his ethical level or spiritual accomplishments but because of his material acquisitions. Such a lifestyle is not only demeaning, it is also downright dangerous, and in the wrong place and time, surrounded by people who begrudge another his fortune, it can and has led to the most disastrous results.

"We Are Guilty"

> *And [the brothers] said to each other, "Indeed we are guilty concerning our brother [Yosef] in that we saw his anguish when he pleaded with us and we ignored him; therefore, this trouble has befallen us." (Breisheet 42:21)*

After degrading and then selling Yosef into slavery, his brothers felt grief but not guilt. They were anguished at the pain they caused their aged father, and mourned their loss and his sadness. But at no time did they feel that they had done something wrong or even immoral. On the contrary, the sale of Yosef was to their thinking an unfortunate necessity: unfortunate because of its effect on Yaakov and a necessity because they genuinely believed that Yosef endangered the future viability of their family.

The issue was neither their jealousy of Yosef nor his dreams of greatness, which he imprudently shared with them. Rather, the brothers observed that in their family history, there was always one child who was different, who could not comply with the program established by Avraham and had to be excluded, sent away for the benefit of the survivor. Just as Avraham had to banish Yishmael to protect Yitzchak, and Yitzchak had to separate Esav from Yaakov, so too the brothers had to intervene – as their grandmother Rivka did when Yitzchak could not perceive Esav's true nature – and save their family from the evil they thought Yosef portended. The brothers believed that Yosef had hoodwinked their father – just as Esav had bamboozled Yitzchak – into thinking that he was righteous and a worthy heir to the legacy of Yaakov. On the contrary, they maintained, the Yosef who was arrogant, self-centered, obsessed with his looks and misconstrued their own conduct in order to blacken their reputations in the eyes of Yaakov would surely drive a wedge between Yaakov and his other sons and undermine the family.[330]

Rashi says mystifyingly that "God did not reveal [Yosef's fate to Yaakov] because the brothers had decreed excommunication [*cherem*] on anyone who would reveal what they had done, and they enlisted the Holy One, blessed be He, with them."[331] One way of understanding Rashi's comment is that they all recognized – even Yaakov, and even his sons – that God had a plan, and that God's plan would ultimately prevail.

But another way of understanding Rashi's explanation is that the brothers were so convinced of their own righteousness that they assured themselves that God was on their side and supported their decision. This conclusion – that God must support what one is doing because the motivations are sincere – is not an uncommon one among leaders and laymen. It is an especially deadly form of rationalization, as it leaves the perpetrator no room for repentance or even reevaluation. If God "supports" this conduct, then to reassess means to oppose God's will.

Thus, the brothers felt no guilt – until now, when they sat in prison contemplating this strange turn of events and still unaware that the viceroy who was tormenting them was their brother Yosef. But note the precise nature of their guilt: they still did not feel that the sale of Yosef was wrong and sinful; that would not come until later. Now, in prison, they had only one regret: "we saw his anguish when he pleaded with us and we ignored him." They had thrown Yosef in the pit, ignored his cries for help, even sat down to eat while

---

[330] Breisheet 37:2, with Rashi's commentary. To the brothers' credit, Rashi notes (37:4) they were not hypocrites, did not hide their displeasure at Yosef's demeanor and did not pretend to like him. "Their feelings and their words were the same."

[331] Rashi, Breisheet 37:33, citing Tanchuma 2.

he was pleading with them. They were guilty of a lack of compassion, but still did not question either their motivations or their plan.

There are times when we are so convinced of our sincerity that we can swear that God is on our side. It is on those occasions when we are best off consulting someone objective in order to get a fresh perspective. We may "feel" that an act is warranted, even noble, but "feelings" are usually not the best judge of morality.

The world has had no dearth of despots who felt that God was with them in their crimes against humanity. This attitude can be traced to Pharaoh, if not even earlier. It is dangerous to feel that "God is on my side," as it can lead to all sorts of despicable acts being perpetrated under color of holiness and rectitude. We have to be capable of greater objectivity in our responsibility for our own actions and not hastily invoke the Almighty as support for our side.

Perhaps Abraham Lincoln said it most eloquently: "I do the very best I know how – the very best I can; and I mean to keep doing so until the end. If the end brings me out all right, what is said against me won't amount to anything. If the end brings me out wrong, ten angels swearing I was right would make no difference."[332] The brothers convinced themselves that they were on the side of the angels. They felt no guilt about the outcome, only the process.

Still, it was a breakthrough. At least they began thinking that something about what they had done was remiss. It was the first step – admittedly a small step induced by their incarceration – toward the greater acknowledgment of wrongdoing and acceptance of responsibility that would come later.

Fools Can't Be Trusted

> *And Reuven said to his father, "You can put to death my two sons if I do not return [Binyamin] to you." ...And [Yaakov] said, "My son will not go down with you..." (Breisheet 42:37, 38)*

> *And Yehuda said to Yisrael his father, "Send the boy with me.... I will guarantee him, you can demand him from my own hand. If I do not bring him back and stand him before you, then I will have sinned against you for all eternity." (Breisheet 43:8, 9)*

Rashi explains that Yaakov utterly rejected Reuven's argument without directly addressing it, as if it were not worthy of a formal response: "He said,

---

[332] Cited in Francis Bicknell Carpenter, *The Inner Life of Abraham Lincoln: Six Months at the White House* (Lincoln, Nebraska: University of Nebraska Press, 1995), 258–59.

'My firstborn [Reuven] is a fool. He said I should kill his two sons: are they his sons and not also my sons?'"[333] But what did Yehuda say that Reuven didn't, that made Yehuda's suggestion immediately acceptable to Yaakov?

The answer is that the level of personal responsibility that Yehuda accepted far exceeded that claimed by Reuven.[334] Yehuda was willing to forfeit his share of eternal life, to be deemed a sinner forever, if he was unsuccessful in restoring Binyamin to his father. Those were more than mere words, or the idle (and ludicrous) threat of Reuven. In fact, Yehuda's earnestness became clear when he offered himself to Yosef as a slave in exchange for Binyamin's freedom;[335] from that perspective, Yehuda willingly sacrificed his life in this world – a life of bondage in the depraved environment of Egypt – in order to fulfill his pledge to Yaakov and retain his share of eternal life.

Yaakov realized from Yehuda's words that his commitment was reliable and transcended the foolishness of Reuven's plea. Indeed, the declaration by Reuven was so preposterous – and inherently unenforceable[336] – that it called into question Reuven's seriousness and his own ethic of responsibility. Reuven never articulated what he felt should be his own punishment if he failed to bring back Binyamin; rather, he proclaimed that he would punish his sons. Punishing someone else for one's own failing is not unknown in life, but is the exact opposite of personal responsibility.

Yehuda's self-sacrifice underscored his guarantee to Yaakov, who felt more confident that this son would succeed. It was that greatness of spirit – manifested again and again by Yehuda – that qualified him for the timeless leadership of the Jewish people, a leadership that is rooted in personal responsibility.

---

[333] Rashi, Breisheet 42:38.

[334] Heard from Rav Yisrael Chait. See also Rav Chaim Shmulevitz, *Sichot Musar*, maamar 23.

[335] Breisheet 44:32–33.

[336] By what standard of justice would the sons of Reuven have merited execution if their father had failed to fulfill his proposition to Yaakov?

Vayigash

FATEFUL APPROACH

And Yehuda approached [Yosef] and said, "If it please my master, may your servant say something in my master's ears, and let not your anger flare up at your servant…" (Breisheet 44:18)

Yehuda's intervention on behalf of Binyamin climaxes this disturbing episode of the sale of Yosef and also represents the pinnacle of Yehuda's transformation into leader of the tribes and paragon of personal responsibility.

Yosef's plan worked to perfection. Yet many are troubled that Yosef did not reach out to his brothers when they first came and, instead, harassed them psychologically with his seemingly erratic behavior and impulsive requests. But Yosef was motivated by one factor in which the fulfillment of his dreams was only a part. He had to determine whether the brothers truly had remorse, and whether their antagonism toward him was generated by Yosef's own failings or the animosity of the sons of Leah toward the sons of Rachel. The only logical test was to place the brothers in a situation in which the remaining son of Rachel would be endangered and they would have to rescue him. And so it was.

Yosef first insisted that Binyamin be brought to him,[337] a capricious request about which Yehuda elaborates here: "Then you said to your servants, 'Bring him down to me, that I may set my eye upon him.' And we said to my master, 'The lad cannot leave his father, and should he leave his father he will die…'" (44:21–22).[338] Yehuda recognized that Yosef's conduct toward

---
[337] Breisheet 42:20.
[338] Who "will die"? While most commentators understand the subject to be Binyamin (see Rashi to 44:22), Rav Avraham ibn Ezra (as understood by Ramban) suggests it was Yaakov who would die because he would not be able to tolerate the death of his other child from Rachel. That would leave him with no legacy from Rachel at all. (Rashi mentions this point as well in 44:32.) Thus, Binyamin

these grain purchasers from Canaan was unlike the way Yosef treated other customers – but after much cajoling by his sons, and with no good alternative, Yaakov acceded to the request and sent Binyamin down to Egypt with the sons of Leah.

In Egypt, Yosef broke down emotionally when he saw that his brother was still alive and proceeded to conduct his test to determine how the brothers would react after Binyamin was framed for theft of the royal goblet, found culpable and sentenced to slavery. It was the perfect test for several reasons. Yosef wrapped himself in the mantle of justice and rectitude, telling the brothers that he would not enslave all of them but just the thief himself.[339] And the brothers had to contemplate this as well: they knew Binyamin was innocent, but there was a family history of stealing – Mother Rachel had stolen her father Lavan's idols and concealed them![340] In the language of one Midrash, some of the brothers started beating Binyamin, calling him a "thief the son of a thief"![341]

They had every reason to abandon Binyamin to his fate. In addition, Yehuda's plea[342] referenced all the questionable behavior the brothers had experienced or in which they had engaged – the money twice restored to them by Yosef, the goblet, the incidents with Tamar, Bilha and Dina, and even the sale of Yosef. "If we say to you that we sinned, it is certainly obvious that we did not sin; yet if we say to you that we have not sinned, God has uncovered the sin of your servants."[343] We are guilty, and God has come to collect His debt from us, but we are unsure of what precisely is our sin, so "we are [all] ready to be slaves to my master" (44:16).[344]

It was at this point that Yehuda stepped forward and took responsibility on behalf of all the brothers and Binyamin. Note that he had guaranteed Binyamin's return to Yaakov by pledging to forfeit his eternal reward; he said nothing then about slavery and loss of a meaningful life in this world. But that was his intention: he would acquire no eternal life and completely abnegate the life of the soul as a slave in the Egyptian palace if that became the only option available to him.

---

is referred to several times as the "lad," even though he is now thirty years old with ten children of his own (Breisheet 46:21)!

[339] Breisheet 44:17.
[340] Breisheet 31:19.
[341] Breisheet Rabba 92:8; Midrash Yelamdenu Breisheet 175.
[342] Breisheet 44:16.
[343] Breisheet Rabba 92:9.
[344] Rashi, Breisheet 44:16.

Yosef's fears for his and Binyamin's future were assuaged by one statement of Yehuda's that changed the entire dynamic: "for your servant *took responsibility* for the lad from my father, saying, 'If I do not bring him to you, then I will have sinned against my father for eternity. Now, let your servant remain as a slave in place of the lad, and let the lad ascend with his brothers'" (44:32–33).

As soon as Yehuda offered his life for Binyamin's, Yosef realized that the family dynamic could be healed and the sons of Rachel and Leah could coexist. Within moments, he cleared the room, beckoned his brothers to come forward and cried, "I am Yosef. Is my father still alive?" (45:3). Soon, Yaakov would entrust Yehuda with safeguarding the family's spiritual destiny in the Egyptian exile – the only son to whom he could turn for that critical task.[345]

THE DAY OF JUDGMENT

And Yosef said to his brothers, "I am Yosef. Is my father still alive?" And his brothers could not respond to him because they trembled before him. (Breisheet 45:3)

Yosef's revelation stunned his brothers, to put it mildly. In an instant, their world had been turned upside down. Everything they thought was true was in fact false. Yosef the menace had become Yosef the ruler. The dreams that they had perceived as pretentious and arrogant had all been realized. The self-righteousness they had felt from the beginning – that the sale of Yosef had been necessary, even if unpleasant – now dissipated when they heard the simple words "I am Yosef." The anguish they had caused their father, which certainly weighed on their consciences, now became an even heavier burden to bear: "Is my father still alive?" Could Yaakov really have survived this trauma?

The Midrash declares: "Woe to us for the day of judgment; woe to us for the day of rebuke. Yosef was [thought to be] the most insignificant of the brothers, and they could not stand up to his reproof: 'his brothers could not respond to him because they trembled before him.' When God comes and reprimands each and every one of us, how much more so [will we tremble]?"[346]

The Beit Halevi[347] explains that there is a difference between the "day of judgment" and the "day of rebuke." We will all be judged for the sins for which

---
[345] Breisheet 46:28, with Rashi's commentary.
[346] Breisheet Rabba 93:10.
[347] Rav Yosef Ber Soloveitchik of Brisk, nineteenth-century *rosh yeshiva*, Breisheet 45:3.

we have not repented; that is the Day of Judgment. But for each of our sins we will surely have explanations and rationalizations – as did the brothers for theirs – but they will all be exposed as meaningless and contradictory. Yosef said, in effect: you, Yehuda, claim that you wish to spare Binyamin his justly deserved fate out of compassion for your father? Where was your compassion for him when your other brother disappeared? "Is my father still alive?"

For each and every misdeed, the "day of rebuke" comes to eviscerate our rationalizations and expose the inconsistencies of our actions. "You rejected a request for charity because you claimed limited funds and unlimited demands? …So on the Day of Reproof we will be shown many instances in which we squandered money to pursue honor, an illicit pleasure, to engage in strife, etc."[348]

"All of man's ways are upright in his eyes, but God resides within his heart."[349] The *seichel hayashar* ("honest intuition") that God bestowed upon us is usually a good guide as to the probity of any act, but it can occasionally become blurred and unreliable. The days of judgment and reproof are then divine gifts, reflecting His will that man live with decency, integrity and meaning. Those days are manifestations of the Divine Presence.

One should not think that those days arrive only after we depart this earth. Often, the days of judgment and reproof happen during our lifetime, when evildoers are exposed and sinners shamed. Repentance obviates the harshness of these days, and that is only possible when we hold ourselves accountable for our failings. To wait – to deny – is to bring upon us the shock of the days of judgment and reproof that overwhelmed Yosef's brothers at this moment.

Communal Responsibility

> *And they said [to Yaakov], "Yosef is still alive, and indeed he is ruler over all the land of Egypt," and his heart skipped a beat for he could not believe them. But when they related all the words of Yosef to them, and he saw the wagons that Yosef had sent to transport him, the spirit of Yaakov was revived. (Breisheet 45:26–27)*

What was so special about the wagons that convinced Yaakov that Yosef was still alive? A more basic question is this: did Yaakov ever ask Yosef what

---
[348] Ibid.
[349] Mishlei 21:2.

happened to him?! It would seem that would have been a natural conversation, and yet the Torah has no record of it! And if Yosef was now the ruler in Egypt, and Yaakov would soon discover that Yosef had been viceroy for nine years already, did Yaakov ever ask – or did Yosef ever volunteer – why he never attempted to contact his father during their years of separation, especially after Yosef had the ability to do so?

Rashi cites the Midrash[350] that Yosef sent a sign to his father that when Yosef was sent away to look after his brothers, Yaakov and Yosef had been studying together the chapter of *egla arufa*, the axed heifer.[351] That new bit of information relieved Yaakov's skepticism upon first seeing that Binyamin was not with them and hearing the news of Yosef's elevation to power.

The Midrashic comment is both anachronistic and puzzling. The Torah had not yet been given, so how could father and son have been studying that portion? And why that portion in particular, which is seemingly unrelated to the events at hand except through the phonetic similarity of the words?

Our Sages are conveying a very deep message as to how Yosef sensitively, delicately broached and resolved the looming questions surrounding his original disappearance and long absence. The *egla arufa* is a fascinating rite that is carried out when a slain corpse is found between two cities, "and it is not known who murdered him."[352] The elders of the city nearest to where the body was found are obligated to go out, take a heifer that has never been worked, and break the neck of the heifer in an unsown valley. And they must declare: "Our hands did not shed this blood…. Atone for Your people Israel that You have redeemed, God. Do not place innocent blood in the midst of Your people, Israel."[353]

In essence, the case of the "axed heifer" reflects an acceptance of communal responsibility for a crime for which no one takes individual responsibility.[354] There are occasions when no one person is responsible for a crime, and then society takes responsibility.[355] There are other occasions – such as here – when

---

[350] Breisheet Rabba 94:3.

[351] Devarim 21:1–9. The Hebrew words for wagon (*agala*) and heifer (*egla*) are phonetically similar.

[352] Devarim 21:1.

[353] Devarim 21:7, 8.

[354] If the murderer is found before the heifer is killed, the heifer lives and grazes freely in the fields. If a murderer is found after the heifer is killed, the murderer is tried and executed. But the ritual is only performed if the assailant is unknown (Rambam, *Hilchot Rotzeach* 10:8).

[355] That is one reason the death of the *kohen gadol*, high priest, frees from the cities of refuge those who were convicted of criminally negligent homicide, for the high priest "should have prayed for mercy for his generation – that such a deficiency should not have happened" (Masechet Makkot 11a; Rashi, Bamidbar 35:25).

everyone is responsible for the catastrophe. In such a case, everyone takes responsibility, and there would only be harm in pursuing the truth and exposing each person's failings.

The "axed heifer" can only take place when after an initial investigation, no perpetrator is found. The investigation stops. Further inquiries are halted, although witnesses can come forward on their own initiative. The entire society is to blame – even the elders who can swear that they did not shed this innocent blood, nor did they allow the victim to leave their city without a proper escort.[356]

Yosef sent his father a subtle message that was designed to end the speculation and recriminations forever. The family of Yaakov was a mini-society here, and the disaster that befell them was a joint effort. Yosef realized his brashness and insensitivity in ratting on his brothers and prattling on about his dreams in their faces. Yaakov erred grievously in showing blatant favoritism to Yosef above all his other sons, and prompting Leah's sons to resent the sons of Rachel and act imperiously to the sons of Bilha and Zilpa. He had also unwisely sent Yosef alone to see his brothers in Shechem – tempting them to rid themselves of their nuisance brother. And the brothers sinned equally grievously by letting their envy overcome their decency, disposing of Yosef in a heartless way that they thought would solve their problem, leave no traces and mend their family.

That is also why Yosef never contacted his father during his years in Egypt, and certainly when he had the capability to do so in the palace of Pharaoh. The young Yosef was impetuous and self-centered, two qualities that had to be purged from him if he was to assume his rightful role as leader. To have contacted his father – and certainly to inform his father how he happened to be in Egypt (*because your other sons sold me into slavery*) – would have irrevocably split the family. Yaakov would have had no other option than to banish his malevolent, malicious and misguided sons from his home. Such individuals were as bad as Esav or Yishmael and would deserve no share in the house of Yaakov.

That severance of the relationship of Yaakov and his other sons would have delighted the young Yosef, who loved to tweak his brothers about the special bond he had with his father. It would also have been the height of selfishness, the hallmark of the teenage Yosef. But the new, improved, matured and chastened Yosef – the one known as Hatzaddik (the righteous), the one

---

[356] Rashi, Devarim 21:7, from Masechet Sota 48b.

who humbly perceived himself as a creature of Providence and not an actor in his own right, the one on whom rested the divine spirit, enabling his success and preservation in the heart of Egyptian society – that Yosef could not have jeopardized his entire family in order to justify himself, and even in order to alleviate his father's grief. Had he done so, Yaakov would have regained one son, but would have lost another ten sons.

The only way to escape that fate was to hint to his father that the events that led to his disappearance should not be investigated for the benefit of all concerned.[357] Responsibility for what happened should be shared by all; there was enough blame to go around that finger-pointing was unnecessary. Yaakov's spirit was revived, in knowing not only that Yosef was alive but also that he had reconciled with his brothers and that the family of Yaakov was again whole.

Surviving Egypt

And they said [to Yaakov], "Yosef is still alive, and indeed he is ruler over all the land of Egypt..." (Breisheet 45:26)

In a similar vein, Rav Yosef Dov Soloveitchik[358] explained that Yaakov was greatly agitated by an inconsistency in the report brought to him by his sons. He was told that "Yosef is still alive, and indeed he is ruler over all the land of Egypt." But how could Yosef be alive – still the same pious Yosef – and simultaneously be the "ruler of Egypt," a land renowned for its debauched and depraved citizenry, and with a governing entity that routinely practiced cruelty and dehumanization?

The *egla arufa* was the signal to Yaakov that Yosef had not lost the instincts he inherited from his holy household. The elders who perform the ritual accept responsibility on behalf of the entire society. As Yaakov soon learned, that was Yosef's assignment in Egypt – he was the "provider" (42:6) who distributed vital sustenance to all of Egypt and to the world's poor, the one who had devised the plan to save the world from famine.

When Yaakov heard that Yosef was the viceroy of Egypt, he worried about his spiritual state. But when he saw the *egla arufa* – the symbol of the societal

---

[357] That is not necessarily to say that Yosef and Yaakov learned the portion of *egla arufa*. Our Sages often speak in coded terms to convey profound ideas. "*Egla arufa*" was the code they used in order to transmit to us the means Yosef used to reunite his family with the minimum repercussions possible.

[358] The Rav, twentieth-century United States, cited in Rabbi David Holzer, *The Rav Thinking Aloud on the Parsha: Sefer Bereishis* (Miami Beach, FL: Holzer Seforim 2010), pp. 420–23.

responsibility that is assumed by worthy leaders – he was comforted, revived and regained the divine spirit that had been missing during his years of grief.[359]

Private Property

And Yosef acquired all the land of Egypt for Pharaoh, for every Egyptian sold his field because the famine had overwhelmed them. And all the land became Pharaoh's. (Breisheet 46:20)

Desperate times call for desperate measures, and Yosef, brought in to steward the economy through a terrible crisis, successfully averted the potential catastrophe of the famine. And something else: he consolidated all wealth and power in Pharaoh's hands. Yosef horded Egypt's grain and then sold it gradually to the Egyptians and all comers once the famine started. When the people's money supply was depleted, Yosef "purchased" (with grain as the medium of exchange) all their land, and then leased it back to them in exchange for a 20 percent federal tax: one-fifth of their crops had to be awarded to Pharaoh. In effect, the people became sharecroppers on what was once their privately owned land and all land was actually owned by Pharaoh. "Only the land of the priests was not purchased, since the priests lived off the stipend that Pharaoh had given them. Therefore they did not sell their land…" (47:22). Yosef did not want to antagonize the other power structure in Egypt and left alone the clerical elites. The clergy were supported by Pharaoh but also retained their private property interests.

Yosef also engaged in massive population transfers; "and [Yosef] moved the people to the cities" (47:21). This maneuver accomplished two things: first, Yosef's brothers would not feel like aliens in a foreign land, because almost every Egyptian was new to his community;[360] and second, the people would not immediately regret the confiscation of their land, since they were resettled in other places anyway.

Yosef managed to secure and increase Pharaoh's fortune, despite the famine, and to guarantee his own position in the palace. But, ultimately, it came at a cost – Yosef's diminishing popularity and the enmity that the Jewish people experienced in Egypt for well over a century after Yosef's death. The famine lasted only two years,[361] and it wasn't long after that the Egyptian people

---

[359] Rashi, to Breisheet 45:26.
[360] Rashi, Breisheet 47:21, citing Masechet Chulin 60b.
[361] Midrash Breisheet Rabba 89:9; Sifrei, Parshat Ekev, 38.

realized that, effectively, all their private property was gone and they were now wards of the state. Whereas during the famine they had felt that they should become "serfs to Pharaoh" (47:19), once the crisis passed, the loss was keen.

The 20 percent tax rate that Yosef imposed seemed magnanimous at the time; Yosef could have imposed an 80 percent rate as Pharaoh was now the landowner.[362] But such magnanimity was soon forgotten.

Yosef's standing in the palace declined so much that he had to petition Pharaoh through an intermediary to leave Egypt and attend his father's funeral.[363] And Yosef's immense contributions to Egyptian life were "forgotten" by Pharaoh, either by a new king who sought to uproot any memory of Yosef or perhaps even the same Pharaoh who now had to distance himself from Yosef's legacy.[364] And Yosef's people, the Jews, began to suffer inordinately under the yoke of the Egyptian despot, now liberated from any feelings of gratitude toward Yosef.

Private property ownership is indispensable to the functioning of civil society. One who owns something – anything, but especially real property – feels grounded, rooted and fully part of his community. For similar reasons, the American government has long encouraged private home ownership through various tax benefits given to homeowners. Such ownership is good for the community and good for the individual. It gives him a stake in what happens to others and an abiding interest in assuring the stability of his neighborhood.[365]

Without private property, people feel rootless and transient, and, indeed, find it much easier to move away and much more awkward or unnecessary to participate in civic life. Transients just do not care as much, as they live in a place while never really intending to stay permanently. Often, their rented domicile and its four cubits are the limits of their sense of kinship with others.

The Netziv comments that Yosef meant well and reasoned that if the government now owned everything then the government would be responsible for supporting its citizens if their farming was unsuccessful.[366] In theory, it sounds great, but in practice the people had once been "free men"

---

[362] Ramban, Breisheet 47:19.

[363] Breisheet 50:4.

[364] Shemot 1:8, with Rashi's commentary that cites Masechet Sota 11a.

[365] Sometimes that encouragement takes a remarkably foolish turn. The American housing crash in 2007 resulted from decades of the government subsidizing home purchases for – and forcing private banks to lend money to – people who had no means of repaying those loans. See Thomas Sowell, *The Housing Boom and Bust: Revised Edition* (New York: Basic Books, 2010).

[366] *Ha'amek Davar*, Breisheet 47:20.

(or as "free" as anyone could be in the land of the Pharaohs) and were now one step removed from being serfs.

The ownership of private property engenders a greater sense of responsibility for one's own destiny and for that of others as well. The opposite leaves one to the tender and mercurial mercies of government, and that has not always been a desirable fate for mankind.

Vayechi

Influence

> *And Yaakov dwelled in the land of Egypt for seventeen years…*
> *(Breisheet 47:28)*

The Torah is usually specific enough and could have noted that Yaakov actually dwelled in the land of Goshen (a territory of Egypt) for seventeen years and not merely the land of Egypt, especially since it seems that he never left Goshen once settling there. In fact, his son Yosef, the viceroy, was compelled to travel to Goshen when he wanted to see his father. Why then does the Torah record Yaakov's domicile as "the land of Egypt"?

Rav Meir Simcha of Dvinsk[367] wrote that "there are people who live for themselves, or for their families, or for their cities, or for the entire world, and about the latter it is written, 'The righteous [one] is the foundation of the world' (Mishlei 10:25)."[368] Yaakov physically lived in Goshen, but his influence was felt throughout Egypt. When he arrived in Egypt the famine stopped, while he lived there the nation was blessed, and after he died the entire country mourned him. How was Yaakov able to accomplish this singular feat?

The *Meshech Chochma*[369] explained that there are two ways an individual can influence other people. One way is limited to average people – not outstanding Torah personalities or people renowned for their righteousness – who are observed by their peers withstanding pressure to sin. It could be a simple merchant who struggles to eke out a living and yet manages his business with complete integrity, or someone who is gregarious and friendly but is scrupulous about not indulging in *lashon hara* (disparaging talk about

---

[367] Early twentieth-century Torah commentator.
[368] *Meshech Chochma,* Breisheet 47:28, cited in *Dorash David,* Breisheet, p. 339.
[369] Ibid., *haftara* for Parshat Devarim, cited in *Dorash David.*

others). People would say about him what they might not say about a *tzaddik* perceived as spiritually superior to them: *If he can do that, so can I.* In this way, someone who is not exceptional can have a tremendous impact on his environment.

The other way that a person influences another is the method of the spiritual giant. It is much more difficult to attempt to duplicate his deeds, because those are unique to him and his personality. One who tries that will often stumble. But the *tzaddik* and the *talmid chacham* can influence people through their words. They have the stature that commands attention and respect. We may not be able to do what they do – who can learn Torah every day for twenty-two hours like the Vilna Gaon did? – but they can inspire others with their words about Torah study, *mitzvot*, good deeds and pursuit of holiness.

Yerushalayim was destroyed, the *Meshech Chochma* wrote, because "they did not rebuke one another" and "they vilified Torah scholars."[370] That they did not rebuke one another means they did not seek to learn from their peers, and that they belittled the Torah scholars means that they ignored the teachings and exhortations of their spiritual superiors. Both sounded the death knell of that society.

Yaakov influenced Egyptian society both ways, exhorting his sons before his death to lead exemplary lives (something that was noticeable to the Egyptian people) and setting an example for his contemporaries as to how to overcome hardship and suffering and still retain faith in God.

Sometimes the greatest example we can set for others is not by anything that we say, but simply by living virtuous lives. Quietly, others will notice, be inspired by it and sometimes even transformed. Some might be shocked by the influence a neighbor at home or in shul can have on an impressionable child – for good and for not-so-good. Yaakov succeeded in that, and was deemed to have lived throughout the land of Egypt even though his residence in Goshen never changed.

Consequently, the loss the Egyptian people felt at his death was suitably and understandably intense.[371]

---

[370] Masechet Shabbat 119b.

[371] Breisheet 50:11.

The Oath

> *"...Please do not bury me in Egypt. I will rest with my fathers, and you will carry me up from Egypt and I will be buried in their burial site." And [Yosef] said, "I will do as you say." And [Yaakov] said, "Swear to me," and [Yosef] swore... (Breisheet 47:29–31)*

Yaakov's request – to be buried in the ancestral grave in the holy city of Hevron – was so reasonable that we might wonder why he required Yosef to take an oath that he would fulfill his father's request. Why didn't Yaakov just trust Yosef to carry out his will?

Rav Soloveitchik explained that Yaakov realized that he was putting Yosef in a precarious position. Here was Yosef, viceroy of Egypt and fully accepted in an Egyptian society that was the dominant empire in the world and its cultural center. He had long since overcome feelings of estrangement and alienation from that society. He was well respected, even admired. And now Yosef was confronted with a new situation – one that later generations of Jews would encounter many times: his elderly father, who had never assimilated, was still attached to the old world. Burial in Israel would call attention to Yosef's origins and roots in a different society and nation.

Yaakov's insistence on an oath – the commitment to fulfill an obligation that is conflated with one's relationship with God – was designed to impress upon Yosef the seriousness with which Yaakov held this desire to be buried in the land of Israel as well as to afford Yosef the inner strength to deal with the inevitable charges of dual loyalty and the emotional discomfort they would raise.

Personal responsibility means doing the right thing – and following through on one's commitments – even when the challenges seem overwhelming.

Rachel's Death

And when I came from Padan, Rachel suddenly died on me in the land of Canaan, just a short distance from Efrat, and I buried her there on the way to Efrat which is Bethlehem. (Breisheet 48:7)

This second visit of Yosef to his elderly father elicited Yaakov's blessings to Yosef's sons, but was preceded by Yaakov's account of Yosef's mother Rachel's premature death in childbirth. Rashi explained that Yaakov had to assuage Yosef, for he was insisting that Yosef carry his body back to the land of Israel even as Yaakov did not carry Rachel to Hevron but buried her at the side of the road near Bethlehem.

Certainly, this situation was unique, but generally, do parents owe children an explanation for their actions? When a child is young such explanations can be counterproductive, as the child's immature intellect may not be able to grasp every nuance of the parent's approach. But when a child is older, those same explanations can also be perceived as disrespectful. The parent and child do not coexist on the same plane, and a parent should not have to earn a child's respect, which should be innate, a reflection of simple gratitude for being brought into this world.

Nonetheless, there are occasions when parents should justify their decisions to their children, not in order to win their children's approval but so that the children should learn from parents how to make decisions, how to weigh different and sometimes competing factors, how to think through a problem and on what basis to make decisions. It is important for children to realize that not every question has a black-and-white answer and that some decisions are made based on the best possible, albeit imperfect approach.

That can only help the child acquire the necessary skills to make decisions, maintain them and carry them out.

Yosef's Sons

Efraim and Menashe will be like Reuven and Shimon to me. (Breisheet 48:5)

What was so exceptional about Efraim and Menashe that they merited this special consideration? From a practical perspective, the two sons of Yosef were deemed by Yaakov as two of the twelve tribes of Israel and received portions in the land of Israel. This acknowledged Yosef's rightful place as the true firstborn, the eldest son of Yaakov's intended wife, Rachel.

But there is a deeper aspect to this designation as well. Of all the children and grandchildren of Yaakov, only Efraim and Menashe were raised in a completely foreign environment, typically inimical to a full Jewish life. They dressed in Egyptian garb like their contemporaries, to the extent that they were unidentifiable to Yaakov when they appeared before him.[372] Yet Yosef was able to reassure Yaakov that they were *"my children*, righteous and God-fearing" despite their exotic upbringing.[373]

Without doubt, our place of birth and the community in which we are raised play a significant role in determining our course in life. The odds favor a person being raised in a religious community becoming religious and one raised in a secular community becoming secular. But by no means is this dispositive, nor is a person's spiritual destiny decreed by his origins. Recent history is replete with examples of great Jews and Torah scholars who were raised in secular communities and even attended public school in their youth. And that is the powerful lesson taught to us by the upbringing of Efraim and Menashe.

They – or their father, Yosef – never used the excuse that nothing of any spiritual significance should be expected from them because they were not raised in a religious Jewish environment. Rather, Yosef took responsibility for making the best of a difficult situation and instilled in his children the traditions of Yaakov. He even sent Efraim to learn with Yaakov when he arrived in Egypt.[374] They challenge all those raised in small towns away from Jewish communal centers to create their own religious atmosphere that positively influences their offspring and others.

It is certainly not easy, but what is required to succeed is building an environment of love, nurturing, kindness, education, values, and above all, a strong Jewish identity in which the children always recognize their Jewishness as *the* distinctive element of their personalities. They have to know they are essentially different, even if they are similar in other, secondary ways to their neighbors.

Then, "the angel that guarded me from all evil will bless the lads and call their names after my name and that of my fathers Avraham and Yitzchak, and may they flourish like fish in the midst of the earth" (48:16).

---

[372] Breisheet 48:9, with commentary of Malbim to 48:8–9.

[373] Ibid.

[374] *Ha'amek Davar* (Netziv), Breisheet 48:14, notes that Efraim was spiritually superior to Menashe, and that is why Yaakov reversed his hands in blessing the brothers and placed his right hand on Efraim's head.

Sibling Rivalry Revisited

And [Yaakov] blessed [Efraim and Menashe] that day, saying, by you shall [the people of] Israel bless, saying, "May God make you like Efraim and Menashe," and he placed Efraim before Menashe. (Breisheet 48:20)

Wasn't Yaakov concerned about (again) singling out the younger child for more favorable treatment than an older child? It was the error that had torn asunder his family and the impetus for the current exile in Egypt. So how could Yaakov do this again?

What is more interesting, and resolves the dilemma, is the reaction of Yosef's two children, Efraim and Menashe. Unlike every other example in the book of Breisheet, in which different treatment accorded to brothers resulted in conflict, enmity and occasionally violence, Efraim and Menashe here accepted their distinctions with equanimity. Efraim was blessed with greater spiritual qualities, and Menashe was greater in worldly affairs and even assisted his father in governance. They each saw the intrinsic worth of the other, a fulfillment of the prayer of the *baalei musar* that we should always merit seeing the virtues of our friends and never their deficiencies. Together, Efraim and Menashe became the realization of the vision of Yitzchak when he sought to bless Esav, of two brothers employing their respective talents and gifts for their mutual benefit. Their relationship is a welcome coda to the strife often displayed in Breisheet.

While sibling rivalry is ordinarily a normal aspect of childhood, as each child "competes," in effect, for the parents' attention, if left unchecked it can tarnish childhood, ruin adulthood and destroy families. According to one report, as many as 45 percent of families struggle with some form of adult sibling strife.[375] When rivalry becomes jealousy and hostility, each party has the obligation to seek reconciliation and mend the rift in the family.

It is certainly emotionally wearisome to reconcile, but it can be done if each focuses on the positive qualities of the other (rather than their poorer characteristics and the sources of friction) and tender memories of their pasts, and each considers the conflict from the perspective of the other. If they then take the initiative to heal their wounds, are not defensive about their own actions, and indeed are capable of mutual apologies (usually, the roots

---

[375] Jeanne Safer, PhD, *Cain's Legacy: Liberating Siblings from a Lifetime of Rage, Shame, Secrecy and Regret* (New York: Basic Books, 2012), 2.

of discord are not found in only one side), then the possibility of a pleasant relationship exists.[376]

As in many areas of life, determination is the most important quality necessary. If both parties desire a relationship more than they do holding on to their respective grievances, then reconciliation is very possible. Rivalry need not be the default position of siblings. It took the greatness of Efraim and Menashe to recognize that different treatment is not necessarily unequal or unfair. Indeed, while Yaakov switched his hands, he did not reposition the brothers, which would have been the simpler approach. He wanted Menashe on his right side, and he wanted his right hand on Efraim's head, in order to recognize – and inculcate in each of them – their respective realms of greatness.[377]

It was not at all a "mistake" on Yaakov's part; rather, "he maneuvered his hands" with "intelligence and wisdom" to impress upon them that he knew exactly what he was doing.[378] And the brothers accepted their grandfather's decision with humility and grace, exactly what we want for our children, which is why Jewish parents from time immemorial have blessed their sons saying, "May God make you like Efraim and Menashe."

THE EVIL EYE

...and may they flourish like fish in the midst of the earth. (Breisheet 48:16)

Yaakov's blessing to his grandsons Efraim and Menashe requires some analysis. What is the virtue in multiplying like fish? And how do fish multiply "in the midst of the earth"? The opposite is the case! Fish cannot survive on land and can only proliferate in water. What, then, was the essence of Yaakov's blessing?

Rashi cites the gemara that the descendants of Yosef are not subject to the "evil eye," just like fish who reproduce outside the disapproving gaze of the evil eye.[379] The Talmud even mentions that Rav Yochanan had the unusual practice of sitting outside the *mikve* and blessing the women who exited that they should merit having children with his beautiful countenance; he, too, as a descendant of Yosef, was not afraid of the evil eye. What is the nature of the

---

[376] See Safer, *Cain's Legacy*.
[377] *Ha'amek Davar*, Breisheet 48:4.
[378] Breisheet 48:14, with Rashi's commentary.
[379] Masechet Berachot 20a.

"evil eye" that has so many Jews today living in fear and seeking all sorts of talismans, strings and amulets to keep it away?

The cult of the "evil eye" is unfortunately pervasive in Jewish life, even in communities that pride themselves on their sophistication and modernity. Jews who mock paganism and idolatry hesitate little in attributing powers and protective ability to objects of their own creation, objects that cannot even protect themselves. What is the concept of the "evil eye" as our Sages understood it?

Rav Soloveitchik taught that the "evil eye" is the eye of society, and it is "evil" when it is allowed to dominate. There are people whose entire self-image and self-esteem are dependent on how others view them; they are preoccupied with what others think or say about them, and cannot live without their approval. To them, the social reality is the most powerful force that they encounter – and those people are indeed subject to the "evil eye," which, sadly, cannot be dispatched with a red thread or a mystical hand hanging on the wall.

Anyone who so craves the approval of others lives as a perpetual victim, psychologically paralyzed and incapable of living a normal life. Such people have relinquished their egos to the world at large and will bend over backwards to satisfy their needs for attention and acclaim.

Yosef was such a person as an adolescent, always seeking his father's approval and even that of his brothers whom he nonetheless offended with his dreams. His personality did not change even in captivity. He longed for the esteem of Potifar and then the prison warden – until he was cured of this malady (by his disappointment in the chief cupbearer) and was worthy of leadership. In prison, Yosef became an individual – independent, strong, defiant, confident and self-sufficient, and subservient only to God. He became his brothers' equal regardless of what they thought of him, and eventually earned their respect as well.

This was the blessing that Yaakov conferred on his grandsons and the descendants of Yosef – the strength of character to "flourish like fish in the midst of the earth." Fish are not subject to the "evil eye," because fish are the only creatures in our world that live in a completely different environment from ours. All other creatures share our atmosphere, but fish are not at all dependent on what we do on land. They live in their own realm, alone in the water. So Yaakov told his grandchildren to be like fish – but "in the midst of the earth." Live in society and interact with society, but do not be dependent on others for their approval. Determine your behavior based on the objective standards of the Torah, and not based on what others think or say.

Rav Yochanan lived in the world of absolute reality – not the world of pettiness and small-thinking, the world of personalities in which people look at others with the "evil eye" and try to avert its glare. Certainly, this does not mean that we do not care at all about what others think about us; on the contrary, "He in whom people delight, God delights."[380] The opinion of society is often an accurate barometer as to the essence of our personalities. We should never act in a way that causes others to think ill of us – but that is different from being utterly dependent on the opinion of others for our emotional well-being.

For most people, it is difficult to buck prevailing trends or to distinguish themselves from the masses morally, spiritually, culturally or politically. It is easier just to blend in with the majority than to suffer their disapproving glances when one deviates. But to be a "Yosef" or among his descendants means to be proudly Jewish even in a foreign land, to defend our rights as Jews in the exile or our claim to the entire land of Israel despite the occasional unpopularity, and to stand up for the objective morality of Torah even when the winds of moral relativism swirl around us.

And even from a religious perspective, it is ultimately unhealthy for a person to observe the *mitzvot* simply because the community will otherwise condemn him, rather than for the purpose of fulfilling God's will. The lower level might be the first step – even the level of a child – but adults need to outgrow that mindset and embrace the Torah and its way of life because it is divine and right and good, and for no other reason.

That was the strength of Yosef and the legacy that Yaakov left to his descendants.

The Blessings

> *Gather yourselves and listen, sons of Yaakov, and listen to Yisrael, your father. (Breisheet 49:2)*

The exhortations of Yaakov to his sons are called blessings at the end of the process, but do not present as "blessings" throughout. Instead, Yaakov is harshly critical of Reuven, Shimon and Levi, laudatory of Yehuda and Yosef,

---

[380] Masechet Avot 3:13.

and relatively sparse in his comments to his other sons, underscoring a particular quality that each possessed. How, then, were these "blessings"?

A blessing points out the true nature of an object or event and defines its essential quality. Truth itself is a blessing, and coming from Yaakov, his charges to his sons were not mere recriminations but rather admonitions and especially challenges. Yaakov highlighted to each son the unique feature of his personality, the specific element that each son would contribute to the Jewish nation as a whole. "[Yaakov] blessed each one with the blessing [appropriate] for [each of] them" (49:28).

The twelve sons of Yaakov possessed different personalities and temperaments. The idea that all Jews must dress the same and think the same way is a relatively modern convention. Later, the tribes would each carry their own flags with a color combination unique to them. Each tribe had different proclivities and talents, and each would benefit the nation as a whole by utilizing those abilities for the common good. For some tribes, Yaakov pointed out their weaknesses so they could harness their energies and improve, or rein in destructive habits; for others, Yaakov indicated their strengths so they could fully develop the aptitudes they possessed.

Certainly, it is critical for a parent to talk to children honestly about their abilities and about the parents' expectations for them. But why wait until the end of life? Rav Avigdor Neventzal commented that Yaakov was understandably reluctant – as was Moshe at the end of the Torah – to identify shortcomings in his children until the brink of death.[381] He cites the comment of Rashi: "Moshe waited until his death neared before rebuking the tribes. He learned this from Yaakov, who said to Reuven that 'I hesitated to criticize you before, lest you leave me [in anger] and cleave to Esav my brother.'"[382]

From the simple understanding, it would seem that Yaakov did not have much confidence in his eldest son. Did he really fear that Reuven would run away and join Esav – the murderer, the marauder, the antithesis of everything Yaakov deemed sacred? Conversely, the parent who is reluctant to reprimand a child when necessary runs the risk of that same child straying from the path of righteousness. How else can children learn right and wrong but from their parents – and, if necessary, with a timely rebuke from them?

Rav Neventzal answered that Yaakov did not genuinely fear that Reuven would defect to Esav, but rather that Reuven would be embarrassed by a stern denunciation and lose faith in himself. Yaakov desperately wanted to avoid the

---

[381] Rav Avigdor Neventzal, Breisheet, Parshat Vayechi, sicha 33, pp. 347–53.
[382] Rashi, Devarim 1:3.

awful scenario that both his father and grandfather had to deal with: the loss of the firstborn to the family traditions. So Yaakov was extra-sensitive with Reuven.

A parent has to be fully cognizant of the limits of effective criticism and especially be mindful of time and place for that criticism. Some people are perfectionists who demand the same from their families; they are usually hardest on their spouses and children. Others are dissatisfied with their own lives and seek to live vicariously through their children. Neither prospect is salutary to the family dynamic or to the production of happy, well-adjusted, honorable children.

One who wants to fulfill the commandment of "you shall love your neighbor as yourself"[383] must first love himself. People who are filled with complaints against themselves – they do not earn enough, learn enough, they are not handsome or athletic enough – will have exponentially more complaints against those in their inner circle in whom they see the same shortcomings.

Above all, Yaakov knew what his children needed. For some children, a gentle, well-timed admonition is a blessing, especially when it comes from a parent without an ulterior motive (as before the parent's death), and especially when it is delivered with love and respect for the child based on a realistic expectation of the child's capacities. For others, untimely criticism of a sensitive child delivered stridently can be disastrous to that child, as well as to the child's relationship with the parent.

The saintly Chofetz Chaim,[384] asked to give a blessing to someone to raise children properly, demurred and said that raising children does not require a blessing, but rather *mesirut nefesh* (self-sacrifice). It requires dedication, hard work, vigilance, a bit of *mazal* too,[385] and, as generations of parents can attest, a lot of prayer. There are no shortcuts or guarantees, and no one method works for every parent and all children.

The essence is to recognize that Yaakov "blessed each one according to the blessing [appropriate] for [each of] them" (49:28). That is the responsibility of parents – and of children.

---

[383] Vayikra 19:18.
[384] Rav Yisrael Meir Kagan, late nineteenth-early twentieth-century Europe.
[385] Masechet Moed Katan 28a.

The Midlife Crisis

All these were the twelve tribes of Israel, and this is what their father spoke to them and blessed them; each according to his blessing, he blessed them. (Breisheet 49:28)

It is impossible not to notice that the grammatical number changes from the singular ("his") to the plural ("them") within the same verse. Rashi explains that at the conclusion of his blessings, Yaakov included all his sons in each of the individual blessings. They (the nation) would benefit from the special qualities of each individual. In so doing, the nation itself would thrive, and not just its constituent elements.

There is a deeper idea here as well that has enormous ramifications for today. It is sadly not unknown in the general world, and in our small corner of it, that adults in their thirties or forties suddenly lose interest in their marriages, families or lifestyle. Some – a small number, to be sure – simply get up and leave their spouses and children behind. Others struggle with the passage of time and become despondent. It is the peculiar phenomenon known as the "midlife crisis." It exists even though most people who make the choice to dramatically change lifestyles wind up less happy than before, even ruining their lives in the process. Yet it persists – the ultimate in the abdication of personal responsibility. Why does it exist, and what can be done to avert it?

During our thirties, we are usually at the height of our physical prowess and ability to fulfill our fantasies and yearnings in life. But since "no one leaves this world fulfilling even half of his desires,"[386] the realization dawns around the end of one's fourth decade of life that many (most?) of one's desires will not be fulfilled. Panic sets in. In the healthy individual, maturity tempers desire and one accepts that most of those fantasies were unbecoming or unrealistic in any event. For others, the panic leads to frustration and often rash decisions because of an inability to accept that one has achieved what life has to offer, and, in fact, it is quite good, with more of the same to come. That lack of awareness engenders the belief that what we really want is *out there somewhere*, and we need only go out there and find it. While trying to find himself, the person in the throes of a midlife crisis often loses everything he cherished as the family and lifestyle that were once his pride now become encumbrances preventing the achievement of his goals.

---

[386] Midrash Kohelet Rabba 1:13.

What a dreadful mistake! Our need to conquer the world exists not as a goal *per se* but only as a means to better serve God and perfect His world. The life of Torah is a gradual, steady climb up the mountain. The healthy person at age thirty is filled with strength, but at age forty acquires understanding – the ability to apply his knowledge and deal with setbacks and frustrations. At age fifty, he acquires the experience needed to counsel others.[387]

The modern world rebels against the Torah's vision of the simple enjoyments of life, of pleasures that slowly grow and are incrementally experienced. "But the wicked are like the driven sea that cannot rest…there is no peace for the wicked, says God."[388] The wicked, here referring to people who fantasize after the illicit, find no satisfaction in the stable delights of everyday life but are constantly seeking new experiences, embracing extreme highs and lows rather than consistency. That explains why so many people are drawn to danger – skydiving, bungee jumping and the like – when they should know better, as if life finds its meaning only when it is at risk of being lost. Likewise our society's romanticization of the new and different explains why others abdicate their parental and spousal roles and disappear in search of new horizons.

When each of our forefathers died, an identical phrase is used to record their deaths: "and he was gathered to his people" (25:8; 35:29; 49:33). To be "gathered to one's people" is a stark reminder that we do not live for ourselves. Only a person who lives for ideals, a nation or a family beyond himself can be "gathered to his people." When the current of the times glorifies the individual, his choices and strivings, and extols the "virtues" of self-gratification and self-fulfillment, one who instead chooses to live for something beyond the self and to touch eternity is on a different, higher plane of existence.

In life, God blesses us with the opportunity to serve Him in a variety of different settings and situations – in youth, middle age and older age, while single and while married. One who rails against the natural changes in life's circumstances will be induced to abandon what he holds dear in pursuit of a chimera. Few things are sadder, and few choices are as guaranteed to ruin a person's life.

Our world is a world of limits, a fact that is as liberating to some as it is burdensome to others. When Yaakov concluded the blessings of his sons, he reiterated the blessings, "each according to his blessing, he blessed them." But if they all received each other's blessings, then why didn't Yaakov just bless

---

[387] Masechet Avot 5:25.
[388] Yeshayahu 57:20.

them in the collective? Why did he individualize the blessings? The answer is that the capacity identified belonged to the individual son, but he was told to use it for the benefit of the nation. If so, then there was no deficiency in the nation if everyone was not as strong as Yehuda or as fleet as Naftali – as long as *they* were actualizing their unique gifts. Each tribe was just asked to contribute its share.

In other words, we cannot do everything and be everything in life – but we do not have to. That is why we are surrounded by others – a spouse, a family, a community, a nation – which in the aggregate possess all the qualities that the individual needs for a successful, fulfilling life. The man who can love his wife as he loves himself, honor her more than he honors himself, guide his children properly and give of himself to others knows only peace and tranquility in his world.[389] Of him it is written: "And you will know that your tent is at peace, and you will visit your home and find nothing amiss."[390]

That harmony and contentment is the true blessing of the Jewish home, and is attainable by all who want it, and want to labor to produce it. That is the responsibility of the heads of households, and the end result is the glory of the Jewish people.

Reconciliation

> *[The brothers] instructed that Yosef be told, "Your father commanded before his death, saying thus you shall say to Yosef: 'Please, please forgive the iniquity of your brothers and their sin that they did evil to you....' And Yosef cried when they spoke to him. (Breisheet 50:16–17)*

After Yaakov's death, the brothers perceived – whether or not accurately is debatable – that Yosef's attitude toward them had changed, and they feared that the day of retribution was at hand. They sought to preempt that by fabricating a message that Yaakov was purported to have intended to send to Yosef – a message that contained a complete apology, a confession of wrongdoing, and a plea for mercy.

Why did they suspect Yosef of preparing his moment of revenge? Rashi states that after Yaakov's burial, the brothers were no longer invited as

---

[389] Masechet Yevamot 62b.
[390] Iyov 5:24.

frequently to dine at Yosef's table as they had been in the past.[391] Of course, while Yaakov was alive, Yosef acted out of respect for his father, but after Yaakov's death, Yosef did not wish to increase his brother's discomfort by reinforcing their dependence on him. So, too, the Midrash suggests that the brothers noticed Yosef's detour during the funeral procession to the pit into which the brothers had thrown him; to them, it was a not-so-subtle reminder of the payback to come, but Yosef merely wanted to thank God (reciting the blessing "who performed a miracle for me in this place") for saving him from the pit.[392]

Notice how simple acts can be interpreted antithetically, and even innocuous gestures take on greater significance when the parties have a troubled history and are programmed to analyze the clues in different ways. Thus, one has to be careful not only to do the right thing, but also to be mindful that others might react negatively – often because of their own failings or guilt – to the most innocent activities or comments.

It is certainly heartbreaking that after years of interactions with Yosef – more than seventeen years after he poured out his heart to them and reassured them, "Do not be distressed or rebuke yourselves for selling me here, for God sent me ahead of you to be a provider" (45:5) – the brothers are still insecure enough in their relationship with Yosef that they concoct a story that contains not only penitence and contrition but also a fabricated posthumous message from Yaakov as a further inducement. Such was the trauma caused to the family by the sale of Yosef, and such was the extent of the guilt felt by the brothers. They lied in order to assuage Yosef, playing on Yosef's closeness with Yaakov and hoping that would suffice.

The Talmud avers that "it is permissible to deviate [from the truth] for the sake of peace."[393] The brothers did it here, albeit with ulterior motives as well, but even God did it by modifying Sarah's comment about Avraham's age.[394] Truth is a primary value in Jewish life, but peace is a greater value. In ordinary human relations, truth must give way to peace and to kindness or else it would be impossible to live in a civil society. If everyone always said everything that was on his mind without any filter, life would be unbearable.

---

[391] *Gur Aryeh* (Maharal), Breisheet 50:15.
[392] Tanchuma 17, cited by Chizkuni here.
[393] Masechet Yevamot 65b, quoted in part by Rashi here (50:16).
[394] Breisheet 18:12–13.

The truth is filtered through the demands for peace and friendship, a corollary of the adage that "it is better to be kind than to be right."

The responsibility for ending any feud – among spouses, families, friends or communities – rests with each party. Certainly the one that is more "guilty" bears a greater responsibility for ending it, but it is still not completely a unilateral obligation. Any dispute involves two parties, and both have roles to play in defusing tensions and then resolving the outstanding issues.

How can acrimonious quarrels be resolved? The way that usually never works is to rehash the arguments and try to persuade the other side why and how he was wrong. That usually intensifies the dispute instead of diminishing it. What is most indispensable is the capacity to look at the dispute from the perspective of the other party, to put yourself in the other's shoes. That is finally what the brothers did when they prostrated themselves before Yosef and cried to him, "We are ready to be your slaves" (50:18). They, who had made Yosef into an unwilling slave, were now ready to suffer the same fate. They, who had shattered their father's life and his relationship with Yosef, now invoked his memory in order to assuage Yosef's feelings.

It is interesting that – contrary to our expectations and childish notions of forgiveness – Yosef did not agree to let bygones be bygones, nor did he say to his brothers, *I know you meant well and it was all a big misunderstanding.* The opposite occurred: "Although you intended to harm me, God meant it for good in order to bring about, as on this very day, sustenance for many people" (50:20). Rather than resolve the clash on the personal level – a back-and-forth of who did what and why – Yosef universalized their disagreement. Your motivations *were* impure, you *did* mean to injure me – but, in the end, we are all creatures of Providence, and you, like me, were fulfilling a role that God ordained for us. Thus, "Do not be afraid, for am I in place of God? …Do not be afraid, for I will sustain you and your young ones" (50:19, 21). And with these words, Yosef "consoled them and spoke to their hearts" (50:21). These were more than mutual regrets and sorrows but rather a shared realization that the focus on the personal aspect of their history completely obscured and missed the bigger picture – the will of God.

Any two disputants who momentarily step back from the arena of conflict and ask themselves, honestly, "What does God want?" will find it much easier to resolve any lingering differences and restore amicable relations.

At the end of Breisheet, the family of Yaakov is again whole, a unity that was crucial as the bitter exile in Egypt began. And the relationship of Yosef and his brothers was restored to the point that Yosef entrusted them with his destiny: "When God will indeed remember you [and bring you out of this exile] you will bring up my bones from here [to the land of Israel]" (50:25). There would be dark days ahead, but the oath of Yosef and his brothers – the symbol of their reconciliation and reciprocal responsibility for the future of the Children of Israel – would strengthen them in Egypt and inspire them to yearn for their return to the land of Israel.

Shemot

The Book of Exodus

Shemot

Redemption

And these are the names of the children of Israel who came to Egypt… (Shemot 1:1)

This Torah portion is replete with stories of the great personalities of Jewish life who were active, not passive, and looked beyond themselves – some even risking their lives – to assist or save others. The midwives incredibly defied Pharaoh and refused to put to death the newborns they had brought into the world. Moshe left the comforts of the palace to see and try to ameliorate the suffering of his brethren, killed the Egyptian taskmaster who was beating a Jew, intervened to try to break up a fight between Jews, and, in Midian, single-handedly stopped the persecution of the daughters of Yitro by other shepherds. Bitya, Pharaoh's daughter, reached into the Nile River to rescue the infant Moshe and brought him to the palace. And the Jewish police refused to enforce Pharaoh's decree that they smite the Jews who were lagging behind in the performance of their duties, and instead were beaten by Pharaoh's forces.

The Book of Redemption, as the book of Shemot is called,[395] is the story of the redemption of the Jewish people from slavery and their manifestation as God's nation on earth that would bear His name and observe His law. Redemption itself – in its manner and substance – required the assumption of personal responsibility by a number of individuals who were integral to the story and became legendary figures and role models for the nation of Israel.

---

[395] Ramban and Don Yitzchak Abravanel, in their respective introductions to Shemot.

Gratitude

And a new king arose over Egypt who did not know Yosef.
(Shemot 1:8)

How is it possible that just decades after Yosef's historic contribution to the Egyptian people a king should arise over Egypt without knowledge of Yosef's heroic deeds?

Rashi quotes the well-known Talmudic statement that contrasted two rabbinic opinions as to the meaning of the word *new* in the verse cited: "One said it was actually a new king, and the other said that [it was the same Pharaoh but] he made new decrees, and he pretended not to know Yosef."[396]

On the surface, neither approach is comprehensible. How would it be possible for a new king to deny Yosef's existence immediately after his death? Surely he would be familiar with the recent history of Egypt. Even more inexplicably, how could the same Pharaoh renounce Yosef and still retain his credibility in front of his people, who were well aware of Yosef's role in saving and strengthening the Egyptian empire? If, indeed, it was the same Pharaoh, then he was the one who in desperation related his dreams to Yosef, impulsively elevated this Hebrew slave to royalty and even called him *"avrech"* (father and advisor)![397] *That* is a short memory. But how was it possible?

The answer explores a fascinating psychological dimension that many of us occasionally encounter and that overwhelmed Pharaoh here.[398] Certainly, the simple explanation is that the Pharaoh in Shemot was literally new to the job, a successor to Yosef's Pharaoh,[399] but found it morally expedient and politically convenient to deny Yosef and thereby bolster his own credentials. There are leaders who are so insecure that they seek all credit for themselves for the good – fearing that sharing credit with others (or even acknowledging the contributions of others) diminishes their own standing – and deflect blame for anything unpleasant during their tenure to predecessors or to chance.[400] This new Pharaoh, feeling threatened by the rise of the Jewish people, could

---

[396] Rashi, Shemot 1:8, citing Masechet Sota 11a.

[397] Breisheet 41:43; Rashi, ibid.

[398] Heard from Rav Yisrael Chait.

[399] Yosef lived seventy-one years after Yaakov came to Egypt, and thus another fifty-four years after Yaakov died. There were approximately 140 years from the time of Yosef's death (aged 110) until the redemption from Egypt. If the Pharaoh here was truly the "same" Pharaoh, he would have had to have been well over two hundred years old by the time Moshe was born.

[400] President Ronald Reagan kept a plaque on his desk that read: "There is no limit to the amount of good you can do if you don't care who gets the credit."

not tolerate any residual goodwill that his citizens might feel toward Yosef's people, and therefore was forced to deny that Yosef ever existed. Rather than acknowledge the good that they did, Pharaoh claimed that these "people" were dangerous threats to public order that might "join our enemies and wage war against us" (1:10), a fifth column, traitors who were "stronger than us" (1:9). Note that the Hebrew word *mimenu* (than us) can also be interpreted as "from us," i.e., they have grown powerful and wealthy at our expense.[401]

The Talmud, though, offers a second possibility – that this Pharaoh was the same old Pharaoh who partnered with Yosef and now was disavowing his very existence. Why?

Pharaoh projected an image of omnipotence that was threatened when his dreams disturbed him and the specter of the coming famine was revealed to him. If Pharaoh could not control nature – could not even get the Nile to provide Egypt's sustenance – then how powerful or divine was he in reality? Pharaoh compensated for that by clinging to Yosef and merging their identities almost completely. Yosef became, for Pharaoh, just an extension of Pharaoh – indeed, the savior that Pharaoh himself found.[402] With Yosef at his side, Pharaoh was again, in his own mind, the most powerful person on the planet, even a deity.

When Yosef died, all of Pharaoh's fears were reawakened. He knew, of course, that he was not all-powerful, and the famine still loomed large in his thinking. Without Yosef as his "savior," Pharaoh resorted to a common psychological tool – repression. He wrote Yosef out of the story, as if Yosef never existed ("who did not know Yosef"), and in his mind, Pharaoh was once again a god.

To further imprint this new interpretation of reality, repression of Yosef was followed by oppression of Yosef's people, as if to say that not only did this people not help Egypt, but they were actually dangerous to Egypt and deserved enslavement and persecution.

The virtue of personal responsibility extols the capabilities of the individual to act, carve out his own destiny, and transform the world – but it should never be understood as fostering the illusion that others cannot assist or that occasional dependence on others is not warranted. On the contrary, the very nature of a society means that we must rely on each other – on people

---

[401] If these accusations sound familiar, they are nearly identical to the arguments used against the Jews by the Nazi Party during their rise to power in Germany – that the Jews were traitors aligned with Germany's enemies, who had become wealthy by plundering German assets.

[402] No mention of the chief cupbearer is made after he brought Yosef to Pharaoh. That would have reduced the "credit" due Pharaoh for navigating this crisis.

performing their roles competently and properly. Only a megalomaniac like Pharaoh cannot tolerate the contributions that others play in our lives and in our success.

To be sure, we cannot sit back and let others take care of us or make decisions for us, but we should always appreciate the assistance of others and naturally express our gratitude for the good that other people do.

CHOSEN PEOPLE

And [Pharaoh] said to his people, "Behold, the people, the Children of Israel, are more numerous and stronger than us." (Shemot 1:9)

For the first time in history, the family of Avraham was now perceived as a "people," a nation unto itself, and not simply a family, a group of relatives. Our numbers had grown inordinately, and our way of life and concern for each other had been noticed by our Egyptian neighbors. Our refusal to assimilate and simply blend in with the rest of Egyptian society was conspicuous. Pharaoh, in his wicked, aggressive paranoia, suspected that his regime might be destabilized by the presence of a nation that did not view him as divine and that had a living memory of how their ancestor, Yosef, saved the Egyptian people from famine. To Pharaoh, we were no longer just the "Children of Israel," but a "people."

Rav Zvi Yehuda Kook observed that the chosenness of the Jewish people is not based on any individual but on the nation as a whole.[403] No one individual or even group of individuals is responsible for that lofty designation, which refers to our society, the *klal* or *tzibbur* themselves, the community and not any person. That is why we bless God Who distinguished "between Israel and the nations"[404] – Israel as a nation – and why God's praise of our essence is also related in terms of the nation, as in "I formed this people for Myself, that they will relate My praise."[405]

Certainly, great individuals shape the destiny of the Jewish people, and their influence is felt long after their physical passing. But Jewish identity is the province of every Jew; no one can add to it and no one can take it away. And the relationship of God to every single Jew exists in potential and is limited

---

[403] *Sichot HaRav Zvi Yehuda* (edited by Rav Shlomo Aviner), Shemot, pp. 14, 30.
[404] Text of the Havdala blessing.
[405] Yeshayahu 43:21.

only by the fidelity of the Jew to God's Torah, and even in the worst-case scenario, God's compassion is inscrutable and enormous. That Jewish identity remains a unique feature of every Jew, and his province simply by virtue of his membership (through halachic criteria) in the Jewish people. As a popular expression puts it, "ten simple farmers form a *minyan*, but nine people of the stature of the Vilna Gaon cannot."

THE COURAGE TO SAY NO

And the king of Egypt said to the midwives…, "When you deliver the Hebrew women, and you see them on the birthstool, if it is a son then you will kill him, and if it is a daughter she can live." But the midwives feared God and did not do what the king of Egypt told them, and they let the boys live. (Shemot 1:16–17)

The officers of the Children of Israel, whom Pharaoh's taskmasters had appointed over [the people] were beaten, saying, "Why did you not complete your quota of bricks, like yesterday and the day before, yesterday and today?" (Shemot 5:14)

Midwives are correctly presumed to be among the most compassionate individuals, dealing, as they do, with mothers in childbirth and newborn children. Rashi notes that their names reflected their kindness. They were not called by their given names, Yocheved and Miriam, but "Shifra and Puah" (1:16), reflecting their tender treatment of the babes physically and psychologically. Why, then, did Pharaoh sense that these women – of all people – would repress their natural feelings of empathy and instead kill the male infants?

Rav Moshe Zvi Neriah[406] suggests that Pharaoh's intelligence officers had informed him that the Jewish people were so dispirited by their persecution that they assumed that even midwives – broken by despair – would betray their professional ethics in order to carry out Pharaoh's will.[407] The very fact

---

[406] Twentieth-century author of *Ner La'maor*, 1913–1995, founder of the Bnei Akiva youth movement.
[407] *Ner La'maor*, p. 164.

that Pharaoh made this request reveals that he assumed the people were in a morally degraded state.

He was wrong. The Jewish people, even in the depths of the Egyptian bondage, were lauded by our Sages – and deemed worthy of redemption – "for not having any informers among them,"[408] a state of affairs that has not always characterized Jewish life, in both ancient and modern times. The people remained faithful to their identities and their sense of camaraderie, even patriotism, and the midwives rebuffed Pharaoh. They turned toward each other and not against each other.

This situation achieved its apex when Pharaoh's taskmasters appointed Jewish overseers to enforce Pharaoh's evil decrees, similar to what the Nazis did in appointing Jews to the *Judenräte* ("Jewish councils") or as concentration camp *Kapos* – both in order to render Jews the first enforcers of Nazi orders. But, unlike (for the most part) during the Holocaust, the Jewish police in Egypt refused to cooperate with the Egyptians and willingly absorbed the blows from the Egyptian taskmasters that otherwise would have fallen on the backs of their brethren. That self-sacrifice reflected the renaissance of Jewish pride and individual initiative, and a spiritual reawakening that was the harbinger of the redemption to come.

That spirit of concern for others even at the risk of one's own safety was eloquent testimony to the readiness of the individual to sacrifice for the nation. What characterized the midwives and the Jewish officers is the same spirit that animated Matityahu in the story of Chanuka and countless other Jewish heroes.

Finding a Spouse

> *And a man from the house of Levi went, and married the daughter of Levi. (Shemot 2:1)*

Why was it necessary for the Torah to state that the man from the house of Levi "went" and then married Levi's daughter? Why not simply state that he married?

Avraham ibn Ezra, the great literalist, suggests that the Jewish people were scattered over a large geographical area that necessitated this illustrious

---

[408] Midrash Vayikra Rabba 32:5.

groom (identified as Amram, father of Moshe) to find his mate in a distant place. And so he did.

My beloved son Ari Pruzansky pointed out that marriage – finding a spouse – requires initiative on the part of the groom who must "go out" in search of a bride. The Talmud states unequivocally that *"darko shel ish l'chazer al isha"* (it is the way of man to seek after woman).[409] One must be active and vigorous in this process, rather than passive.

Yet the modern ethos has glorified passivity, and some men routinely sit back and wait for others to screen worthy candidates. They are often provided with lists that set forth the names of women who presumably meet all their requirements. Such a process is as demeaning to the women as it is emasculating of the men. Our world, which apparently has reached levels of squeamishness under the guise of modesty that were unknown to – or at least went uncelebrated in – the Talmud, has unwittingly made men haughtier, and less desirable, and less manly in the process.

Sometimes finding a spouse requires traveling out of town, and even living out of town. It is remarkable how many couples do not marry simply because one party does not wish to leave the comforts of "home" (i.e., the parents' community), failing to recognize that "home" is where the couple will live. "Therefore a man will leave his father and mother and cleave to his wife…"[410]

The "man" here "went" to another city to find his wife, and history was never the same.

The Enemy of the Good

And a man from the house of Levi went, and married the daughter of Levi. (Shemot 2:1)

Of course, the bride and groom here were not newlyweds, but Amram and Yocheved, long married but recently separated. As the Talmud states, the "man went" and followed his daughter's advice.[411] After Pharaoh decreed that all male newborns had to be drowned in the Nile (1:22), Amram – the spiritual leader of the generation – separated from his wife and encouraged others to do the same. They would simply refuse to procreate and therefore not feed Pharaoh's killing machine.

---

[409] Masechet Kiddushin 2b.
[410] Breisheet 2:24.
[411] Masechet Sota 12a, cited by Rashi here.

Shortly thereafter, Amram's young daughter Miriam said to him: "Father, your decree is harsher than that of Pharaoh, for his decree only affects males whereas yours affects males and females; his decree relates only to this world, whereas your decree affects this world and the world-to-come. Pharaoh is wicked, so his decree may not be fulfilled, but you are righteous, and your decree will certainly be fulfilled!"[412] That argument proved persuasive, and Amram "went and remarried"[413] his wife. Others did the same.

What did Miriam know that Amram did not know? Certainly, Amram knew that his own decree was absolute – no children would be conceived or born. That would, over time, spell the end of the Jewish people. So why did he, the "great one of his generation," decide to divorce his wife? And how did Miriam convince him to retract his decision?

Amram's contention was, on the surface, a cogent one. "We are toiling in vain"[414] if we produce sons that Pharaoh will murder. If we succumb to Pharaoh's diktat and compromise in the slightest, then we are already lost. If so, there is only one alternative: to rely on God. My dear son-in-law Rabbi Ari Ginsberg added that Amram was trying to avoid a situation of abject despair that would devastate the nation if the women gave birth to sons who would immediately be executed.

Miriam disagreed. What sounds pious is actually self-defeating and self-destructive. Amram's passivity would leave the people without the pain of loss, but also without any hope or positive vision for the future. If girls are born, they will live – and there will still be a future. The suggestion is not perfect, but, paraphrasing Voltaire, "the perfect is the enemy of the good."[415] It would be illogical – and, if Pharaoh's real intention was the extermination of the Jewish people, too accommodating to him – to completely halt the production of children. Absent a miraculous intervention, Amram's course would effectively terminate Jewish existence – in this world and in the next.

The youthful Miriam's great strength was seeing beyond the troubles of the moment and focusing on the brighter future. Amram's fear of national demoralization was well taken, but his plan had no loophole, no escape hatch, but for divine intervention. But we are adjured never to rely on miracles,[416] as

---

[412] Ibid.

[413] Ibid.

[414] Ibid.

[415] Voltaire actually wrote, in his poem "La bégueule," that "the better is the enemy of the good" (*le mieux est l'ennemi du bien*).

[416] Masechet Pesachim 64b. Our Sages (Talmud Yerushalmi Masechet Yoma 1:4) base this on the prohibition of "testing God" from Devarim 6:16.

that presupposes our suitability for having miracles performed for us. We live in a world of activity, in which we are enjoined to act in our own best interests, and those actions, appropriately carried out after utilizing our divinely given faculty of reason, meet with divine favor in accordance with His will.

Miriam, in a moment, transformed the destiny of the Jewish people and engendered faith and hope in place of desolation and despair. Often, we paralyze ourselves by waiting for perfect conditions to arise until acting, or for a foolproof, risk-free plan that may never materialize. Such an approach stops progress in its tracks and breeds failure, lethargy and ultimately inaction that usually exacerbates the situation. Miriam convinced her father of the logic of her thinking, and to his credit, he immediately realized his error and acted upon his daughter's suggestion. The birth of Moshe, redeemer of Israel, was now at hand.

Moshe

And the boy grew up and [his mother] brought him to Pharaoh's daughter and he became a son to her, and she called him Moshe, and she said, "for I drew him from the water." (Shemot 2:10)

Bitya, Pharaoh's daughter, herself took a great risk in rescuing the infant Hebrew from the Nile, satisfying a deep maternal longing that had been thwarted. She found a Hebrew wet nurse – Moshe's natural mother! – and then at a young age brought him to the palace. There, she named him Moshe, "the one who draws [water]."

But the name she bestowed upon Moshe was not quite precise, even assuming that Moshe is the Hebrew equivalent of the Egyptian name she used. The infant Moshe was not "the one who draws"; he was actually the one "who was drawn." If she drew him from the water, and so named him, then Moshe should have been called Mashui, "the drawn," rather than Moshe, "the drawer." Why, then, did she use a different form? After all, *she* was the *moshe* (technically, the *mosha*), not he.[417]

It might be argued that Bitya immortalized her role in Moshe's salvation by naming him after herself – the "drawer." But another possibility presents

---

[417] Chizkuni comments that perhaps Bitya converted to Judaism (she did leave Egypt with the Jewish people) and thus used the Hebrew word, or perhaps that Moshe was named by Yocheved, who explained the etymology to Bitya, who approved.

as well, and is recorded here by the medieval commentator Rav Chizkiya ben Manoach.[418] Moshe was so named because his mother and stepmother did not want to raise someone who would be an object – *mashui* (drawn) – but rather envisioned greatness for the young child as a *moshe*, a drawer. It is as if to say: "Just as he was once drawn, so he will merit drawing others," especially to withdraw the Jewish people out of Egypt.

We can affect a child's destiny in very subtle ways. Mystics argue that a child's name itself is a portent of his or her future, but one need not embrace the esoteric in order to understand this concept. What we call a child makes an impression on him. Modern thinkers are insistent that a misbehaving child never be called "bad," but rather one who "did something bad." At times, this tap-dancing can sound like an abdication of responsibility, but it is more an attempt to shape a child's self-definition. A child who sees herself as "bad" or as a "failure" will, not surprisingly, engage in further conduct that tends to confirm that conclusion. A child who sees himself as an object (a *mashui*) always controlled by others and never allowed to make even a small decision for himself, sometimes well into adulthood, will be handicapped his entire life and never be able to assume responsibility for his own actions or to lead others. He will be a sheep but never a shepherd.

Yocheved and Bitya had greater expectations for Moshe, as we should for our children, and named him – and then raised him – accordingly. Moshe was groomed for leadership and became the leader par excellence of the Jewish people.

Prince of Egypt

> *And it came to pass in those days that Moshe grew up and went out to his brethren and observed their suffering. And he saw an Egyptian man beating a Hebrew man, from among his brethren. (Shemot 2:11)*

It is a measure of Moshe's greatness that despite being raised in the palace of Pharaoh he never felt estranged or distant from his Jewish brothers and sisters. He was not corrupted by the depravity of Egyptian life nor desensitized to slavery despite the fact that slavery was Pharaoh's policy, the law of the land and fairly standard in the ancient world. In a word or two, he "grew up." To

---

[418] Commentary of Chizkuni, thirteenth-century France.

"grow up" means to take less interest in oneself and one's needs and exhibit greater concern for the needs of others, even at huge personal risk.[419] This was Moshe's essence.

When he saw the "Egyptian man beating a Hebrew man," he recognized the injustice being perpetrated before him.[420] When the next day he saw two Jews fighting, he also could not restrain himself. When he fled to Midian, sat at the well and witnessed the harassment of Yitro's daughters by the shepherds, "Moshe rose and saved them" (2:17). Again, he intervened on behalf of the victim. The good person finds it impossible – or at least extremely difficult – to remain mute on the sidelines when injustices are being perpetrated anywhere, and certainly when they are right in front of him. It is not always the healthiest approach – evil people resent being stopped – but it is near impossible to do nothing. Silence is not an option.

The Midrash elaborates that Moshe witnessed the oppression and immediately lent a hand to his brethren, literally helping them carry their burdens as well, and then alleviating some of Pharaoh's excesses by reassigning workloads to be more suitable to each person (e.g., lighter for women, children and the elderly).[421] His concern was not just verbal or emotional. His empathy had a practical focus. He did not simply lament suffering, try to raise consciousness about it or begin a petition drive. He sought to reduce the hardship and then to end it.

It is important to note that Moshe had his share of disappointments with the Jewish people, not only during the sojourn in the wilderness but even at this early stage. He was forced to flee when his killing of the Egyptian was disclosed by the fighting Jews, leading Moshe to exclaim, "Indeed, the matter is known" (2:14). What "matter"? Not only the execution in question, but also, as Rashi remarks, Moshe said to himself that now it was known to him why these people are singled out for harsh servitude unlike all other nations: because they have such masochistic informants among them.[422]

Yet Moshe never refrained from involving himself in the people's plight and never hesitated to challenge any injustice that he perceived. Neither his

---

[419] Rashi states that Moshe had been appointed by Pharaoh the administrator of palace affairs, and in that capacity he sought to help his brethren. One Midrash (Shemot Rabba 1:27) suggests that Moshe had just turned twenty years old.

[420] Ibid. The beating wasn't random, but the result of a tawdry triangle in which the Egyptian had forced himself on the innocent Hebrew's wife.

[421] Midrash Shemot Rabba 1:27.

[422] Rashi, Shemot 2:14. This scandalous act, attributed to Moshe's nemeses Datan and Aviram, was the exception to the general praise of Israel that there were no informers among them, cited above.

comfortable life in the palace nor the hardships of the life of the fugitive deterred Moshe from this very basic aspect of personal responsibility: concern for the welfare of others.

ROD OF ACTION

> *And God said to [Moshe], "What is that in your hand?" And he said, "A staff." And [God] said, "Throw it to the ground," and he threw it to the ground and it became a serpent, and Moshe fled from it. (Shemot 4:2–3)*

> *And God said to [Moshe], "Bring your hand to your bosom," and he [did], and then he withdrew it and behold it was leprous like snow. And He said, "Return your hand to your bosom," and he returned his hand to his bosom, then he removed it, and behold it had returned to be like his flesh. (Shemot 4:6–7)*

Moshe spent a full week arguing with God over his perception that he was unfit to be the savior of Israel. His arguments were sound, as befits such a high-stakes dialogue: the people will not believe him; he has been away from Egypt for decades; he has not suffered as much as they did, and so will not have any credibility with them; he is physically incapable of being the spokesman; his brother Aharon will be slighted and is better suited to the tasks at hand; and even that he fails to see how the Jewish people merit redemption.

Each argument was deflected by God, as one can imagine, but there is a subtext to this entire conversation that bears mention: a fundamental disagreement on tactics.

Rav Yaakov Ariel suggests that God's relationship with the Avot, as described in the Torah, was purely "natural."[423] There were no open miracles performed for them recorded in the Torah, and Divine Providence remained hidden to them, as indicated by the use of the divine name El Shaddai (6:3). In Egypt, God's relationship with their descendants changed dramatically and was based entirely on explicit miracles that impacted across society. The question is which course of divine action is greater, the miraculous or the natural?

This was the dilemma with which Moshe wrestled. His resistance to God's demand that he assume the responsibility to persuade Pharaoh to let

---
[423] Chief Rabbi of Ramat Gan, Israel, in his *Me'ohalei Torah*, p. 97.

the Jews leave Egypt was based on his contention that only the miraculous, indisputable demonstration of God's existence could detach the people from the impurities of Egypt. Moshe saw – from his own experience – that the Jewish people in Egypt were spiritually deprived, and that Pharaoh would not respond to diplomatic appeals. But even if such efforts were successful, that type of liberation, Moshe contended, would extract the Jews from physical bondage but have little effect on their spiritual state. It might even embolden the Jews to glory in their own powers of persuasion and resourcefulness, as well as Moshe's genius, and still leave them distant from God.

Thus, Moshe first asked God: "What is His name?" (3:13) – with what method will God liberate the Jews from Egypt, through miracles or the natural order?

When God answered "I will be that I will be" (3:14), that His relationship with the descendants of Avraham will continue for eternity despite the tribulations of the future,[424] Moshe was still unsatisfied. Even when God shortened the message to "I will be" (3:14) – they will perceive My existence – Moshe still wanted tangible proof to bring to the people.

Both possible modes of redemption – the supernatural and the natural – present potential problems of belief. When miracles are "hidden," i.e., when there are no overt deviations of nature but God's hand is visible behind the scenes, then man's participation is required to initiate, act and move the process forward. Such was the very basis of the stories of Purim and Chanuka, and the hallmark of the modern return to Israel. Man feels closer to God when he is an active partner in furthering God's will, and man is spiritually exalted when he participates in perfecting the world. Conversely, when man is passive in the redemptive process, the redemption itself remains incomplete. The spectator is not quickly changed by what he sees; the activist is usually changed by what he does. A passive redemption would not have brought about a fundamental change in their worldview, and would have left that redemption lacking. "And the saviors will come up on Mount Zion";[425] the Jewish people of the future redemption are called "saviors," and not the "saved."

Yet one would think that miracles are clearer manifestations of God's presence; they certainly do vividly draw man's attention. We are impressed with miracles, at least on the surface. But great people do not require miracles to verify their faith in God, and lesser people are quickly inclined to attribute even the miraculous to "natural causes." This became apparent during our

---

[424] Rashi.
[425] Ovadia 1:21.

years in the wilderness, during which the splitting of the Red Sea, the daily provision of heavenly bread and even the Revelation at Sinai did not long sustain the people's loyalty to God. Miracles have a short-term effect and are soon followed by a reversion to the mean. Without a deeper basis for faith, the influence of miracles is fleeting.

God taught Moshe that the redemption from Egypt would involve both aspects – the people would have to "earn it," i.e., perform actions that would involve them directly in redemption,[426] as well as passively view the plagues that God would visit on Egypt, which culminated in the splitting of the Red Sea. This dichotomy was symbolized by the rod that Moshe grasped which became a serpent, and Moshe's hand which became leprous and was quickly healed. From one perspective, Moshe's rod would be the catalyst for a number of miracles performed in Egypt and beyond; it would be the symbol of God's mastery of nature, as conveyed to mankind through His faithful servant. From a different perspective, Moshe is simultaneously advised that to sit on his hands and do nothing – with his hand "in his bosom" – is not a formula for leadership or success. It brings impurity, spiritual stagnation and despair.

It was imperative that Pharaoh be afforded the opportunity to make his own decisions and even realize the corruption at the core of his kingdom. Human beings are not robots, but free-willed creatures of God. And God knew that Moshe's innate humility would preclude the people from ascribing any divine powers to him.

Usually, the supernatural route is not desirable. Here, it was indispensable that the miraculous work in tandem with the practical in order to both introduce the people to God "Who took [them] out of Egypt" (20:2) and to acquaint them with the necessity to take responsibility for their own destiny, now and forever.

In Egypt, the supernatural power of God predominated; thenceforth, and certainly, in the postbiblical era, the role of the people in building God's world and safeguarding Israel would take center stage and become the story of our history.

---

[426] Especially the preparation of the Korban Pesach, the paschal offering, that was set aside several days before the Redemption, in defiance of the religion of Egypt, and the splattering of blood on their doorposts and lintel which marked their public separation from Egyptian society.

Control of Emotions

...And [God] said, "Isn't there Aharon your brother the Levite? I know he can speak. And behold, he is going out to meet you and he will see you and rejoice in his heart. (Shemot 4:14)

Moshe's brother Aharon had every reason to feel wronged – and jealous of Moshe. Moshe spent decades away in a distant land, far from the maltreatment afflicted by the Egyptians on the Jews, while Aharon had to deal with their growing sense of desolation and hopelessness. Aharon was Moshe's older brother and had a natural empathy for people. Indeed, the Jews always loved Aharon, and they often barely tolerated Moshe.[427] Moshe's plea that Aharon accept the mission in Moshe's place was not inherently unreasonable. Yet God chose Moshe, and even more astoundingly, the Torah testifies that Aharon will meet Moshe in the wilderness, and "rejoice in his heart" – not only exhibit external signs of joy, which most people can fake, but actually feel joy in his heart. Aharon rejoiced with a full heart over seeing Moshe and learning of his ascension to leadership.

The Talmud states that because Aharon demonstrated such magnanimity of spirit, he "merited wearing the Choshen Mishpat (the priestly Breastplate) on his heart."[428] But what is the connection?

The breastplate contained the precious stones that served as the letters for the Urim v'Tumim, the vehicle for the quasi-prophetic transmission of divine messages through the auspices of the High Priest. A person – usually, a politician like the king – would come to the High Priest with a question about some policy or burning issue, and the various letters engraved on the stones, the names of the tribes of Israel, would be illuminated and spell out the answer. Nonetheless, it was still necessary for the High Priest to interpret those letters and make them into words or a sentence. And that required complete objectivity; any predilection, predisposition or bias would taint and distort the divine message.

Aharon's greatness was that he was the master of his emotions. He did not allow himself to react as most others would – with jealousy here or with palpable grief when his two sons Nadav and Avihu died in the Tabernacle[429] – but retained enormous (and, from a modern perspective) almost superhuman

---
[427] See, for example, Shemot 5:21, 15:24, 16:3, 17:4, etc.
[428] Masechet Shabbat 139a, with commentaries of Rashi and Maharsha.
[429] Vayikra 10:3.

self-control. He did not impose his bad moods on others, nor did he expect any special deference or understanding because "bad things" had befallen him. Rather, he responded as a perfect servant of God, bending himself before God's will, and even rejoicing when God's will challenged what others might have expected.

The great scholar of twentieth-century Baghdad, Rav Yosef Chaim, further explained that Aharon's joy was not momentary but permanent.[430] That is, one might have expected the happiness in seeing his brother Moshe after so many years to temporarily overwhelm any feelings of envy Aharon might have had at being bypassed by God, but that jealousy would overtake him at some future point. But that *never* happened; Aharon's heart always remained jubilant at Moshe's good fortune.

It is not always easy to rejoice in another's success. Paradoxically, the closer one is to another person – siblings, relatives, close friends, neighbors, etc. – very often the more intense the envy. That is because we identify more with those nearest to us, compare ourselves to them, and can be troubled when they attain certain things that we want for ourselves or for which we deem ourselves more deserving.

Adults are responsible for their emotions and not just their actions. Aharon reminds us that, whatever the personal difficulties involved, such self-control is possible and even mandatory. A parent does a disservice to a child by indulging moodiness, and certainly when a child evinces an inability to celebrate another person's achievements. Aharon overcame that natural tendency and merited the permanent revelation of the divine word through the breastplate that rested on that perfected heart.

The Walking Dead

> *And God said to Moshe in Midian, "Go, return to Egypt, for all the people who sought your life are dead." (Shemot 4:19)*

Two points should be underscored in this verse. Rav Meir Simcha of Dvinsk[431] suggests that Moshe could now return to Egypt because the miscreants who wanted him dead were now themselves deceased. Does that imply that if they were still alive, Moshe would have been exempt from his divinely mandated

---
[430] Ben Yehoyada, Masechet Shabbat 139a.
[431] From his commentary *Meshech Chochma*.

mission? He answers in the affirmative. Moshe was not obligated to risk his life, which, after all, is man's most precious resource.

Moreover, it bears mention that God Himself informed Moshe of the demise of his tormentors. But couldn't God have just protected Moshe from them if they were still alive, or killed them if they came to harass Moshe once he returned to Egypt? Indeed, He could have, but that is not the way God operates. Moshe accepted the mission and assumed certain risks. The righteous person lives in reality and does not anticipate a miracle or a divine intervention if he deviates from accepted norms and places himself in danger.[432] We are accountable for our actions and even divine commands must be carried out in a responsible way. Moshe's fears about his enemies in Egypt had to be assuaged, especially since Moshe had promised his father-in-law Yitro that he would not endanger his life and leave his wife a widow by returning to Egypt while his enemies were still extant.[433]

There is another dimension to this verse as well. Rashi comments that the "dead" in question – Datan and Aviram – were actually alive but had lost their wealth and were reduced to insignificance: "the poor are equivalent to the dead."[434] Why should that be? Does this view not equate wealth with life and poverty with death, a most materialistic way of viewing the world?

Certainly, the wealthy are better positioned to fully live – to help others, to extract the most out of life. But the poor have another deficit beyond simply a dearth of money. Maharal states that "life is defined by self-sufficiency. One who cannot support himself to the extent that he always has to take from others is deficient. That deficiency has a flaw that is similar to death."[435]

The constant taker does not truly live. It is grueling, not to mention demeaning, to live with one's hand always extended, palm up, waiting for support to come. Indeed, our Sages made this same point in a different context, describing one of the three people "whose lives are not really lives" as the person "who is dependent on his friend's table" for his daily sustenance.[436]

Certainly, this is not meant as even a slight criticism of people who suffer hardship or deprivation and require the assistance of others, but rather of those who make a lifestyle, a career and even a virtue of living off public (or

---

[432] Similarly, the prophet Shmuel feared that King Shaul would kill him if Shmuel went and anointed the son of Yishai as the new king, as God had commanded him. Shmuel did not presume that God would save him just because his mission was divinely ordained (I Shmuel 16:2).

[433] Rashi, Masechet Nedarim 62b.

[434] Rashi here, citing Masechet Nedarim 62b.

[435] *Gur Aryeh*, Shemot 4:19.

[436] Masechet Beitza 32b.

even private) support.⁴³⁷ It is not the way of Torah, and leaves the recipient akin to one who no longer exists.

Moshe's adversaries were still walking and breathing, but their ability to sow dissension and make trouble had disappeared along with their money. Money does provide the ability to influence others, if not always productively. Without their wealth, Datan and Aviram could be safely ignored. To Moshe's chagrin, they would recover their wealth and try his patience in the wilderness, until they were killed by God for their role in the rebellion of Korach.⁴³⁸

God's Many Agents

And it came to pass on the way, in an inn, that God encountered [Moshe] and preferred his death. (Shemot 4:24)

This strange story begins and ends abruptly. During Moshe's return to Egypt, his wife Tzippora gave birth to their son Eliezer, and Moshe, reluctant to postpone the fulfillment of his mission even temporarily, neglected to circumcise the infant. With Moshe suddenly in the throes of death, Tzippora herself took a sharp stone and circumcised their son, in the process saving her husband's life. But how is it comprehensible that God would kill Moshe for this sin, after convincing Moshe that only he – of all people – could carry out the lofty assignment of redeeming the Jewish people from Egypt?

Rav Shamshon Raphael Hirsch explains this anomaly in stark language: "The same God Who had just sent him out with such a great message… suddenly…preferred to let him die."⁴³⁹ The Jewish people introduced to the world the whole idea of circumcision – of submitting to God's law the most intimate areas of our life. Should Moshe then be allowed to bring into this nation an uncircumcised child? God has many agents, and no human being – not even Moshe! – is indispensable. God does not overlook any flaw in His messengers. "That point is here, right at the beginning, made very clear."⁴⁴⁰

It is unfortunately not uncommon for leaders to take liberties with the law, either to profit illegally from their public activities or benefit their loved ones,

---

⁴³⁷ Certainly there is a very small minority of people who require permanent assistance because of some malady or impairment, and every civilized society provides a safety net to those people.

⁴³⁸ Bamidbar 16.

⁴³⁹ Rav Shamshon Raphael Hirsch, Shemot 4:24 (translated by Isaac Levy, *Hamishah Humshei Torah* [1960], p. 49). Rav Hirsch interprets *va'yevakesh hamito* not as "sought his death," the more typical translation, but as "preferred his death."

⁴⁴⁰ Ibid., p. 50.

or even just to disparage people in their inner circle, saving their charm and charisma for their adoring public. Some may adhere to acceptable standards of public behavior but feel that in their private lives neither law nor morality pertains to them. They are so involved in the big issues of the day that they discount the importance or relevance of probity in one's personal affairs.

This episode of Moshe and Tzippora is a telling reminder that God expects faithfulness to the Torah from all Jews but especially from Jewish leaders, and is far more compassionate with the sinning layman than with the straying leader. The leader is accountable for all his deeds, both public and private, and no individual's contributions to the nation are so invaluable that God overlooks a fundamental disregard of His law.

Moshe was taught this lesson, and brought back from the brink of death by his faithful wife.

Va'era

The Price of Exile

And Moshe spoke accordingly to the Children of Israel, and they did not hear Moshe due to the shortness of spirit and the arduous labor. (Shemot 6:9)

On the surface, it seems surprising that the Jewish people disregarded Moshe's words of inspiration. Although his initial diplomacy had been unsuccessful, and had even exacerbated the people's plight, they did not have any realistic alternative. Yet all the hope and goodwill that had pertained on Moshe's arrival had now dissipated. The people accused Moshe and Aharon of making them "loathsome" (5:21) in Pharaoh's eyes. Now, worse than the loss of enthusiasm, and worse even than rejection, was the people's apathy. "They did not hear Moshe due to the shortness of spirit and the arduous labor."

How did they lose faith so quickly?

The Egyptian exile took a terrible toll on the Jewish people, certainly physically (with the servitude and persecution) but also spiritually. Their "descent to the forty-ninth level of impurity"[441] – one level above complete disappearance – meant that they had become almost completely indistinguishable from the Egyptians in their values and worldview. They had largely succeeded in retaining their unique identity, but now that was also vanishing, and quickly. They were adopting the fatalistic, materialistic view of the Egyptians – then the dominant political and cultural power in the world – that had left ancient man without any notion that a better, freer life was even possible, and without any awareness that there was a transcendent force Who had created the world and conveyed to it His moral code.

---

[441] *Zohar Chadash*, Parshat Yitro.

"Without vision, the people become unrestrained."[442] The inability to visualize anything more profound than the next day's labor and a fresh supply of bricks bred hopelessness, despair and apathy. Indeed, that typified the society in which the Jews were enslaved. There was no greater vision than living day-to-day, serving Pharaoh, feeding one's family, and dying. The absence of spirituality – or the substitution of an ersatz spirituality for the real thing – is the price of exile. The influences on us are as overpowering as they are subtle. Even in more enlightened exiles, it is hard to stand against the tide and much easier to believe that the cherished values of the nations are really our values as well. That induces the desire to modify, reform and refine the Torah along the lines of the conventional wisdom and prevailing morality of that era and locale. Spirituality abhors a vacuum even more than nature does. We have a constant obligation to ensure that we do not have a vacuum; hence, Rav Moshe Isserles begins his commentary on the *Shulchan Aruch* with this verse: "I have set God before me, always."[443] It is the awareness that we are to carry within us always that we are standing before the King of kings, Whose glory fills the earth, and Who sees every deed and knows every thought.[444]

The "shortness of spirit" was even worse than the "arduous labor," and that spirit was no longer amenable to conventional appeals and idle promises. The only way to regain the people's attention – and faith – was the introduction to the world of God's mighty hand and outstretched arm.

Marriage Check

> *And Aharon took as his wife Elisheva the daughter of Aminadav, the sister of Nachshon… (Shemot 6:23)*

Why does the Torah mention that Elisheva was the sister of Nachshon? Rashi, quoting the Talmud, states that this teaches that "a person who marries a woman should [first] investigate her brothers."[445] Apparently, the character of the brothers will be duplicated in the children.[446] But is that necessarily so? Even if it were true occasionally, why would we think that it is such a

---

[442] Mishlei 29:18.
[443] Tehillim 16:8.
[444] Rema, *Shulchan Aruch*, Orach Chaim 1:1.
[445] Masechet Bava Batra 110a.
[446] Rashbam, ibid.

categorical imperative that such an investigation should be a prerequisite to marriage?

What seems to be a slightly unreasonable quest actually reveals the depths of our Sages' insight into human nature, and even the extent to which we have gone awry in our own inquiries while contemplating marriage. The study of a woman's brothers enlightens us as to the parenting skills of the future in-laws. We can observe, superficially of course, how they raised a female (the prospective wife) and a male (her brother). The values of the parents (as revealed by the type of children they raised) are an indicator, albeit imperfect and inexact, of the home in which our children will be raised and educated. That inquiry certainly affords a greater apprehension of a family's character than questions that seem to be more common today, such as the type of tablecloth used by the family on Shabbat, the type of hat (if any) worn by the father, whether the furniture is covered by plastic, and the extent of their assets.

Thus, we are obligated to make our own efforts to find a spouse and to research appropriately, but only in important matters such as character, religious commitment, etc. Why then has finding a spouse – which seems so uncomplicated – degenerated into what is called a crisis? Other points have already been addressed on this topic.

Rav Eliezer Melamed[447] was once asked if love is a prerequisite to marriage. He answered that it is, but not in the way we later think about love after marriage. Love before marriage is *"shivui de'ot"* – a convergence of personalities, thinking and the way of looking at life. Note that the couple's worldviews need not be identical; they only have to converge. This union comes first from the head, and only after the couple merges does it penetrate the heart. What often delays marriage inordinately and deceives people (both men and women) into passing over worthy opportunities to marry is the failure to recognize the two types of love and to acknowledge that love after marriage grows and matures and is wholly unlike the love that exists before marriage.

Moreover, the waiting, the gamesmanship, the endless playing of the field, the relentless investigation into inanities and the background checks that uncover the tiniest flaw in the most perfect among us all engender doubt, hesitation and deferral of fully living one's life. All this is as unnecessary as it is depressing for so many people.

---

[447] Rav of Beit El Aleph, columnist in the Israeli weekly *B'sheva*.

Ultimately, our fundamental life choices are made based on our understanding of personal responsibility. The Midrash cites the verse "it is good for a man to bear the yoke in his youth" (Eicha 3:27) and references the three "yokes" in a person's life: the yoke of Torah, the yoke of marriage, and the yoke of gainful employment.[448] They are "yokes" not in the sense of albatrosses that weigh us down but rather as guides that keep us on the right path and enable us to live complete lives.

It is good to bear the yoke when we are young, only because it enables us to live more fully and have a greater impact on family, community and society. The postponement of the complete life – by construing Torah study as incompatible with marriage or work, or by incessantly delaying the study of Torah, marriage or employment – is at the core of the discontent of many of our youth, and more a failure of their education than of their personalities.

The Torah offers a simple guide to marriageability: look at the character of the sons and daughters reared by the parents of your prospective spouse. That encompasses almost every area that needs investigation; the rest is a matter of the meshing of personalities and worldviews. Obsessive investigations are usually just pretexts that try to conceal an inability to commit, a flight from personal responsibility, and sometimes the parents' own egos that require the "other side" to be worthy of them – often an unreachable standard.

The difficulties that prolong dating and hinder marriage are often, from this perspective, contrived, self-inflicted and unnecessary. And, somehow, I think we know that already.

Loss of Free Will

And I will harden Pharaoh's heart, and I will multiply my signs and wonders in the land of Egypt. (Shemot 7:3)

One of the most profound questions of Jewish philosophy is raised by this verse and this course of action. How could God have hardened Pharaoh's heart? The Midrash states that this provides the heretics with a legitimate grievance, as Pharaoh was deprived of the opportunity to repent.[449] As Rambam expressed it, the "great pillar" of the Torah is that man has free will, makes his own decisions and is rewarded and punished accordingly. If man's actions were decreed or foreordained, then how would reward and punishment be feasible?

---

[448] Midrash Eicha Rabba 3:9.
[449] Midrash Shemot Rabba 13:2.

Man would be no more than an automaton responding as he was programmed to do.[450] How then was Pharaoh's heart hardened by God, implying that his decisions were not completely free-willed?

Rambam himself explains that this was part of Pharaoh's punishment. After repeatedly rejecting Moshe's pleas for mercy and an end to his people's suffering, Pharaoh's free will was impeded in order that he should receive the full measure of punishment due him under the circumstances. Some sins can be so heinous that even the option of repentance is foreclosed.[451] Even here, Pharaoh's heart was not hardened for the first five plagues, when he of his own volition rejected God's demands.

Yet that answer does not fully satisfy, as it seems to leave Pharaoh – even in his extreme wickedness – an aggrieved party who cannot help himself. Rashi seems to imply that Pharaoh's case was *sui generis*, because, since his evil was so heinous, any repentance (and consequently the absence of any punishment) would have been misinterpreted by the nations of the world as a victory for Pharaoh.[452] Thus, the hardening of Pharaoh's heart was necessary to allow God's miracles and wonders to penetrate the consciousness of the world. Still, Pharaoh's plight is troubling, and perhaps the solution lies in understanding the meaning of a "hardened heart."

Rav Yosef Ber Soloveitchik explained that "hardening Pharaoh's heart" does not mean that his free will was completely removed.[453] A human being without free will is not a human being. Rather, something else took place here: Pharaoh was deprived of the natural response that human beings have to troubling events.

Usually, a person is able to learn from stimuli, especially painful ones. A child who touches a hot stove learns the hard way about the consequences of "hot." Those consequences circumscribe our future choices and tilt the scale of "free choice" in the direction of avoiding the pain. The choice is not completely "free" if one knows that a particular choice will result in intense pain.

That capacity – to internalize the consequences of poor choices – was removed from Pharaoh, so in effect the scales of free choice were completely balanced each time he made the decision. That was the definition of "hardening the heart"; his heart was so constricted that he did not feel the pain, the crisis, even the impending catastrophe that was befalling his nation. As his servants

---

[450] Rambam, *Hilchot Teshuva*, chapter 5.

[451] Ibid. 6:1–2. And see the continuation of the Midrash cited earlier, Shemot Rabba 13:2.

[452] Rashi, Shemot 7:3.

[453] Beit Halevi, Parshat Shemot, p. 12 (heard from Rav Yisrael Chait).

later said to him: "Do you not yet know that Egypt is lost?" (10:7). In fact, the calamity did not fully register with him as it would have with a normal functioning heart. Each time, Pharaoh was able to decide with the scales of choice evenly balanced, and each time his megalomania and Jew hatred led him to reject Moshe's entreaties.

That is what Rambam means when he writes that Pharaoh's sin was so enormous that justice demanded that his "heart be hardened" so repentance became impossible for him, even though theoretically it remained an option.

From Pharaoh's extreme case, we see a confirmation of the import of free will as the very underpinning of personal responsibility. Actions have consequences, choices dictate results, and lives are shaped by people's own decisions. Certainly there are manifold factors that play into the decision, and sometimes the decision seems to be a foregone conclusion. Yet "permission is given"[454] to choose freely, and no person can ever say he was compelled to act one way or another. That notion is the very essence of the freedom that animates the servant of God.

Plagues

> *...I shall put My hand upon Egypt, and remove My legions, My people the Children of Israel from the land of Egypt with great judgments. And all of Egypt will know that I am God when I stretch out My hand over Egypt. (Shemot 7:4–5)*

The ten plagues visited upon the Egyptians "introduced" the King of kings to His subjects. The gods of Egypt were all natural forces – the sun, the Nile and the animal kingdom. The world learned through the people of Israel that the true God, Creator of the universe, is not a force of nature but controls nature and bends it to His will. The plagues shattered the complacency of the Egyptians in every sphere of life and wherever they looked – on the ground and in the water, on their bodies and in the atmosphere. And they were so successful that when the Jewish people left Egypt, hordes of others, a veritable "mixed multitude" (12:38), joined them in pursuit of the Jewish future, but with decidedly mixed results.

The miracles, ironically, had less of an impact on the Jews, and they were slow in embracing the process of redemption. The early wonders of Moshe

---

[454] Masechet Avot 3:19.

attracted their attention and initial enthusiasm but then faded. The elders who had welcomed Moshe when he returned to Egypt and marched with him to Pharaoh disappeared before he arrived at the palace.[455] The people saw the miracles as well but were not steadfast in their faith.

What went wrong? Why was the loyalty of the Jews so difficult to win and so easy to lose?

Rav Avraham Blass[456] wrote that it is easier for people to believe in God's powers and capabilities than it is for them to believe that God gave man power and taught him how to use it properly.[457] Thus, as Rashi notes, the plagues had another purpose as well: to teach the Jewish people the ways of war, military tactics and all.[458] They had to learn that when an army lays siege to a town, it first tries to capture its water supply (the plague of blood), then it sounds its trumpets and bugles to try to intimidate the enemy (the plague of frogs), etc. With each plague, another maneuver was taught until, finally, when the enemy refused to surrender, its leaders were killed (the death of the firstborn) and the battle was clinched.

From this perspective, the mighty hand of God during the Exodus was not designed to induce passivity but to train the people to seize their own destiny (at some future time). In a similar vein, the saintly Chofetz Chaim reportedly opposed the not-unfamiliar practice of some young European Jews of maiming themselves in order to avoid service in the Polish army. He argued that not only was such mutilation a violation of the Torah, but also that Jews who were martially dormant for so many centuries had to learn military strategies and fighting skills in order to conquer and protect the land of Israel. The era of the "birth pangs of Moshiach," which would require the conquest of the land of Israel, was at hand. The attempt to avoid service, he felt, was shortsighted.[459]

A nation of slaves found it difficult to believe in itself and its inchoate capabilities. There is something comforting about relying on God's dominance winning every battle and defeating every foe. It is comforting, but that is neither the world God created nor the purpose of the nation He formed in order to

---

[455] Rashi, Shemot 5:1.
[456] Twenty-first-century Israeli rabbi, founder of the Jerusalem Talmud Institute.
[457] "The Message behind the Plagues" [Hebrew], *B'sheva*, January 10, 2013, p. 27.
[458] Rashi, Shemot 8:17, citing Tanchuma Bo 4.
[459] See *Sichot of HaRav Zvi Yehuda: Devarim* (edited by Rav Shlomo Aviner, Jerusalem, 5765), p. 263, where Rav Kook tells this story that he heard from a disciple of the Chofetz Chaim. Apparently, the Chofetz Chaim felt that a Jew could withstand the rigors of customary conscription and, more importantly, the Jewish nation would derive an enormous benefit from it.

spread His word throughout mankind. That requires a nation of activists, leaders and noblemen confident in their mission and the tools provided to carry it out.

Moshe benefited tremendously from being raised in Pharaoh's palace, and there learned leadership and diplomacy. So, too, the Jewish people were to glean from the ten plagues knowledge that would assist them as well in their national future. Fortunately, Moshe was a better student in the palace than the people had to be – then – in the field of battle.

The Limits of Gratitude

And God said to Moshe, "Say to Aharon, 'Take your staff and stretch forth your hand over the waters of Egypt…and they shall become blood.'" (Shemot 7:19)

And God said to Moshe, "Say to Aharon, 'Stretch out your staff and strike the dust of the land [of Egypt], and it shall become lice throughout the land of Egypt.'" (Shemot 8:12)

Aharon's involvement in initiating the plagues of blood, frogs and lice is noteworthy, as in most other plagues Moshe was the sole instigator. Here, in both places, Rashi makes a similar comment. Aharon's staff turned the waters of the Nile into blood (and elicited the frogs), "because the Nile protected Moshe when he was thrown into it [as an infant]; therefore, he did not strike it."[460] So, too, Aharon hit the earth because "it was improper for the ground to be struck by Moshe, as it defended him when he killed the Egyptian [and buried him in the sand.]"[461]

Gratitude is so important that, apparently, we are enjoined to be thankful not only to human beings who act kindly toward us but even to inanimate objects, like water and earth! But what is the benefit of that? Gratitude toward people evokes a response and even reciprocity; but what does gratitude toward nature accomplish?

Our Sages taught us that a person should not throw stones into a well that once provided him with water.[462] Our personalities are largely shaped by

---

[460] Rashi, Shemot 7:19.
[461] Rashi, Shemot 8:12.
[462] Masechet Bava Kama 92b.

our deeds. The *Sefer Hachinuch* understands this as the essential reason that the Torah has so many commandments that direct our behavior: "A person is galvanized by his actions; his heart and thoughts are [drawn] after the actions that he does, for good or evil."[463]

We habituate ourselves to good behavior by repeated performances, even when the outcomes of those performances have no direct impact on people other than ourselves. If Moshe were oblivious to the benefits he obtained from the water or the ground, such would reflect a character flaw that eventually would manifest itself in a lack of gratitude toward human beneficiaries.

It should not be, but it is difficult enough to say thank you to people who help us. It is not easy for many people to admit even momentary dependence on others. But gratitude is perhaps the most fundamental attribute of the healthy soul. One who cannot express appreciation for others will be deficient in his relationship with God, parents, teachers, spouse and society. Ingratitude is a cardinal flaw, born of arrogance, a sense of entitlement, and flippancy toward others. It was deemed to be an unpardonable aspect of man's very first sin, when Adam blamed Chava for the fruit and practically dismissed Chava's importance to him by referring to her as "the woman You gave me,"[464] as if she meant nothing to him. "Here," Rashi writes, "[Adam] was ungrateful."[465]

Rav Eliyahu Dessler wrote that just as one's soul is shaped by ideas and deeds, so too one's character is shaped by ideas, deeds and emotions.[466] We might think that since the inanimate has no feelings then there is no harm in displaying ingratitude toward stones, water or earth. Our sages perceived the matter differently. Ingratitude, even to the inanimate, breeds insensitivity, even to people. Character traits are very fragile entities, influenced very subtly and gradually, both negatively and positively.

And note that Moshe would have been obeying God's command had he struck the water or the ground. Often, there is no better rationalization for the expression of bad character than the fulfillment of a *mitzva*! It is possible to use the *mitzvot* as clubs and sticks with which to pound others, or as a means to display arrogance, cruelty or jealousy under the cover of righteousness.

The Torah insists we cultivate a gracious spirit by subtly acknowledging even the facets of nature that provide us with benefit. A person who will not

---

[463] *Sefer Hachinuch*, Mitzva 16.
[464] Breisheet 3:12.
[465] Rashi, ibid.
[466] Twentieth-century *mashgiach ruchani* in the Gateshead and Ponevezh yeshivot, in his *Michtav Me'Eliyahu* (10th ed., Bnei Brak, 5737), vol. 3, pp. 98–101.

strike the earth and water that protected him will be very receptive to the requirement to express sincere gratitude to people who benefit him as well.

BUSINESS OPPORTUNITY

> *The fish that were in the river died and the river became foul; and Egypt could not drink the water from the river, and there was blood throughout the land of Egypt.... And the Egyptians dug around the river for water to drink because they could not drink from the waters of the river. (Shemot 7:21, 24)*

The first plague turned all of Egypt's water into blood, which represented not only a physical hardship but a direct challenge to Egypt's national pride and religious doctrines. The Nile, source of Egypt's prosperity, was worshipped as a deity,[467] and one of the Pharaoh's primary responsibilities – and prerequisites for leadership – was the ability to control the Nile. In the most outrageous expression of this, Pharaoh conflated the Nile with himself: "The river is mine, and I have made it."[468]

How did the Egyptians manage to survive without water for seven days? The Midrash suggests that the Egyptians procured their water from a most unusual source: they bought it from the Jews! "The Jews became wealthy from the plague of blood, for if a Jew and Egyptian would drink from the same basin, the Jew would drink water and the Egyptian would drink blood. But when the Egyptian paid the Jew for his water, it remained water. Thus, from here, the Jews became wealthy.[469]

What seems mercenary in the extreme actually taught the Jews a very important lesson. My son Ari Pruzansky explained that the plagues had two fundamental goals – certainly to punish the Egyptians, but also to allow the Jews to become a free people. The Jewish people had to overcome the psychological shackles of slavery in order to be liberated and become God's nation. Usually, the slave owns nothing and the master is responsible to provide for the slave's needs, especially food, in exchange for labor. Here, the tables were turned, and the slaves became the providers to the "masters." With

---

[467] Rashi, Shemot 7:16.
[468] Yechezkel 29:9.
[469] Midrash Shemot Rabba 9:10.

the very first plague, the process of redemption began, as Israel began to break away from those who had enslaved and dehumanized them.

Free enterprise certainly facilitates that goal. The classic American dream of owning one's own business and working for oneself motivated generations of Americans and led to the greatest era of creativity, ingenuity and prosperity on earth. The technological revolution of the last century was spearheaded by people with scientific knowledge, dreams and ideas, and the capacity to carry them out. The dependent – who waits expectantly for support from others[470] – does not really live freely and remains a slave to others. The sale of water enabled the Jews to shatter their self-image as slaves and dependents.

Yet we are taught elsewhere that the real wealth of the Jews came from the spoils that were taken from the homes of the Egyptians before the Exodus, at God's command, and from the valuables lost by the Egyptians at the Red Sea.[471] How, then, can the Midrash contend that Israel became wealthy here, from the plague of blood?

The answer is that there are two ways of acquiring wealth – to earn it on our own or to be given it by others. Even as the former gives one a sense of pride and accomplishment, the latter often breeds resentment and dependency, as generations of old-moneyed families can attest. Money given but not earned is easily squandered. If the Jewish people's wealth had only come to them through the spoils of Egypt and the Red Sea, they would have still felt indebted to the Egyptians. They would not have been able to break away, as they always would have attributed their bounty to the efforts of others. Through the plague of blood, God enabled the Jews to become entrepreneurs who sold the Egyptians a desirable commodity and thereby made money the old-fashioned way: they earned it.

This was their very first venture into freedom, which was founded, as we see, on economic liberty and free enterprise. The wealth they acquired later only added to this foundation, laid here, as free people taking responsibility for their financial destiny.

---

[470] Masechet Beitza 32b.
[471] Mechilta Bo, 13; Bamidbar Rabba, Naso, 13; See also Rashi, Shemot 15:22.

SANCTIFYING GOD'S NAME
...so that you will know that I am God in the midst of the earth.
(Shemot 8:18)

The Exodus had a purpose even broader than the founding of God's nation. Several times, in similar forms, the Torah enunciates that the plagues and wonders were designed to let the Egyptians "know that I am God in the midst of the earth," not only the Creator but also the Master of the universe Who remains engaged with His creation. Before the Exodus, God engaged directly with certain individuals but was generally concealed from others; during the Exodus, God manifested His involvement in the affairs of nations in an open and miraculous way. The plagues were not merely punishments but means of enlightenment, to inform the world of the reality of God's existence.

And after the Exodus? God's existence is demonstrated through the lives of His chosen people. The Jewish people offer to the world living proof of God's existence, a walking, breathing, thinking and perpetual reminder of the Exodus from Egypt. That is one reason we are obligated to remember the Exodus every day, morning and night.[472] Through our lives, we are enjoined to make others aware of God's existence so that all will "know that I am God in the midst of the earth."

This idea is at the very heart of the *mitzva* of *kiddush Hashem*, the sanctification of God's name. In its most extreme form, *kiddush Hashem* requires us to martyr ourselves in certain limited circumstances,[473] but the more expansive obligation of *kiddush Hashem* is fulfilled through a person's life and not his death: integrity, kindness, sensitivity to others, respect for others and increasing love of God.[474] Each individual action should be weighed based on whether it sanctifies or desecrates God's name, whether it elevates or diminishes God's profile in the world.

What the plagues in Egypt accomplished at the time of the Exodus in a very contrived and forceful way is what each and every Jew is mandated to effect in our time in a persistent and pleasant way – to make others aware of God's existence and moral code. That can only be done if we ourselves live in a way that evinces a constant awareness of God's existence and the embodiment of His moral code.

---

[472] Masechet Berachot 12b; Rambam, *Hilchot Keriat Shema* 1:3.
[473] Masechet Yoma 82a; Vayikra 22:32, with Rashi's commentary.
[474] Masechet Yoma 86a.

The Circle of Fault

And Pharaoh sent and called for Moshe and Aaron, and said to them: "This time I have sinned. God is righteous and I and my people are the wicked ones." (Shemot 9:27)

The plague of hail chipped away at Pharaoh's armor, and for the first time he takes responsibility, admits his complicity and even his failings. "*This* time I have sinned."

Yet this breakthrough was incomplete, as proven by the continuation: "*I and my people* are the wicked ones." What did the *people* do? There were few rulers in history as autocratic as Pharaoh. The people were not consulted at all about the affairs of state; the people only bore the brunt of the suffering wrought by the plagues. In fact, even among Pharaoh's servants, "those who feared God chased his servants and cattle into the house" (9:20) in order to avoid the effects of the fiery hail. Why then did Pharaoh refer to the wickedness of "my people"?

This is another example, fairly common in life but especially in politics, of a half-hearted, desultory acceptance of personal responsibility. The wrongdoer admits his own complicity, but deflects complete responsibility by including others – innocent others, especially – in the circle of fault. The guilty party will use the word *we* when the word *I* suffices. He will include his staff and advisors in the flawed decisions that "were made" (passive voice). He will call for national soul-searching when personal soul-searching is more than enough. He implicates others in order to escape responsibility, not in order to embrace it.

It is a neat rhetorical trick, which is one reason it is employed so frequently. It sounds like an apology and an act of graciousness when in fact it is an attempt to avoid culpability and recriminations. Even Pharaoh's partial confession convinced Moshe, who quickly ran to halt the plague of hail. But once the storm passed, Pharaoh "continued to sin, and he hardened his heart, he and his servants" (9:34). God did not have to harden Pharaoh's heart here; the circle of fault was a shrewd tactic, not a genuine act of remorse.

From another perspective, Pharaoh here displayed the situational contrition that also typifies the wicked of all stripes. The Midrash comments that "as long as the wicked are suffering, they humble themselves; but once the trouble passes, they return to their depravity."[475] According to this approach,

---
[475] Midrash Shemot Rabba 12:9.

Pharaoh was never sincere; even his partial confession was disingenuous, the utterance of mere words that did not emanate from the heart.

The true penitent – even the average person who has done something wrong and wants to make amends – does not defend himself, rationalize his conduct, broaden the circle to impute guilt to others, or otherwise flee from responsibility. The first step toward repentance is always the acknowledgment our own shortcomings rather than those of others.

Bo

The Process

> *And God said to Moshe, "Come to Pharaoh, for I have hardened his heart and the heart of his servants so that I may place My signs in his midst, and so that you may relate to your children and grandchildren that I made a mockery of Egypt, and My signs that I placed among them, and you will know that I am God." (Shemot 10:1–2)*

The process of redemption took almost a year from the time Moshe arrived in Egypt until the Exodus itself. Why so long? If the killing of the firstborn was the plague that broke Pharaoh's will, then why not start with that and end the enslavement more quickly?

Man is impetuous, and a process that involves stages with twists and turns, ups and downs, is inherently frustrating. Yet our Sages taught that the world was created with ten utterances, although it could have been created in one; there were ten generations from Adam to Noach, and ten from Noach to Avraham, and ten plagues in Egypt – even though everything could have happened sooner and in a more linear fashion.[476]

We can understand the Torah's approach by pondering one of the world's famous and more peculiar landmarks, the Leaning Tower of Pisa. It is a testament to man's obstinacy, foolishness and self-absorption. The tower started to lean immediately after the first three stories were constructed, beginning in 1174, but they kept building it anyway. Most of the construction took place after the tower was already leaning! Why continue to build a tower that is already leaning? Because change is hard, and admitting error is even harder. But when the foundation is crooked, nothing straight can be created.

---

[476] Masechet Avot 5:1–3.

Rav Shlomo Aviner wrote that life is a progression, a process of growth.[477] The world was created so that man should be able to ascertain and uncover the stages in creation – to make the development of the world accessible to human knowledge. The Exodus took place in stages for the same reason, one plague at a time, until the Jewish soul became enriched through knowledge of God and awareness of our mission, and until Pharaoh slowly understood the new divine Force with which he was dealing.[478] Spiritual revolutions cannot take place overnight. Just as there are stages in pregnancy and in the birth of a child, so too there are stages in redemption, in the birth of a nation.

The whole process seems to move in slow motion until there is an abrupt jump. After seeming to dawdle forever, and after a crisis of faith in the possibility of redemption itself, the Jewish people left Egypt "in haste."[479] All positive development has to be progressive in order to ensure that the foundation is concretized. If the foundation is crooked, then it becomes hard to correct; even worse, there can be a conscious desire not to correct a warped foundation, and instead to deem it "the way it is supposed to be," since, after all, it was the foundation laid by the founders.

"The righteous grow like a palm tree,"[480] slowly but sturdily. In the secret of the Exodus lies a basic message of life itself and the task of every Jewish parent – to nurture palm trees, to make certain that the foundations are straight, to correct mistakes as soon as they appear, and to never despair when setbacks arise.

That is our obligation toward ourselves, our families and our history.

CHILDREN

> *And [Pharaoh] said…, "Who is going?" And Moshe said, "With our young and our old, we will go, with our sons and our daughters, with our sheep and our cattle, because for us it is a festival of God." (Shemot 10:8–9)*

After the plague of locusts, Pharaoh's resistance is eroded to the extent that he agrees to let the Jews have a few days of worship, only to react negatively when Moshe informs him that Jewish worship requires participation of young and

---

[477] *Tal Chermon*, Parshat Bo.
[478] For Pharaoh, God was a new Force: "I did not know God" (Shemot 5:2).
[479] Devarim 16:3.
[480] Tehillim 92:13.

old, boys and girls. Pharaoh is incredulous and suspects bad faith: "Your evil intent is on your faces. Now, let the men go and serve God, for that is what you really seek" (10:10–11). A religion that had a place for youngsters in divine worship was unknown and unknowable to Pharaoh, who said that "children are not part of religious service."[481]

Pharaoh's attitude is not completely unknown to Jews, either, although it might not be as vehemently expressed. Do children have a role in divine service, especially young children who cannot understand, cannot sit, and should not be expected to act like mini-adults? Moshe's response is clearly an ideal – young and old, male and female, everybody. It sounds good on the surface, but in practice? The children will need to be fed, entertained, humored and napped. How then can they be taken to Sinai, or to synagogue? And if they do come, what kind of spiritual experience will adults have if they cannot fully focus because the children are around and need their attention?

The spiritual life of a child is different from that of an adult and does not utilize the same mechanisms or institutions. An adult can derive a lot from a shul – a center of prayer, Torah study, acts of kindness, community involvement, etc. These things are not alluring for a child, for whom the shul becomes a place to hang out, get candy, see friends and play.[482]

How, then, does a child develop a spiritual life and a relationship with God? At times, he will find that in school, but the primary locus of religious enrichment is in the home, and that is accomplished through absorbing some ideas but mostly values, etiquette and good character traits, for which the parents are primarily responsible.

The *mitzvot* are the outer garb to the inner person, and the inner person can only be developed through perfecting character – that is, through refining how we treat other people, how we talk to (or about) someone else, and how we build sensitivity to the world around us. This central importance of *middot* is not necessarily taught in a classroom, but is rather conveyed by living it and by touting its virtues to our young as much as we would good grades on the report card.

We can spend years filling our children's heads with ideas and facts, but it is far more important to shape their emotions, imaginations, desires and deeds until goodness becomes second nature to them.

This was Moshe's response to Pharaoh, who saw children as adjuncts, appendages to adults, lacking any spiritual integrity at all and with no reason

---

[481] Midrash Shemot Rabba 13:5.

[482] Occasionally it is exactly the same for an adult, especially if we substitute "liquor" for "candy."

to believe they can even relate to God or develop a spiritual personality. Moshe disagreed: "with our young and our old, we will go, with our sons and our daughters…" The divine service of children is not the same as that of adults, but it is nevertheless divine. Encouraging the spiritual life of children is the obligation of parents that supersedes everything else in life, for the only true festival is when the young and old are together.[483] Only then can the young be filled with the spirit of their forefathers, their nation and their Torah.

Light in the Darkness

And Moshe stretched forth his hand to the heavens, and there was a thick darkness of three days across the land of Egypt. (Shemot 10:22)

Rashi states that the plague of darkness had an ulterior motive beyond just further tormenting the Egyptians and enabling the Jews to scout the Egyptian homes for the valuables that would constitute reparations: "There were wicked Jews in that generation who did not wish to leave Egypt, and they died during these three days so that the Egyptians should not be cognizant of their demise and say that 'the Jews were afflicted just as we were.'"[484]

The verse and commentary have frightening implications, because the numbers were devastating. As much as 80 percent – if not more – of the population perished during this time period![485] From this perspective, the Exodus does not seem so glorious; most Jews were not redeemed.

Perhaps our Sages are making a different point, one to which we have grown accustomed even as we also rummage through the world acquiring valuables. Historically, most Jews have been lost to the Torah world, and in every generation only a remnant remains. This is one reason the Jewish population has not grown measurably since antiquity; we have consistently lost large number of Jews to assimilation, as well as to the sword of our oppressors. When Rashi says that these Jews "died," he need not mean that they stopped breathing. There are forms of death that also afflict the living.[486] Here, millions of Jews were swallowed up by the darkness of Egypt, assimilated and lost forever to the people of Israel.

---

[483] Commentary of *Yismach Moshe*.
[484] Rashi, Shemot 10:22.
[485] Rashi, Shemot 13:18.
[486] Masechet Nedarim 64b.

In her seminal work *Off the Derech* (Devora Publishing, 2005), Faranak Margolese traces the multifaceted reasons why young Jews abandon – temporarily or permanently – the faith of their families. There is no one reason that will explain everything and no panacea for this most vexing problem, but looking at the data reveals a pattern that can be reversed.

The number one cause of religious drop-outs according to Margolese's survey was unfavorable and unpleasant experiences with other religious Jews. Exposure to ostensibly religious Jews who profess their religiosity and are observant of some *mitzvot* but fall woefully short in their decency, sincerity or integrity was damaging to youthful spirituality. The drop-outs were keenly aware of people who were perceived as just going through the motions, which the genuine searcher or questioner refuses to do.

Some of these youngsters were, unfortunately, hurt by teachers who did not hesitate to humiliate a student publicly for perceived shortcomings. Others were troubled by the empty spiritual lives of the observant Jews around them – people who could come to shul faithfully but not really daven, and who in their conversations were oblivious to the sanctity of the shul. Small things make a big difference.

It is certainly easy to blame others for one's own defection and flaws, and it is the responsibility of these people to find their way back despite whatever obstacles or disappointments they faced in life. But it is also just as easy to ignore the unwitting role each of us can play in turning people on or off to Torah. Negative relationships or experiences with practitioners of Torah will engender a negative attitude toward Torah.

In Egypt, according to this thinking, too many Jews despaired of redemption because they saw nothing unique or special about their brethren, nothing that would merit redemption or divine favor. They saw that the Jews could be as pagan as were the Egyptians, and that, given the chance, the Jews could be as brutal and as repressive. During the days of darkness – in an era permeated by moral darkness and an inability to see beyond the morass on the surface – they just blended in and were lost to us forever. A similar process unfolds today.

Every Jew has an obligation not only to reach out to the wayward, but also to be a role model who inspires others instead of repelling them, who draws people near to Torah rather than driving them away. Poor impressions can be made in a moment of thoughtlessness that cannot be retracted, or in patterns of behavior that may be perceived as wrong or hypocritical to the observer.

This can happen at home or in shul, in the workplace or on the roads, whether we are aware or unaware that others are watching and learning.

There are few greater areas of personal responsibility than the realization of the impact we have on our surroundings and on observers, whether knowingly or unknowingly. It requires little more than to take what we do seriously, going beyond being mere "practitioners of Judaism" to become a kingdom of priests and a holy people.

Time

This month shall be for you the beginning of the months, the first of the months of the year for you. (Shemot 12:1)

The very first commandment given to the Jewish people as a nation was the *mitzva* to sanctify and control time – to declare the New Moon and therefore the beginning of months, years and holidays. Moshe was taught which particular shapes of the moon were considered to be "new," representing a new month. Why was this *mitzva* – essentially the prerogative of the Sanhedrin and not the laity – the very first commandment?

Rav Yaakov Ariel places this commandment in context.[487] The Jewish people were a nation of slaves, centuries removed from any semblance of control over their own lives. A slave, by definition, loses dominance over his body – and over time itself. A slave's time is not his own but belongs to his master, which helps explain why certain slaves are exempt from time-bound commandments.[488] A slave lives at his master's beck and call. Indeed, a slave has no "free time," as such. Even his non-working hours are hostage to his master's need. He cannot arrange his time to maximize his productivity or develop other interests. He is a slave.

"This month shall be *for you*..." As a prelude to redemption, God gave us the gift of time. It is a generous gift – time is man's most precious and fragile commodity – but a gift that carries with it tremendous responsibilities. Most people are controlled by time, creatures of habit and circumstance. But we were commanded to control time. Controlling time means to prioritize, to organize our daily activities so as to be most productive. One who works for others will frequently cut corners and give less than a full effort; one who works for himself is a free person who must master the fluidity of time.

---

[487] *Me'Ohalei Torah*, pp. 111–13.
[488] *Shulchan Aruch*, Orach Chaim 17:2.

Only those who can manage time are free enough to be deemed "servants of God." Modern man particularly suffers from the malady of time mismanagement. That is apparent not only from the ubiquitous courses in time management offered to executives but also in the pervasive distractions that are one legacy of the technological advances in the modern world. The Internet provides unlimited opportunities to waste time, and the entertainment options available are infinite. People can spend hours of their lives doing very little (some estimates have office workers wasting up to half the workday on idle Internet activities).

The modern conception of freedom is not so much the biblical concept of *herut* (liberty, freedom) as it is *hefkerut* – wantonness, a life without responsibilities, concerns, obligations or limits. That is not freedom, but rather enslavement to one's passions. The "free person" lives within limits and knows the constraints of time, but knows as well the opportunities in life afforded those who have mastered time, who fulfill their obligations and use their time to enrich their souls.

Judaism demands the mastery of time. It is the very essence of freedom and responsibility, and the very foundation of the Exodus.

Spoiled by Wealth

> *And the Children of Israel did as Moshe commanded, and they requested from the Egyptians vessels of silver and gold, and garments. And God gave the people favor in the eyes of the Egyptians, and they gave them what they requested – and they emptied out Egypt. (Shemot 12:35–36)*

God had promised Avraham that, after his descendants would be enslaved in an alien land centuries in the future, "afterwards they [would] leave with great wealth."[489] And so it was. The land of Egypt was drained of its wealth, and people claimed valuables that brought them great riches and a sense of vindication that their years of hard labor were not for naught.

Wealth, as is not uncommon, comes at great cost – in time, energy, effort and spiritual attainment. It can easily lead one to profligacy, pursuit of luxuries and ethical minefields. Moshe himself attempted to defend the Jewish people's sin of the golden calf by blaming it on the excess gold they procured from Egypt and the spoils of the Red Sea, telling God: "The calf was constructed

---

[489] Breisheet 15:14.

because of the gold and silver with which You showered them until the people said 'enough!'"[490] What sounds like a poor argument of a desperate criminal defense attorney was actually accepted by God: "I lavished silver on them and the gold they used for Baal."[491] Does that not sound like a cop-out? How is it God's fault that the people sinned?

The Talmud teaches that "a person would rather have one measure of his own than nine that belong to his friend."[492] People feel more comfortable and more satisfied with their own accomplishments than with unearned gifts. Rashi comments that "a person's earnings are more precious to him because he exerted himself for them, and he prefers his own single measure to the nine measures that someone else has that he can buy from him,"[493] and certainly more than if simply given to him.

Do not underestimate either the importance of or the satisfaction inherent in individual achievement. People feel little attachment to gifts, to unearned endowments. That is why the Jews felt little hesitation in squandering their precious metals on an idol. They did not feel the wealth was theirs. Likewise a child feels better having produced a project on his own that is imperfect than having a parent produce something of superior quality to submit under the child's name.

In fact, it has become more and more common for some parents to actually do their children's homework for them, rather than have them learn it on their own, make mistakes and be corrected. It is easier – and quicker – for the parent just to solve the problems and complete the assignment rather than to explain and correct the work the child has done. But that does a great disservice to the child, who not only will never learn the material but will also never derive the sense of accomplishment that arises from succeeding at something after struggling with it. Such children often struggle with failure later on in life and find it harder to overcome difficulties than their peers who wrestled with lessons on their own.

People who are given too much never learn to strive on their own, and never learn that a sense of responsibility grows only in a person who stumbled and then recovered, who had setbacks and overcame them.

The wealth of Egypt was necessary to fulfill the promise to Avraham and avert possible feelings of resentment over the uncompensated slavery in

---

[490] Masechet Berachot 32a.
[491] Hoshea 2:10.
[492] Bava Metzia 38a.
[493] Rashi, ibid.

Egypt. It was imperative, as well, Rav Kook wrote, in order to lift their spirits and shatter their self-definition as slaves.[494] But the people took too much for their own good, and without any sense of obligation, the wealth became an unfortunate catalyst for their spiritual decline.

Parenting Skills

> *And it shall come to pass when God will bring you to the land of the Canaanites as He swore to you and your fathers, and He will have given it to you… (Shemot 13:11)*

A similar problem developed when the Jewish people were "given" the land of Israel. Rashi hastens to add that "you should always construe the land of Israel as if it was given to you today, and not see it as an inheritance from your fathers." But, of course, we were given the land because it was promised to our forefathers, so how can we perceive it otherwise?

In fact, God earlier promised us that "I will bring you to the land that I have lifted My hand to give to your forefathers, and I will give it to you as a legacy" (6:8). Our rights and connection to the land do emanate from our relationship to our fathers, and yet here we are told the exact opposite – that we are not to consider it an inheritance from our forefathers. Which is it?

From one perspective, our Sages here articulated the tension that exists between two modes of parenting that generally produce two different results: giving everything to a child versus encouraging the child to earn what he wants.

There are parents who sincerely do not want their children to experience any hardship or sacrifice and do not want them to feel any want or deficiency. Whether it is because they have ample wealth to distribute, because they endured hardship as children and want to spare their children any deprivation or simply because their love is all-encompassing, the result is the same: they take pride and pleasure in giving. Some children receive because they are good and decent, others because they breathe and share the same last name as their parents – but everything comes to them from their parents. And the children learn a simple lesson: just ask, and it shall be granted. And if the child does not ask, the parent will anticipate the need and the child will receive what he wants even without asking.

---

[494] *Ein Ayah*, Masechet Berachot 1:114.

Conversely, there are parents who essentially deprive their children of nothing, but still require the children to earn what they receive by performing household chores or pursuing gainful employment outside the home. They encourage their children to strive and to work, even to do without, until they can have the satisfaction of succeeding on their own. "To eat from the toil of your own hands is good for you," in this world and the next.[495] These parents are very generous, as long as children do not ask or expect – or worse, develop a sense of entitlement.

The second way seems healthier, but there are advantages and disadvantages to both. Creating artificial hardship seems contrived, even as it inescapably avoids nurturing the entitlement mentality that is wreaking havoc on this generation. We want children to earn their way, to learn independence, but by the same token, to realize that there is a safety net that always stands ready to help them.

Rav Moshe Zvi Neriah wrote that God made two distinct promises to the Jewish people, each at a different time in completely different circumstances.[496] When we were still reeling from the blows of the Egyptian taskmasters, God reassured us that our future was bright and secure, and the land of Israel would be granted to us as a "legacy" from our forefathers. Those were words of comfort intended to lift the spirits of people who were beaten down, broken and despondent.

But by the time the verse cited above was told to the people, the Jews had already left Egypt. We were like a young person whose future is before him, filled with opportunities that we want him to seize on his own so he should not be led into passivity, slothfulness, and apathy. Here, God wanted to challenge us, so we were told that all the blessings of life were being given to us but we were not to construe them as an inheritance. Rather, we must continue to earn the land, to be worthy of it, and to strive to uphold it – or it can be forfeited. As a result, each day we look at those blessings as if we had just received them and must justify our share in them.

In truth, both modes of parenting have some validity – it just depends on what, when, how often, how much and at what stage in life. The goal remains the same – to instill in our offspring a sense of responsibility for their future and for the future of the Jewish nation, which, after all, will merit redemption in its time or even earlier – if we deserve it.[497]

---

[495] Tehillim 129:2, as interpreted by Masechet Berachot 8a.

[496] *Ner La'maor*, Parshat Bo.

[497] Masechet Sanhedrin 98a.

Beshalach

Armed but Not Ready

And God turned the people toward the wilderness, to the Red Sea, and the Children of Israel were armed when they went up from Egypt. (Shemot 13:18)

At first glance, the verse cited is making a contradictory declaration. On the one hand, the people were armed and fully capable of defending themselves; but on the other hand, God chose for them the path of least resistance. Instead of guiding them north and then east, crossing into Sinai and journeying to Israel on the Via Maris (the ancient trade route that hugs the Mediterranean coast), the Jewish people were directed to the south to avoid contact with the Philistines. As it subsequently turned out, the Jewish people were unprepared for any military conflict with the Egyptians as well. So why did it matter that we were "armed"? The weapons were not to be used at all.

The Talmud Yerushalmi[498] understands the word *chamushim* (armed) to mean that the Jewish people were armed with five different types of weapons: swords, bows and arrows, shields, clubs and spears. While they obviously lacked the chariots of the Egyptian or Philistine armies, they were equipped to challenge the enemy in hand-to-hand combat and could inflict much harm. It would have been a battle in which their superior motivation and the absence of any alternative for the Jews could have been decisive – much like Israel's wars ancient and modern. But if they were not to fight, and were specifically told not to confront any enemy but instead to head to the relative safety of the wilderness, why were they armed at all?

When the Jewish people left Egypt, they tasted freedom for the first time, and freedom includes the right of self-defense as well as the right to bear arms.

---

[498] Yerushalmi Masechet Shabbat 6:7, cited by Rashi here.

Historically, the first act of putative dictators always is to confiscate the weapons of the citizenry, as all despots seek a monopoly on the exercise of strength and authority. That notion underlies the Second Amendment to the United States Constitution, the much-debated and highly controversial right to bear arms that is afforded American citizens. It reinforces not only the idea that free people have a right to defend themselves against unjust attack but also that free people have an obligation to do so. Man is first and foremost charged with the responsibility to protect himself and his loved ones from harm, to the best of his ability. That obligation is often delegated to others, but to completely relinquish one's responsibility in that realm is unwise and immoral.

Here, as the Jews left Egypt, they were immediately informed of one central aspect of any nation's existence: they would eventually have to fight for their survival, for the conquest of the land of Israel and for its preservation. They had grown accustomed to God's miracles sustaining them and liberating them from Egypt, and would grow even more accustomed to that in the wilderness. But that is not the ideal. Even if as newly freed slaves they were incapable of confronting their attackers, the ideal was that they eventually would be free and independent – not beholden to their erstwhile Egyptians masters – and eagerly awaiting the day when God's blessings would enable them to prevail in the battles that their armies would fight.

It is never too soon to learn that individuals and nations are charged with defending themselves and their interests, and so the Jews left Egypt "armed" with weapons they would not use immediately but that began the process of preparing them for their eventual use. That would not take long; a little over a month later, Amalek attacked and the small Jewish army repulsed them.[499]

Don't Wail, Do Something!

> *And God said to Moshe, "Why are you crying to Me? Speak to the Children of Israel and let them journey forward." (Shemot 14:15)*

As Moshe was standing and praying to God for salvation, Rashi states here that God told Moshe quite forcefully, "Now – when the Jewish people

---

[499] Shemot 17:8–16.

are in distress – is not the time for long prayers."⁵⁰⁰ But isn't it? Are we not traditionally educated to believe that prayer is always propitious, and certainly when danger lurks?

Rashi continues with a second interpretation: "Why are you crying to Me? Is this matter up to Me and not to you? Tell them to journey forward and the merit of their forefathers and their own faith in Me will bring salvation."⁵⁰¹ As the Talmud puts it: "My beloved [children] are [almost] drowning in the sea, and you are praying?!"⁵⁰²

The Ohr HaChaim⁵⁰³ frames the difficulties in the original question quite eloquently. "To whom should they cry out but to God, and certainly during a time of distress when we are taught to call out to God? And if you argue that they need not pray too long, [we are also taught that] as long as the prayers have not been answered, then we are to continue praying. And regarding God's command that they "journey forward," to where should they go? The Egyptians are to their rear, and the sea is in front of them! God should have said to Moshe, "Lift up your staff" (14:16) and only then told the people to "journey forward."

God's rhetorical question to Moshe – "Why are you crying to Me?" – is the refutation to the idealization of passivity that became a staple of parts of the Jewish world in the last two centuries and lingers today.⁵⁰⁴ It affirms that we need do nothing to defend ourselves, to fight our enemies, or to safeguard our land and our values. Do nothing – and God will take care of all. In one version of this philosophy, reference is made to the Talmud's dictum that "Torah at all times protects and saves"⁵⁰⁵ and active self-defense is deemed to be almost unfaithful to God.

Of course "Torah protects and saves," but does that idea necessarily mean that we are obligated to forego any type of self-defense? Jewish history – from the Crusades through the Holocaust and into modern Israel – is unfortunately replete with examples of great Torah scholars who were murdered during wars, pogroms, liquidations and terrorist acts. "Torah protects and saves" means that there is a special measure of Divine Providence that attaches to those who

---

⁵⁰⁰ Rashi, Shemot 14:15.

⁵⁰¹ Ibid.

⁵⁰² Masechet Sota 37a.

⁵⁰³ Rav Chaim ibn Attar, eighteenth-century rabbi in Morocco and Eretz Yisrael.

⁵⁰⁴ See a graphic, if unduly harsh and perhaps even exaggerated description of this mindset in Chaim Nachman Bialik's poem "City of Slaughter" ("*B'ir Haharega,*" 1903), written in the wake of the Kishinev pogrom.

⁵⁰⁵ Masechet Sota 21a.

engage in the study of Torah – but not that those scholars therefore benefit always from a suspension of the rules of nature, warfare or politics.

The Ohr HaChaim explains – and Rashi alludes to this as well – that there is one prerequisite to God's deliverance: an act of self-help on our part. Some initiative is required in order to activate the divine plan.[506] Here, the Jewish people were miraculously redeemed from Egypt, but at each stage in the process had to do an act – something – that exemplified their faith in God, whether it was the setting aside of the paschal lamb, the splattering of blood on the doorposts, etc. The Jews in Egypt were also idolaters and had largely renounced circumcision;[507] by what merit would they continue to benefit from God's wonders? Justice demanded accountability.

"Speak to the Children of Israel and let them journey forward." If the people would gird themselves with faith and march forward into the sea, then the divine response would be forthcoming. "It is not only up to Me," God said. "As much as I desire a miracle, if the people are not worthy, the attribute of justice will thwart any miracle and even mercy cannot overcome it."[508] The people would have to demonstrate some *hishtadlut*, some effort on their own behalf.

As the Talmud relates, the Jewish people marched forward to the sea – and then stopped. In a great leap of faith, Nachshon the son of Aminadav jumped into the sea, followed by the entire tribe of Yehuda and/or Binyamin – and the sea split.[509] Salvation was at hand, spurred not only by prayer but by prayer combined with action. The ultimate success or failure of any venture is decided by God; prayer and deeds are the tools we use in order to evoke divine compassion.

The Malbim similarly writes that God said to Moshe: "You don't need prayer, because the miracle and the rescue are already prepared. You just need some merit…that will demonstrate the people's faith and trust in God."

That was the Torah way in ancient times, and that is the Torah way today as well.

---

[506] An identical point is made by Rav Yosef Chaim of Baghdad, in Ben Yehoyada, Masechet Pesachim 56a: "A man should not rely completely on miracles but should perform whatever natural act of salvation he can perform."

[507] See *Meshech Chochma*, Shemot 12:22.

[508] Commentary of Ohr Hachaim.

[509] Masechet Sota 36b–37a.

Religious Cop-out

And Israel saw the great hand that God inflicted upon Egypt, and the people feared God, and they believed in God and in Moshe, His servant. (Shemot 14:31)

At the Red Sea, the Jewish people were privileged to behold the *yad hagedola* (great hand) of God smite the Egyptians. But in Egypt, they witnessed not the *yad hagedola* but rather the *yad chazaka* (mighty hand; 6:1, 13:9, etc.). What is the difference between the "great hand" and the "mighty hand" of God?

Rav Yosef Ber Soloveitchik, the *Beit Halevi*, taught that there was a profound difference between the two hands that reflected the different levels of the Jewish people in Egypt and at the Red Sea. In Egypt itself, the people saw God's "mighty hand" punish the Egyptians with ten plagues, but the Jews themselves lacked any merit. They were brought to the precipice of redemption by a "mighty hand" and the shock waves it unleashed in Egypt. But at the Red Sea, we had already fulfilled several *mitzvot* and gained divine favor; the hand that was perceived was "great" and not just mighty, a reflection of God's compassion.

The *Beit Halevi*'s great-grandson and namesake Rav Yosef Dov Soloveitchik expanded on this point. A "mighty hand" is all-powerful. It astounds, it grabs people's attention, it is formidable – but it neither inspires nor uplifts. By contrast, a "great hand" uplifts. It changes the observer. One who gazes at a strong man will not become stronger, but one who gazes at a great man can become greater.

Something changed in the Jewish people. When the "mighty hand" was active in Egypt, we were completely passive. We did nothing. We watched. We were passive beneficiaries of the plagues.[510] But at the Red Sea, as noted above, we finally became active. We had to move forward and jumpstart the impending miracle. Nothing happened until we initiated it. In Egypt, we were spectators at the miracles; at the Red Sea, we were participants and thereby merited the prophecy that resulted in the sublime song that was chanted jubilantly in the aftermath of the miracle, the song that we sing daily in our prayers.

Our response at the Red Sea should be a constant reminder of how the Jewish people are supposed to react to turmoil and instability. The Talmud

---

[510] The meritorious actions in Egypt (e.g., the Korban Pesach, the blood on the lintel) qualified us for redemption, but we were completely passive during the redemption itself.

presents a horrific picture of the world in pre-Messianic times: "In the footsteps of Moshiach, insolence will proliferate, honor will dwindle, the government will turn to heresy with none to rebuke it; morality will be privatized, the meeting place of the scholars will become a house of lewdness, their wisdom will degenerate, and those who fear sin will be despised. The truth will disappear. Elders will be embarrassed by the young, and a son will not be ashamed in front of his father. And on whom can we rely, but our Father in Heaven?"[511]

Indeed, it is a litany of dreadfulness, most of which is already recognizable in modern times. But the Rav, Rav Soloveitchik, quoted Rav Chaim Volozhin as saying that even the last clause – "On whom can we rely, but our Father in Heaven?" – is also part of the anguish. If a Jew looks around the world and times are bad, morality is receding, and all he can say is "on whom can we rely, but our Father in Heaven?" then he has failed in his divine mission.[512] He has not fulfilled his responsibility as a faithful servant of God.

If a Jew looks at the world and sees an abundance of rudeness, then he should first teach his children manners. If the government denies God and society rejects elementary morality, then do not despair but preach it to them and to all. Fill our homes, schools and airwaves with God's word. If the wisdom of scholars degenerates, then they should redouble their efforts and seek new audiences. If children are disrespectful, then raise them better. If truth is in danger of disappearing, then proclaim it again and again.

In essence, Rav Chaim Volozhin taught, "on whom can we rely, but our Father in Heaven?" is a cop-out clothed in lofty, pious-sounding garb. Do something, speak out, don't be afraid, even jump in the sea if necessary. That is what God wants – not the songs and chants of the inert and inactive, and not the sounds of the sheep, but rather the voice of the shepherd and the dynamism of the leader. That does not at all diminish the will of God; indeed, that is the will of God.

The Gift of Certainty

This is my God and I will exalt Him... (Shemot 15:2)

Our Sages underscored the word *this* and stated that "what a maidservant saw at the Red Sea was not perceived by Yechezkel or Yeshayahu."[513] The prophecy

---

[511] Masechet Sota 49b.
[512] Holzer, *The Rav Thinking Aloud*, p. 103.
[513] Rashi, Shemot 15:2, citing Mechilta of Rabbi Shimon bar Yochai, Beshalach 15.

was that real and that intense. What was so unique about the miracle at the Red Sea? After all, people had seen wonders in Egypt – and the prophets themselves lived through miraculous times.

There was one aspect of the splitting of the sea that stands out in history. It was unprecedented and has only rarely been duplicated. To the saintly Chofetz Chaim is attributed the aphorism "For the believer, there are no questions; for the non-believer, there are no answers." Both sides of the equation require understanding.

To be sure, the non-believer finds no answers. The unfaithful are trapped in darkness, in a chaotic void that is governed by randomness and unpredictability. As they say, "Life happens," as if that ultimately explains anything. In the poignant language of the Midrash, "all are presumed to be blind until God illuminates their eyes."[514] For the non-believer, the world remains dark and forbidding.

But do the faithful really have no questions, as the Chofetz Chaim implies? At first glance, the opposite seems to be true. Avraham and Moshe both questioned God – but having questions did not at all diminish their faith or affect their service of God except to the extent that it made them more humble, devoted and compassionate.

Life always presents questions but answers – about personal matters, national matters or global matters – are not always as readily forthcoming. In this world, we only have a visceral response to what is construed as joyous or tragic; hence we have separate blessings for each.[515] Man longs for moments of absolute clarity, in which everything makes sense and all is explicable. Those moments are exceedingly rare, but one such moment occurred at the Red Sea. Suddenly, everything was clear – God's promises to our forefathers, the travails of Yosef, the persecution and slavery, etc. The divine plan that unfolded before the people was impeccable.

"What a maidservant saw at the Red Sea was not perceived by Yechezkel or Yeshayahu." It is not that the maidservants were more intellectually gifted than the greatest prophets; that is obviously untenable. Rather, the maidservant enjoyed that moment of absolute clarity – of seeing the divine justice inflicted on our enemies and all wrongs righted.

---

[514] Midrash Breisheet Rabba 53:14.

[515] Masechet Pesachim 50a: "Rav Acha ben Chanina stated: This world is not like the world to come. In this world, for good tidings we recite the blessing 'He is good, and does good,' while for bad tidings, we recite the blessing "the Judge of truth." But in the world to come, [we will recite for both] only 'He is good and does good.'"

The prophets Yeshayahu and Yechezkel prophesied about the future with sublime visions of Jewish life and the Messianic era, but they did not live to see the fulfillment of their visions, which remained abstract. The prophets saw the destruction and the exile and gazed prophetically into the redemption of the future – but they did not see it.[516] Like the Jews who left Egypt, Yeshayahu and Yechezkel witnessed the suffering of slavery and exile but they never enjoyed the exhilaration of triumph and redemption, and could never exult "this is my God and I will glorify Him" in a tangible way. Indeed, for many of the righteous, such transparency is limited to the next world.[517]

At the Red Sea we enjoyed that moment of perfect clarity, and so we recall its commemorative song every morning in our prayers as the last in the introductory praises of God. It reminds us that we have a responsibility to ask questions and seek answers – but never to let those questions and answers divert us from our life's task: service of God and the pursuit of moral and intellectual perfection.

SMALL THINGS

> *...There [at Marah, God] established for [the people] a statute and an ordinance, and there He tested them. (Shemot 15:25)*

The euphoria over the rescue at the Red Sea faded fairly quickly. Within days, the Jewish people complained to Moshe about water, and soon after that, about food.

In response, God showed Moshe a tree and had him throw it into the bitter water, which sweetened and became potable. And then God gave the people "a statute and an ordinance," laws. But they asked for water, not laws. Why did God give them laws?

Conversely, didn't it occur to the people that the God Who had just liberated them from slavery and from annihilation at the Red Sea would also provide them with food and water? Why didn't they just *ask* Moshe about the future plans? Instead, "the people complained against Moshe" (15:24). Why is it that people who seemingly have everything to be happy about are too often unhappy?

---

[516] Rashi, Shemot 6:3, offers a similar idea in a different context.
[517] Masechet Taanit 31a.

Rashi notes that the people were punished for complaining: "They should have asked Moshe to evoke [God's] compassion but instead they whined."[518] Indeed, just because a person is distressed – even understandably distressed – doesn't give him the right to act boorishly to another person. We are not entitled to inflict our bad moods on others. What happened here that the people's closeness to God seemed to evaporate within days?

The Torah is about great things but not only about great things. It is about "small" things too. Rav Kook noted that just as a Jew is trained to say "how great are Your deeds, God" (Tehillim 92:6), we must also constantly remind ourselves to say "how small are Your deeds, God" – to recognize how the Torah deals at substantial length with the mundane aspects of life.[519] No area of life is beyond the Torah's scrutiny – family life, business, interpersonal relations, conversation, dress, shopping, etc. We are enthralled by the majesty of the heavens, but the Torah also obligates us to look around us and see divine sparks – and divinely ordained obligations – in every venue. Every refined character trait is as much an expression of the divine light that permeates us as are the luminaries above us.

That was the test of Marah. If you look for God only at the Red Sea, He will be found there, but that will not necessarily make you a better person. Perceiving God only in the "big things" in life will not always connect you to God any more deeply – and when the stupendous event passes, you will be left deflated, even vacant. The euphoria passes pretty quickly, as we see in many of the great and joyous events in life (such as weddings and births) that are often followed by feelings of despondency.

We make many important and transformative decisions in life – such as whom to marry, when to have children, what profession to enter and where to live. All those decisions shape us, but not as much as how we then fill in the blanks ourselves: what kind of spouses are we; how do we want to raise our children; how will we divide our time between family, work and Torah; how will we spend the money that we earn; what will we give to the community in which we have chosen to live; and even what benefit does our community offer that we are not fully utilizing.

At Marah, the Jewish people were introduced to the world of details, the particulars of daily living that define our lives. We were taught about Shabbat, the red heifer and a smattering of monetary laws,[520] and even gently reminded

---

[518] Rashi, Shemot 25:25.

[519] *Orot HaTorah* 3:8.

[520] Rashi, Shemot 25:25.

about etiquette and polite ways of redressing grievances. People are unhappy not just when the big picture is unclear, but especially when the small details are overlooked and undervalued and our quality of life is impaired.

This is the greatness of the Torah system. We were not punished at Marah so much as we were educated. The Torah, compared to a living tree, sweetened the bitter waters.[521] God has the capacity to sweeten what is bitter even if it inherently remains bitter, like the waters of Marah. God could have given us sweet water. Instead He gave us bitter water that could be sweetened. The Chofetz Chaim once said that a Jew should never say that "life is bad," rather that "life is (occasionally) bitter." The bitter can be made sweet.

And we learned as well that finding the sweetness in life is the heritage of every Jew, but only if we "surely listen to [His] voice…, do what is right in His eyes, obey His commandments and observe all His decrees" (15:26). Our choices in matters both small and great define our lives and quantify our enjoyment of life itself.

Manna from Heaven

And God said to Moshe, "Behold, I will rain down for you bread from heaven, and the people will go out and collect each day's portion, so that I can test them whether or not they will follow My teaching." (Shemot 16:4)

What was the test of the manna? Apparently, our Sages perceived it as so essential to the Torah personality that the Talmud teaches that "the Torah was only given to those who eat manna."[522] Yet what proof of righteousness does consumption of this special substance offer? It does not seem to have required much more than gathering it in every morning (with a double portion on Friday) and not seeking it on Shabbat.

The consumers of manna – the Jews who received the Torah in the wilderness – were completely dependent on God for their sustenance. Indeed, reliance on God to provide our daily needs is a core principle of Judaism. "You open Your hand and satisfy the desire of every living being."[523] The Talmud teaches that man's annual income is apportioned every year on Rosh Hashana,

---

[521] Mechilta D'Rabbi Yishmael, Shemot, Beshalach, s.v. "*va'yasa*" 1.
[522] Ibid, s.v. "*va'yasa*" 2; quoted here by Sforno and others. See also MidrashTanchuma, Beshalach 20.
[523] Tehillim 145:16.

with the only exceptions his expenses for Shabbat and *yom tov* and for his children's education; "if he skimps on them, his income is diminished; if he is generous with them, his income is augmented."[524]

It is difficult to live a full Jewish life and dedicate most of that life to earning money. Much is lost – Torah study and public prayer, time with spouse and children, even the sundry pleasures the world has to offer. One's health is often sacrificed, and the strain of sustaining a luxurious lifestyle induces life-shortening stress. It is mindboggling when men (it is usually men) in their eighties and nineties show up at the office every day for work. Although one's career can provide immense personal satisfaction, even a career should not become an end in itself and the primary focus in life. "No one ever dies wishing they'd spent more time at the office."[525] The "consumers of manna" know that God looks after our true needs, and that we do not need as much as we think we do in order to live productive and happy lives.

Work and wealth do provide security. The Talmud declares in several contexts that "there is no comparison between one who has bread in his basket and one who does not."[526] "Bread in the basket" means that his desires can be readily satisfied and the stresses of earning a living reduced dramatically. But, more importantly, the Talmud also teaches that "one who has bread in his basket and frets 'what will I eat tomorrow?' is a person of little faith."[527] In such a circumstance, either he has overextended himself with luxuries or has become unnaturally obsessed with wealth. Interestingly, the Talmud (in Sota) adds that even righteous people can have "little faith" in this area.[528]

And yet, even as we know intuitively that God provides – and nothing symbolizes God's provision of our daily bread more than the manna of the wilderness – we are not allowed to remain passive and expect our sustenance to come to us. In fact, receipt of the manna was conditioned on the beneficiaries going out "each day" and collecting that day's allotment. The Manna did not come to them; even though little work was involved in its retrieval and preparation, the people still had to "go out" and find it.

What should be obvious – that everything worthwhile in life requires *hishtadlut* – effort – is not universally accepted in Jewish life. Reliance on God, for some, means doing nothing, even living off the dole, and construing that

---

[524] Masechet Beitza 16a.
[525] Quotation attributed to the late publisher Malcolm Forbes.
[526] Masechet Yoma 67a.
[527] Masechet Sota 48b.
[528] Ibid.

as God's will. Indeed, there are mendicants who view their beneficiaries as the instrumentality through which God sends them their sustenance – and they are correct! But anyone who argues such a lifestyle is desirable, normal or in accord with Torah values is mistaken.[529]

In our daily prayers, we beseech God for a number of different needs that we have – knowledge, forgiveness, salvation, health, sustenance, the ingathering of the exiles, etc. Few would argue that we can attain knowledge by sitting and doing nothing, or seek forgiveness without repenting, or maintain our health without seeking professional care, or return to the land of Israel without packing up and physically going. Well, maybe some would, but every blessing we seek requires our initiative. Why would sustenance be any different?

Just as the manna was accompanied by the application of Jewish law – manna-specific laws like going out every morning except for Shabbat, or not leaving leftovers overnight – so too the world of employment has laws that are meant to be implemented and not merely studied – laws of merchants and buyers, borrowers and lenders, builders and homeowners, courts and marketplaces.

To believe that God provides for us is not the same as maintaining that we are thereby freed from our own exertions. The Torah was given to a generation that consumed heavenly bread but accepted their role in obtaining it. Those who take responsibility for themselves and seek to be self-sufficient are still the repositories of Torah.

SHABBAT

See that God has given you the Shabbat; therefore He gives to you on Friday a double portion... (Shemot 16:29)

For good reason, observance of Shabbat is one of the defining characteristics of the Torah-faithful Jew. The acknowledgement of God as the center point of our lives is perpetual, but achieves a different dimension of awareness on Shabbat itself. On that august day, we refrain from creative labors in order to pay homage to the Creator of all. The term *shomer Shabbat* (Sabbath observer) is not just a description of a person and a set of behaviors but a status that

---

[529] Indeed, in the Grace after Meals (Birkat Hamazon), we entreat that God should not oblige us to "be dependent...on the gifts of flesh and blood."

entails certain rights and privileges in the Jewish community; indeed it is the hallmark of the Jewish people.

Our Sages presented two statements about the momentousness of Shabbat that on the surface seem to conflict with each other. "Rabbi Levi said: if the Jewish people would observe even one Shabbat properly, the son of David would come."[530] The Talmud, though, quotes Rabbi Shimon bar Yochai as saying that "if only the Jewish people would observe two Sabbaths according to law, they would immediately be redeemed."[531]

What is the difference between the observance of one Shabbat and the observance of two? What does the second add that the first doesn't have?

From one perspective, to celebrate one Shabbat – in fact, to do almost anything once – is an "experience." It is exciting, interesting, different and culturally unique. Once is a phenomenon – but twice is a commitment. "Twice" means that the person is now responding not merely to curiosity but to the call of a higher authority. It means that Shabbat spoke to him, drew him in, and now his observance is much more profound and real. So why then did Rabbi Levi aver that even one Shabbat suffices in order to merit the coming of the Messiah?

The Maharal of Prague[532] explained that the proper observance of even one Shabbat distinguishes the Jewish people from the nations of the world.[533] We, as a nation, are sanctified and elevated by the day, which is one reason Shabbat begins with Kiddush (sanctification) and ends with Havdala (separation). After one Shabbat, we are already a changed people; for Rabbi Levi in the Midrash, that sufficed as a prerequisite for ultimate redemption.

Rabbi Shimon bar Yochai required the proper observance of two Sabbaths, as the first one defines and elevates, but the second one confirms and reinforces the commitment. The Messiah comes when we embrace our uniqueness, but full redemption is possible only when the entire nation is exalted and internalizes our destiny.

Shabbat can be the most uplifting day of the week – or it can be, Heaven forfend, dark, depressing, overbearing and even devoid of spirituality. The latter happens when parents transform Shabbat from a day of blissful joy and spiritual warmth into a day of "nos," "don'ts," "can'ts," and prohibitions.

---

[530] Midrash Shemot Rabba 25:12.

[531] Masechet Shabbat 118b.

[532] Rav Yehuda Loew, sixteenth-century Prague.

[533] Ibid., commentary to Masechet Shabbat 118b. A similar approach is found in *Dorash David*, Shemot, pp. 131–32.

When the emphasis is on what is forbidden rather than on what is mandatory and enriching, then Shabbat takes on a gloomier tone. In some families, the Shabbat meals bring out the worst in the participants, and the Shabbat table is filled with strife, gossip, tale-bearing, mundane talk and personal grievances. That is a shame.

It is hard to imagine something sadder than the misuse of Shabbat, given to the Jewish people as a gift direct from God's treasury.[534] Perhaps the only thing sadder is the extent to which the true and enriching observance of Shabbat is unknown to most of our brethren today, for who would knowingly refuse a gift that is intended to enhance their lives and increase their happiness?

Every Jew – especially every parent – is obligated to make Shabbat the high point of the week, the culmination of all our work, and the central celebration of family and Torah. A family with a satisfying Shabbat will produce children who love Torah, Shabbat, and their parents as well. Of course, the type of Shabbat we are able to create is a very personal decision, and in retrospect, when the adult looks back at his childhood, a crucial component of Jewish parenting. Moreover, families that enjoy and properly celebrate this holiest day of the year form communities that do the same, and those communities are the building blocks of the Jewish nation that will see its redemption coming in the wake of the full observance of Shabbat.

Filling the Void

> *And he called the place Massah u'Meriva, because of the contentiousness of the Children of Israel and their test of God, saying, "Is God in our midst or not?" (Shemot 17:7)*

The *Zohar* asks the obvious question: "Were the Jewish people fools?" After seeing all the miracles and wonders in Egypt and the Red Sea, the well and the manna, how could they ask "Is God in our midst or not?"[535] Their whole world – their entire existence – depended on God. Rashi compares them to a child who, while being carried on his father's shoulders and having a number of kindnesses done for him by the father, asks a stranger, "Have you seen my father?"[536]

---

[534] Masechet Shabbat 10b.

[535] *Zohar*, Beshalach, 64b.

[536] Rashi, Shemot 17:8.

The use of the word *ayin* – literally, nothingness – is interesting. Earlier, when God says to Moshe that He is testing the Jewish people to see "whether or not they will follow My teaching" (16:4), the word *lo* is used for "not." What is the difference between *ayin* and *lo*?

Lo is the opposite of *ken* (yes); that is to say, there are two options for the people. They can follow the Torah, or they can refrain from following the Torah. *Ayin* is a different sensation – nothingness, emptiness, a vacuum in life that cannot be filled. When Rachel cried out to Yaakov, that "without children, I am *ayin*,"[537] she was articulating the heartrending reality that there is nothing that can fill that void. "The advantage of a man [without Torah] over an animal is *ayin*…"[538] Without Torah, man is just another instinctual creature. Even *yesh* (something) does not contradict *ayin*; a person can have "something," even plenty that still leaves him feeling that he has nothing. What were the Jewish people missing?

The *Zohar* continues that they did not know whether they would still relate to God on the highest level – the *atika stimaa* – or on the lower, mundane level of *ze'eir anpin*. They had seen God wage war on their behalf against the most powerful empire in the world and effect a global revolution. And now? God was being "reduced" before their eyes to the Provider of bread, water and meat. At this point, before they received the Torah, the people had little else in life. They were deflated, with a frustrating sense of *ayin*, a lack of meaning and deeper purpose. It is a feeling with which we are quite familiar; modern man is often tormented by prolonged feelings of *ayin*, spiritual emptiness.

As noted earlier, a Jew has to be able to see God's hand in the big things and in the small things. After the Six-Day War, the Satmar Rebbe wrote a sequel to *Vayoel Moshe* (his original anti-Zionist tract) called *Al Hageula v'al Hatemura* in which he posited that no miracles occurred during that astounding victory, and indeed, any success was the work of Satan.[539]

It is possible to be so trapped by ideology that one can no longer see the *atika stimaa*, God's great accomplishments, and only see "small things," if that. One who disparages the miracles of modern Israel could also disparage the

---

[537] Breisheet 30:1.

[538] Kohelet 3:19.

[539] See Rav Yoel Teitelbaum, *Vayoel Moshe*, Maamar Shalosh Shavuot, chapters 45–48; Rav Yoel Teitelbaum, *Al Hageula v'al Hatemura*, Introduction, pp. 6–7. See also Rav Shlomo Aviner, *Aloh Naaleh: Response to Vayoel Moshe* [Hebrew], ed. Rav Mordechai Zion (Beit El: Hava Books, 2012), pp. 177–81. See also Rav Menachem Kasher, *Hatekufa Hagedola*, chapter 15, in which he posits that one who attributes the wonders of Israel to natural forces and even to the *sitra achra* essentially denies the role of Divine Providence in the national life of the Jewish people.

miracles of Chanuka and denude of any divine influence the plagues in Egypt and the splitting of the Red Sea. Those are intellectual choices we make – to look for God's hand is a choice, and perceiving it is also a choice. To be permeated by God's works and not to see them is essentially to ask "is God in our midst or not?"

The *ayin*, though, would not be the presence of God but the *ayin* within us. Our Sages taught that "God wished to confer merit on the Jewish people so He gave us a plethora of Torah and *mitzvot*."[540] God benefited us with Torah so that we can lead purposeful lives and so that we can look up from the pettiness and hardship of life and see greatness, His presence, and His protective hand. We should never ever feel emptiness or a lack of deeper meaning. That is why our lives are always full of obligations and opportunities to serve Him. He is not benefited at all by our service, but we are enriched, inspired, perfected and gain eternity through it.

---

[540] Masechet Makkot 23b.

Yitro

LONELINESS

> *And it was on the very next day that Moshe sat to judge the people, and the people stood before Moshe from morning to night. And Moshe's father-in-law saw everything that he was doing for the people, and he said, "What is this that you are doing, sitting alone and the people stand over you from morning until night.... You shall surely become worn out..." (Shemot 18:13–14, 18)*

Yitro made an instantaneous judgment that Moshe's governance of the people was flawed. "On the very next day," he observed that Moshe was sitting alone and judging the people. Obviously, Moshe was an indefatigable leader of his people, but what could Yitro have seen in one day? It is not possible to perceive a pattern in one day. So how did Yitro know that Moshe would "surely become worn out" if he maintained that pace?

Moshe's father-in-law noticed – immediately – that Moshe was sitting "alone"; or worse, he was not alone but lonely, even though he was surrounded by people. He was lonely without a support system, with no one on whom he could rely or trust or to whom he could even pour out his heart. Moshe's position made him a lonely person, and that, surely, would erode his strength over time. Yitro the outsider saw something that insiders don't always see – one can be lonely in a crowd, and it is painful to be lonely.

Moshe's family life was unconventional (his wife and sons had just rejoined him) and his relationship with God was unprecedented. He had no peers, and his isolation would only grow over time. The solution for Moshe's loneliness, Yitro said, was to find "men of valor, God-fearing men of truth, who despise money" (18:21) – men who possessed inner strength and unshakeable convictions, who were grounded in a different reality, whose ideals were not for sale, and whose values could not be bought – and to make them leaders of groups of thousands and hundreds and fifties and tens of people.

Every person is called upon to contribute to the world beyond his own personal four cubits. Clearly, some are called upon to do more than others – some to lead tens and others to lead thousands. But we all have something to do. The realization that there are others who share our views and values is comforting and inspiring; we need not have perfect symmetry of opinions and approaches to join forces with others to accomplish great things in service of God and His people. Too often we find ourselves handicapped in cooperating with others because we exaggerate the differences and lose sight of the commonality of interests that we have.

Insiders tend to identify and overstress minor distinctions much more than do outsiders, who routinely see a group's similarities and shared destiny. Where the world sees just "Jews," we see a variety of sects, ethnicities, factions and camps divided sometimes by religiosity but more commonly by external appearances only.

Yitro perceived Moshe's plight and alleviated it by creating a cadre of leaders that would assist Moshe, a support system that would wage Moshe's battles and transmit the Law he would receive. It is not weakness to acknowledge the support system that surrounds us – spouse and children, family and community, rabbis and friends – and enables us all to look beyond ourselves and seek the greater good for others.

Abundant Kindness

And you will warn them regarding the statutes and the teachings, and you will make known to them the path on which they shall walk and the deeds that they should do. (Shemot 18:20)

The Talmud expounded this verse to include the fundamental practices of loving-kindness: "'the path' – those are acts of kindness; 'they shall walk' – that refers to visiting the sick; 'on which' – this refers to burial."[541] But how did these admittedly virtuous acts become the definition of "the statutes and the teachings"? One might have expected that the thrust of Yitro's advice to Moshe would reflect not the universal norms of kindness but the more particular

---

[541] Masechet Bava Kama 99b.

aspects of Torah – the *mitzvot* that govern our lives and define our practice of Jewish law.

Although we are accustomed to perceiving Moshe as the man of Torah, for whom "the law bores through the mountain,"[542] Moshe was introduced to us as a performer of acts of loving-kindness. He first went out to his brothers and "observed their suffering" (2:11), and then he killed an Egyptian taskmaster who was cruelly beating a Jew.[543] In Midian, Moshe saved the daughters of Yitro from their tormentors,[544] and found a wife in the process. That was Moshe, the man of kindness.

Chesed – kindness – comes in different forms. There is a type of *chesed* that is simply utilitarian: *I'll do something nice for you, so you will do something nice for me.* Undoubtedly, that, if practiced regularly, would make the world a better place, but that is not the Torah's conception of *chesed*.

Moshe's kindness was based on love of justice, and that type of kindness was exemplified in Moshe's life. We see a modern example in the following story. During World War II, a Nazi officer boarded a train in Italy and arrested a Jewish girl. A pregnant Italian woman stood between the Nazi and the Jewish girl and refused to let the Nazi arrest her. She said forcefully, "You can kill me if you want, but look at the faces of these passengers here. You will never leave this train alive." And the Nazi backed down. That gallant Italian woman was the mother of Silvio Berlusconi, who many decades later became Italy's prime minister.[545] Her kindness was the *chesed* of justice.

But the Torah's *chesed* demands even more from us – to be affirmative and fearless, and to seek *chesed* that is motivated by *ahavat Hashem*, love of God. Rav Zvi Yehuda Kook was once walking in Yerushalayim and saw a young woman who looked lost. Upon inquiry, he realized she needed directions and he informed her: "Left, left, straight, right, right," to which she replied that she always hears directions like that, and always gets lost. So Rav Kook walked her to her destination.

Arriving home late, he told his inquisitive wife that he walked a young woman to her destination. She asked him who it was, and Rav Kook answered that she was a young woman from HaShomer Hatzair, the secular Socialist-Zionist movement in Israel.

---

[542] Masechet Sanhedrin 6b.
[543] Shemot 2:12.
[544] Shemot 2:17.
[545] Nick Squires, "Silvio Berlusconi in Tears over Hero Mother," *Telegraph*, February 4, 2010, http://tinyurl.com/ydegcuj.

Rav Kook's wife then asked, "Was she wearing pants?" Told that she was, Rabbanit Kook continued, "Isn't it enough that people are constantly attacking you, criticizing you and sullying your good name – that now they will say that you were seen in public walking with and talking to a woman in pants?"

Rav Kook answered, "If a person doesn't want to do *chesed*, there are always plenty of reasons – great reasons and petty reasons – not to do it."[546] Indeed, there are always reasons *not* to do something. Apathy is almost a default position in life. And there is only one good reason to do an act of kindness – another human being created in the image of God needs help.

Berlusconi's pregnant mother could have sat on the train and said nothing, just as Moshe could have ignored the Jewish victim of the Egyptian master and the plight of Yitro's daughters. But Yitro imparted to us that *chesed* is not a part of Torah, but rather the very foundation of the Torah. The Talmud did not offer a homiletic discourse on "the path on which they shall walk" but rather defined precisely what it is.

The Talmud referred to the Giving of the Torah in a most pithy but inspiring way: "Let the good come and receive the good from the Good and give it to the good."[547] That is to say, let Moshe, who is all good, receive the Torah, which is defined as good, from God, Who is described as good, and give it to people who are good.

We can be cautioned about the "statutes and the teachings," but if we do not see "the path on which [we] shall walk" then we will have missed the whole point of the Torah, our tradition and the very creation of the people of Israel. Opportunities for *chesed* abound. They define our nation and the purpose for our having been given the Torah, and it is the responsibility of each person to pursue acts of kindness and to perform them.

The Community's Torah

And you shall be for Me a kingdom of priests and a holy nation… (Shemot 19:6)

The Torah, as we shall see shortly, was given to individuals but not only to individuals. The fundamental context of Revelation was to a nation and not just to a group of individuals. The Torah is the repository of the nation and not of any single group, and it is the definitive component of Jewish identity. In the

---

[546] Rav Shlomo Aviner, *V'halachta Bi'drachav* (Beit El: Hava Books, 2009), pp. 216–17.

[547] Masechet Menachot 53b.

words of Rav Saadia Gaon, "Our nation, the Children of Israel, is a nation only by virtue of its Torah."[548]

The ramifications for the individual are dramatic. The Talmud suggests that one reason the Jewish people were exiled was that, although they studied Torah, "they did not first recite the blessing over the Torah."[549] Rav Zvi Yehuda Kook[550] explained that the ignominy of that failure to recite the Birkat Hatorah was that Torah study must be prefaced with the words of that blessing, which begins by thanking God "Who chose *us* from among the nations…" Those who studied Torah derived individual pleasure from it, but they did not perceive their Torah study as emanating from their share as part of the nation of Israel. Theirs was an individual learning; the nation was an afterthought, if that.

Every individual Jew must accept the Torah, but must also recognize that the Torah was not given only to him. He must take responsibility for the community and ensure that Torah study permeates that community and not just his own four ells. And he must never forget that the Torah was given to the nation and through the nation to him, and do his share to uphold the honor and the obligations of a "kingdom of priests and a holy nation."

By the same token, the fact that the Torah is the possession of the nation benefits each individual. We can each strengthen each other, and each member of the nation lightens the load of the others. "A burden that is heavy for one is lighter for two [people], and what is heavy for two is lighter for four."[551] That is why the Torah could only be given to a nation that arrived at Sinai "like one person with one heart,"[552] a most unprecedented and unduplicated phenomenon in Jewish history.

The Talmud expounds that the generation of Rav Yehuda son of Rav Il'ai was cherished – as the "God-fearing woman is praised"[553] – because they were so poor that six men had to share one cloak, and still they involved themselves in Torah study.[554] But how is it possible for six men to share one cloak? Rav Chaim Shmulevitz explains that such is not possible if each one is only concerned with his own personal comforts, for if so, each will pull the cloak

---

[548] *Sefer Emunot v'De'ot* 3:7.
[549] Masechet Bava Metzia 85a; Masechet Nedarim 81a.
[550] Rav Zvi Yehuda Kook, *Sichot on Talmud Torah* (Beit El: Hava Books, 2010), pp. 18–19, 58–60.
[551] Midrash Vayikra Rabba 1:4.
[552] Rashi, Shemot 19:2.
[553] Proverbs 31:30.
[554] Masechet Sanhedrin 20a.

to get the maximum benefit until it is torn to shreds.[555] The uniqueness of Rav Yehuda's generation was that each person was concerned about the comfort of the *other person*. In such an environment, it is indeed possible for six people to share, because each one is looking after the needs of his friends.

In the ideal world of Torah, each Jew is concerned with the other and takes responsibility for the spiritual welfare of others. Certainly this notion underlies the *kiruv* (outreach) movement, numerous charitable organizations and aid societies, as well as Jewish intervention in other countries to safeguard the lives of persecuted Jews. Communities that insulate themselves from other Jews and think that only their Torah is authentic and meaningful do themselves a disservice and enervate the bonds that keep our people together. In the end, their acceptance of the Torah suffers, as an essential element of Jewish nationhood is undermined.

Jews prepared for Revelation by joining together "like one person with one heart." That might be an elusive goal, but it remains the ideal of Jewish nationhood for which we strive. And every individual helps make that a reality.

LIMITS

> *You will set boundaries around the mountain saying to the people, "Beware of ascending the mountain or touching its edge; whoever touches the mountain shall surely die." (Shemot 19:12)*

God demanded that man not ascend or even draw near to Mount Sinai at the Revelation, on pain of death. Moshe himself – right before the Revelation – guarantees God that the people "cannot ascend Mount Sinai, as You warned us, saying, 'Make a boundary around the mountain and sanctify it'" (19:23). Note the shift in the verses; the cited verse literally asks that Moshe "set a boundary around the *people*," whereas Moshe states accurately that the border was drawn around the mountain. The distinction is telling.

People need limits; inanimate objects do not need limits. God's law speaks directly to people, who are told to exercise self-control and even to restrain their religious enthusiasm when inappropriate – as it would have been had they stormed the mountain to come "closer" to God. A person who does not recognize limits will usually be forced to rationalize bad behavior or worse, revise the Torah (or secular law) in order that it should conform to his desires.

---

[555] *Sichot Musar*, maamar 36.

Man could not ascend or even touch Sinai during the Revelation, as man played no role in the authorship and revelation of the Torah. If Sinai were not partitioned, man would inevitably claim a partnership in the Torah, if not sole authorship. At the very least – and as has happened repeatedly down to modern times – man would commingle his ideas with those of God, and claim that what he says is also God's word. As Rav Shamshon Raphael Hirsch comments, the fundamental nature of Revelation was that God's word came *to* the people, not *from* the people.[556]

The whole Torah teaches us about limits – what we can or cannot do, say, eat, think and be. It is the very essence of surrender to God's word that is the hallmark of the faithful Jew. Modern man who recoils at any encroachment on his personal autonomy invariably clashes with God's law – *the* point of conflict between those who *say* they accept the Torah's law as divine and those who really do accept it, and live accordingly.

The limitations that delineate objective right and wrong define our lives and provide responsible people with a framework against which they can measure the morality of each activity – a morality that does not change from era to era and from place to place.

Beneath the Mountain

And Moshe brought out the people from the camp toward God, and they stood at the bottom of the mountain. (Shemot 19:17)

Indeed, our Sages famously note that the Jewish people did not stand at "the bottom of the mountain" but as the words can be interpreted, "beneath the mountain." The Talmud comments that God suspended the mountain over the people's heads like a cask, essentially coercing their acceptance of the Torah, saying, "If you accept the Torah, fine; but if not, there will be your burial place."[557]

Certainly a forced acceptance of the Torah negates much of the majesty of the Jewish people responding to God's offer with "we will do and we will listen" (24:7), the wholehearted embrace of the Torah that presumably defined our commitment. But Rav Avraham Yitzchak Kook explained the metaphor of the inverted mountain as meaning the impossibility of refusal rather than the necessity of acceptance. Man has free will, but "man does not have free

---

[556] Commentary to Shemot 19:10–13.
[557] Masechet Shabbat 88a.

will whether or not to have free will."[558] As the Torah is the essence of the Jewish soul, the Talmud's description of the compelled acceptance reflects not an actual event but a characterization of the intimate bond the Jewish people have with God and the Torah.[559] The nation of Israel could not reject the Torah due to its intrinsic characteristics as a nation, notwithstanding the divine miracles and wonders they experienced in Egypt that also made repudiation of the Torah impossible.[560]

That idea alone conveys the inherent connection between the Jew and God's Torah as the foundation of our lives. There was a deep and compelling inner will to accept the Torah that could not be suppressed, and that coexisted with the reality that the Jewish people had to accept the Torah in order to fulfill God's will for His universe. The individual who studies and internalizes the Torah uncovers his essence as a human being, in addition to serving God.

Rav Yaakov Ariel notes that the Torah underscores that the Jewish people "stood" even though they were "at the bottom of" or beneath the mountain.[561] How does one "stand" underneath something? He answers that the tension in the verse illuminates a unique dimension of our lives. Even at Sinai, we "stood." We were not crushed, broken or bent, nor did we lose our autonomous selves. In fact, the opposite was true. We "stood" in the sense that we remained independent beings, thinking and feeling and assessing the situation before us. Nonetheless, we remained standing "beneath" the mountain, a sign of humility and subservience.

Only a man who recognizes his true nature and limitations and is humbled before the presence of God can stand on his own and desire to reach the mountain top. "In the midst of the trembling, man's personality remains firm."[562] Such a person strives for more, is open to new ideas and is willing to learn from others. Conversely, those who see themselves already on the mountain top looking down on others and feeling they have achieved all they want to or ever will achieve can easily lose their footing and find themselves humbled morally, spiritually and intellectually.

Every detail of the Revelation conveyed critical ideas to the Jewish people about ourselves, the Torah, our relationship to God, and the expectations that He has for us as the people of Torah.

---

[558] *Ein Ayah*, ibid.
[559] *Zohar* 3 73a.
[560] Tosafot, Masechet Shabbat 88a, s.v. *"modaa rabba."*
[561] *Me'ohalei Torah*, Parshat Yitro, pp. 127–28.
[562] Ibid.

Individual Acceptance of the Torah

I am the Lord your God Who took you out of the land of Egypt, from the house of bondage. You shall have no other gods before Me. (Shemot 20:2–3)

As noted above, the Torah was given to a nation and not just to individuals. Yet we must recognize that the Decalogue itself is phrased in the singular, not the plural. All the pronouns, "your" and "you," are in the Hebrew singular; even the phrase "Who took you out of the land of Egypt" is singular. Why?

Ramban addressed this question explicitly, and explained that the use of the singular "comes to warn us that each individual is punished for his sins, that God spoke to each one of us, and one should never think that [only] the majority is punished and the individual will be spared [because of the group]."[563]

Man often feels that there is "safety in numbers." If "everyone" is cheating, stealing, speeding, talking in shul, etc., then the illegality is somehow mitigated. After all, one does not want to "separate from the community"![564] There is a measure of truth in the statement; the reality of modern life is that "everyone" cannot be arrested and incarcerated, and if that is the only measure of rightful conduct, then a transgressor will find refuge in the criminality of the mob.[565]

Such an attitude is the death knell to all spiritual aspirations. Just because "everyone" is doing something does not make it right, and is often a pretty good guide to what is wrong. We are first and foremost responsible for our own conduct, which must be based on objective moral norms and not the current mores or cultural climate in the general society or even in the Jewish world.

It is hard to resist the pressure of peers and friends who are doing something improper and seeking our assistance or participation. In such a situation we are obligated to remember that God spoke to each of us as individuals, and that each of us as individuals accepted His Torah and bound ourselves to His law. And that one truth supersedes all the social pressure than can be brought be bear.

---

[563] Ramban, Shemot 20:2.

[564] As in Rambam, *Hilchot Teshuva* 4:2 or *Shulchan Aruch*, Yoreh Deah 345:5.

[565] Witness the modern crime of the "flash mobs," wherein a large group of people will suddenly invade a store, steal its merchandise, and disappear within minutes, overwhelming the store's minimal security staff.

The Right Ideas

What appears to be a declaratory statement was perceived by most Jewish authorities as a commandment. For example, Rambam records as the very first positive commandment that we are "commanded to affirm [or believe in] the Deity, to affirm that there is a First Cause to all of reality, as He said, 'I am the Lord your God.'"[566] He begins his Code of Law with a similar expression: "The foundation of all foundations and the pillar of all wisdom is to know that there is a First Cause that brought all of existence into existence…. And knowing this is a positive commandment, as it says, 'I am the Lord your God.'"[567]

It is frequently asked, How can the Torah mandate faith, which in any event seems to be a prerequisite to the Torah generally? We can certainly understand the regulation of behavior, a general function of law, and therefore the commandments of the Torah, but how can the Torah command a person to believe something, and especially to "know" something?

The renowned *rosh yeshiva* of Ponevezh in Bnai Brak, Rav Elazar Menachem Mann Shach,[568] explained that we are commanded to use our God-given intellects in order to "know God" to the limits of our intellectual capacities.[569] That entails at least a limited study of philosophy and the various rational proofs of God's existence that have been proffered over the millennia.[570] *Emuna* (faith) begins only at the point where our intellectual capabilities have been exhausted. Nonetheless, each person is obligated to undertake the process and engage in that study.[571]

This idea explains a famous statement of our Sages that "all who prolong the word *echad* (One) [in the recitation of the Shema] have their days and years prolonged."[572] What is so special about "One" that we could not apply the same reward to someone who elongates, for example, the words *Shema* or *Elokeinu*?

---

[566] *Sefer Hamitzvot*, Mitzvot Aseh 1.

[567] *Hilchot Yesodei HaTorah* 1:1, 6.

[568] Twentieth-century Israel.

[569] In his commentary *Avi Ezri*, *Hilchot Teshuva* 5:5 (page 48), citing the Brisker Rav, Rav Yitzchak Zev Soloveitchik in the name of his father, Rav Chaim Soloveitchik.

[570] One, of course, emerges from this verse. The *Sefer Hakuzari* (1:11–27; cited here by Avraham ibn Ezra in his commentary to Shemot 20:1, who asserts that he provided Rav Yehuda HaLevi with the answer) asks why God began the Revelation by stating that He was the God Who took the Jewish people out of Egypt rather than the God Who created the heavens and the earth. The Kuzari answers that God spoke to the Jewish people who had witnessed His wonders, rather than refer to creation to which no one was an eyewitness. In essence, we know of God's existence through His deeds and the miraculous story of the Jewish people throughout history. History, itself, is His-story.

[571] Heard also from Rav Yisrael Chait.

[572] Masechet Berachot 13b.

Rav Shach answered that every day we recite the essence of the Decalogue in the recitation of the Shema: "I am the Lord your God" parallels "*Hashem Elokeinu*" (our Lord, God),[573] and "you shall have no other gods before Me" parallels "*Hashem echad*" (God is One). It is the latter phrase that is elongated, not the former, as God's essence (I am the Lord your God) is ultimately beyond man's complete comprehension. We can, however, comprehend the negation of all other powers (you shall have no other gods before Me). When we acknowledge God's existence, we realize our limitations; this is the point at which faith predominates. But when we enunciate "God is One," we are able to prolong the word *One* to emphasize to ourselves that we are indeed able and obligated to uproot and eradicate all thoughts of other "powers" from our minds and hearts.

Every Jew is required to study the Torah in all its elements: its laws, its ideas and its values. The observance of Torah requires more than just the control of our actions, as difficult as that is; it requires as well the shaping of our thoughts and a correct understanding of God. As Rambam notes, a Jew who professes that "God has a body or physical likeness" is a heretic who has no share in the world-to-come.[574]

We can control what we think, and we are required to fill our minds with positive and accurate ideas that perfect our souls and govern our actions.

The Father Figure

Honor your father and your mother so that your days may be prolonged on the land that the Lord your God has given you. (Shemot 20:12)

Parents are the primary source of the *mesora* (Jewish tradition) for their children, and bear the major responsibility for conveying it. For that reason, this fifth statement of the Decalogue is connected to the laws between God and man and not to the second quintet, which discusses laws between man and man.[575] Parents provide their children with their physical existence, but also serve as the bond with the Jewish past.

---

[573] Devarim 6:4.

[574] *Hilchot Teshuva* 3:7. Raavad excuses such unintentional errors drawn from a misunderstanding of texts as wrong but not heretical.

[575] Rav Shamshon Raphael Hirsch, Shemot 20:12.

That notion is at the heart of this commandment, in addition to the elementary value of gratitude. A child must always appreciate that it was his parents who brought him into the world and who – together with God[576] – are responsible for his existence. They exerted themselves in order to raise and guide him properly; gratitude for that is everlasting.[577] Generally, and specifically in this instance, gratitude leads to longevity, in the sense that it provides a quality of life that is sublime and rewarding.

But our Sages broadened the definition of parenting here beyond the simple words of the text. The Talmud states that the individuals for whom respect is mandated in the verse include step-parents and older brothers – i.e., anyone in a position to offer guidance.[578] Elsewhere, the Talmud notes that a person who teaches his friend's son Torah is considered as if he gave birth to him.[579] Nurturing a person's spiritual growth is no less important than enabling his physical existence; spiritual life is as essential as physical life, and endures even longer.

Thus, the parental figure is more than the person who procreates and contributes genes to the child. Modern society has, unfortunately, no shortage of "parents" who procreate and evaporate, who deliver children but abandon them shortly thereafter (and sometimes, in the case of fathers, even before the birth). There are many social dysfunctions that are directly attributable to this lamentable phenomenon. Add to that the astounding number – currently hovering at around 40 percent,[580] rising to as high as 72 percent among the minority population in the United States[581] – of children born out of wedlock to single parents, and it is obvious that the meaning of "parent" has been diluted, or at least transformed. True parents provide much more than sperm and egg to their offspring.

The American thinker Dr. William Bennett made this point in an intriguing way. The Latin language has two words for "father." *Genitor* means a biological father, as in the word *progenitor*. But *pater* – the root of father – means the

---

[576] Masechet Kiddushin 30b; Masechet Nidda 31a.

[577] *Sefer Hachinuch*, mitzva 33.

[578] Masechet Ketubot 103a.

[579] Masechet Sanhedrin 19b.

[580] According to the CDC, in 2011, 40.7 percent of all births in the United States were to unmarried women. Joyce A. Martin, Brady E. Hamilton, et al., "Births: Final Data for 2011," *National Vital Statistics Reports* 62, no. 1 (June 28, 2013): 9, http://www.cdc.gov/nchs/data/nvsr62/nvsr62_01.pdf.

[581] In 2011, 72 percent of births to non-Hispanic black women were to unmarried women. Ibid.

father who takes responsibility, who oversees the upbringing and nurturing of his children. That *pater* is the father who deserves the most respect.[582]

Jewish law recognizes the obligation of a child to honor even the parents who gave birth to him, the biological father and mother with whom he might have no meaningful contact thereafter. That is the simplest expression of gratitude. But far more gratitude and respect are owed to the mother and father who raise their children, teach them Torah, provide them moral guidance and give them a sense of their connection to the Jewish people. Those individuals – often but not always the biological parents – are the real *patrēs*, and the very foundation of the Jewish home and the Jewish people.

Homicide

You shall not murder. (Shemot 20:13)

Do we really need the Torah – God's word – to command us not to murder, or for that matter, not to kidnap others, steal what is not ours, or commit adultery? These are defined, even by Jewish thinkers,[583] as natural laws, i.e., rational laws that man could deduce through his reason. Nevertheless, even these laws will occasionally pose complex questions on the margins that require divine guidance;[584] for example, is abortion, euthanasia, or suicide identical to homicide? Generally, though, these laws are universal, and not particular to Jews.

Yet our Sages debated the purpose of enshrining these laws, and especially in the Decalogue. Two of the most illustrious teachers of *musar* discussed this very issue. Rav Simcha Zisel Ziv, the Alter of Kelm, posited that we see from the Decalogue the great dichotomy in man's nature – how this creature who possesses such intellectual gifts and spiritual potential can still succumb to such base instincts that he would steal and murder and the like. Even a nation that had been liberated by God Himself from bondage and witnessed His miraculous hand – even *they* had to be warned not to murder, steal, commit adultery, testify falsely, etc. That is the nature of man – as great as he can be, he can stumble in the most grotesque and vulgar ways.

---

[582] William Bennett, *The Moral Compass: Stories for a Life's Journey* (New York: Simon and Schuster, 1995), 488.

[583] E.g., Rav Saadiah Gaon, *Sefer Emunot v'De'ot* 3:1–4.

[584] Ibid. 3:4.

The Alter of Slabodka, Rav Nosson Tzvi Finkel, strenuously disagreed, and embraced a completely different approach to the Decalogue: "The way of the world precedes the Torah."[585] Do we need a Torah to command us not to deny God, not to murder, not to steal, not to testify falsely? That is common sense! Common sense tells us not to commit those acts. Does it make sense to say that God took us out of Egypt, performed for us miracles and wonders, and gathered one nation at Mount Sinai at which He revealed Himself – all to say "you shall not murder," and other matters that are elementary to any thinking person?

Rather, the Torah aimed higher – or at least aimed higher for us. The Torah starts its real teaching only when "the way of the world" does not suffice. The prohibitions of the Torah are meant literally, but not only literally – they are meant for us to probe deeper into our natures and uproot the impulses that drives us in that direction.

Therefore, our Sages taught that not only is idolatry forbidden in the literal sense, but also that habitually becoming angry[586] or exhibiting arrogance[587] is tantamount to idolatry. Or, embarrassing someone publicly is the equivalent of murdering him.[588] The Alter of Slabodka took for granted that the flagrant, brazen violations of the Torah could not occur – who could be so uncouth? His focus was on the unconscious, on the inner world of the Jew, on his thoughts, feelings and passions.

Shlomo Hamelech said of the words of the Torah: "Bind them on your necks, and inscribe them on the tablets of your hearts."[589] We must always wear the Torah like a shiny necklace, so people should see and admire it. That requires *more* than merely not murdering, stealing or desecrating Shabbat, but rather that people should see the Torah come alive in our personalities. To "inscribe them on the tablets of [our] hearts" means not only to do or not to do as the Torah commands, but a higher level: to *be*, to have the Torah penetrate one's interior being. That was the heart of the acceptance of the Torah at Sinai more than thirty-three centuries ago, and remains the heart of the acceptance of Torah by each individual today.

---

[585] "*Derech eretz kadma l'Torah*," found in similar form ("*Kadma derech eretz et haTorah*") in Midrash Vayikra Rabba 9:3.

[586] *Zohar* I, Breisheet 27b.

[587] Masechet Sota 4b.

[588] Masechet Bava Metzia 59a.

[589] Proverbs 3:3.

Torah from Heaven

You have all seen that I spoke to you from heaven. (Shemot 20:19)

The definitive aspect of the Revelation was not necessarily the substance of the laws, as important as they are for human progress, but primarily their divine origin. Rambam classifies this as the eighth fundamental principle of Judaism – "that the Torah we have in our possession today is the Torah we received from Moshe, and all of it came from the Almighty."[590]

The divine origin of Torah ultimately defines Jewish life as well as the very nature of our divine service. Rav Yaakov Ariel frames the essential question with precision: does man serve God according to the criteria and moral norms established for eternity by Him, as acceptance of the divine origin of Torah implies? Or does man serve himself and his own ethical conclusions that will vary from person to person, generation to generation and locale to locale, as a rejection of that principle requires?[591]

How that fundamental question is answered – whether man will be theocentric or anthropocentric in his moral framework – is *the* critical determinant of the core and consistency of our value system. There are people who believe in God's existence and His providence but reject His laws and moral code. They cannot bring themselves to subordinate their will to that of a Higher Authority and so perceive God as the Creator of life but not its Governor. Often that reluctance stems from arrogance, but not always; it can also be a reflection of awareness of man's innate potential in the realms of reason, knowledge and morality.

The fact that we witnessed "that I spoke to you from heaven" – the only divine revelation to an entire nation in all of history – sets the Torah apart as the word of God. Millions of non-Jews also recognize the Revelation experienced by the Jewish nation, but it poses a special obligation on Jews to never let the reality of that event slip from our consciousness. Ramban even posits that we are commanded as one of the 613 commandments not to forget the Revelation at Sinai – what we as a nation saw with our own eyes – but to always keep the idea vibrant and relevant.[592]

---

[590] Rambam, Mishna, Sanhedrin 10:1.
[591] *Me'Ohelei Torah*, pp. 123–24.
[592] *Hasagot haRamban* to Rambam's *Sefer Hamitzvot*, Mitzvot She'shachach Harav ("Prohibitions the Rambam Forgot"), Mitzvot Lo Taaseh 2.

The root of personal responsibility rests on our awareness that God created us in His image and communicated to us His moral code that regulates our personal lives and our interactions with others. No other idea is more profoundly important to mankind, and no other idea bears such momentous consequences for our lives and our world.

Fairness

And Moshe said to the people, "Do not be afraid, for God has come in order to test you…" (Shemot 20:17)

There are people who often lament that "life is unfair." Certainly, children can be born into poverty or affluence, freedom or tyranny, into families where knowledge is prized or others in which knowledge is scorned. There are children and adults whose native lands are wracked by war, poverty, disease and repression – and others who live in tranquility, prosperity, health and luxury – all through no fault, and sometimes no choice, of their own.

In our world, there is unfairness of opportunity, geography, intellectual gifts, material attainments, physical prowess; it is a world of unfairness. And there is unfairness of levels of perception – some trials we see coming, or we know will come; others pounce on us suddenly, without warning. Yet we pay homage to "the Rock, Whose works are perfect, for His ways are all just."[593] Those who affirm that God micromanages the world and all its affairs bow our heads in submission to the greatness of God and His inscrutability.

The concept of "fairness" is a moral one and applies only to the world of human interaction and not to creation itself. Regarding the physical world – and the infinite variety of circumstances that can befall a human being, both good and bad – we say that we cannot control, for the most part, what happens to us. *We can only control how we respond.* No person is immune from the travails of life nor does one get to choose the particular challenge he would want. This is how our Sages urged us to look at life and the variety of ordeals that come our way.

Ramban explained eloquently in his commentary on this verse that "fortunate is the man who withstands his trials, because there is no creature that is not tested. The wealthy are tested to see whether they will open their hands to the poor, and the poor are tested to see whether they can endure

---

[593] Devarim 32:4.

suffering."[594] The robust are tested to see how they will utilize their vigor, and the frail with how they will respond to their frailties; the free and the unfree, the young and the old, the male and the female – we are all put in a variety of situations to measure our responses, our faith, our commitment, our receptivity to others and our loyalty to the Creator. Life is a revolving door of experiences that challenge our faith, test the limits of our empathy, expand the horizons of our goodness and challenge us to assume responsibility for our personal destinies.

---

[594] Ramban, Shemot 20:16. In context, Moshe tells the people that God is subjecting them to the ultimate test. Having witnessed His revelation to an entire nation, can they dedicate themselves to being God's cherished possession on earth?

Mishpatim

The Mentsch

And these are the laws that you will place before them. (Shemot 21:1)

Rashi comments that the conjunctive *vav* (meaning "and") implies that these laws "add to the prior ones; just as the prior ones were from Sinai, so too these are from Sinai."[595] There are fifty-three *mitzvot* contained in this Torah portion, and thousands of laws that are derived therefrom. Why would we think that these are any less divine than the ones God spoke to the entire nation at the Revelation? The whole Torah is of divine origin!

The answer presents itself as we study the portion. The various topics discussed – the Hebrew slave and maidservant, the laws of torts and borrowing, criminal law and procedure – do not seem "religious" as we commonly understand the term. Where do we find the divine inspiration in something as mundane as the case of the goring ox? Certainly such rules are needed for a civilized society, but are they inherently religious notions? All societies formulate laws to deal with such matters.

We return again to the fundamental concept of "*derech eretz kadma laTorah*" (the way of the world precedes the Torah). In this context it means, simply, being a *mentsch*.[596] A *mentsch* is a person with *derech eretz* who embodies "*derech eretz kadma laTorah*." To have *derech eretz* doesn't simply mean to comport oneself with proper etiquette as colloquially understood today, although that is certainly part of it. It means being part of the civilized world – to act decently, morally, to have respect for others. *Derech eretz* means

---

[595] Rashi, Shemot 21:1.
[596] See Rabbi Berel Wein and Rabbi Warren Goldstein, "Being a Mensch," in *The Legacy: Teachings for Life from the Great Lithuanian Rabbis* (Jerusalem: Toby Press, 2013), for an exposition of this ideal.

earning a living, maintaining personal hygiene, dealing honestly with others, and developing good character.

The sense of being part of the world with others is indispensable to Torah – it "precedes the Torah." The Torah can never take root in a person without it; on the contrary, Torah in possession of one who holds himself aloof from the world or condescends to his peers will be corrupted.

The thousands of details that govern Jewish civil law only find relevance in people who are out in the world, and can only be tools for perfection for people who are engaged in *derech eretz*. The Mishna states that "whoever has [knowledge of] Torah and Mishna, and *derech eretz*, will not quickly sin."[597] Through *derech eretz*, each person makes a profound contribution to the world, and without it (and without Torah and Mishna) we are not even considered civilized.[598]

Somehow, we have gotten off the track. Many people suggest that segregation from the outside world is the Jewish ideal. Perhaps that notion can be traced to the truism that the world can be a hazardous place for spiritual growth. Out there in the world, we are going to run into unsavory people, and occasionally their oxen and cars, and deal with employees and employers, borrowers and lenders, thieves and tortfeasors, and even witches (22:17) and other mean and lowly people that we would never encounter in the house of study. And we are going to be tempted to respond in kind – to look at *derech eretz* as a religious discretionary area, a free-fly zone, where what we *feel* is right and just is more important to us than what *is* right or just. And we are going to be tempted to say – "what does God have to do with any of this? I know how to handle this situation on my own."

Rashi informs us that the "and" in "And these laws" shows us that they add to the prior ones; "just as the prior ones are from Sinai, so too these laws."[599] The same God Who commanded us about Shabbat, homicide and honoring parents is the One Who, at the very same time, at Sinai, also instructed us how to treat others, how to deal with our enemy's donkey collapsing under its burden, how to be gracious, and how to be *mentschen* in a world where the savages often have the upper hand.

---

[597] Masechet Kiddushin 1:10. Rambam defines *derech eretz* here as "social interactions that are refined and dignified," whereas Rav Ovadia Bertinoro understands *derech eretz* in a business context, "honest dealings with others."

[598] Masechet Kiddushin 1:10.

[599] Rashi, Shemot 21:1.

The extent to which we comply with those laws is a truer indication of our acceptance of the Torah than any other of the Torah's laws. The ritual laws are a critical component of Jewish life, but not as indicative of a person's true spiritual level as is compliance with the civil laws that govern relationships between people. One can attempt to purchase righteousness on the cheap by embracing stringencies in *kashrut* and the like. As the Talmud states, "whoever wants to be considered pious should fulfill the laws of damages."[600] Adherence to those laws creates the *mentsch* on whom Jewish society depends and which the God-fearing Jew yearns to be called.

SLAVE MENTALITY

> *When you acquire a Hebrew slave, he shall work for six years, and in the seventh he shall go free, without payment.... If the slave says, "I love my master, my wife and my children; I will not go free," then his master brings him to the judges and brings him to the door or doorpost [of the court] and his master shall pierce his ear with an awl, and he shall be his servant forever. (Shemot 21:2, 5–6)*

We shall soon see that this passage contains of the most important lessons for our study, but it first behooves us to examine slavery itself. The modern reader often recoils from the Torah's discussion of slavery, an institution that is rightly construed as immoral and degrading. It was especially so in the ancient world, and even in the modern world until very recently. Slavery dehumanizes and degrades other human beings. How did the Torah ever countenance such an institution?

It is important to remember that the Torah was given to a nation that lived in a milieu with social norms that were considered quite reasonable. It was to that world – and the Jewish people who lived in it – that the Torah was given and had to be accepted. Every nation had slaves that were essentially treated as chattel and brutalized; certainly the Jewish people, just weeks after their own liberation from slavery, knew that. Slavery was a given; what the Torah did was refine and limit its extent and application, such that the institution in a Torah context was unrecognizable to the commonly practiced forms of slavery then extant.

---

[600] Masechet Bava Kama 30a.

For example, the Hebrew slave was not a slave per se, but usually a debtor paying off his obligations.[601] Even so, his tenure was limited to six years. He had to be fed and housed commensurate with the host family's wealth, exactly the same as other members of the family, leading the Talmud to declare that "he who acquires a Hebrew slave has acquired a master for himself."[602] The more common Canaanite slave was essentially an indentured servant, and even obligated in some aspects of Jewish ritual life. As the Torah will soon note, if the master strikes his slave even accidentally and knocks out even a tooth, the slave goes free.[603] That prevented the physical abuse of slaves that was so common in ancient and recent times.

Without sugarcoating the institution too much, it would not be far-fetched to posit that slavery in the general world was intended to demean and debase human beings who were often considered subhuman, while the Torah's view of slavery was a convention that was intended to take the public's outcasts and misfits and civilize them so they could properly function in decent society.

The Hebrew slave who is the subject of this passage was mandated to perceive his years of servitude as finite, or he had to suffer the indignity of a perforated ear. "God says, 'The ear that heard at Sinai that the Children of Israel are servants to Me, and not servants to servants, and still this one went and acquired another master for himself, that ear should be pierced.'"[604] Why would a rational human being choose servitude over freedom?

The physical abuse usually associated with slavery diverts us from the enormous "benefits" that the life of slavery provides. Essentially, the slave is responsible for nothing. He need not make any decisions in his life about anything. His time belongs to his master, as do his possessions. He need not support his wife and children; that is his master's obligation.[605] He is fed, clothed, and housed by his master, and if he is unmarried, he can even be mated by his master to a Canaanite maidservant, an indication of the degraded state to which he has fallen.[606] Every major decision in his life is delegated to someone else.

---

[601] Rashi, Shemot 21:2, s.v. "*ki tikneh*."
[602] Masechet Kiddushin 20a.
[603] Shemot 21:27.
[604] Masechet Kiddushin 22b; Rashi, Shemot 21:6.
[605] Masechet Kiddushin 22a.
[606] Rashi, Shemot 21:4, based on Mechilta. If the slave is married to a Jewish woman, the master has no control over her at all.

That is slavery – and is that state of affairs really so uncommon today? There are people who will delegate major decisions in their lives to others – career, choice of spouse, marriage, community, when to have children and how many, names of children, investments and other business decisions, medical care and all other personal issues. Often, in segments of our society, the decisions are delegated to spiritual leaders or mystics, but the bottom line is the same: a person who chooses not to take responsibility for his own life is a slave, and a slave to human beings is an inferior servant of God, if indeed he is a divine servant at all.

That typology is often cultivated in socialist societies, in which there is an expectation that government will care for a person's needs from cradle to grave. He need not own anything, nor is personal ambition a desirable attribute. The individual trapped – sometimes by his own choice – in such a system lives a static rather than dynamic life.

A young person once explained to me, in the form of a question: "why should I have to make a decision about anything if someone else can make it for me?" The answer is that some people desire slavery – a slave has all decisions made for him – but the Torah wants us to be free people because only a free person can be engaged in Torah.[607] The adult, the free person, thinks through the issues, and seeks advice and guidance from family, Rabbis, experts, wise people and then decides. To yearn for someone else to make a decision *for you* is embracing the life of the slave, and nothing less than an attempt to relieve yourself of the consequences of your own decisions. If someone else decides for me, then I can never be wrong, I am never responsible, I am never accountable – it is always someone else.

One who forfeits his decision making to others – or voluntarily transfers it – has wittingly or unwittingly chosen a life of servitude. Freedom and free will are divine gifts to mankind. The former is a natural right, and the latter is the distinguishing mark of humanity. God afforded us all the tools necessary to enable us to make our own decisions and to live as free people – functioning intellects, the support system of family and community, and even the wise counsel of spiritual leaders who should guide and inspire rather than categorically determine the personal choices of others.

---

[607] Masechet Avot 6:2. The Bnei Yissaschar (Maamarei Chodesh Nisan 4:4) explains that God brought us out of Egypt to freedom so that we should be "truly free people, beholden only to Him, His Torah and His commandments." That is true freedom. Those who are still enslaved to other entities – people, desires and especially to the pursuit of wealth – physically "left Egypt in vain" because they are still slaves to Pharaoh. Only free people could accept the Torah.

"For the Children of Israel are servants to Me; they are My servants whom I brought forth from the land of Egypt."[608] We do ourselves a disservice and undermine our very humanity when we choose servitude and flight from personal responsibility rather than embrace freedom and accountability that enables us to succeed, and occasionally stumble, on our own. That is the only way that we can live *our* lives rather than have others live *their* lives through us. In that sense, the institution of slavery is not a relic of a bygone era but is still very much with us, in concept and application.

Flying Solo

If he comes by himself, he will leave by himself; if he is the husband to a woman, then his wife shall leave with him. (Shemot 21:3)

The Torah uses an interesting expression for the single, unmarried man: *b'gapo*, "by himself," but literally meaning "like a wing." The single person flies with one wing; that is to say, he lacks roots in the community of Israel. Marriage, by definition, creates roots with other neighbors and families that soon coalesce into a community, and the conglomerate of communities constitutes the nation. It is no great secret that a collection of singles struggles to form a cohesive community, and even to contribute to the greater community; that type of involvement usually stems from the family structure.

Certainly, this characterization primarily refers to singles-by-choice and not involuntary singles whose marriages have ended through death or divorce. And it is clear that many singles seek to make a contribution to society and serve the Jewish people in any number of ways. But single status does impose limitations, which is why the Torah is biased in favor of marriage, and why the contemporary norm that sees young people often delaying marriage well into their twenties and thirties in order to pursue their career ambitions or "find themselves" does not accord with traditional Torah values.

Marriage is not for the selfish, nor is it an institution that concerns only two people, man and woman. The Jewish marriage is a communal event and a national celebration. Thus, the Ashkenazi bridegroom customarily receives an *aliya* to the Torah the Shabbat before his wedding (Sefardi bridegrooms are called to the Torah the Shabbat after the wedding); that allows the community

---

[608] Vayikra 25:55.

to celebrate with him. The wedding ceremony and the recitation of the special seven blessings both require the presence of a *minyan*, a quorum of ten adult males who symbolically represent the nation of Israel.

The responsibility to marry and have a family is not just the product of self-actualization, or the fulfillment of a paternal/maternal need. It serves the national interest, as families are the basic building blocks of the nation.

One who is unmarried can fly – he/she has a "wing" – but to fly solo leaves us incomplete and without the partner who completes and complements us. It leaves the nation deficient. Conversely, one who marries fills his life with happiness, blessing and goodness, fulfills God's will and strengthens the people of Israel.[609]

Man and His Torts

> *If a man smites another and he dies, he shall surely be put to death.… If a man shall uncover a pit or if a man shall dig a pit and not cover it, and an ox or donkey falls into it, the owner of the pit shall pay restitution… (Shemot 21:12, 33)*

Our Sages articulated man's responsibility for his conduct toward others in one pithy expression: "*Adam mu'ad la'olam*" – a human being is considered permanently warned as to the consequences of his actions.[610] In short, we are always responsible for our deeds, unlike an animal, which is considered to be a *tam*, innocent or unwarned, until repeated conduct labels the animal (really, the animal's owner) as "warned," and full liability results.[611]

The extent of human liability depends on the nature of the conduct – whether intentional, negligent or accidental. A complete accident – caused by force majeure or an action that is compelled by others – exempts a person from any liability.[612] The intentional murderer is executed, but the criminally negligent killer who was careless in his conduct and took a human life is nonetheless responsible for his deed. He is exiled to the city of refuge and banished from civilized society.[613] The limits of liability vary – but the liability

---

[609] See Masechet Yevamot 62b.
[610] Masechet Bava Kama 3b.
[611] See Yalkut Shimoni, Mishpatim 339, for some distinctions between the "warned" and "unwarned" animal.
[612] Masechet Bava Kama 28b; Rambam, *Hilchot Issurei Bi'ah* 1:9.
[613] Shemot 21:13.

is there, and in some cases where human adjudication is impossible, then one is liable to Heaven and God works out the details, "caus[ing the harm] to come to his hand."[614]

The Torah takes a dim view of people who blame others for the harm they themselves caused or could have prevented. The legal system is based on the fundamental principle that people can and must guard themselves and their property from inflicting damage on other people or things. It is an elementary rule of life. To say "it was an accident!" is not always an acceptable excuse. The frightening number of people who drive vehicles while intoxicated itself testifies to the lack of concern and lack of personal responsibility common in modern life.

Every human being is on permanent notice to pay attention to his limbs, clubs, axes, ladders, oxen and vehicles to ensure that another person does not suffer from his carelessness. And that diligence recognizes our obligation to God and to our fellow man, created as we were in God's image.

An Eye for an Eye

An eye for an eye, a tooth for a tooth, a hand for a hand, a foot for a foot. (Shemot 21:24)

This classic biblical punishment is derided by modern "moralists" as primitive and cruel. Of course, it is well known that this measure-for-measure punishment was never imposed on the guilty, even in pre-Talmudic times, but was always interpreted as requiring monetary compensation for the tortious loss of organs or limbs. Indeed, there are several hints in the verse that indicate that the tortfeasor should pay compensation rather than lose his own limb or organ.[615]

The question is obvious: If the Torah never intended this type of bodily retribution to be exacted from the guilty, why was the mandate phrased in

---

[614] Rashi, ibid, s.v. "*v'ha'Elokim ina l'yado*," in which God causes one who murdered without witnesses and therefore cannot be prosecuted to come to an inn where he becomes the victim of a criminally negligent homicide, perpetrated by one who killed negligently but also without any eyewitnesses. Each now receives the appropriate punishment.

[615] E.g., the word *tachat* (for, or in place of) is elsewhere in the Torah used to mean "compensation" (Masechet Bava Kama 83b); additionally, the letters *ayin-yud-nun* (eye) are followed in the *aleph-bet* by *peh-kaf-samech*, which, rearranged, spell out *kesef* (money; Gaon of Vilna, cited in *Tallelei Orot*, Shemot 21:24).

such literal terms? Why didn't the Torah simply express the law itself, as in "monetary compensation for an eye," etc.?

Rav Ovadia Sforno answered that the punishment *should have been* literal.[616] An "eye for an eye" is the appropriate payback for someone who was so incautious that his actions cost another person his sight or the use of a limb. But for the impossibility of perfect justice being executed through this type of penalty – e.g., what if a one-eyed person injured a person with two eyes, or how do we measure partial loss of vision or utility? – the punishment for such laxity would have been literal, measure for measure.

The unvarnished truth is that the tortfeasor herein *deserves* to lose his limb or organ, and that is why the Torah highlighted his liability in the most graphic language possible. One should never think that money is full compensation and the harm inflicted is thereby forgotten after payment, as if now bygones are bygones. The money is a necessity but not full atonement. Just as an animal offering is really brought in place of the one who offers it, compensation is proffered in lieu of the warranted penalty.

This idea is underscored by the Talmudic opinion that maintains that the eye that is evaluated for compensation is not the eye of the victim (which is the final law) but the eye of the victimizer![617] In other words, the assessment is not based on how much the eye is worth to the victim, but instead on how much the victimizer would pay to keep his own eye. Invariably, that evaluation would be much higher. Even though that is not the *halacha*,[618] the message is clear: *responsibility for one's actions is absolute*. Grace is offered here for technical but not moral reasons. One who blinds or wounds another deserves to be treated in kind, and that will ensure due care in his dealings with others.

De-fueling the Fire

If a fire breaks out and finds thorns, and stacks of grain, standing corn or a field is consumed, the one who kindled the fire shall make full restitution. (Shemot 22:5)

Perhaps even deadlier and more destructive than the arsonist of property is the social arsonist who stokes the flames of discord, acrimony and rancor, sometimes for cause and sometimes for pleasure.

---

[616] Sforno, Shemot 21:24.

[617] Masechet Bava Kama 84a.

[618] See generally, Rambam, *Hilchot Nizkei Mamon* 11:1; the reason is that the victim needs to be made whole for his loss, so the valuation is made based on his diminished state.

The prolific Chida expounded our verse homiletically as relating to the disputes that occasionally roil Jewish communal life. "If a person initiates a conflict, and then the quarrel is seized by other people or groups [thorns] and expanded, such that it consumes righteous people [stacks of grain] or people's wealth [standing corn], or causes a decrease in Torah study [a field], then you should not think that the one who *began* the conflict is not liable for all that followed after his initial attack. Rather, those who first sow discord are responsible [shall make full restitution] for all escalations, even those they could not necessarily foresee. They pay double for what they began and what unfolded later."[619]

The primary guilt for any dispute clearly rests on those who started it, even if the direction of the argument takes on an unanticipated direction. They cannot later say that they did not intend that, but it all spiraled out of control. But it takes two to quarrel, and each side is responsible for its share in the dispute and in the resolution. Those who constantly bicker, criticize and find fault with anything and everything bear primary responsibility for the tensions that are created, but others have a concomitant obligation to cool passions, defuse those tensions, and make peace among couples, families and communities.

The Optional Requirement

> *If you lend money to My people, to the poor with you, you shall neither be a demanding creditor nor levy interest upon him. (Shemot 22:24)*

Rashi comments that this is one of the three places in the Torah where the conjunctive *im* (if) is not optional but actually means "when," as in "when you lend money to My people." That the impoverished will occasionally need loans from the well-to-do is a given and obligatory, and not simply a discretionary act of kindness. So why then does the Torah utilize the equivocal language of *im*?

The Maharal explains that there are certain commandments that, although mandatory, must be performed willingly and with a full heart. If one lends money to a fellow Jew only because the Torah commands it, as if he is merely fulfilling a divine decree, then his performance of the *mitzva* is flawed. Rather,

---

[619] Rav Chaim Yosef David Azulai, eighteenth-century Israel and Europe, in his *Pnei David*, Parshat Mishpatim.

"It is required that the commandment of lending money be done voluntarily and goodheartedly."[620] Consequently, the word *im* is used, implying that there is an optional aspect to this commandment.

Nevertheless, the Torah does not intend that the *mitzva* should be completely elective, for then the possibility exists that a society like Sodom could emerge in which such acts of kindness were nonexistent. The performance of this deed cannot be left to the discretion of the individual, and yet it cannot be fulfilled with a sense of coercion either. How do we navigate that balance?

Rav Kook wrote that the ideal is self-arousal – that a person activate his natural ethical sense but then allow the Torah to expand, enlarge and direct his good instincts into the most productive sphere possible.[621] Just as a person who feels forced to perform acts of kindness will eventually do them grudgingly, so too one who merely relies on his own good instincts will eventually find them leading him in an improper and unwholesome direction. "It is forbidden for a God-fearing person to allow his natural ethical sense to be displaced."[622]

To serve God properly requires that we assume responsibility for both our attitude and our performance, and especially when it concerns our responsibility for other people.

The Cult of the Victim

Do not glorify the destitute by showing preference in his grievance. (Shemot 23:3)

This admonition challenges one of the hoary shibboleths of liberal society – the idea that the poor have ipso facto been mistreated by their contemporaries and therefore deserve special treatment in every aspect of civil life, including the legal system. This patronizing attitude demeans and demoralizes the poor, who, after all, suffer from a condition that can usually be ameliorated by the opportunities of a free society. Showing favoritism to the poor in a lawsuit – deciding in his favor, as Rashi says here, because he is poor and the other party is rich – corrupts the notion of equality under the law that functions as one of the foundations of civil society. Worse, it fosters in the poor the expectation of sympathetic but biased consideration in other areas of life and, in effect, glamorizes the life of the victim.

---

[620] *Gur Aryeh*, Shemot 20:22.
[621] *Musar Hakodesh*, Rosh Davar, 27.
[622] Ibid. See Rav Yaakov Ariel's *Me'ohalei Torah*, p. 130.

In truth, as Rav Hirsch comments here, outside the court of law nothing could be a greater *mitzva* than showing great honor to the poor. But inside the courtroom, both parties must be treated alike, and one cannot render verdict in favor of the downtrodden simply because he is downtrodden, if the facts and the law do not support such a verdict.

Indeed, the notion of judging people based on external characteristics – not on their virtues or lack of same but on their wealth, race, height, sex, status, etc., should be anathema to all thinking people. To bend the law in favor of a particular group is promoting equality for some at the expense of inequality to others, a morally dubious proposition.

Victimization, and the sense of entitlement it creates, is the very antithesis of personal responsibility. Those who embrace it, and those who advocate for them, are prolonging their suffering and doing them a great disservice. They would do better to encourage true fairness, self-help and moral discipline. It is far preferable to temper the letter of the law with personal kindness than it is to distort the law in the first place.[623]

The Burden of Enmity

> *If you see your enemy's donkey crouching under its burden, you may not refrain from helping him; you shall surely help him. (Shemot 23:5)*

Later the Torah will discuss helping the donkey's owner load the burden back onto the fallen donkey,[624] but here the emphasis is on removing the burden that rests on the donkey of one's enemy. Certainly, the avoidance of inflicting pain on animals is meritorious, and according to many opinions even a Torah commandment.[625] But why would a Jew consider another Jew an enemy, and how can that be rectified?

The Talmud offers perhaps the only cogent and justifiable circumstance wherein one can legitimately hate another Jew: if he sees him sin (there are no other witnesses), warns him against a recurrence, and the warning is blithely ignored.[626] But even that situation – with all its practical limitations –

---

[623] There are many stories of great rabbinic judges who ruled against the poor but then gave them money to pay for the judgment. This is the law being upheld while simultaneously allowing for personal compassion.

[624] Devarim 22:4.

[625] Rema, *Shulchan Aruch*, Choshen Mishpat 272:9.

[626] Masechet Pesachim 113b; Rambam, *Hilchot Rotzeach* 13:14; *Shulchan Aruch*, Choshen Mishpat

is designed by the Torah to be temporary, not permanent, and the Torah's majesty is apparent in the methods it offers in order to alleviate such righteous passions. One such method is this commandment.

The Midrash expounds the verse in Psalms extolling God's qualities: "Mighty is the King, He loves justice. You established uprightness…"[627] How does God maintain both "justice" – the law – and "uprightness" – a sense of fairness? The Midrash continues with, as an example, this very *mitzva*: "A man is traveling on the road and sees his enemy's donkey crushed under its burden. He goes [since the Torah demands it] and helps his enemy. The enemy then goes to an inn and wonders, 'I thought that person was my enemy [and here he helped me]!' What caused these two enemies to become friends? The Torah…; thus does God 'establish uprightness.'"[628]

This reconciliation occurs notwithstanding the "justification" for the original hatred! The Torah gives us a mechanism whereby we can resolve all our feuds, and certainly the ones that are based on trivialities that have little if any justification. We need not persist in our anger at personal slights; we can let go. The mighty person – the one who really is able to subdue his inclinations[629] – is "the person who can turn his enemy into his friend."[630]

And the best tool to let go is to perform an act of kindness for the other person. It immediately reduces tensions and enables both people to see their erstwhile foes in a different light. It also reduces stress that impairs our health. The means to diminish and then eradicate animosity toward others was provided to us by God, Who "established uprightness" as the cornerstone of His Torah. It is our responsibility to embrace it, internalize it and act upon it.

Living in the Moment

> *And God said to Moshe, "Ascend to Me on the mountain and be there…" (Shemot 24:12)*

The Baal Shem Tov wrote that a person *is* where his thoughts *are*. The request that Moshe climb Mount Sinai and "be there" – for forty days, as Rashi

---

[272:11.]

[627] Psalms 99:4.

[628] Yalkut Shimoni, Tehillim 99, remez 852.

[629] Masechet Avot 4:2.

[630] Avot d'Rabbi Natan, chapter 23.

comments[631] – meant that Moshe had to be entirely there. All his thoughts and energies were devoted to ascertaining God's word and receiving the Torah.

Rav Kook explained the verse "in all your ways you shall know Him"[632] as meaning that man serves God in a variety of different settings – in prayer, Torah study, *mitzvot*, acts of kindness, family life, business, etc. – but in each setting, man must be completely present and not have his mind diverted to other possibilities.[633] At prayer, we focus on the prayers, and not on a Torah question we are pondering – and vice versa. When we are doing something, we should not be doing or thinking of something else that could be done at that moment. Divine service requires no multitasking but instead prefers a singular focus on the matter at hand.

It is human nature, but often a sign of immaturity, to want to do something else when we are doing anything. But whatever we are engaged in at the moment is the matter on which we should concentrate. It makes as little sense to think of family when we are at work as it does to think of work when we are with family, but how often do we succumb to that mistake? Often, a person learning one area of Torah will be filled with a desire to stop and learn some other area of Torah, with that desire arising with each new area of study.

"To everything there is a season, and there is a time for each desire under the heavens."[634] The rhythms of Jewish life are regulated by the Torah, and each season or event provides us with the appropriate means of divine worship. To sit in the *succa* on Pesach is a contrived and ultimately empty spiritual experience. In each sphere of life, we find opportunities to serve God – in the home and the synagogue, in the workplace and house of study. But those opportunities cannot be commingled or they are essentially lost.

Personal responsibility, in that sense, means to live in the moment, to seize the opportunity to serve God in line with the demands of that moment. Rabbis, for example, are often confronted with the necessity of officiating at funerals and weddings, and sometimes within minutes of each other. The only way to way to handle such a range of emotions is to exercise control over them, and be 100 percent present at each event. As Moshe was told, "and [you will] be there." Wherever we are, we take the most apposite thoughts and feelings, and we are "there" with all of our heart.

Certainly, it takes self-control, discipline and willpower, but those are all staples of the Torah personality.

---

[631] Rashi, Shemot 24:12.
[632] Proverbs 3:6.
[633] Rav Avraham Yitzchak Kook, *Musar Avicha* 2:2.
[634] Kohelet 3:1.

Terumah

THE INNER WORLD OF PRAYER

Speak to the Children of Israel and have them take for Me a teruma offering; from each person whose heart is stirred to donate shall you take My teruma. (Shemot 25:2)

The mandate here is unique in that God demands that the donor's "heart [be] stirred" to contribute to the Mishkan (Tabernacle), otherwise the offer is unwelcome. Few commandments are similarly circumscribed. We are never ordered to observe Shabbat only if our heart is in it, eat kosher food only when our motivation is pure, or learn Torah when we are in the mood. Those are all absolutes; but here, the Torah constrains those who will perform this *mitzva* and authorizes acceptance of their donations only when they are heartfelt. Why?

The divine service implicit in Temple service and its modern substitute, prayer, are dependent on and defined by the engagement of the heart. The Talmud asks, "Which is deemed service of the heart?" and answers, "Prayer."[635] To connect with God through the intellect and the emotions requires more than deeds; it requires accessing our inner world.

There is a passage in our daily prayers that underscores this prerequisite. In the blessing of *avoda* (service) in the daily Amida, we recite, "*U'tefillatam b'ahava tekabel b'ratzon.*"[636] This is alternately translated in the popular *siddurim* today as "You should accept their prayer with love and favor" (ArtScroll); "accept their prayer, lovingly and willingly" (Metzuda); or "accept in love and favor their prayer" (Koren). But none of the translations are precise, as the

---

[635] Masechet Taanit 2b.
[636] The issue of whether this is an independent clause or linked to the prior phrase "*v'ishei Yisrael,*" which is debated by the early authorities, is not germane to this discussion.

clause actually reads "and their prayers [offered] with love, You should accept with favor."[637]

Clearly, the meaning here is different, and most pointed: our prayers have to be offered with love. If they are not offered with love but by rote and without feeling or thought, then how can we ask God to find favor in them? Prayer that is not offered out of love is mere words, and a contribution that is given to the Mishkan from which the heart is absent – that is, given perfunctorily, without feeling, sensitivity and gratitude – is both unwelcome and unworthy.

Rav Kook wrote that the study of Torah is considered divine service with our minds and intellects.[638] Torah study develops and perfects our minds in line with God's word. But prayer is divine service with our emotions, which is another dimension of the human personality. To be sure, the intellect is more reliable and more exalted than the emotions, and so Torah study is therefore the word of God coming to us. But the emotions are usually a more credible determinant of who we are and of how we perceive ourselves. We sometimes *know* things that we do not internalize, that do not animate us and that do not even speak to us. It is the "inner light" that we bring to our prayers that renders them either vacuous and mechanical or meaningful and heartfelt.

That inner world is known only to us (and to God). The externals of prayer – the words, the melody, and for the so-inclined, the swaying – are easily faked. Too often, those external manifestations of prayer are all we see and all we ask for, in our children and students, to their detriment. The inner world – of thoughts, aspirations and values – is the very essence of prayer and our relationship to holy places, like the Mishkan, the Beit Hamikdash or the synagogue. It is our direct line to God.

We are responsible for that inner world, which is our core, and it is the greatest indicator of our spiritual state.

---

[637] See Rav Shimon Schwab, *Rav Schwab on Prayer* (Jerusalem: Mesorah, 2001), p. 506, for a similar formulation. "Love" and "favor" are separated here by "you shall accept," not linked together as they are, for example, in the Shabbat prayers: *"v'Shabbat kodshecha b'ahava u'v'ratzon hinchaltanu."*

[638] *Orot Hakodesh* 1:252.

The Precious Stones of Individual Initiative

Shoham stones and stones for the settings for the Apron (Ephod) and the Breastplate… (Shemot 25:7)

The Mishkan required many different elements of animal, vegetable and mineral origin – gold, silver and copper, different skins and wools, oils and spices, and then a variety of precious stones: diamonds, emeralds, pearls, rubies and others "for the Apron and the Breastplate." Interestingly, these precious stones – the most expensive of the commodities used in the Tabernacle – are mentioned last, not first. We would have thought that if the Torah first mentions precious metals – gold and silver – instead of skins, it would have been more logical to start with the most valuable items needed. So why were the precious stones mentioned last?

And from where did a nation of newly liberated slaves procure precious metals and stones? The gold, silver and copper were part of the spoils of the Egyptian army at the Red Sea.[639] What about the great variety of precious stones?

The Or Hachaim cites the Talmud that these precious stones were carried to the Jewish people from Heaven with the manna by the divine clouds, and literally fell into the hands of the princes who donated them to the Mishkan.[640] "Since the stones came directly from God's table, they acquired them without much exertion or toil, and donated them without feeling any out-of-pocket loss. For this reason, the stones were listed after all the other components of the Mishkan."[641] The contributions to the Mishkan had to come from the heart, from a voluntary, benevolent spirit – and these stones did not, so they were mentioned last in the Torah.

It is a basic truism that if a person does not work for something and toil and struggle himself – if there is no "sweat equity" – then he can lack a full appreciation for it. Something you get without working for it is yours, but not really yours. There is a certain pleasure provided in "eat[ing] from the labor of your own hands."[642] Rav Chaim Shmulevitz quotes the fascinating and much

---

[639] Rashi, Shemot 15:21. Rashi also states that they also acquired the precious stones from the spoils of war.
[640] Masechet Yoma 75a.
[641] Or Hachaim, Shemot 25:7.
[642] Psalms 128:2.

ignored statement of the Talmud that a person prefers one measure of what he worked for himself than nine measures of what he can get from someone else.[643] "The labor of our own hands" is part of us. It represents the investment of time and energy, our most precious commodities. When we then give it away, it is a true measure of our generosity. Those who gave away their animals and their metals – which they had attained themselves – were on a higher level than the princes, who merely gave away stones that had fallen into their laps.

That "a person prefers one measure of his own" is a presumption in the Gemara, but is, sadly, widely ignored today. It is not only in financial matters that our "own measure" is sometimes less attractive than "the nine measures of our friend"; it is in life as well. To enjoy our "own measure" means seeking independence of thought and judgment on major personal decisions in life.

"A person prefers one measure that belongs to him than nine measures belonging to his friend." Character is developed through independent action, struggling in the arena of life, through success and failure and then success again. That is how one develops a personality and worldview, instead of just borrowing or renting the personality and worldview of someone else.

From the "*Shoham stones and stones for the settings,*" we learn that true worth is determined not by market value but by exertion and energy – the investment of all of our spiritual and emotional resources in life and its decisions, in service of God and pursuit of freedom according to the Torah. There are enough limitations in life without imposing others on ourselves. And only in that life of the free-willed Jew – who chooses to serve and to give and to help others and to learn Torah and do *mitzvot* – that every person finds his purpose in life and the divine presence finds its resting place on earth.

Our Torah

And you shall place into the Ark the [Tablets of] Testimony that I will give you. (Shemot 25:16)

The Tablets of Testimony on which the Decalogue was engraved that Moshe would receive from God were placed in the Holy Ark, constructed according to the most precise specifications: the Aron was composed of wood and gold alternating, three separate compartments topped by a *kaporet*, a cover itself made of gold with golden cherubs perched on top as guards. And that Ark was

---

[643] *Sichot Musar*, Parshat Terumah, pp. 211–14, citing Masechet Bava Metzia 38a.

housed inside a segregated area called the Holy of Holies, ten by ten cubits, partitioned off by a *parochet* (curtain), consisting of a variety of heavy wools that hung down from a bar that stretched across the top – itself covered by an array of thick animal skins. The Ark of Testimony was placed there, inside a small area to which one person would have access just one time a year.

It seems like a lot of effort for very little return. If Moshe went to such great lengths to bring down the tablets, which were "the handiwork of God" (32:16), then we might think that they should be featured more prominently in our divine service – an artifact that could always be seen and thereby inspire us. Instead, it was kept hidden, *never* to be taken out. By contrast, if a museum had a precious relic that was *never* displayed, such a museum would not attract visitors. So why were the tablets hidden?

Indeed, we treat our Torah scrolls in the same way. The Torah is also concealed from us, resting in the Holy Ark until we read from it. It is removed from the Ark with pomp and restored with ceremony. But, for the most part, it is out of sight.

This, of course, is intentional. The paradox of the Torah is that it was given to us, but it has to be protected from us as well. Men and women are often too eager to place their own imprint on the Torah, to redefine it – to reform it – in their image. If we had ready access to the Tablets of Testimony, it would not have been long before some brazen person came forward and begin chipping away at it – erasing some of the prohibitions while adding some of his own pet causes. Given the chance, man would carve his own initials on the *luchot*, notwithstanding that they were written with the "divine script" (32:16) and perhaps precisely *because* they were written with the "divine script."

Our Torah is the same way. Granted, the Torah "is not in Heaven,"[644] but that does not give man a license to distort the Torah and conform it to every modern trend and personal whim. We take the Torah out with great honor, walking it among us for people to touch and kiss – and then to put it back, away, so we cannot tamper with it, and so it thereby remains the immaculate word of God.

Once, in the Beit Hatalmud in Kelm (the renowned *musar* yeshiva), the student leading the public prayers accentuated the word *l'avdecha* (to serve You) in the phrase "and purify our hearts to *serve You* in truth." The *rosh yeshiva*, the Alter of Kelm, Rav Simcha Zissel Ziv, took him aside afterward and said if you want to emphasize one word, emphasize *b'emet* (in truth). The

---

[644] Devarim 30:12.

search for truth – the labyrinthine, tortuous, tangled search for truth – is much more indicative of our spiritual state than is our desire "to serve You." Serving God, unfortunately, is not always done "in truth." Divine service can at times be motivated by fear, guilt, desire for reward, self-aggrandizement, pleasure or the like – and not pursuit of truth.

The great *musar* sage Rav Elya Lopian wrote that the whole purpose of "and they shall make for Me a Sanctuary" (25:8) is for the Torah that rests in the Holy Ark. So, too, every Jew must make himself into a resting place for Torah.[645] "Prepare yourselves to learn Torah," the Mishna states.[646] It is not enough to learn Torah; first, we have to prepare ourselves to learn by internalizing respect, proper character traits, true ideas about Torah and the appropriate reverence for the word of God.

Only then can we be fitting vessels to receive the Torah and to serve God "in truth," and only then can we properly safeguard and transmit the Torah from generation to generation.

The Permanent Joys of Youth

> *And you shall make two cherubs of gold…and the cherubs shall have their wings spread upward, sheltering the cover with their wings, and their faces turned toward each other… (Shemot 25:18, 20)*

The cherubs rested atop the holiest object in Jewish life – the Holy Ark of the Covenant. For a Tabernacle that was designed to counter the allure of idolatry, it was certainly an unusual choice of representation in the Holy of Holies – images of children, infants even.[647] Our Sages discuss whether the cherubs had the appearance of a boy and a girl or that of two boys. But why were "two" necessary? Why not just one? And why does the Torah emphasize the unusual locution of *shnayim keruvim* for the "two cherubs" instead of the more commonly used *shnei keruvim*?

George Bernard Shaw, the Irish playwright, famously said that youth is wasted on the young. Rav Kook disagreed and pondering the purpose of youth, he raised this question: Is the function of youth just to prepare a person

---

[645] *Lev Eliyahu*, Parshat Terumah, pp. 200-6.
[646] Masechet Avot 2:17.
[647] Rashi, Shemot 25:18.

for adulthood – i.e., is youth just a bridge from a lower state to a higher state – or does youth have an inherent value, a sublime and mighty purpose all to itself?[648]

To those who perceive the essence of life as material productivity – doing work and earning money – then clearly youth is just a stepping-stone, and a young person is just a lump of clay that can be molded into a proletarian who serves others, produces and adds to society's material bounty. But for those who value purity above all else, youth is perhaps the most precious time of life. Our Sages averred that "the world is sustained only because of the breath of children who study Torah," because "it is without sin, pure and holy in its essence."[649] That purity of thought and of mind, the Gemara says, an adult – even the greatest of sages – cannot have. An adult becomes jaded, has seen and heard too much, is not easily impressed, and considers himself formed (if not perfected). Youth, Rav Kook maintained, is "a precious unit of life all to itself,"[650] and not merely a means to an end. Therefore, God says, "do not touch My anointed ones,"[651] the children who study Torah.[652]

That purity is what safeguards the Torah, and that is the image that adorns the cover that sits atop the Holy Ark – an image of innocence, wholesomeness and virtue.

But youth represents something else as well – something on which the Torah and Jewish life depend for its continuity and its revival in every generation: enthusiasm, exuberance, a willingness to embrace an ideal in its purest, undiluted form and a yearning to actualize it in the real world. That vibrancy is a positive force, notwithstanding that it occasionally signals a clash of generations. That enthusiasm is what enables nations to send young people into battle; that enthusiasm is what dispatches young Jewish teenagers to seize hilltops and protect the land of Israel even from their elders – despite great personal suffering and cost; that enthusiasm is what drives Jewish youngsters to eschew the allures and distractions of the modern world and focus their energy on Torah study and spiritual growth; and that enthusiasm ensures that an old nation does not weary, pack in its towel, and lose faith in its mission and its destiny.

---

[648] *Maamarei Hare'iya* I, p. 230.
[649] Masechet Shabbat 119b.
[650] *Maamarei Hare'iya* I, p. 230.
[651] I Chronicles 16:22.
[652] Masechet Shabbat 119b.

Those young people also adorn the Torah and guarantee its vitality. The Torah demands "two cherubs" – "two" as *shnayim* and not just *shnei*, because *shnei* implies a similarity, an identity – a pair of something. *Shnayim* is not a pair, but one plus one, or two individual entities – because two people's passions are never the same.

To be sure, there are other young people who are fervent about the most frivolous things imaginable. But Jewish enthusiasm must be permanently affixed to the Torah. Within Jewish life and even within the Torah world, passions run in a variety of shades on the spectrum, and the sensitive Jew recognizes and appreciates those differences.

There are ideas and values that can be learned from every group in the Torah world (and maybe even outside, but that is a different point). There are things we can learn from the Modern Orthodox and from the Chasidic world, from the Religious Zionists and from the non-Zionists, from the giants of the Sephardic world and the Lithuanian *roshei yeshiva* – and to think otherwise is not only foolish but also shortsighted.

"And you will make one cherub from the end at one side, and one cherub from the end at one side…and their faces turned toward each other" (25:19, 20). Those cherubs not only protect the Torah but also enrich our lives and enable us to experience more fully the seventy facets of Torah. We are in a much stronger position, both intellectually and morally, if we try to extract the good from each of the faces of Torah, rather than try to find points of disagreement from which we can take offense and become disgusted and disenchanted – as if we are trying to kick the other cherub off the top of the Holy Ark.

Constantly finding fault with everything and everyone is a debilitating way to live. Our young people are rewarded when they witness the faces of the Torah world "turned toward each other," and not turned away from each other. And only we can make that a reality.

Tetzaveh

SELF-EFFACEMENT

And you shall command the Children of Israel… (Shemot 27:20)

Moshe's name is not mentioned at all in this Torah portion, a point noted by Rav Yaakov Baal Haturim[653] and attributed by him to the fact that Moshe, in mounting a defense to the Jews' sin of the golden calf, exclaimed that he would rather be erased from the Torah than see the Jews destroyed: "Erase me, please, from the book that You have written" (32:32).[654] "Even a conditional curse uttered by a scholar comes to fruition";[655] Moshe's utterance against himself – that he should be erased from the Torah if God does not forgive the Jewish people – was fulfilled in this portion, where the word *you* is repeatedly used rather than Moshe's name, which does not appear at all.

What sounds like a punishment – the exclusion of Moshe's name – is actually a badge of honor. Moshe perceived his responsibility for the Jewish people as all-encompassing. His protection of them – notwithstanding his occasional criticisms and perhaps in light of them – was absolute and heartfelt. He understood his very mission as tied to their fortunes, such that without the nation that left Egypt to receive the Torah en route to the land of Israel, his life itself had little purpose.

This self-effacement – the dedication to a cause with heart and soul – is known in Hebrew as *mesirut nefesh* (literally, giving one's soul) and was a legacy

---

[653] Commentary of Baal HaTurim (thirteenth-fourteenth-century Germany and Spain), Shemot 27:20. He notes that this is the only time in the Torah from the record of Moshe's birth that his name is omitted from a *sedra*. In fact, Moshe's name does not appear in Parshiyot Ekev, Re'eh, Shoftim and Ki Teitzei, presumably because Moshe himself was the sole speaker.

[654] Interestingly, this chapter and verse each number 32, or *lev* (heart) in Hebrew, an indication of how Moshe perceived his essence and his total commitment to the Jewish people.

[655] Baal Haturim, Shemot 27:20, citing Masechet Makkot 11a.

to Moshe from Bitya, Pharaoh's daughter, who, in rescuing and raising the infant Moshe in defiance of her father's homicidal commands, demonstrated the same quality.[656]

Concern for the welfare of others is a cardinal Jewish trait and typifies the moral outlook of the individual who centers his life on service of God and fidelity to His will. It is so fundamental that this idea will shortly recur in this very *sedra*.

CLOTHES MAKE THE MAN

And you shall make sacred garments for Aharon your brother, for glory and splendor. (Shemot 28:2)

The garments of the priesthood – the tunic, miter, breastplate, turban and so on – were indeed splendid, and by modern standards somewhat ostentatious. They were colorful and difficult to miss, stamping the person as a *kohen*, a minister of God. To modern eyes, unused to such pomp in sacred service, that special garb might seem a little strange. So why was this unique clothing mandated? And for whose "glory and splendor" were they made?

Clothing does not make us who we are nor does it define who we are essentially. Many people wear special garments that they feel furnish them with gravitas or status in Jewish life, with black clothing being the sartorial choice now for several centuries among many European Jews and their offspring. They are superficially deceptive, much like in Talmudic times when some wore *tefillin* the entire day in order to induce others to presume them to be people of integrity.[657] When their customers learned otherwise to their chagrin, our Sages began to frown on public wearing of tefillin the entire day, i.e., anytime outside the context of *tefilla*. The custom changed so as not to enable the deceitful dressed in the clothing of piety to defraud the innocent.

Nonetheless, it would be an error to conclude that clothes do not matter at all, with some Jews even minimizing or disregarding the injunction to wear special dignified clothing on Shabbat.[658] People do have a reasonable expectation that doctors, lawyers, rabbis and members of other professions

---

[656] Rav Chaim Shmulevitz, *Sichot Musar*, Parshat Noach, p. 12.

[657] Yerushalmi Masechet Berachot, 2:3, cited in Beit Yosef, Orach Chaim 37:1. It is one reason why wearing tefillin the entire day ceased being the norm of Jewish life. See also Masechet Sota 22b for another list of various poseurs.

[658] Rambam, Mishneh Torah, *Hilchot Shabbat* 30:3, based on Masechet Shabbat 113a.

will dress appropriately, however defined, and are nonplussed when those expectations are unmet. Why is that?

The Talmud quotes the great Sage Rav Yochanan as calling his clothing "that which honors me."[659] Choice of clothing does not say anything substantive about ourselves – except how we seek to define ourselves. Those who dress immodestly, for example, are informing others that they perceive themselves – their essence, in fact – as their body and are inviting others to take notice of it. Conversely, those who dress with dignity, class and refinement invariably see themselves as dignified, classy and refined. It is not uncommon for the uniform itself to function as a reminder to the wearer that he represents more than himself to the outside world but represents also the traditions and values of what that uniform symbolizes.

The priests wore garments that reflected the royal vestments of the time so that they should see themselves – servants of God in the Temple – as kings and princes. The "glory and splendor" were not theirs, but for the "honor of God Who dwelled amongst them" and the glory of the people of Israel whom they represented.[660] The *kohen*'s garments projected his self-image, the grandeur of the human being and his potential as a servant of the Creator.

In that sense, we can understand how each of the garments of the priests atoned for a particular sin. "The pants atoned for immorality, the turban for haughtiness, the robe for gossip, the headplate for brazenness, etc."[661] The garments were unlike the sacrificial order that atoned for specific sins; rather, they were "atonement" for potential sin, a preemptive atonement. Life teaches us that anyone can sin and that no one is perfect; all human beings are driven by fantasies and desires. But sin can be thwarted not just by effective law enforcement, but primarily by constant reminders of our potential, of the kind of people we can be if we strive appropriately.

People who saw the garments and understood their deeper meaning realized that improper thoughts and deeds are part of the human experience, but not an essential part. Simply seeing the *kohen* garbed in his "sacred garments" raised Jews to a high level of spiritual awareness.

As we are told to see ourselves as a "kingdom of priests" (19:6), we too have a self-image (as individuals and as a nation) that we seek to project to the world. It is found not necessarily in the color of our clothing, but certainly in our deportment and in the codes of ethics, integrity, purity and modesty that

---

[659] Masechet Shabbat 113b.
[660] Ramban, Shemot 28:2.
[661] Masechet Zevachim 88b.

guide our lives. Ultimately, it is not our attire that is for "glory and splendor" but the way we live our lives.

On Our Hearts

And Aharon shall bear the names of the Children of Israel on the Breastplate of Judgment on his heart when he enters the Sanctuary, as a constant reminder before God. (Shemot 28:29)

The Breastplate (Choshen) worn by the high priest contained a variety of stones on which were engraved the names of all the tribes. Certainly, it reminded Aharon and his successors that they represented the entire nation in their divine service. But they were to be constantly reminded of something else as well.

Aharon was the great lover and pursuer of peace who strove to reconcile feuding parties.[662] His heart was filled with love of Jews and concern for their well-being. He grieved during their suffering and rejoiced in their celebrations. And yet even he was commanded to keep on his heart a constant physical reminder of his love for them.

Rav Chaim Shmulevitz noted that sharing in the pain of other Jews is an even greater indication of one's love and identification than sharing in their joy.[663] Too often, the ill, suffering or despondent are abandoned by former friends for whom a continued relationship is too strenuous or painful. But to share the burdens of others – as Moshe did when he "went out to his brethren and observed their suffering" (2:11) or assisted the nation in their battle with Amalek (17:12)[664] – is indispensable to leadership. It is also indispensable to nationhood.

The twentieth-century sage Rav Zalman Sorotzkin taught that in Megillat Esther, when the plot to exterminate the Jews began to unfold, Mordechai went to the king's courtyard in sackcloth, knowing he couldn't enter the palace.[665] So why did he go to the courtyard if he couldn't enter the palace? Furthermore, why not dress normally? Rav Sorotzkin answered that it was because Mordechai wanted to share in the suffering of the people, and not

---

[662] Masechet Avot 1:12.
[663] *Sichot Musar*, Parshat Tetzaveh, pp. 118–19.
[664] See Masechet Taanit 11a.
[665] Esther 4:2. During most years, the holiday of Purim is celebrated the week after Parshat Tetzaveh is read.

stop, even for the moment he entered the courtyard. Nor did he want to divert the attention of all – even passersby in the king's courtyard – to the impending decree. His identification with the people was complete.

Aharon's responsibility for the welfare of the Jewish people was so complete that the Torah commanded that "the Breastplate may not be loosened from the Apron" (28:28). He was not allowed to detach the Breastplate containing the stones that carried the names of the tribes from the Apron to which they adhered.[666] But what applied to Moshe and Aharon applies to all Jews. To share in each other's suffering and to help others carry their burdens is a fundamental component of brotherhood and mutual respect. Those who carve out for themselves exemptions from sharing that burden – and this applies on some level to every Jew in every community, from the person who chooses not to go to minyan every day to the person who fails to respond to a communal charity appeal or to the obligations of national life – are constricting their feelings of brotherhood, separating from the community, and are missing an essential element of the Torah personality.

Our hearts are big enough to include room for caring for others outside ourselves and our immediate circle of friends and family. The Jewish heart is big enough to be concerned about all mankind – but certainly in the first instance about our nation, its needs and challenges.

The Ideal, Part I

And you will take the anointing oil and pour it on [Aharon's] head… (Shemot 29:7)

Aharon and his sons were only ready for divine service in the Mishkan after they were anointed with oil. Rashi here clarifies that the oil was not exactly poured on Aharon's head, but that it was applied to two places – on his head and between his eyes – and connected like the Greek letter *chi*, our letter *x*. So, too, the Torah says that the vessels of the Mishkan also had to be specially anointed.

The question is why? Why the ceremony? The world is filled with such coronation, inauguration or investiture ceremonies – oaths, hands on Bibles, kneeling, etc. – but what does that have to do with us? Aharon was designated

---

[666] Indeed, this is one of the 613 commandments, number 100 according to the count of the *Sefer Hachinuch*.

by God as the *kohen gadol*, the high priest; what more is required? And why an *x*?

Aharon and his sons, and later the kings of Israel, were anointed with special oil in order to make them radiant, separate them from others, and have people point to them and say, "These are our exemplars of human greatness and majesty. They sparkle because they were chosen by God to serve Him and to guide His people." And their aura radiates, Rav Hirsch said, like an *x*, in all directions – not just in one or two limited areas of life, but in everything they do, in their very being.[667]

This is what is expected of us, as we are "God's anointed people." We also have that *x* on our heads, and we too are observed from all sides and in every move we make, both the positive and less positive. The prophet Yechezkel said, "Tell the family of Israel of the Temple and let them be ashamed of their sins…"[668] Only one who is anointed can feel shame; only one who perceives himself on a high level can be embarrassed when he lets himself down. Only a person with standards can sense when he has fallen short of those very standards.

In that sense, guilt can be a productive emotion; even better are the self-control and personal responsibility for one's actions that diminish the quantity of our sins and serve as perpetual reminders of the princely status that compels us to set our standards high and our sights even higher.

The Ideal, Part II

And this is what you shall offer on the Altar: two sheep less than a year old every day, perpetually. (Shemot 29:38)

The copious and meticulous details governing the construction of the Mishkan culminate, finally, in the first practical application of the Mishkan: "this is what you shall offer…every day." The renowned commentator Don Yitzchak Abravanel[669] questions the use of the phrase "and this," which implies that the offerings on the Altar were limited to the daily schedule of two sheep in the morning and afternoon.[670] But, in fact, far more was offered on the Altar than just the *korban tamid*, the continual offering; there were also sin offerings,

---

[667] Rav Shamshon Raphael Hirsch, Shemot 29:7.
[668] Yechezkel 43:10.
[669] Fifteenth-sixteenth-century Portugal, Spain and Italy
[670] Don Yitzchak Abravanel, Shemot 29:38.

burnt offerings, peace offerings, etc. None are mentioned here – only "this." Why?

Don Yitzchak answered that if the Torah had immediately discussed *all* the offerings – especially the sin offering – we would have inevitably concluded that God has forced us to have sinful natures. If a regular, recurring and expected part of the Temple service were sin offerings, we might think that it was God's intention that we sin and repent. To counter that view, the Torah speaks only of the daily offering, which is "praise and gratitude to God."[671] The Torah only mentioned the other offerings that relate to sin and atonement after the episode of the golden calf when our propensity for sin was revealed. For now, "this is what you shall offer on the Altar: two sheep less than a year old every day." What is the function of this daily service?

The construction of the Mishkan culminated in the instructions for the daily offerings because those reflected our service on the highest level – the ideal: a daily attempt to draw near to God in a much more vivid and striking way than merely through the articulation of words. Every offering is always brought in place of the person who himself wished to approach. It was a substitute for the person; it was the person himself but in a different form. That was *avoda*, the divine service in the Tabernacle and Temple. That internal process can be simulated in prayer, but it is not as profound or as intense as the Temple service. That is what we are missing, but that is what we can recapture too.

Prayer is so often mechanical to us– say these words and sway this motion and turn this page and stand up here and sit down there – that it loses its sense of *service*. It is the verbal offering of the individual who wants to concentrate all his resources and energies on drawing near to God. That is why *tefilla* – properly done – is primarily an experience of the soul.

It requires accessing our inner world, and its beauty lies in its regularity. How so?

"You shall offer the one sheep in the morning, and the second sheep you shall offer in the afternoon" (29:39). What strikes us as a most prosaic verse is actually the subject of one of the most sublime expositions about life itself. Our Sages discussed the following proposition: which one Biblical verse is the *pasuk kollel* – the one verse that encapsulates the essence of Judaism?[672] Ben Zoma cited – as could be expected – "Listen, Israel, the Lord is our God, the Lord is One," the first verse of the *Shema*.[673] Ben Nanas quoted another

---

[671] Ibid.
[672] Introduction to *Ein Yaakov*.
[673] Devarim 6:4.

famous verse as the essence of the Torah's message: "And you shall love your neighbor as yourself."[674] Both of those are all-embracing concepts – the former our testimony to our affirmation of God's existence, and the latter our commitment to doing justice and acts of kindness to our fellow man.

But the third opinion – that of Ben Pazi – mentions the present verse. The all-encompassing verse that defines Judaism is "you shall offer the one sheep in the morning, and the second sheep you shall offer in the afternoon." Surely this requires an explanation; how can this verse reflect the overarching philosophy of Judaism?

Rav Sholom Gold[675] taught that it refers to the importance of self-sacrifice in Judaism. The commitments to obeying the laws between man and God and between man and his fellow man must be undertaken even at personal sacrifice. It is easier to espouse the ideals than to live them. It is in the divine service in the Temple that we find the extent of our commitment to both ideals.

Perhaps another suggestion is also appropriate. The daily service in the Temple – the sheep in the morning and afternoon, every day without exception – reminds us that our faithfulness to God and His law must be consistent and omnipresent. The beauty of the Jewish lifestyle is found, in part, in the regularity of our obligations. *Tefillin* and *tzitzit* every morning, prayer three times a day, ubiquitous blessings, consumption only of kosher food, Shabbat every week, integrity at every moment and so on.

The citation above concludes with this comment: "The law follows the opinion of Ben Pazi!" The verse that encapsulates all of Judaism is, indeed, this one: "You shall offer the one sheep in the morning, and the second sheep you shall offer in the afternoon." Every day we fulfill our obligations to God and to man. Every day, without exception.

A friend of mine, a Sabbath-observant lawyer, was once asked by his partner to attend an important meeting with a client that would take place on Shabbat morning. He said: "You've known me for fifteen years already. You know I don't work on the Sabbath." To which the partner retorted, "Yes, I know, but I thought just this one week you could make an exception." My friend declined the suggestion!

That is the most significant commitment the Jew can make: to embrace the Torah in all its aspects and to fulfill all its obligations as required when required. There are no vacations from God's service.

---

[674] Vayikra 19:18.

[675] Illustrious twentieth-twenty-first-century *rav* in Canada, the United States and currently in Jerusalem, Israel.

Ki Tisa

My Share

> *This is what they shall give – everyone who is counted in the census – a half shekel of the sacred shekels, twenty geras to the shekel, a half shekel as a portion to God. (Shemot 30:13)*

Rav Shamshon Raphael Hirsch comments that the basic obligation of the Jew toward the Sanctuary is to annually donate a half shekel, and specifically not a full shekel. No person should ever feel that he has accomplished everything. "No person dies with even half his desires fulfilled."[676] So, too, no person should ever feel that he must do everything or the task will not be completed properly. "It is not for you to complete the work, nor are you free to desist from it."[677] As Rav Hirsch notes, "the most complete and most perfect work of any single individual is never the whole of the work...[;] the work of any single person will always remain but a fragment."[678]

What we are therefore asked to do is to make our contribution to the whole, and not deem it unimportant. If twenty *geras* are the equivalent of one shekel, then the individual responsibility is ten *geras*. "The rich shall not give more and the poor shall not give less than a half shekel" (30:15). The rich should not give more and feel that their contributions afford them some proprietary control over the Sanctuary. The poor should not give less and feel that their contributions don't really matter at all.

We are not expected to do everything but nor are we allowed to abstain from doing anything. In our personal and communal lives, we each must do our share and not rely on others to do our work for us. It is as true of marriage

---

[676] Midrash Kohelet Rabba 1:13.
[677] Mishna Avot 2:21.
[678] Rav Shamshon Raphael Hirsch, Shemot 30:13 (translated by Isaac Levy, *Chamishah Chumshei Torah* [1960], p. 578).

and parenting as it is of volunteering for our local synagogue or yeshiva or making our appropriate contributions to the security and prosperity of the State of Israel.

The annual tax of the half shekel was "the ransom for [our souls]" (30:12). Every Jew justifies his membership in the people of Israel by making this symbolic offering, the same for everyone.

The Holy Shekel

What makes one shekel holier than any other that the Torah should three times describe this donation to the Tabernacle as a "holy shekel"?

Our Sages taught that the production of the shekel was one of four things that Moshe had difficulty fully comprehending.[679] It was so abstruse that God had to show Moshe a "shekel of fire" so that he would understand what had to be made.[680] Similarly, Moshe, also flummoxed by the Menora, had to be shown "a Menora of fire."[681] But what was so complicated about the shekel and the Menora – and why were they both shown to Moshe in the form of fire?

Fire is one of the most fascinating substances on earth. It is multifaceted, useful, productive, at times indispensable – and yet also intensely dangerous. Fire provides heat and light; it is the engine of creativity. And yet it can also burn out of control, destroy and devastate lives and property.

There are two areas of human endeavor where the desired objective is both necessary and vital but also quite hazardous. They are knowledge and money, and the question of how each can be employed in God's service challenged Moshe. The Menora, Rav Hirsch wrote, is the symbol of wisdom.[682] The branches of knowledge are seemingly disparate, but all emerge from the same source. The Talmud states that "knowledge is so great that it was given between two of God's names."[683] All wisdom has to be constrained, so to speak, bounded by God's names on each side. If wisdom is detached from its divine source it becomes "fire," so dangerous that it can easily burn out of control.

---

[679] See Rabbeinu Bachye, Bamidbar 8:2. He lists the four as Menora, Korbanot (the Temple offerings), shekel and the New Moon. The Talmud (Menachot 29a) mentions three: Menora, the New Moon and *sheratzim* (the unclean reptiles), and adds a potential fourth – the laws of kosher slaughter. There are other lists, as well, but the most reported three are Menora, shekel and Rosh Chodesh, the latter not relevant to this discussion.

[680] Rashi, Shemot 30:13, citing the Mechilta.

[681] Rashi, Shemot 25:40, citing Midrash Bamidbar Rabba 15:10.

[682] Rav Shamshon Raphael Hirsch, Shemot 25:39.

[683] Masechet Berachot 33a.

Surely the sophisticated murder machines invented by civilized and educated people in Nazi Germany and elsewhere in the twentieth and twenty-first centuries are adequate testimony to that proposition. Man can destroy himself and others.

Knowledge enables us to conquer nature and to achieve new heights of human accomplishment – but that same knowledge, devoid of God's limitations, can produce wickedness and terrible human suffering. No wonder Moshe found it difficult to properly assign knowledge its place in the Tabernacle.

Wealth is the same way. Fabulous things can be achieved with money – human suffering can be alleviated, holiness can be nurtured, people can enjoy life. And yet, like wisdom, wealth is also fire; it can reduce meaningful life to ashes; it can corrupt, surely but insidiously. Wealth can become an end in itself, until otherwise decent people come to cut corners, take shortcuts, and engulf themselves in the fantasies of abundance. It is not that Moshe found the actual shekel difficult to fashion; the challenge rather was how to make the "half shekel" into a "holy shekel." A "holy shekel" sounds like a contradiction in terms; yet the Torah refers to it three times.

It is not easy to make our *shekalim* holy. One can't just give a half shekel to the Temple, spend the rest of it on hedonistic excess and construe that shekel as holy. Nor can a person indulge every thought or pursue knowledge detached from its connection to God, the Source of knowledge. Both are, literally, playing with fire.

God had to take Moshe by hand and show him how to incorporate wisdom and wealth in the lives of a holy people, so that it warms, animates, and arouses – but doesn't corrupt, degrade and degenerate. Indeed, those are two areas that challenge modern man as well. Exercising control over our money and our ideas – our assets and our thoughts – is essential to building character and maintaining our values.

Stage One Thinking

> *When [God] finished speaking to [Moshe] on Mount Sinai, He gave him two Tablets of Testimony, stone tablets inscribed by the finger of God. (Shemot 31:18)*

> *And Moshe turned and descended from the mountain with the two Tablets of Testimony in his hand, tablets inscribed on both sides...and the tablets were God's handiwork, and the script was God's script, engraved on the tablets. (Shemot 32:15–16)*

These verses that describe the tablets of stone read as if they should be juxtaposed, but in fact they are separated by the narrative of the sin of the golden calf. So how did the Jewish people surrender to idolatrous desires so soon after Sinai?

They were guilty – among other things – of what the noted economist Dr. Thomas Sowell called "stage one" thinking.[684] People often act without regard to the immediate – much less the long-term – consequences of their actions. All they see is the first stage, which at times is the gratification of the initial impulse.[685] The rebels exclaimed: "Rise up and make us a god that will go before us" (32:1). And then what? They had not really thought it through, so "they arose to revel" (32:6).[686]

Whenever people act impulsively and precipitately, it is invariably the result of stage one thinking. It sounded good, polled well, and tested well in focus groups! That is all that matters. They assumed it would all just work itself out.[687] Naturally, it did not.

God gave Moshe the "two Tablets of Testimony, stone tablets inscribed by the finger of God" (31:18), before Moshe left the mountain. At that point, that is all we needed to know about the tablets – that they were inscribed by the finger of God. But when the people sinned, they did so because they did not recognize another aspect of these tablets – that they were "inscribed on

---

[684] Thomas Sowell, *Applied Economics: Thinking Beyond Stage One* (New York: Basic Books, 2003).

[685] Usually, stage one thinking utilizes an attractive slogan like "Health care for all!" The second stage constitutes the details and the difficulty of how that worthy goal is to be subsidized and implemented, a less attractive proposition.

[686] Rashi (32:6) notes that their "revelries" included sexual immorality and homicide.

[687] Israel's retreat from Gaza and the expulsion of the Jews who lived there is a classic example of stage one thinking, never really seeing beyond the "advantages" of the retreat to the likelihood of that territory being transformed into a base for terror, as indeed happened.

both sides…and the script was God's script." Our Sages taught on this verse, comparing the similarities of the Hebrew words for "engraved" and "freedom," that "the only free person is the one who is involved in Torah."[688] The tablets liberate man. How?

Rav Kook wrote that man is composed of a "holy soul" and an "impure soul" that vie for supremacy in every human being.[689] Each one wants to dominate, and at first, each one that is indulged leaves the other unsatisfied. It is an internal struggle; when we are drawn to the spiritual good, then the body demands pleasure. When we indulge our sensual side, our conscience is activated. How do we overcome this dichotomy, this tug-of-war? How do we get past stage one thinking?

"The only free person is the one who is involved in Torah." The tablets were inscribed on both sides, and readable from both sides. The people were taught that the Torah accounts for all aspects of the human personality and enables man to find satisfaction with each part of the soul. Can a person make good choices and find satisfaction without Torah? Yes, but he will never be a "free person." He will always be struggling, always at war with himself, and always in danger of stumbling.

If the people knew what the tablets were, they could not have sinned, and certainly they would not have acted so impetuously. But they did, with the result that those tablets were broken. That battle continues – in our personal lives, in our nation and around the world – to be neither one committed to stage one thinking nor one who prefers not to commit at all, but rather to make the choices between truth and falsehood and between good and evil and to take responsibility for them.

STUNTED GROWTH

And the people saw that Moshe had tarried coming down the mountain, and they assembled around Aharon and said to him, "Rise up and make for us a god who will go before us, for this man Moshe who brought us out of Egypt, we do not know what happened to him." (Shemot 32:1)

How did the Jewish people fall so abruptly from the majestic heights of Sinai to the nadir of idolatry and paganism? Rashi cites the Talmud, which

---

[688] Masechet Avot 6:2.

[689] *Orot Hakodesh* 3:135, discussing the *nefesh kedosha* and *nefesh temeia*.

records that Satan himself confused the Jewish people by showing them the image of a deceased Moshe in the clouds.[690] The people, in their sadness and bewilderment, surrounded Aharon and demanded a new leader – of gold, which would not decay or die. Satan's involvement adds another perplexing element to this already baffling and tragic story.

To be sure, Satan is never construed as an external being but rather as an internal force that reflects our instinctual drives and the part of man that desires non-spiritual gratification. Elsewhere, the Talmud understands Satan as a synonym for the *yetzer hara*, the "evil inclination" that is certainly an internalized dimension of man.[691] This is the case here as well.

For all the magnificence of the Revelation, there were elements in the Jewish people that were completely committed neither to the Torah nor to Moshe's leadership. They conjured images of a dead Moshe, seeing what they wanted to see, and it was they – a relatively small group of people – who were largely responsible for this debacle. But how could even that small group deny what their eyes had seen at Sinai and what they themselves had experienced in Egypt that they should say of their freshly manufactured calf "this is your god, Israel, who took you out of Egypt" (32:4)?

Rav Chaim Shmulevitz explains that from the time the people left Egypt – and even for a year before then – all they knew was Moshe. He led them, he guided their every move, and only he had knowledge of their future travels. They were completely dependent on Moshe.[692]

Once the people assumed that Moshe was dead, they panicked. All they saw was "darkness, fog and confusion."[693] They lost their ambition, energy and motivation. Immediately, they began to flounder and lost their self-control. In one fell swoop, they fell prey to the idolatrous impulse and acted on it.

Certainly, as events unfolded in Egypt and thereafter, there was no other option open to Moshe. He *had* to lead. He was the only one who had access to the divine message, and the dependency happened quite naturally. In the wilderness, the people's total reliance on Moshe was unavoidable and their fall in his absence was steep.

The same phenomenon can occur in our lives as well. There are parents who, overprotective of their children, do not allow them to make age-appropriate decisions. These parents do not want their children to make mistakes, which often deprives them of the capacity to make decisions or to

---

[690] Rashi, Shemot 32:1, citing Masechet Shabbat 89a.
[691] Masechet Bava Batra 16a.
[692] *Sichot Musar*, 5731, chapter 55, pp. 234–35.
[693] Masechet Shabbat 89a.

learn from their mistakes. It then happens that when the parent leaves the scene, the child is completely lost and helpless. Like the proverbial husband who cannot find the refrigerator in his own kitchen and therefore starves in his wife's absence, these children are handicapped by their upbringing and struggle to function as adults, spouses, parents or wage-earners.

Parents thus have an obligation to ensure that their children learn personal responsibility and appropriate decision-making skills. Children can be allowed to stumble and even fail on their own every now and then, without the parents displaying horror and disappointment.[694] The earlier that is done in a child's life, the sooner he or she will mature and be able to lead a healthy, independent life. The great pioneer of outreach, Rav Noach Weinberg, once said, "People often avoid making decisions out of fear of making a mistake. Actually, the failure to make decisions is one of life's biggest mistakes."[695]

Moshe never contemplated his demise (at this point) and had prepared no succession plan. A fickle public – three months removed from slavery – that could not think for itself dealt with his disappearance in the worst possible way: by renouncing the very essence of their leader's ideals by engaging in the worship of a molten calf. A person or child unschooled in the art of decision making will invariably make bad decisions when suddenly bereft of the decision maker.

That is the background to this sin that would forever shape Jewish history.

QUICK SLIDE

[And God said to Moshe], "They have strayed quickly from the path that I have commanded them, and made for themselves a molten calf…" (Shemot 32:8)

The decline was as precipitous as it was sudden. Forty days after the Jewish people received the Torah, God revealed to Moshe that his people had already

---

[694] Modern culture has taken to calling the two types "alpha parents" and "beta parents." Alpha parents seek to govern their childrens' lives, fill every waking moment with activities, are overprotective, require equitable outcomes (as in "everyone gets a trophy") and generally have plotted out the course of their childrens' lives. Beta parents are more relaxed in their parenting, allow children to plan their own activities and act in ways appropriate to their ages, and are much more comfortable with granting their children autonomy (at all ages, but of course only when appropriate). For a sample of the former, see www.thealphaparent.com, and of the latter, www.freerangekids.com. Obviously, neither mode of parenting is perfect or has all the requisite answers!

[695] Rabbi Noah Weinberg, "Way #4: Introduce Yourself to Yourself," 48 Ways to Wisdom, http://www.aish.com/sp/48w/48970096.html.

sinned grievously: "Go down, for the nation you brought up from Egypt has degenerated" (32:7). But how could this have happened so suddenly? The Talmud says that the tactic of the "evil inclination" is usually more gradual and subtle: "Do a little [sin] today, something else tomorrow, until you are ready to serve false gods."[696] It is never "do this now," a sudden impulse, but rather the "evil inclination" seeps slowly into our minds – with doubts, cynicism, a little rebelliousness – until it completely permeates our thought processes, and "suddenly" we are completely corrupt.

How, then, did the people sin here so hastily?

Rashi blames the *erev rav* (mentioned in Shemot 12:38), the mixed multitude of non-Jews that accompanied the Jewish people from Egypt: "It was the *erev rav* that came up from Egypt who gathered against Aharon, and who built [the golden calf], and who afterwards enticed the Jews after it."[697] But everyone stood at Sinai and heard God's injunctions against idols and graven images. Should the mixed multitude really be "blamed" for this debacle?

Modern thinkers speak of something called "social contagion," the idea that individual behavior is influenced by group dynamics. People feel the need to applaud when others do, or drink alcohol because their friends are imbibing – in both cases, even if they themselves do not really want to indulge in either behavior.

In another context, the Talmud teaches that it is forbidden to socialize before morning prayers, and "whoever does, it is as if he has built an idolatrous altar."[698] What is the connection?

Our Sages are teaching us that everyone's life is governed by a value system – a set of principles that animates him, shapes his reactions and molds his character. Ideally, our values are drawn from the Torah. It is God's ideas that give us life, meaning, direction and a true concept of reality.

That is the ideal. For most people, though, the most powerful force that shapes their lives and attitudes is other people – the social reality. The desire to be liked compels them to assimilate and internalize the attitudes of others only so that they become part of a desired group. To them, the social reality is even more powerful than the reality of God's existence. Both the gratification and the harm are more immediate. In the worst case scenario, people are seduced into self-destructive behavior because others in their social circle are doing likewise. *That* is tragic.

---

[696] Masechet Shabbat 105a.
[697] Rashi, Shemot 32:4.
[698] Masechet Berachot 14a.

The Jewish people sinned here, even though the *erev rav* built the idol, because the basis of the sin was succumbing to the blandishments of man. They could not resist doing what a large group of people were doing;[699] after all, how could so many people be wrong? Social contagion is a powerful force. Left alone, man would ordinarily have to work himself into an idolatrous frenzy – slowly – in order to yield. Here, "they have strayed quickly from the path." They abandoned their most cherished principles, and in a hurry.

Our Sages insisted that we "stop considering man, for what is he?"[700] One who socializes before davening (and obviously all the more so during davening), is clearly moved by an alien value system in which popularity with people matters more than God and divine service.

Personal responsibility requires the strength of character to say yes and no to others who might be expecting no and yes. Our guides are truth, kindness and friendship grounded in the real world that God created and not the artificial one that we create.

ONE MAN

[And God said to Moshe…] "And now, leave Me alone, and let My anger flare against them and I will destroy them, and I will make you into a great nation." (Shemot 32:10)

How did Moshe, in fact, avert this terrible decree? Moshe never claimed that the people did not know what they were doing, had lost their heads, and would never do it again. (The sad fact is, they would, and multiple times.) God's recommendation – "I will make you into a great nation" – is logical; this nation is hopelessly compromised. It is far better to start over again with a new nation.[701]

Moshe offered no guarantees, took up residence outside the camp of Israel, spent a few more months at Sinai, received the ultimate personal revelation of God, and then the Jewish people moved on. But what exactly did Moshe say or do? How did he transform the crisis into an opportunity and preserve our existence?

---

[699] Shemot 32:29 notes that a total of three thousand idol worshippers were killed by the tribe of Levi out of a population of approximately, six hundred thousand males.

[700] Ibid., citing Yeshayahu 2:22.

[701] This is reminiscent, in a whimsical way, of the twentieth-century German playwright Bertolt Brecht's statement about a certain political crisis, pithily paraphrased: "The people have lost the confidence of the government, and a new people must be formed" ("Die Lösung," c. 1953).

Without a doubt, Moshe's refusal to abandon his people – "if You forgive their sin, [fine]; but if not, blot me out from the book that You have written" (32:32) – is one of the most heroics acts of personal responsibility in history. But there is even more to the story.

Rashi comments here that Moshe perceived an opportunity. God said "leave Me alone," but Moshe had not yet prayed on the people's behalf. "Here God informed Moshe that there was an opening – that the [fate of the people] was dependent on him; if he prayed for them, they would not be destroyed."[702]

Even one great person can redeem an entire generation, or inspire thousands, or save an entire nation. The Jewish people survived because Moshe left the camp, dwelled alone, merited the knowledge of the thirteen divine attributes that marked him as a superior human being, learned the ways of God, and became – if nothing else – an example for others of what Jews can be. Soon, "the skin of his face shone" (34:29).

The movers and shakers of Jewish life, together with all of history's greats, are always individuals who carve out a new path, take intelligent risks, blaze new trails in Torah, divine service and our national lives – and all despite the harping and the criticism they receive, and the imperfections that they may themselves have.

Moshe prayed for a stricken and undeserving nation. He offered no guarantees of future righteousness; he only offered himself, from the realization that, in Rashi's words, everything was "dependent on him." He reached the highest level of human perfection attainable, and saved His people.

That acceptance of responsibility is true greatness, and the very definition of leadership.

The Minority

> *And Moshe stood in the gate of the camp and said, "Whoever is for God, come to me." And all the Levites gathered around him. (Shemot 32:26)*

If anyone can be called heroic in the catastrophic sin of the golden calf, it is the tribe of Levi who stepped into the breach, heeded Moshe's call, and avenged God's honor. Avraham ibn Ezra comments here that it was natural, since the Levites were Moshe's family, that they all came out to support Moshe; but they

---

[702] Rashi, Shemot 32:10, citing Masechet Berachot 32a.

were also Aharon's family. What was the essence of the greatness of the tribe of Levi?

Rav Soloveitchik once contrasted the two most consequential sins in the Torah – the sin of Adam and the sin of the golden calf. Adam's sin, he said, resulted from an inflated ego. Man perceived himself – rightly so, from one perspective – as the crown of creation, but imagined that he would have divine qualities if he ate from the tree of knowledge. Man was induced to sin because he overestimated his worth.

The sin of the golden calf was exactly the opposite. The people here had no self-confidence, but rather were diffident and afraid: "this man Moshe who brought us out of Egypt, we do not know what happened to him" (32:1). With the disappearance of Moshe, the people felt they could not go on as before.

Indeed, that is the conundrum of life: Adam sinned because he felt he was too important, and here the people sinned because they felt they were too unimportant. How can we decide how to act if we are prone to being too sure or too unsure of ourselves?

The answer is that both can coexist. In the famous epigram attributed to Rav Simcha Bunim, the Rebbe of Peshischa, he said that one should always keep a paper in each pocket, with one reading "the world was created for me"[703] and the other "for I am but dust and ashes."[704] The test of life is to know when to pull out one and when to pull out the other, when assertiveness is required and when humility is required.

It is never easy being in the minority, as the majority offers the security of numbers and a greater ability to hide. One can readily conclude that he is nothing but "dust and ashes" and abstain from any communal involvement or from any decision that requires a difficult choice. Such a life can be lived on the sidelines and can masquerade as humility.

The tribe of Levi was called upon to decide – and not just the tribe as a whole but each individual in the tribe, as "all the Levites gathered around him." That was an act of faith that was not necessarily predictable, foreseeable or even explicable but one that emanated from the momentary feeling that "the world was created for me"; there are certain things that only I can do; I must be the one to make the difference.

Choosing can be hard. Similarly, the prophet Elijah gave his contemporaries a difficult personal choice as well: "for how long will you straddle both sides

---

[703] Masechet Sanhedrin 37a.
[704] Breisheet 18:27.

of the fence; if the Lord is God, follow Him; if the Baal, then follow him."[705] Sometimes, there is no default position and no safe ground above the fray; one cannot simply vote "present" and avoid the tough choices. That is when the individual with a proper sense of self and an awareness of the demands of the moment steps forward and changes the course of history, as the Levites did here.

THE BOOK AND THE SWORD

> *...and [Moshe's] servant, Yehoshua son of Nun, a lad, would not depart from the tent. (Shemot 33:11)*

The portrait of the young Yehoshua painted by this verse is that of a novitiate learning from and ministering to Moshe, a disciple so singularly dedicated to learning from his master that he never left Moshe's presence. Yet this is not the first reference to Yehoshua in the Torah; the first reflects a much more pugnacious lad – not an uncertain adolescent but a warrior leading men into battle.

"And Moshe said to Yehoshua, 'Select men for us and go wage war against Amalek…'" (17:9). The battle against Amalek occurred several months before this later description of a Yehoshua who only clings to Moshe, accompanying him up to Sinai and back to the camp to witness the horrors of the golden calf, and who is now depicted as his diligent attendant. But if Yehoshua never left Moshe's tent – the tent of study – how then did he lead the army of Israel in the war with Amalek?

The question presupposes an exilic attitude in which the values of Torah study and military service are deemed incompatible. In the Bible, the greatest of our spiritual leaders often went to battle, when necessary. Avraham fought the four kings, Moshe fought against Og (and oversaw the battle with Amalek, praying for and inspiring his people), and King David famously fought numerous times. None of this was considered out of character or a concession to the times, but rather a natural part of serving God.

When the Torah related that Avraham "armed his disciples who had been born in his house,"[706] Ralbag comments that Avraham specifically chose those who had been "trained in Avraham's way since their youth." Those were the most appropriate brothers-in-arms for Avraham in his wars. Yaakov, too,

---

[705] I Kings 18:21. Not coincidentally, this is the designated *haftara* for Parshat Ki Tisa.
[706] Breisheet 14:14, with Ralbag's commentary thereon.

on his deathbed, praised his sons Yehuda, Yissachar, Dan, Gad, Yosef and Binyamin for their martial abilities.[707]

King David's fighters – Benayahu ben Yehoyada, Adino Ha'etzni – did not represent a power structure that rivaled the Sanhedrin; they *were* the Sanhedrin, the greatest Torah sages of their generation. The Talmud even suggests that David himself was "Adino Ha'etzni," so called (in a play on words in Hebrew) because when he was involved in Torah study, he was supple like a worm, but in battle he was hardened like a spear.[708] The exile robbed us of that, and over the centuries we made – perforce – a virtue out of passivity, pacifism, and even weakness.

That is the message of Yehoshua bin Nun. Did he really never leave Moshe's tent and was only engaged in the study of Torah? How then did he wage war against Amalek?

Rav Zvi Yehuda Kook explained: "The Torah personality *is* the fighter who brings us into the land of Israel; it is all one related matter."[709] Only the greatest Torah personalities can fully conquer the land of Israel. The Yehoshua who received the Oral Tradition from Moshe[710] is the same Yehoshua about whom Eldad and Medad prophesied "Moshe will die and Yehoshua will bring the Jewish people into the land of Israel."[711] That concept is actually normal; it is a dedication to Torah and divine service that is complete and not bifurcated. That is not *bittul Torah* (the nullification of Torah), but rather *kiyum Torah* (the fulfillment of Torah); yet the idea that one can be a scholar and a soldier – a Torah giant and a defender of the Jewish people – is repudiated by segments of the religious world today who see a chasm between "the book and the sword."[712] That chasm might exist in the exile, but the dichotomy is foreign to the Jews of the land of Israel and was completely alien to the biblical giants who routinely combined both aspects of Jewish nationhood in their service of God – the spiritual and the physical – and perceived the protection of Jewish life and the settlement of the land of Israel as integral parts of their Torah commitment.[713]

---

[707] Breisheet 49.

[708] Masechet Moed Katan 16b.

[709] *Sichot on the Torah*, Parshat Vayechi, 2, cited by Rav (Col.) Eliezer Chaim Shenvald, *rosh yeshiva* of Yeshivat Meir Harel in Modiin, in his *Tzava V'Yeshiva*, p. 71, from whom these ideas are drawn.

[710] Avot 1:1.

[711] Masechet Sanhedrin 17a.

[712] Masechet Avoda Zara 17b.

[713] Also deserving honorable mention in this context is the eleventh-century Spanish Jew Rav Shmuel Hanagid, who was the *rosh yeshiva* and leader of Spanish Jewry at the same time he was a general

Consequently, it has become quite common today to redefine the giants of Jewish life – from Avraham to David, from Yehuda the Maccabee to Rabbi Akiva – and render them into unidimensional figures that will conform to our preconceptions. But that ultimately diminishes their greatness instead of enhancing it. The exile took such a toll that we have had a hard time re-acclimating ourselves to the normalcy of Torah, idealizing the division of responsibilities, and incapable of merging the "book and the sword." Hence the ongoing conflict in the State of Israel regarding the balance of Torah, military service and participation in the work force – the debate over "equality of burden."

Every Jew is responsible for his own welfare and that of all others. Ideally, every Jew would be engaged in Torah study, national service and self-sustenance. Those who fight wars and never study Torah miss the mark as do those who learn Torah and never fight in Israel's battles. The true giants of Jewish life do both, like Yehoshua who never left Moshe's tent even as he fought Israel's battles and advanced our destiny.

---

commanding the Muslim (!) army of Granada.

Vayakhel

THE NATIONAL PROJECT

And Moshe gathered the entire assembly of the Children of Israel… (Shemot 35:1)

In the wake of the sin of the golden calf, the Jewish people embarked on a national project with enormous consequences: the construction of the Tabernacle in which God's presence would dwell in a discernible way. Everyone was enlisted in this endeavor and the services and/or contributions of all were critical to its success; hence, Moshe gathered "the entire assembly of… Israel."

The men contributed their possessions and their skills; the women came as well, with "all the women that were wise-hearted" offering their expertise at spinning wool (35:25–26). Materials spanning the gamut of creation were employed in constructing the Tabernacle, and the variety of labors reflected the apex of human creativity. But there was another process under way here, as well.

Rav Yosef Carmel[714] wrote that the construction of the Mishkan required a revolution in the mindset of this nation of ex-slaves.[715] Slaves do not make decisions, nor do they make plans or possess an intellectual life of any substance. Their lives do not belong to them but to another, their master, whose instructions they are bidden to carry out. They are, obviously, unfree beings.

All that changed abruptly, first with the Exodus itself, but certainly here when they were thrust into positions of responsibility. *They* were the ones who had to donate – the "entire assembly," men and women, and *they* were the ones who had to lend their talents to the process. Every person had a

---

[714] Twenty-first-century Torah sage in Yerushalayim and *rosh yeshiva* of Eretz Hemdah.

[715] This is drawn from his commentary found in *Hemdat Yamim*, Parshat Vayakhel, 5773.

share, and every person had to do something. There was no reliance on others, nor any shirking of personal responsibility. Everyone was invested in this venture. It was a powerful message to this nation of ex-slaves that we are not just accountable as individuals for our deeds and misdeeds, but also that as a nation we are obligated to build and maintain a spiritual center with an orderly mode of operation.

Of course, the sacrificial order highlighted the fact that we as individuals are also accountable for our individual actions. Accountability for sins and mistakes is the sign of an organized nation that has expectations and demands of each of its citizens, and a mandatory standard of behavior. Freedom to choose suggests also the responsibility to atone for one's poor choices.

Amid the "entire assembly," we retained our individuality in one context while in another becoming part of a greater entity. It was the Tabernacle project that cemented the realization that we were no longer a random collection of former slaves but a structured nation – responsible to each other and to ourselves.

Centrality of Shabbat

For six days work may be done, but the seventh day shall be holy for you. (Shemot 35:2)

Even in the context of the construction of the Tabernacle, the Torah underscores the centrality of Shabbat in our lives. Rashi comments that this admonition is given here before Moshe relates the protocol for building the Tabernacle to teach us that even building the Tabernacle does not supersede Shabbat. The ends do not justify the means. The Temple is important, even crucial for propagating God's message to Israel and to the world – but Shabbat still takes precedence.

Yet *once* the Tabernacle or Temple was built, the laws of Shabbat were in fact superseded by the divine service therein. One could even argue that a Shabbat in the Beit Hamikdash did not seem very Shabbat-like! An observer would see animals being led in and out and slaughtered, with blood all around and carcasses being burned on the Altar. Musical instruments were played and numerous Shabbat laws were breached.[716] Yet the Torah makes clear that

---

[716] It is not impossible to foresee that when the Beit Hamikdash is rebuilt and the divine service resumed there will be people protesting, yelling "Shabbos, Shabbos!" during the proceedings. That is how unusual it will look to us.

"two male lambs less than a year old"[717] were to be offered every Shabbat. This is the "*olah* offering of each Shabbat on its own Shabbat."[718]

Why is that? Why did the laws of Shabbat supersede the building of the Mishkan, but once it was built, then the *avoda* superseded Shabbat? And why do we derive the types of forbidden labors on Shabbat – the thirty-nine *melachot* – from the variety of labors that were performed in the Mishkan?[719]

Rav Shlomo Aviner writes that there is an apparent conflict between creation and nature.[720] We only see the effects of nature; in fact, we are mandated to investigate, study, conquer and subdue nature, which operates according to the specific and rigorous laws that God ordained. Obviously, each generation since the beginning of time has advanced our knowledge of the natural order, and in the last century we have made tremendous strides.

But we are no closer now than we were millennia ago to understanding the divine life force that animates all of nature. If a person were to say, "I see how God causes the tree to grow," we would think him insane. We measure nature's results, but the processes implicit in natural law are hidden to us. Nevertheless, we intuitively sense and recognize that there is such a life force. We see grass grow, we see animals run, we see the sun shining, and we see the streams flowing. We sense that there is something that brings nature to life.

Pagans saw the same thing, and imagined that each entity was divine in its own right – and so they worshipped nature: the sun, moon, stars, trees and mountains, animals, minerals, and finally, man himself. They could not understand that there was one non-physical Creator "Who in His goodness renews all of creation every day."[721] We, as Jews, were taught before anything else that there is only one force in the universe – the Creator – but that force is hidden from view. We do not see the life force or the intrinsic connection between the Creator and nature. Why not?

Rav Aviner suggests that perhaps our perception is limited to allow for the existence of free choice. If God's hand were visible in nature instead of implicit, man's free choice would not be completely free. We would be overwhelmed by the reality of His presence, and our role as partners in creation through our exercise of moral judgment would be undermined and minimized.

---

[717] Bamidbar 28:9.
[718] Bamidbar 28:10.
[719] Masechet Shabbat 97b.
[720] *Tal Chermon*, Parshat Vayakhel, section 2.
[721] From the blessings before Kriat Shema in the daily prayers.

As the first Shabbat approached, God's creative processes stopped, "for on [Shabbat] He abstained from all His creative labor."[722] The world of creation stopped and the world of nature began. It is as if God's presence "went on strike"[723] and was hidden from us in the natural world. All we see today is the physical, but we do not see what animates and sustains it.

We were commanded to build a Mishkan in order to consecrate all of nature to God's service. Every aspect of the animal, vegetable and mineral world is utilized, sanctified and dedicated to that goal. Every type of constructive, creative human activity was employed in its construction. Since we are generally the masters and conquerors of nature, a right given to man by God,[724] on Shabbat we acknowledge our subservience to the God of nature and refrain from those very same labors. Abstention from *melacha* (forbidden work) testifies that God is the ultimate Master of nature – and so the Tabernacle could not be built on Shabbat.

But how do we acknowledge that God is the present life force of all creation, and not just the original Creator? How do we recognize His hiddenness, even on Shabbat? Through the sacrificial order in the Temple. When we detach a living creature from life, we return its life to the Giver of all life. God exists in the world of nature, where His presence is hidden, and even in the world of man's free choice, in which God allows man control. We humbly admit that God, unseen in nature, continues to be the animating force of all life and all creation; thus, the divine service in the Temple supersedes Shabbat.[725]

At the center of Jewish life is the recognition that there is only one power in the universe, and that we serve Him according to His will. His law governs our lives, His ideas govern our thoughts and His hand guides our history. The world itself was created in such a way that free choice, the very foundation of personal responsibility, is at the heart of human existence. The laws of Shabbat are a constant reminder of this.

Every Shabbat thus reinforces our core identity as thinking, free-willed creatures blessed with an intimate relationship with the Creator of all.

---

[722] Breisheet 2:3.

[723] The word *shavat* (abstained) in modern Hebrew has engendered the word *shvita* (strike, as in "labor strike").

[724] Breisheet 1:28.

[725] Masechet Yoma 85b.

The Wise-Hearted

And let every wise-hearted person among you come, and do everything that God commanded. (Shemot 35:10)

One of the simplest, most beautiful, profound and comprehensive statements about the obligations of Jewish life is concealed under the guise of an exhortation for wise people to come and participate in the building of the Tabernacle.

The *Pardes Yosef*[726] explained that the greatest wisdom a person can have is to not be too much of a *chacham* (a wise person) but simply to do what God commands. That is the greatest wisdom known to man: ascertain what God has commanded, and then just do it.

It is when we deviate from that simple formula that all our problems emerge, and the Torah becomes muddled and the *mesora* becomes an ideological football. We start to unnecessarily question – and sometimes quite pugnaciously – what does God want? What does the Torah really say? What do our Sages say – the Sages of the past and the Torah scholars of today – and did they really mean what they said?

Modern man seems especially troubled by these questions and the requirement to subordinate our knowledge and conclusions to God's will. There are some issues that do not engage the emotions of the participants (stem-cell research, for one example) and can be analyzed more dispassionately, and others that easily arouse people's ire, like the debate about the woman's role in the Torah world, because they involve people's aspirations, self-definition, and worldview – and those views are not always shaped by the Torah and are often heavily influenced by societal norms.

In truth, the innovator, on whom the burden of proof rests to demonstrate the legitimacy of his innovations, always has to ask, "Am I serving God – or am I serving myself, a constituency, or an interest group?" So, too, the activist has to realize that Jewish law is not made nor is our tradition shaped by what will make people happy in any given generation, but rather by how we perceive the essence of our divine mandate.

"And let every wise-hearted person among you come, and do everything that God commanded." The greatest wisdom is just to do what God says, and for that we turn to our tradition and to our Sages – not to our journalists or polemicists. Beyond all our calculations, machinations, rationalizations,

---

[726] Rav Yosef Pachanovsky, early twentieth century Poland, in his Torah commentary here.

improvements and so-called sensitivity, the greatest wisdom is to find out what God wants and to do it. That is the true acceptance of the Torah that is required of every Jew and that brings us the merit of the Divine Presence.

HESITATION

And the princes brought the shoham stones and the stones for the settings of the Apron and the Breastplate. (Shemot 35:27)

Where were the "princes" (the leaders of the tribes of Israel) until now, that they brought the stones, one of the last items that were needed for the construction?

Rashi comments that the princes reasoned that the people should donate whatever they could, and they – the princes – would make up whatever was lacking.[727] To their chagrin, nothing was lacking, as the donations to the Tabernacle exceeded what was required. They atoned for this misstep by volunteering to bring the first offerings on the day of dedication of the Tabernacle. "But because they exhibited laziness at first, the Torah spelled their title [the Hebrew word *nesi'im*] defectively [without the letter *yud*]."[728] Laziness is the classic trait of the shirker of responsibility, always delaying until tomorrow what should be done today – with "tomorrow" sometimes never arriving.

The princes' mistake was troubling from two perspectives.

Rav Yitzchak Zev Soloveitchik, the Brisker Rav, noted that when a person is obligated to fulfill a *mitzva*, he must discount all calculations and just do what God says.[729] Moshe commanded that the people donate their personal property to the Tabernacle. That should have sufficed for the princes. Others emphasize their role as *leaders*.[730] A leader by definition cannot wait for the masses to act, but must be out front – that is to say, leading.[731] The princes failed in this regard but atoned for it later.

Few communal endeavors are successful when the natural leaders defer their involvement until the end of the project. Under those circumstances, the "end" is rarely reached as the project fails long before completion. Those

---

[727] Rashi, citing Midrash Bamidbar Rabba 12:16.
[728] Ibid.
[729] Cited in *Tallelei Orot* on this verse.
[730] Cited in *Iturei Torah* on this verse.
[731] A modern American president's staffer coined the locution "leading from behind" to illustrate that president's hesitant conduct of foreign affairs, although he meant it as praise, not criticism.

who aspire to leadership must inspire others to act. In so doing, they take responsibility for their actions and for those of others as well.

Happiness

And they said to Moshe, "The people are bringing more than enough for the labor of the work that God has commanded." (Shemot 36:5)

The Jewish people plunged into the Mishkan project with remarkable enthusiasm. They came with all their precious metals, stones, skins, spices – until Moshe was told, "The people are bringing more than enough" (36:5). He then told them, men and women, to stop: "Do not do more work bringing gifts to the Tabernacle" (36:6).

Of course, as our Sages note, the Jews showed the same enthusiasm for the golden calf they had constructed: "'And the nation removed the gold rings that were in their ears and brought them to Aharon' (32:3). They sinned with earrings and they found favor with earrings."[732]

Similarly, it is quite remarkable that when the Tabernacle was erected, the people felt an overpowering sense of joy: "There was great happiness that God's Presence rested among them."[733] But when they built the golden calf, didn't they also rejoice? "And Aharon called out, 'Tomorrow will be a festival to God.' And the people arose early the next day, brought [offerings], and the people sat down to eat and drink and arose to revel" (32:5–6). Apparently, they were quite happy at the golden calf celebrations as well. What is the difference? Why should the people be extolled for their joy at the completion of the Tabernacle?

Certainly there is a difference between the words used to describe their feelings – *tzchok* (levity) in the first instance and *simcha* (happiness) in the second – and undoubtedly there was a benefit in having them channel their energy into something productive and holy after the debacle of the golden calf. But there was more: the people had to learn the meaning of true happiness.

Pursuit of happiness is a great American value, underscored in the Declaration of Independence as an "unalienable right." But its attainment remains so elusive that many people seek the illusion of happiness through the ingestion of chemicals, dangerous thrill-seeking, or the reluctance to invest

---

[732] Midrash Shemot Rabba 48:6.
[733] Ibid. 52:5.

in permanent relationships with a spouse or family. Avoidance of any type of sadness is mandatory.

Yet the true happy life is not one without failures, disappointments, moments of sadness or even the occasional crushing blow. To have no sadness in life means that one has no deep and meaningful relationships, has never attempted anything challenging, never lost a job, never loved – and such a life is empty and essentially unlived.

Setbacks, struggles, even sad events in a sense enrich our lives, perhaps because they are inevitable in life – and to ignore them, drown them, pathologize them, attempt to shop them or drug them away, or foster the notion that it is wrong, embarrassing, unbecoming or unfaithful to feel sad is a terrible mistake. When the people realized the extent of the mistake of the sin of the golden calf and its consequences, "they were grief-stricken" (33:4). And that was a good sign.

The surest way to overcome sadness is to look beyond oneself, to others – helping other people, volunteering in the community – not only because you will find people worse off than you (that is always true) but mainly because helping others is an inherently satisfying act. Happiness is achieved in a life of meaning and purpose and that is always found in doing something for others. The happiest people (even those who endure sometimes unimaginable sadness) are those who find others to help in the community. It could be that finding a job for someone else will bring more joy than finding a job for oneself.

It is not that the Jewish people needed a new project after the great sin to distract them from their misery and rechannel their energies into something noble, but rather that they had to rebuild the sense of community that was shattered. Revelry of the type seen in the golden calf celebrations always engages the individual, but the sense of being a nation with a meaningful existence and a divine purpose had been lost. When Moshe assembled *all* of the people (35:1), he gave them that new purpose, and their hearts opened up to the community. "The people are bringing more than enough" (36:5). It was not too much – but just right.

And so the construction of the Mishkan was followed by an intense and enduring joy, a day of reconciliation and love. This was the day of true joy. For the Jewish people, the highest mountain became even more magnificent because they had lived through the deepest valley. The sin was never forgotten, because it made the divine service that much more precious – as sadness makes life more appreciated. That was complete atonement, and that is a prescription for a meaningful, purposeful and happy life.

Mirror Image

And he made the sink of copper and its base of copper from the mirrors of the legions who gathered at the entrance to the Tent of Meeting. (Shemot 38:8)

Rashi states that Moshe was at first reluctant to use the mirrors for the purpose of building the laver, as they were donated by women who routinely used them to beautify themselves for their husbands. Moshe deemed that use, although proper, sufficiently unholy that it should be disqualified for service in the Mishkan.

God demurred and explained to Moshe that those mirrors were particularly precious to Him because Jewish women in Egypt had used them to prettify themselves before visiting their husbands in the fields, and in so doing had successfully perpetuated Jewish life in the house of bondage. It was therefore most appropriate to utilize them in the Mishkan, especially in light of the use of the laver during the ordeal of the *sota* and the possibility of reconciling the troubled marriage in that scenario.[734]

The mirrors therefore represented the courageous and prescient women of that generation who provided hope when their husbands were discouraged. They took responsibility for the destiny of Israel when the men, under the harsh burdens of their daily labor, had already despaired. Personal responsibility is not the sole province of males. It must pervade males and females, and of all ages and backgrounds. It has to be the underpinning of the entire nation.

In another sense, it is only astonishing by modern standards that mirrors, which symbolize lust, should find their place in the Holy Temple. Desire, properly controlled and directed, is moral, decent and vital to the well-being of God's people. (Uncontrolled desire, of course, is usually catastrophic.) It is an unadulterated good, not a concession to human frailty. We "modern" people are much more judgmental, and usually improperly so. We should rejoice in the celebrations of life and the joys of marriage. They constitute part of the blessings of life with which God has blessed us.

---

[734] Rashi, Shemot 38:8.

Pekudei

The Lingering Sin

> *These are the computations of the Tabernacle, the Tabernacle of Testimony, that were counted according to [the command] of Moshe; the labor of the Levites under the authority of Itamar the son of Aharon. (Shemot 38:21)*

Rashi comments that the Tabernacle was called the Tabernacle of Testimony because the Mishkan was living proof that God had forgiven the Jewish people for the sin of the golden calf. Since now His presence rested in the Tabernacle and among the people, it was clear that all was forgiven and that their repentance was accepted.

But in fact, all was not forgiven. The very end of our verse describes the work in the Mishkan as that of "Levites." This was the case only because the Levites had permanently replaced the firstborn in each family of every tribe, who were originally designated for service in the Mishkan but who had sinned by worshipping the golden calf and had their careers terminated. The *Meshech Chochma* notes that even though the people were forgiven, the firstborn were not restored to divine service but were permanently banned.[735]

Why were the people restored to God's good graces – so much so that the Tabernacle is eloquent "testimony" to their absolution – but not the firstborn? Rav Meir Simcha answers that a priest who brings an offering to idolatry (even once) causes all his future offerings to be rejected even if he repents. His offering is permanently construed as blemished and unfit for the Altar. That permanent ban would seem to contradict our entire philosophy of repentance, which suggests that any misdeed can be forgiven and that every person can start anew. Here, instead, the idolatrous priest is tethered to his past. Why?

---

[735] Rav Meir Simcha of Dvinsk, in his commentary to this verse.

It is true, albeit unpleasant to ponder, that not every wrong can be righted. King Shlomo said in his wisdom that "something twisted cannot [always] be made straight."[736] Certain situations are, sadly, irreversible, like the man and woman who spawn a *mamzer* whose status clings to him his entire life.[737]

For the firstborn, there could not be full repentance and they could not be restored to their positions. If they worshipped idols, then any subsequent act of service on their part would be tainted as well, tinged with the stigma of their grievous sin. Their technical performance could be exceptional, but the personal blemish would remain. Each time they would have brought an offering, they – and other observers – would have recalled their sin.

False ideas corrupt, and most pernicious of all, the wrong ideas taught to children can take a lifetime to undo, if they can be undone at all. A tree that is crooked when planted will never go straight; it has to be uprooted and replanted, and even that doesn't always work.

The reality of life is that some errors cannot be fully rectified, and some sins have lingering effects. People who make mistakes rearing their children can easily sentence them to a lifetime of turmoil and discontent. Marriages and friendships can be unraveled by one impetuous act or statement.

We are thus obligated to think before we speak and before we act. The full consequences of every deed are not always identifiable at the moment of performance. The wise person, states the Talmud, is the one who foresees consequences.[738] That is excellent advice in every sphere of endeavor – personal, familial, parental, financial and, of course, spiritual.

Trust but Verify

> *And from the one thousand seven hundred seventy five [remaining pieces of silver], he made hooks for the pillars…*
> *(Shemot 38:28)*

It was President Ronald Reagan who popularized the Russian slogan "*Doveryai no proveryai*" (Trust but verify), which guided his foreign policy with the

---

[736] Kohelet 1:15.

[737] Masechet Chagiga 9a. A *mamzer* is the product of an illicit union that is considered a capital offense according to Torah, such as incest or adultery. The *mamzer*, among other restrictions, is barred from marrying a natural-born Jew who does not share the *mamzer* status.

[738] Masechet Tamid 32a.

former Soviet Union. One can understand why such was necessary during the Cold War. But with Moshe, the greatest man who ever lived?

The Midrash says that Moshe gave an accounting of every single precious item that was donated to the Tabernacle but could not identify where 1,775 silver shekels had gone. The people were murmuring: "Look how robust Moshe is! He eats, drinks and supports himself off Jewish money!" To which another Jew would respond: "Fool, don't you think that the one responsible for collecting the valuables with which the Mishkan was built would become wealthy?" They suspected Moshe of skimming off the top and pocketing some of the wealth![739]

Immediately, Moshe located the missing shekels. He looked and saw the hooks for the pillars, composed of these small pieces of silver, and he cried out for all to hear, "And from the one thousand seven hundred seventy five, he made hooks for the pillars."[740] That ended the murmuring, at least for a time.

The Talmud states that a Jew is obligated to act in such a way that his deeds are pleasing both to God and to man.[741] It is not sufficient for a person to do the right thing if his actions nonetheless arouse suspicion – and notwithstanding that it is forbidden to suspect a Jew of wrongdoing without credible evidence.[742] Vindication before God – and even before a court of human beings – does not justify conduct that will engender distrust. The priest, for example, who retrieved coins from the Temple chamber with which to purchase animals for offerings on the Altar was not allowed to wear a garment with pockets so he should not be suspected of embezzling.[743]

That is certainly a high standard but one that is expected of every Jew. "And you will find favor and inspiration in the eyes of God and man."[744] No one is allowed to suspect others, but by the same token no person should see himself as if he is above suspicion. Public figures especially have the responsibility to be as transparent as possible and always act with the understanding that access to money arouses a deep and likely unavoidable skepticism among the masses.

---

[739] Midrash Tanchuma, Pekudei 7; Yalkut Shimoni, Pekudei 415.

[740] The eighteenth-century Hasidic Rebbe Reb Menachem Mendel of Rimanov (cited in *Siftei Tzaddikim*) points out the cantillation on the beginning of this verse "and the thousand…" is an *azla geresh*, tantamount to a shriek to get people's attention.

[741] Yerushalmi Masechet Shekalim 3:2.

[742] Masechet Shabbat 97a; Masechet Yoma 19b.

[743] Yerushalmi Masechet Shekalim 3:2.

[744] Proverbs 3:4.

The Midrashim[745] relate that even Moshe, who was explicitly trusted by God – "in My entire house he is trusted"[746] – had to be above the reproach of the people. The awful desecration of God's name that occurs when a member of His people stumbles in this realm, as happens all too frequently, is sufficient reminder that we bear the responsibility to conduct our dealings above board and in good faith so as to preclude even the slightest suggestion of impropriety.

If that mandate applied to Moshe, then how much more so should it apply to lesser mortals?

REPETITION

...and the Children of Israel did everything that God commanded Moshe, so they did. (Shemot 39:32)

Even the casual reader cannot help notice that the Torah, which is ordinarily very precise and sparing in its language, goes to extraordinary lengths to delineate the construction of the Mishkan. The initial command from God to Moshe is described fully, the instructions from Moshe to the people are described fully, and the process of construction and erection are again described fully. The details are repetitive.

Certainly, the redundancy conveys the divinity of the project. Nothing was left to chance or the people's whim; nothing was to leave the impression that the Mishkan in any aspect reflected the input of the people. Otherwise, the danger existed that their worship of God could be rooted in self-worship. Every stage of the process was therefore spelled out completely, with the frequent exhortation "as God commanded Moshe."[747]

There is another important idea as well. In the material world or in popular culture, success is measured by the accomplishment in meeting an objective. Little attention is paid to the effort, the means or the road to the target. "Nice try, but..." doesn't really cut it in business, law or medicine. The emphasis is on *results* – did you get it done or not? Is the report on time, was the brief filed, did you close the deal? That's what matters.

The spiritual world is different. The Talmud cites in the name of Rav Ashi: "If a person thinks of doing a *mitzva* and is prevented from doing it, the Torah

---

[745] Cited above: Midrash Tanchuma, Pekudei 7; Yalkut Shimoni, Pekudei 415.
[746] Bamidbar 12:7.
[747] Such a phrase recurs in this *sedra* well over a dozen times.

considers it as if it were done."[748] In terms of one's pursuit of spiritual perfection, it is enough to "think" about the *mitzva* and plan to do it. Elsewhere, the Talmud states that "God connects a good thought to the deed."[749] Intentions matter. The journey itself matters, and not just arriving at the destination. In spiritual matters, the ends sanctify the means.

The construction of the Mishkan underscores this point. It is not just the final achievement – "and Moshe erected the Tabernacle…" (40:18). We need to hear God's command, how Moshe commanded the people, how the people responded to Moshe, how they set about the task, and how they built the Mishkan over the course of almost half a year. We need to hear of the effort, and we need to hear of the "good thoughts" which in the real world are linked to deed itself.

Much of what we do is defined not by the final product but by our preparation. We prepare for Shabbat and Pesach. We prepare our children for life by gradually imparting to them our wisdom, values and experience. We perfect ourselves gradually through the study of Torah and the fulfillment of *mitzvot*. Our preparations are sanctified, and not just the execution of the task at hand. In fact, we perceive this world, with all its glories and opportunities, as preparation for the next world. In the words of the Talmud, "Whoever prepares on the eve of Shabbat will eat on Shabbat. One who doesn't toil on the eve of Shabbat, from where will he eat on Shabbat?"[750]

Our lives are enriched by the quality of our preparations for all our important tasks. A child prepares for marriage, the married prepare to raise children, parents prepare their children for adulthood, and we all prepare ourselves for eternal life. Those who focus only on the conclusion will find the process itself tedious and cumbersome, and will often start projects and not finish them. If we embrace our preparations then every step in the journey of life is endowed with meaning and significance, and opportunities for growth.

---

[748] Masechet Berachot 6a.
[749] Masechet Kiddushin 40a.
[750] Masechet Avoda Zara 3a.

Between Heaven and Earth

And the cloud covered the Tent of Meeting, and the glory of God filled the Tabernacle. And Moshe could not enter the Tent of Meeting, for the cloud rested upon it, and the glory of God filled the Tabernacle. (Shemot 40:34–35)

The divine cloud covered the Tent of Meeting, and God's glory filled the Mishkan. Yet the cloud brought its own limitations. Moshe could not enter when the cloud rested on the Tent of Meeting. So how did he ever enter? Rashi says that while this verse says he could not enter, another verse says he did enter.[751] That is, when the cloud rested on the Tent of Meeting, he could not enter, but when the cloud would dissipate (i.e., rise), Moshe would then enter and converse with God.

But why did the Mishkan need a cloud? And how did an ethereal and insubstantial cloud inhibit Moshe? How did it manage to keep him out?

Clouds *are* delicate and flimsy substances that are beyond our ability to reach or touch. They represent our aspirations, our vision beyond the immediate and the material. When we say someone is in the clouds, we mean that he is all theory, all dreams, without substance or real weight, lacking a connection to reality. Conversely, there are people who are so enmeshed in the physical that they cannot see above them. They live close to the ground. They have no vision, goal or plan – they are just part of a daily grind. They never see the clouds.

We want to be realists, but we also want to be in the clouds. We want to be able to define what we are living for and then implement it in the real world, in the here-and-now. Without the clouds, we are just cogs in a machine, plugging away aimlessly; with only the clouds, we are dreamers and schemers and fantasists, never changing or improving anything.

The Mishkan could not just become a humdrum, routine, monotonous place of worship where people drop off their *korbanot* (offerings) or their words of *tefilla* and move on unchanged; it was always concealed in a cloud. There was always some unattainable level for which to strive, some ideal beyond our reach. It existed to enable us to grow in holiness, love and consciousness of God, knowledge of Torah, and pursuit of *mitzvot*. Even Moshe could not enter when the cloud covered the Tent of Meeting, because that would imply that he had fused the real and the ideal. Even Moshe could not make that claim.

---

[751] Bamidbar 7:89.

We can never say "I have made it, I have achieved my spiritual potential; now let me rest."

But when the cloud lifted, Moshe could enter. He was the one who was most capable of appreciating the presence of God and bringing the people that ideal vision. Moshe was a conduit between the perfect and the practical.

In a sense, the teacher of Torah is that conduit – not between God and man, but between the aspiration and the reality. The teacher of Torah keeps our feet on the ground and our heads in the clouds. The student of Torah, the faithful Jew and the authentic servant of God – aware of his obligations and imbued with a sense of personal responsibility – lives with that same desire to be a bridge between heaven and earth, to comprehend God's will and the vision of man's true potential and implement it here on earth, in the world of thought and activity, the world of accomplishment.

It is that desire which, when fully embraced by the nation of Israel, will see "the glory of God [that] filled the Tabernacle" again permeate the entire world, and herald the era of God's kingdom on earth, may it come speedily and in its time.

☙❦

לעילוי נשמת יעקב עזריאל בן סימא ואהרן דוד ע"ה

In loving memory of
IRVING D. LIBERMAN, a"h,
Father, teacher and source of eternal inspiration

Sheryl and Aron Liberman
and family

☙❦

In loving memory of our beloved father,
Isidore Feld,
and beloved mother Sylvia Feld

לעילוי נשמת יצחק מאיר בן צבי ע"ה
לעילוי נשמת סימא יטה בת אהרן ע"ה

Rochel and Alan Feld
Andrea and Yosef Nissel

☙❦

About the Author

RABBI STEVEN PRUZANSKY has served since 1994 as the spiritual leader of Congregation Bnai Yeshurun in Teaneck, New Jersey, one of the most vibrant centers of Orthodox Jewish life today. Previously, Rabbi Pruzansky served for nine years as the spiritual leader of Congregation Etz Chaim of Kew Gardens Hills, New York. While in New York, he was President of the Vaad Harabonim (Rabbinical Board) of Queens, and in New Jersey served one term as President of the Rabbinical Council of Bergen County.

Rabbi Pruzansky graduated from Columbia University in 1978 with a B.A. in history and received a Juris Doctor degree from the Benjamin N. Cardozo School of Law in 1981. He practiced law for thirteen years as a general practitioner and litigator in New York City until assuming his current pulpit. Rabbi Pruzansky learned in *yeshivot* in Israel and the United States and was ordained at Yeshiva Bnei Torah of Far Rockaway, New York, under the leadership of Rav Yisrael Chait, *shlit"a*.

He currently serves as Rosh Beth Din L'Giyur in Bergen County, New Jersey, and as a *dayyan* and trustee of the Beth Din of America. Active in a host of Jewish organizations, Rabbi Pruzansky has also received numerous awards, especially for his advocacy on behalf of the State of Israel and the Jewish people. He writes extensively on topics of Jewish interest and has lectured in more than twenty-five countries. Rabbi Pruzansky previously authored *A Prophet for Today: Contemporary Lessons from the Book of Yehoshua* (Gefen Publishing House, 2006) and *Judges for our Time: Contemporary Lessons from the Book of Shoftim* (Gefen Publishing House, 2009).